Bus

A Century of Economics

A Century of Economics

100 Years of the Royal Economic Society and the Economic Journal

Edited by John D. Hey and Donald Winch

Basil Blackwell

Copyright © Basil Blackwell 1990

First published 1990

Basil Blackwell Ltd
108 Cowley Road, Oxford, OX4 1JF, UK

Basil Blackwell, Inc.
3 Cambridge Center
Cambridge, Massachusetts 02142, USA

All rights reserved. Except for the quotation of short passages for the purposes of criticism and review, no part of this publication may be reproduced, stored in a retrieval system, or transmitted, in any form or by any means, electronic, mechanical, photocopying, recording or otherwise, without the prior permission of the publisher.

Except in the United States of America, this book is sold subject to the condition that it shall not, by way of trade or otherwise, be lent, re-sold, hired out, or otherwise circulated without the publisher's prior consent in any form of binding or cover other than that in which it is published and without a similar condition including this condition being imposed on the subsequent purchaser.

British Library Cataloguing in Publication Data
A CIP catalogue record for this book is available from the British Library.

Library of Congress Cataloging in Publication Data
A Century of economics : 100 years of the Royal Economic Society and
  the Economic journal / edited by John D. Hey and Donald Winch.
    p.   cm.
  Includes bibliographical references.
  ISBN 0–631–16745–5
  1. Royal Economic Society (Great Britain)—History. 2. Economic journal (London, England)—History. 3. Economics—Great Britain--History. I. Hey, John Denis. II. Winch, Donald.
HB103.A2C46   1990
330'.06'041—dc20   90–159
                                                                                                        CIP

Typeset in 11 on 12½ pt Imprint
by Photo·graphics, Honiton, Devon
Printed in Great Britain by T.J. Press (Padstow) Ltd.

Contents

Preface   vii

List of Contributors   viii

Part I   History

1. A Century of Economics   3
   Donald Winch

2. Foundation and Early Years   22
   Alon Kadish and Richard D. Freeman

3. Gentlemen versus Players, 1891–1914   49
   John Maloney

4. The *Economic Journal* and Socialism, 1890–1920   65
   Ian Steedman

5. The Attitudes of the Economics Professions in Britain and the United States to the Trust Movement, 1890–1914   92
   Philip L. Williams

6. Reviews by Edgeworth   109
   Peter Newman

7 Keynes as Editor Donald E. Moggridge	143

Part II Recollection

8 Fifty-five Years on the Royal Economic Society Council Austin Robinson	161

Part III Reassessment

9 Editorial Introduction John Hey	195
10 The Theory of Games Revisited Richard Stone	198
11 Expectations Frank Hahn	232
12 Trimming Consumers' Surplus Down to Size Paul A. Samuelson	261
13 The Econometrics of DHSY David F. Hendry, John N. J. Muellbauer and Anthony Murphy	298
14 Reflections on Macroeconomics and Share Systems Martin L. Weitzman	335
Index	355

Preface

In deciding on the most appropriate way of marking the centenary of the foundation of the Royal Economic Society and its official periodical, the *Economic Journal*, the Executive Committee of the Society asked two of its officers, the Publications Secretary and the Managing Editor of the *Journal*, to collaborate in producing a commemorative volume. We have adopted two divergent, but we hope complementary, approaches which can roughly and respectively be described as historical and retrospective and theoretical and prospective. The essays in Part I deal with various aspects of the foundation of the Society and the conduct of the *Journal* during the first three or four decades of its existence. Part II contains a single essay by Austin Robinson based on knowledge of the Society that has been acquired over a period that is longer than half its present life. The authors of the essays in Part III were asked to reflect on seminal articles which they had published in the *Journal* during the last five decades, updating their views in the light of subsequent developments in the fields in question. Taken together, we hope that this volume will convey some idea not only of how economics has developed as a professional pursuit during the last century, but of how it might develop during the next.

Donald Winch
John Hey

List of Contributors

Richard D. Freeman, Imperial Chemical Industries
Frank Hahn, Cambridge University
David F. Hendry, Oxford University
John D. Hey, University of York
Alon Kadish, The Hebrew University, Jerusalem
John Maloney, University of Exeter
Donald E. Moggridge, University of Toronto
John N.J. Muellbauer, Oxford University
Anthony Murphy, Oxford University
Peter Newman, The Johns Hopkins University
Sir Austin Robinson, Cambridge University
Paul A. Samuelson, Massachusetts Institute of Technology
Ian Steedman, University of Manchester
Sir Richard Stone, Cambridge University
Martin L. Weitzman, Massachusetts Institute of Technology
Philip L. Williams, University of Melbourne
Donald Winch, University of Sussex

Part I

History

1
A Century of Economics

Donald Winch

As a serious branch of intellectual inquiry with scope for significant application to the conduct of public affairs, economics is a good deal older than the Royal Economic Society and the *Economic Journal*, the centenary of which provide the occasion for this collection of celebratory essays. But the last hundred years have witnessed most of the crucial developments in the history of economics considered as a *professional* pursuit – one capable of offering a life-time career to those who wished to dedicate themselves to the advancement and dissemination of this branch of social scientific knowledge through teaching and research, as well as through practical application within government and business. It was for this reason that John Maynard Keynes spoke of the founding of the British Economic Association (BEA) in 1890, the organization that became the Royal Economic Society (RES) in 1902, as the beginning of the 'modern age of British economics'.[1] The event was both a reflection of and a means of furthering the wider process of professionalization within learned and scientific communities that burgeoned in the final decades of the nineteenth century.

The history of economics in Britain and the economic history of Britain, though closely intertwined, are by no means coterminous. One of the implications of professionalization is that reaction to political and economic events increasingly becomes mediated by priorities that are internal to the professional community –

amorphous though that community has always been in the case of economics. The headline issues that mark the past century of economic life in this country – two world wars, the apogee and subsequent decline of Britain's imperial role, interwar depression and recovery, abandonment of such nineteenth-century policy verities as free trade and the gold standard, the growth of a welfare state and the inauguration of the immediate post-1945 decades of conscious economic management, entry into the European Community, the return of unemployment accompanied by inflation in the 1970s, the attempt to roll back the state in the 1980s, and the emergence of economic development in the Third World and of environmental degradation as global issues – provide only a rough guide to what has most preoccupied economists, and tell us even less about the way in which economists have pursued their preoccupation.

A different story emerges from the history of economic theorizing, an activity that – when carried out critically, though not necessarily or consistently at its most rarified limits – is particularly characteristic of professional economic thinking. It also follows that the history of economics as a self-conscious discipline or profession brings in yet another set of high and low lights. Told in simple storybook fashion, the century with which we are concerned begins with the absorption and elaboration of what has become known as neoclassical economics, with the consolidation of those developments in the analysis of competitive and non-competitive market allocation and distribution which began with the marginalist revolution of the 1870s. In Britain this chiefly took the particular form associated with the name of Alfred Marshall, whose *Principles of Economics* provides the other reason for a centenary celebration in 1990.[2] It was a revolution in the way in which the problem of value, the behaviour of economic agents at the microeconomic level, and general market interdependence was conceived. In the interwar period this was followed by an equally significant shift of focus towards the economics of imperfect or monopolistic competition as a result of a theoretical debate which featured prominently in the pages of the *Economic Journal* during the 1920s and 1930s. At the same time, beside this new post-Marshallian microeconomic corpus was constructed the macroeconomic revolution that we associate with Keynes's name, where again the pages of the *Journal* saw many of the chief moves in the controversy surrounding the introduction of a new theory enacted.³ Paralleling these changes has been the shift towards greater use of mathematics in the articulation of economic theory and the widespread use of econometric methods in its application or testing. This movement may have begun in the nineteenth century with Antoine Cournot, Stanley Jevons, Leon Walras and Marshall, but it has only come to fruition in the post-1945 period and now represents one of the standard ways in which debate within the economics profession is conducted. It marks a change of direction towards which neither Marshall nor Keynes, despite their own mathematical backgrounds and interests, was particularly welcoming, though both of them gave wholehearted blessing to the use of theory to analyse significant problems of economic life and to the marriage of theory with quantitative evidence.

While the more historically oriented essays in this and the next part of this collection refer directly or indirectly to some of these events and shifts of disciplinary focus, they do not engage in continuous narrative. Still less do they attempt to provide a comprehensive assessment of the changing state of the professional art, then and now. Instead, they deal with key episodes and figures, and other significant features of the history of the Society and its journal, and hence of the emerging profession being served and nurtured, during the first half-century of the Society's existence.

Austin Robinson's personal memoir of his intimate and continuing connection with the Society for well over half the century being celebrated in 1990 provides an excellent reminder, not merely of the obvious fact that all institutions are created and sustained by individuals, but that much of the history of the Society, especially during its first half century and beyond, was dominated by a few exceptional, and exceptionally long-serving, individuals. This is clearly the case with the editorship of the *Journal*. For the first 55 years of its existence, the *Journal* had only two editors: Francis Ysidro Edgeworth and Keynes, working with or without assistance. Keynes himself served continuously from his initial appointment in 1911 at the tender age of 28 until a year before his death in 1946. The essays by Austin Robinson, Peter Newman and Donald Moggridge show just how large, and how idiosyncratic, the contributions of these two eminent economists were to the conduct of the *Journal*.

Austin Robinson's remarkable record of service was matched in length at least during the first half century of the Society's existence by those of James Bonar and Henry Higgs, members of the original Council in 1890 who were still active in the Society's affairs until well into the 1930s, having been born in 1852 and 1864 respectively. But the best illustration of continuity in British economics – of the links between what began life in the late eighteenth century and continued into the nineteenth as 'political economy' and was rechristened 'economics' partly as a result of Marshall's preference for the new term – is provided by George Joachim Goschen, the Society's first President. By 1890 Goschen, after a distinguished career as an economist and a Liberal politician, had risen to the rank of Chancellor of the Exchequer. Born in 1831, his economic studies began in 1852; when he wrote his *Theory of Foreign Exchanges* in 1863 he claimed that the only relevant works he had read were by Aristotle and John Stuart Mill. Although by the 1890s he modestly described himself as an amateur who had, perhaps unwisely, accepted the role of presiding over the affairs of the new association of professional students of economic life, his memories as an economist went back to Mill's recantation of the wage-fund doctrine in the 1860s, the event that presaged the decline in authority of orthodox political economy in Britain. Goschen had also attended the dinner organized by the Political Economy Club in 1876 under the Chairmanship of another Chancellor of the Exchequer, William Ewart Gladstone, to celebrate the centenary of *The Wealth of Nations*.[4] While none of the other founding figures could quite match such longevity, many of the disputes over the legacy of orthodox political economy which continued to rage within and around the new association prior to its formation and during its early years were conducted by those whose introduction to the subject began with Adam Smith, David Ricardo and Mill, however much they may have subsequently been influenced by Jevons and Marshall on one side or by the growing band of late nineteenth-century critics of classical political economy on the other.

The opening essay by Alon Kadish and Richard Freeman re-examines the background to the formation of the BEA and its early years, making use of the wealth of correspondence left by one of the prime movers, Herbert Somerton Foxwell.[5] By November 1890, when the BEA was finally launched, and by March 1891, when the first issue of the *Journal* appeared, the British economic community was, if anything, rather behind the times, judged not merely by foreign examples but by those equivalent bodies in Britain founded by other groups within the scientific and learned community.[6] The American Economic Association (AEA) had been formed in 1885, and a periodical, the *Quarterly Journal of Economics*, had been started at Harvard in 1886. In France there were already two economic periodicals in existence, the *Journal des Economistes*, founded in 1841, and the *Revue d'Economie Politique*, founded in 1887. Since 1872 Germany has possessed a body – the Verein für Sozialpolitik – that had coordinated the work of academic commentators on the role of the state in social and economic policy.

British tardiness can be variously explained. One of the delaying factors was the existence of other bodies that continued to provide a forum and outlet for the work of economists, notably Section F of the British Association for the Advancement of Science (BAAS), a section that had combined economic science with statistics since 1856, and the Royal Statistical Society, a body that had grown out of the London Statistical Society formed in 1834. Added to these was the Political Economy Club, an influential dining club established in 1821 – a private grouping that was too closely associated with classical orthodoxy to provide the neutral setting needed to unite different factions. Between these bodies and the founders of the BEA there was considerable overlapping membership, and their existence helps to explain why creation of a new organization devoted solely to economics entailed deliberation and differentiation born out of growing dissatisfaction and a desire for greater autonomy.

Section F of the BAAS served as an annual forum for economic debate, and while Jevons and others had used the meetings to give important papers, they were miscellaneous in their coverage of statistical and economic topics. Moreover, the occasion had frequently been used to air fundamental disagreements on the nature and method appropriate to the science.[7] It was partly as a result of the virulence of these methodological disputes that a serious, though unsuccessful, attempt was made to abolish Section F in 1878. Despite recovery from this notoriously low point in the history of economics, the BAAS could do little, apart from setting up one or two *ad hoc* research committees, to sustain economic inquiry between annual meetings. Economists were also dissatisfied with the marriage with statistics and with the popular composition of the audience, which often allowed those whom they considered to be cranks and bores to hog discussion. As Henry Sidgwick noted in 1885: 'The profound difficulty of making the talk of this section [F] really scientific is that Statisticians and Economists are yoked together, and the Statisticians are weak or *arriéré* in economic theory. It is worse than if the Physicists and Mechanicians were combined.'[8]

Despite this feeling that most statisticians were rude numerical mechanicals and that the Statistical Society had become dominated by the wrong kind of businessman, anxious to use it for advertising purposes, some of the economist members of the Statistical Society persisted in the late 1880s with attempts to acquire more intellectual space for economics within the society. The failure, or rather luke-warm success, of these efforts was one of the factors that lay behind the decision to press ahead with the BEA. Even so, there was still room for last-minute doubts and hesitations, most of them traceable to Marshall's mixture of caution and desire to outflank opposed conceptions of the form the new association should take. Indeed, the hesitations and disagreements of the founders resulted in the largely Cambridge-inspired *Economic Journal* arriving at the starting line a few months behind its Oxford rival the *Economic Review*.

The two journals were indicative, if not neat embodiments of, the main camps within economics that had emerged since the demise of orthodox political economy in Britain: an approach epitomized, in its most cohesive form at least, by Marshall's attempt to construct a new theoretical-cum-empirical 'organon' and an ethico-historical school of thought that had Christian allegiances and derived considerable inspiration from German example and scholarship. As the coming into existence of two journals illustrates, fundamental disputes as to what kind of science economics was or might become had by no means disappeared in 1890. The relative merits of deductive theory versus inductive evidence, particularly of a historical kind; whether theory could sustain wide claims to relevance regardless of historical or social circumstance; whether economics should be absorbed within a larger sociological scheme of study; whether scientific propositions could be established independently from ethical and political commitments – all these questions continued to be debated, despite the efforts of

Marshall (part tactical, part sincere) to reconcile warring claims, ably abetted by the judicious book, *The Scope and Method of Political Economy*, published by his Cambridge lieutenant, John Neville Keynes, in 1891.

Within the American profession, particularly when the AEA was formed, the balance of influences was tilted more towards the German historical school of thought, and the founders initially took as their model the Verein für Sozialpolitik. Under American circumstances this was associated with a more positive conception of the role of the state in economic life than was characteristic of Marshall's approach. Philip Williams's essay for this volume deals with the elements of convergence and divergence in the attitudes of the infant American and British economics professions towards the trust movement, one of the most important transnational developments occurring in industrial organization at the turn of the century. His essay is therefore an exercise in comparative professional history. It complements the essays by Alon Kadish and Richard Freeman, by Peter Newman on Edgeworth and by Ian Steedman on socialism by showing how much effort was made in the early decades of the RES to keep a window open on continental, transatlantic and imperial developments. It also serves as a reminder of the strength of the Anglo-American connections that have always existed in economics, with leadership passing inexorably to the United States as the century has progressed.

Despite the elaborate attempts made by the BEA and its newfound journal to incorporate historical and inductive work undertaken by the opponents of deductive theorizing, intermittent hostilities continued. Furthermore, a major split – one that *partly* corresponded with the division between economic theorists on one side, and the upholders of ethico-religious positions and critics of orthodoxy from a historical perspective on the other – was provoked by one of the most important political and economic issues of the day: Chamberlain's campaign for tariff reform. The public dispute on this matter helped to resolidify the lines of opposition and keep the temperature in the early 1900s above that required for full reconciliation and mutual tolerance.[9] Nevertheless, as John Maloney shows, considerable effort was made to prevent the dispute from ruffling the pages of the *Journal* unduly.

The demise of the *Economic Review* in 1914 can either be taken as an indication of more successful adaptation to the environment by the RES, allowing it to succeed in the struggle for survival, or as part of another story that eventually led to the emergence of a separate profession of economic historians, towards which the RES was later able to offer some assistance by publishing the *Economic History Supplement*.[10] It can also be treated as part of the background to John Maloney's essay on the slow and uneven process by which a certain kind of 'player' (professional economist) dealt with and gradually ousted a certain kind of 'gentleman' (amateur) in the pages of the *Journal*.

It would be wrong to think, therefore, that the establishment of the *Journal* represented a simple victory for Marshall and a unified Cambridge approach to economics. Those interested in the dissemination of the Marshallian vision of neoclassical economics, and the formation of a Cambridge school around it, will need to employ a good deal of selective hindsight to find supporting evidence in the pages of the *Journal* during its first few decades.[11] For while Cambridge economists were later to proclaim that 'it was all in Marshall', including a good deal of evolutionary theorizing and moralizing which they were *not* interested in pursuing, and while there is no doubt that his *Principles* and later writings provided a model and set standards for some of the early professionals who contributed to the *Journal*, notably perhaps Arthur Cecil Pigou, Marshall's successor in the Cambridge Chair, there was no single undisputed paradigm for the conduct of economic research in the 1890s, or indeed for some time later.

Moreover, it would be a travesty of the intentions of Marshall to depict him as aiming to use the *Journal* as a means of building a home for a new orthodoxy. He went out of his way to combat arguments in favour of restricting membership to those who were 'qualified' by some test that was often mentioned but never clearly defined; and he proclaimed in his address to the inaugural meeting of the BEA that '"orthodox science" was a contradiction in terms'.[12] Marshall's belief that the association should 'include every school of economists which was doing genuine work' left it open to the editor of the *Journal* to interpret what 'genuine' meant. As several of the later essays show, especially that by Ian Steedman, the editorial brief was interpreted sufficiently broadly to include most of the more politically sensitive questions of the day, as well as the main competing schools of thought within economics. Thus while Marshall can be seen, especially in retrospect, to have been the almost-undisputed intellectual leader of the new economics of the 1890s and beyond, he was largely a founder of the BEA by manoeuvre and default. Most of his energies before his retirement in 1908 were devoted to the creation and maintenance of the Economics Tripos at Cambridge, an object that was secured in 1903.[13]

More seriously, perhaps, the essays published here show that a Marshall- or Cambridge-centred view of the first three decades of the RES is in danger of exaggerating the role of theory in the work of economists at this time. It is also worth remembering that one of Marshall's less successful attempts at linguistic legislation was his attempt to replace 'theory' with 'analysis', a term that would, he hoped, help to break the equation of 'economics proper' with theory alone by stressing the need for it to be combined with 'a thorough study of facts'.[14] Edgeworth, the first editor, could sometimes be elaborately deferential to Marshall, but his own work as mathematical theorist and statistician did not conform with Marshall's methodological injunctions, and Edgeworth was not inhibited by his editorial role from placing the results of his own research in the *Journal*.[15] Despite this, Edgeworth, when holding out an olive branch to his Oxford historical colleagues, and when fostering the early catholic mission of the BEA by catering in the *Journal* for the needs of a non-academic non-specialist audience, was carrying out a policy with which he was in wholehearted agreement. It also has to be said that this policy coincided with financial necessity, given the modest dimensions of the academic audience and the equally modest resources available to the BEA.

During its first few decades theoretical issues did not feature prominently in the *Journal*. Even within the academic community, it has to be borne in mind that much of the story of the institutionalization of the British economics must be told in terms of responses to local demand for commercial and industrial education by provincial universities and other educational establishments involved in the adult extension movement.[16] The emphasis of the *Journal* on applied economics in the early decades reflects this fact of life and the mixed nature of the audience being served. The preoccupations of full-time academic students of economics did not begin to dominate the affairs of the Society until the late 1920s, and even then the *Journal* continued to make efforts to cater for a wider audience. Indeed, Austin Robinson's mild complaint against the highly specialized, usually mathematical language of professional economic discourse today, and the failure of the *Journal* in recent years to cater for what he calls the 'working general economist', could be read, in reverse, as proof of just how enduring the aim of meeting the needs of a non-specialist readership has been over the years.

At this point we encounter another persistent problem associated with the professionalization of a discipline such as economics. Like any other subject cultivated largely by university teachers, it had to make its way, partly in collaboration, partly in competition with other branches of specialized knowledge within universities. In this respect, by comparison with other social scientific disciplines, the classic case in Britain being that of sociology, economics was relatively well placed. It had acquired a modest foothold in several universities, but chiefly as a subordinate partner in philosophy and history degrees, notably at Oxford and Cambridge. If the field was to expand and give scope for increasing specialization, however, it had to do more than convince colleagues and/or rivals in related fields to concede space within the curriculum. It was also necessary to create a favourable state of educated public opinion in the world outside universities concerning the subject's scientific claims and educational benefits. Only in this way would there be incentives and openings for serious students of the subject, and hence greater opportunities for those who taught them. As with any self-conscious bid for professional recognition, therefore, the attempt to raise status and morale had to begin with a good deal of firm pulling on bootstraps, accompanied by discreet exercises in public relations.

The state of affairs in the 1890s, and the state of mind which it generated among the early actual and would-be academic professionals, can be gauged from a report produced in 1894 by a committee of inquiry sponsored by Section F of the BAAS, 'On Economic Training in This and Other Countries'. The report emphasized Britain's backwardness compared with European countries as diverse as Austria, Germany, Hungary, France, Holland, Belgium, Italy and Russia.[17] In all these countries economics formed part of the state examinations for the legal profession and the civil service, thereby encouraging the provision of instruction in economics. In the United States, no stimulus was provided by entry examinations, but this was more than compensated by a strong body of popular opinion which viewed economics as a novel field giving access to many of the important social and economic questions that dominated American public life. By contrast with Britain, the report complained,

> The American economists have not to shake off the half-uttered, half-silent opprobrium attached to their subject through the action of the more numerous though less conspicuous of their predecessors in their rigid adherence to incomplete or ill-founded theories. They are fortunate in entering upon their teaching at a time when the need of inductive inquiry and training is more fully recognised. This gives a more systematic aspect to the economic instruction demanded from them than was the case in England.[18]

As in commercial and industrial matters – also the subject of extensive adverse comment during this period – Britain was suffering from the unfortunate legacy of an early and over confident start. A determined attempt to revamp the popular image of economics and press its educational benefits was among the chief priorities of the founders of the BEA. Although elementary economics had become an optional subject in examinations for chartered accountants, and an obligatory one in a voluntary examination recently started by the Institute of Bankers, the partial and uncertain presence of the subject in civil service examinations (chiefly for the Indian Civil Service) was the only official recognition given to economics as a training for other professions in Britain. The early efforts of the BEA to remedy this situation yielded little result. For this reason, despite the quality of the work published by British authors, there was a dearth of serious students and hence of opportunities to develop systematic training along specialist lines. The BAAS report concluded that 'with the two possible exceptions of Oxford and Cambridge, it is difficult to imagine a more complete indifference to the *scientific study* of Economics than that displayed at the present time'.[19]

Another dilemma that seems inherent in the academicization and professionalization of the social sciences expresses itself in tension between scholarly disengagement as part of the case for freedom to cultivate disinterested knowledge, and claims to public utility in the larger non-academic world. Ideally, a delicate mixture of both strategies is required. It is difficult to sustain any durable claims to contemporary relevance without a firm academic and scientific base, and there is always a danger that cases of over selling in the public market-place will rebound and damage that base. Bearing in mind the effect of earlier popularization, this is what the first generation of professional economists in Britain was most anxious to avoid, while at the same time not wishing to be over-modest about the potential benefits of economic knowledge to society at large.[20]

The creation of new institutions and specialized degree courses at the turn of the century, notably at the London School of Economics from 1895 onward, William Ashley's commerce degree at Birmingham in 1899 and Marshall's Economics Tripos in 1903, provides ample evidence of the skills of the early academic entrepreneurs in striking a balance between claims to science, long-term educational benefits and vocational relevance to local and national needs when issuing their prospectuses. Marshall's 'Plea for the Creation of a Curriculum in Economics and Associated Branches of Political Science' (the latter still being thought of as a tactical necessity in Cambridge) is a particularly good example of this contemporary art form, though it was pitched at a higher level of moral earnestness than could be managed by his successors in the 1930s, let alone those preparing themselves for the sharpened inter-university competition for private funding and students in the last decade of the twentieth century. Marshall had long proclaimed his wish to turn out generations of Cambridge men (he was never sure about women students) with warm hearts and cool heads, capable of pursuing their studies with a public-spiritedness that would allow them to penetrate to the root of social problems, to mediate between conflicting interests and encourage 'social responsibility' in businessmen and trade unionists. In an increasingly interdependent world of rapid communications (the telegraph and cheaper international means of transport), economic questions occupied half the time of the legislature, the executive and the diplomatic corps of all countries. International rivalry also meant that 'England's continued existence depend[s] on her keeping pace with the forward economic movement of nations against whom she may need to measure her force' – a statement whose darker implications were reinforced by references to the 'sinews of war' and German imperial and naval competition. Unlike Ashley's commerce degree at Birmingham, Marshall did not wish Cambridge to provide a 'technical' training for businessmen, where this included accounting, but 'the heads of business, of directors of companies, and of the higher public officials' were cited as one of the main groups of likely beneficiaries from an economics education, particularly one that combined it with 'that social training which is afforded by the life of a residentiary university of the Anglo-Saxon type'.[21]

A few years after the publication of the BAAS report, then, institutional provision had improved considerably, though not perhaps to the extent or in the manner hoped for by the academic entrepreneurs involved. Foxwell's boast to American readers of the *Quarterly Journal of Economics* in 1888 that 'half the economic chairs in the United Kingdom are occupied by [Marshall's] pupils' did not amount to much on the ground. Marshall continued to complain about the quality and numbers of students he was able to attract, and Keynes, his prize pupil, emerged from the Mathematics Tripos and only took economics as part of the examination requirements for entry into the civil service.

The situation was much the same for Sidney and Beatrice Webb, the founders of the London School of Economics (LSE), where one of the models they followed was the Ecole Libre des Sciences Politique, a private educational institution in Paris designed to educate French public servants. In its early years, however, largely as a result of demand factors and the sources of finance available, the LSE was closer to being a business school than a training centre for budding public administrators destined to play their part in furthering the cause of bureaucratic collectivism.[22] The Webbs also harboured a plan to 'break up economics' and amalgamate it within a wider, more sociological and institutionalist version of social science, largely designed to train a new breed of scientific public administrator and practical social reformer. Although the LSE provided a home initially for anti-Marshallian tariff reformers and other economic dissenters, under the interwar leadership of Lionel Robbins and Friederich von Hayek it became one of the leading centres of economic orthodoxy. The only signs of break-up that have taken place in economics, at LSE or elsewhere, have chiefly been attributable to shifting borderlines and the finer division of labour within the subject. Collaboration with other social sciences has occurred, but mainly when it comes to application of knowledge to concrete problems. The more common complaint nowadays is one of economic imperialism, as economists extend economic models to the study of law, crime, the family and politics (the study of the behaviour of voters and functionaries).

Although British economists had long played a significant role as policy experts, chiefly through membership of, and by giving testimony before, Royal Commissions and Select Committees, the First World War served as a watershed in providing greater opportunities for direct employment in government. A number of economists, such as Keynes and Hubert Henderson, were brought into government service on a temporary basis alongside others who had already acquired more regular pre-war experience as civil servants, among them Hubert Llewellyn Smith, William Beveridge, Ralph Hawtrey, Josiah Stamp and Arthur Salter. If a report by the Haldane Committee on the machinery of government had been adopted, what became known later as an Economic General Staff might have been created after the war. A version of this idea did come into being in 1930 in the form of the Economic Advisory Council attached to the Prime Minister's office. It became one of the forums in which Keynes advanced his views on economic theory and policy, and it has a place in the history of economics as a profession in Britain by virtue of the fact that Keynes convinced the Prime Minister, Ramsay MacDonald, that a committee consisting entirely of economists should be given a chance to work out an agreed scientific diagnosis and set of remedies for the depression.[23] No less than Marshall then, though in cooler more technocratic language, Keynes discerned the beginnings of 'a scientific age in economics and business'.[24] Unlike Marshall, however, much of the revolution in theory and policy that is associated with Keynes's name pointed to problems of management or 'directive intelligence' on the part of the state – with respect to a crucial range of monetary and fiscal matters at least. This collection of essays only touches on this important episode in the history of economics. But the Society has fully discharged its obligations in this matter by completing, last year, under the editorship of Austin Robinson, Elizabeth Johnson and Donald Moggridge, its 30-volume edition of Keynes's writings.

As is by now well known, it was not until the Second World War and the first two post-war decades that Keynes's views became a regular part of official thinking in this country and abroad.[25] They contributed to a political consensus on the role of the state that can be conveniently, if over-simply, summarized as the Keynes–Beveridge axis upon which so much of the post-war economic order, domestic and international, was constructed. Like most historical episodes the lineaments of this order become clearer as it disappears or is dismantled. Keynes was wrong when he jestingly speculated about the possibilities of economists becoming innocent dentists concerned solely with technocratic repairs to an otherwise healthy body economic.[26] Economists of different persuasions sometimes find or thrust themselves, however briefly, into the political limelight. But for the most part they are to be found behind the scenes in business, financial institutions, government departments, policy think-tanks and international organizations. Larger numbers make their living by teaching and conducting research in universities and other institutions of higher and further education, where they form part of the body of public-sector professionals that those working in higher education have become, particularly since 1945. Judged by the numbers of students now taking economic courses, whether as single honours or in combination with other subjects, in universities and polytechnics, the founders of the RES would have grounds for satisfaction.

Public image is a variable entity, with a large subjective component that makes generalization futile. Some popular misunderstandings persist, the most hardy perennial being that economists seldom agree on anything. Debate within the profession is certainly lively and sometimes heated, not merely when public policy issues are discussed but also when differences of opinion about research priorities and methods are aired. Whereas some of this is not merely inevitable but healthy, the fundamental disagreements about the very nature of the science that made formation of the BEA both difficult and necessary no longer inhibit progress – though one should not expect such progress to be as readily demonstrable as it is in *some* natural scientific fields. It should also be said that the international proliferation of journals has created conditions that favour a healthy pluralism. The variety of positions that had to be encompassed within the pages of the *Journal* in its first decades can now be accommodated separately – though at the cost of reduced communication between specialists, and between specialists and the public at large.

A century of economics provides plenty of scope for observations on changing as well as unchanging fashions. Many incidental observations and conclusions can be found in the essays collected here: others will occur to readers. This introductory survey can perhaps best be closed by mentioning one or two thoughts that might strike a representative economist, 1890s style, when faced with economics, 1990s style. He – it is a source of regret that the chances of him being a her do not seem to have grown remarkably – would be surprised by the extent to which mathematics is now essential to the understanding of over half the articles in the *Journal*. As Peter Newman shows, it has taken 80 years or more for some of Edgeworth's contributions to mathematical economics and statistics to be fully appreciated, but even the most advanced of mathematical economists a century ago would have to learn several new branches of mathematics to appreciate some of the work now published. He might be surprised to find how little the *Journal* still dealt – even dispassionately – with socialistic blueprints for an ideal society, or any overt party programme for that matter. The relative absence of coverage of industrial relations issues, and less markedly of social problems generally, would be striking, although most reports on labour disputes, if they were now given, would contain no great novelty. He would certainly be impressed by the systematic use of sophisticated methods of collecting, interrogating and analysing statistical evidence now employed, especially compared with the casual empiricism of his own day and for some time after.

Although an 1890s observer would be staggered by the scale and complexity of the professional organization of economics today – by the myriad of specialized journals, by the number of different research organizations, private, official and inter-governmental, by the scale of the international ramifications of economics – the continuing hybrid nature of the profession would be less baffling. There are no political worthies, active or retired, adorning the Council of the RES today; but the professional style still follows the non-exclusive habits adopted by the founding fathers in being tailored more to the needs of a learned society whose relations with the public are at best indirect than to those of a scientific academy or qualifying association.

At various stages of its history the RES has been criticized for being insularly British, overly-dominated by Cambridge or Oxbridge, and insufficiently enterprising in such matters as the holding of meetings and the articulation of a clear professional standpoint. Rebuttals of most of these charges can be found in the following pages. Without suggesting that the Society has met every legitimate expectation throughout its career, when the human and financial resources available to it for most of its life are borne in mind, both the apportionment of effort and the results can be defended. Only in the case of the emergence of the Association of University Teachers of Economics (AUTE) in the 1920s, a body largely devoted to serving the need for annual meetings on the part of those engaged in teaching economics, can the Society be said to have passed up an important opportunity. With the AUTE and the RES now in harness together over the organization of annual conferences and in publishing the papers presented, and with an organization of the Heads of Economics Departments as part of a new troika, this too has been remedied. Indeed, in recent years the RES has taken several steps towards becoming an umbrella body for a large range of professional activities, including the need, once more, to articulate the interests of economics and its practitioners wherever they are to be found. As Austin Robinson points out, we have arrived at a situation in which, as the Society embarks on its next century, one of its chief activities, the *Journal*, has become less central, by itself, to British economists: it is a leading international journal among several. By way of compensation, the RES has found other, sometimes more urgent, ways of making itself useful to the life of British economics.

NOTES

1 On the occasion of the Society's jubilee in the *Economic Journal*, 50 (1940), 409.
2 See John K. Whitaker (ed). *Centenary Essays on Alfred Marshall* (New York: Cambridge University Press for the Royal Economic Society, 1990).
3 G. L. S. Shackle, in a work devoted to this period, has dubbed it *The Years of High Theory: Invention and Tradition in Economic Thought, 1926–1939* (Cambridge: Cambridge University Press, 1967).
4 See Viscount Goschen, *Essays and Addresses on Economic Questions, 1865–1893* (London: Edward Arnold, 1905), p.vii, and his Presidential Address on 'Ethics and Economics' for 1893, pp. 328–41.
5 Much of the pioneering work on the origins of the Society and on professionalization generally has been done by A. W. Coats; see especially 'The Origins and

Early Development of the Royal Economic Society', *Economic Journal*, 78 (1968), 349–71; and 'Sociological Aspects of British Economic Thought', *Journal of Political Economy*, 75 (1967), 706–29. His account of the origins was largely based on the papers of R. Inglis Palgrave, which can now be supplemented by the Foxwell Papers.

6 For details of other learned and scientific societies formed during the nineteenth century see P. Alter, *The Reluctant Patron; Science and the State in Britain, 1850–1920* (Oxford: Oxford University Press, 1987), pp. 256–9.

7 For a collection of presidential addresses to Section F on method and scope see R. L. Smyth (ed.), *Essays in Economic Method* (London: Gerald Duckworth, 1962).

8 See A. Sidgwick and Eleanor Sidgwick, *Henry Sidgwick: A Memoir* (London: Macmillan, 1906), pp. 424–5.

9 See A. W. Coats, 'Political Economy and the Tariff Reform Campaign of 1903', *Journal of Law and Economics*, 11 (1968), 181–229.

10 The most recent and thorough study of the relationship between economics and economic history can be found in A. Kadish, *Historians, Economists, and Economic History* (London: Routledge, 1989); see also his earlier work on *The Oxford Economists in the Late Nineteenth Century* (Oxford: Oxford University Press, 1982), and G. Koot, *English Historical Economics, 1870–1926* (Cambridge: Cambridge University Press, 1987).

11 For some recent approaches to this question see J. Maloney, *Marshall, Orthodoxy and the Professionalisation of Economics* (Cambridge: Cambridge University Press, 1985), and David Collard, 'Cambridge After Marshall', in J.K. Whitaker (ed.), *Centenary Essays on Alfred Marshall* (Cambridge: Cambridge University Press, 1990).

12 *Economic Journal*, 1 (1891), 5.

13 See Peter D. Groenewegen, 'Alfred Marshall and the Establishment of the Cambridge Economics Tripos', *History of Political Economy*, 20 (1988), 627–67.

14 See his letter to Edgeworth, 28 August 1902, reprinted in A. C. Pigou (ed.), *Memorials of Alfred Marshall* (London: Macmillan, 1925), p. 436.

15 Edgeworth was also unique in being the only economist to receive the honour of having his articles published under RES auspices during his life-time; see *Papers Relating to Political Economy* (three volumes, London: Macmillan for the Royal Economic Society, 1925).

16 See K. Tribe, 'Political Economy and Provincial Culture in the Later Nineteenth Century', University of Keele, Department of Economics and Management Science Working Paper No. 80-1, January 1988. See also a forthcoming volume on the institutionalization of British economics edited by I. Hont and K. Tribe entitled *Trade, Politics and Letters* (London: Routledge).

17 The committee consisted of William Cunningham, E. C. K. Gonner, F. Y. Edgeworth, H. S. Foxwell, H. Higgs, L. L. Price and J. S. Nicholson; see the report in *Report of the Meeting of the BAAS*, 1894, pp. 365–91.

18 Ibid., p. 381.

19 Ibid., p. 391.
20 Whatever the BAAS report may have said about the advantages enjoyed by American economists at this time, the same dilemmas plagued the early years of professionalization; see Robert L. Church, 'Economists as Experts: The Rise of an Academic Profession in America, 1870–1917', in L. Stone (ed.), *The University in Society* (Princeton, NJ: Princeton University Press, 1975), vol. II, pp. 571–609.
21 As reprinted in C. W. Guillebaud's variorum edition of Marshall's *Principles of Economics* (London: Macmillan for the Royal Economic Society, 1961), vol. II, pp. 160–81.
22 On this point see M. Sanderson, *The Universities and British Industry, 1850–1970* (London: Routledge, 1972), p. 192.
23 For further detail see S. K. Howson and D. Winch, *The Economic Advisory Council; A Study in Economic Advice during Depression and Recovery, 1930–39* (Cambridge: Cambridge University Press, 1977).
24 *The Collected Writings of J. M. Keynes* (30 volumes, London: Macmillan for the Royal Economic Society, 1971–89), vol. 19, p. 726.
25 See Alec Cairncross and Nita Woods, *The Economic Section, 1939–1961; A Study in Economic Advising* (London: Routledge, 1989).
26 In 'Economic Possibilities for Our Grandchildren', in Keynes, *Collected Writings*, vol. 9, pp. 321–32.

2
Foundation and Early Years

Alon Kadish and Richard D. Freeman

The century since the foundation of the British Economic Association (BEA) has witnessed the emergence of economics as a powerful and respected academic discipline capable of supporting an established profession. The period 1890 to 1915 has accordingly been depicted as 'a watershed dividing the predominantly amateur tradition of the eighteenth and nineteenth centuries from World War I, when the professionalization of economics began to gather momentum'.[1] But retrospective knowledge can prove misleading when one is reconstructing the origins and early years of any organization: neither the end result nor the path taken may correspond with the initial intentions of all the founders.

Our reconstruction goes back to the 1880s when political economy, particularly at Oxbridge, was regarded as part of the general educational preparation required of the governing classes. In this guise it was represented in the curricula of Greats and the School of Modern History at Oxford and the Moral Sciences and History Triposes at Cambridge. The study of economics did not entail early specialization or separation from related subjects. On the contrary, it was seen as an important contributory field within philosophy and history. Thus while economics constituted an integral part of some of the most popular degree offerings at Oxbridge, there were few university dons who taught economics alone, and even fewer perhaps who wished to do so. The study of economics was defined more by subject matter than by method, so that the title of 'economist' could legitimately be assumed by members of a number of professions with widely differing educational backgrounds. The common element was an interest in the analysis of some economic phenomenon for whatever reason.

In founding the BEA and in issuing a journal economists were consciously following an academic trend which preceded professionalization, namely a movement towards clearer demarcation and definition of the field of scholarly endeavour. More specifically, they were pursuing the example of philosophy and history, those disciplines with which economics had long been associated within university curricula. The philosophy journal *Mind*, founded in 1876, and the *English Historical Review*, founded in 1886, provided useful models for a new kind of specialized journal, with articles, reviews, specialists' reports, abstracts from foreign periodicals and current notes.[2]

During the early 1880s another influence was at work that was more specific to economics: the revival of fundamental attacks on the subject by radical socialists. This led a number of economists to seek means of establishing more precisely where legitimate and constructive criticism ended and nihilistic attacks began. An effort was made to establish a more catholic core to the subject by drawing together various theoretical and methodological qualifications to the older orthodoxy in an effort to reaffirm the scientific possibilities of studying the economic dimension of human affairs. Many economists were prepared to admit the validity of the grievances voiced by socialists, particularly in the field of income and wealth distribution; they were also willing to grant the need to explore new avenues for government intervention in economic life. But they were not prepared to join their socialist critics in entirely rejecting economics. In this manner some vocal critics of the doctrinal and methodological narrowness of classical orthodoxy were drawn into alliance with those who adopted a more conservative attitude to the past.

One such critic, Herbert Somerton Foxwell, was to become a prime mover in the early attempts to found the BEA, working initially in collaboration with Robert Inglis Palgrave. Foxwell was a Fellow of St John's College, Cambridge, and had been teaching economics within the Moral Sciences and History Triposes for a decade or more. Palgrave was a banker and occasional writer on banking subjects who had held the post of editor of *The Economist* since 1877. A month before the BEA was due to be launched officially, Foxwell recalled that as early as 1883, at the request of Palgrave, who was then President of Section F of the British Association for the Advancement of Science (BAAS), he had drafted the plan for a new association.[3] He was certainly in a position by 1887 to make public to an American audience his version of the prospectus for an 'economic society' to be undertaken partly in emulation of the American Economic Association founded in 1885. It would 'aim at the advancement of theory, at the consolidation of economic opinion, at the encouragement of historical research, and at the criticism and direction of industrial and financial policy'. With time he hoped that additional objectives would be secured – a library, a journal, reprints and translations of scarce works, and the compilation of a dictionary.[4]

The bias towards historical matters reflects the bibliographic and bibliophile enthusiasms of Foxwell and Palgrave; and the library and the dictionary were later to be achieved by their personal initiative alone. Foxwell was a knowledgeable and obsessive collector of rare economic works, the results of which can be found in two of the world's best libraries, the Goldsmith's Library at the University of London and the Kress Library at Harvard. Palgrave was to become the editor of the *Dictionary of Political Economy* which began to appear in 1891, partly, once more, in emulation of foreign models already produced in France and Germany. *Palgrave's Dictionary*, as it became known when it reappeared in the 1920s, contained contributions from many who were to figure prominently in the new Society, though there was also a current of criticism behind the scenes from those who doubted Palgrave's competence as an editor and regretted that the work had not been directed by a committee.[5]

Of the other main objectives, the question of whether the association should precede or follow the creation of the journal remained unsettled while efforts were still being made within the Statistical Society to achieve more autonomy and *lebensraum* for economics. It was only after December 1885, when an attempt to obtain endorsement for a policy of holding regular meetings devoted to economics was defeated, that the two proposals began to come together.[6] As the least controversial of the objectives, the feasibility of the journal was under discussion in Cambridge in 1884, but had still not progressed beyond 'preliminaries and correspondence' by November 1885.[7] Foxwell had made inquiries about likely support from contributors and subscriptions, but the main problem was that of finding an editor 'with sufficient leisure and fortune to work without pay'. And if this condition could be met, there was still the more substantive question of the editor's credentials and acceptability to those who were making the running.

By this stage Alfred Marshall had become involved in the Cambridge discussions. One of his former pupils at Oxford, E. C. K. Gonner, who was teaching at Bristol, Liverpool, and for the University of London extension movement, had written in support of a monthly periodical. Gonner thought that:

> the great difficulty with regard to economics arises from the fact that there is no common recognition of any *scientific* truth. There is still less knowledge of the history of political economy and of the various teachers under whose influence it had attained its present position. Now a monthly magazine would aid in remedying these defects. ... At present political economy really finds [no] utterance in a magazine except to enforce some proposition which has been made the subject of political battle. Consequently very little progress is made.[8]

Progress, in Gonner's view, required contraction in the scope of economic inquiries and withdrawal from normative preaching: 'the student of Political Economy has enough to do without professing to give any decision on other questions, however great though their importance may be.'[9]

In passing Gonner's letter on to Foxwell, Marshall commented that '[Gonner] is not quite first rate, but if the economic magazine is halting for want of an editor, he might perhaps do'.[10] Even without this lacklustre recommendation, Gonner's programme of withdrawal and passivity was unlikely to prove congenial to Foxwell. He agreed that a more limited role should be assigned to theory, but he did not regard political economy as reducible to theory. 'At the same time', he wrote in 1887, 'that [political economy] aims at developing theory, at giving it scientific precision and exactness, it assigns it a more modest place in the solution of practical questions, and treats these latter on a wider as well as a more historical and statistical basis.'[11] Thus broadened, the economist could assume a more active role as an objective guide to public affairs. In reviewing the new *Quarterly Journal of Economics* and the *Revue d'Economie Politique*, he claimed that:

> There can be little doubt as to the salutary influence of such publications. They will lend both to strengthen and to exhibit the substantial agreement which exists between trained economists, and thus enormously to increase the legitimate influence of the study on practical affairs, so long on the wane after a period of perhaps excessive and illegitimate influence. They must also stimulate research, by giving publicity to those technical and detailed investigations so much wanted, but for which it is so difficult to find the necessary audience of experts; as well as by furnishing students with information as to sources of material and authorities. In every way they must tend to advance the science and its influence at a time when the policy of States more than ever turns upon economic considerations, and when, therefore, it is more than ever important that the judgment of those who have given special attention to these matters should obtain due publicity and recognition.[12]

It is hardly surprising, therefore, that Gonner was not considered to be a serious candidate for the editorship of what was intended to be a policy-oriented journal. But in achieving this another extreme had to be avoided: '[A]ny number of men with strong views will volunteer,' Foxwell wrote to Palgrave, 'but these are just the persons we don't want. We want cool heads, keen brains, and impartial judgment. With these are required scholarship, information and if possible knowledge of German. It seems to me a most difficult and delicate post.'[13] The candidate most favoured by Marshall and Foxwell was John Neville Keynes, who despite repeated refusals remained under pressure to take on the delicate task until 1890.[14]

At the more mundane level of finance, Foxwell's inquiries seem to have suggested that the readership was not likely to be large enough for the journal to be self-supporting in its early stages. Early in 1886 there was a possibility of diverting a surplus of some £200 towards the journal from the unexpended balance of a £1,000 grant which had been made by a Mr Millar, an Edinburgh merchant sympathetic to socialism, to fund the Industrial Remuneration Conference held in January of that year. Millar had left the disposal of the £200 to the conference's trustees, one of whom was Foxwell.[15] The money was eventually used to support a series of lectures, but the possibility of private sponsorship brought home the problem of how to ensure the journal's scientific integrity. Marshall was worried that acceptance of Millar's support might lead to undue influence. While the money was still available, he proposed, as a safeguard, that an association with an editorial committee responsible for the journal should be established on the basis of annual subscriptions.[16] This would guarantee the independence of the association and allow it to accept Millar's subvention. In making this suggestion Marshall had effectively come to the same conclusion as Foxwell, who had written in the previous year that the creation of an economic society would 'ensure the catholic character of the review, and prevent it from taking the colour of a particular school or clique'.[17] Henceforth the plans for an association and a journal were joined.

A related problem raised by Marshall was that of cost. He estimated that the journal would cost at least £300 in its first year, perhaps £50 in the second, and 'after a few years it ought to pay its way'. A more detailed calculation was produced by the statistician, Robert Giffen, who estimated that £300 per annum would be needed to pay for printing and paper to produce a 120 page quarterly of 1,000 copies. To this he added £100 for the editor and the same sum for commissioned articles.[18] Similar figures were obtained from inquiries into the costs of the *Quarterly Journal of Economics*.[19] In the event, these figures were over-sanguine: in 1892, the cost was £690 4s 0d, in 1893, £676 16s 2d, and in 1894, £641 16s 5d. In view of the problem of finding a publisher willing to underwrite the venture, with the uncertain hope that it would later earn a modest profit, the link between an association and the journal became vital. As the organ of an association, subscriptions could be made part of the membership fee; or the latter could be used to guarantee the journal against losses.[20]

After 1885 an additional stimulant was provided by the example of similar developments abroad, especially the foundation of the American Economic Association. In 1887 Foxwell complained that 'it is not pleasant to reflect that this country which claims to be the foremost of the commercial countries of the world, now stands distinguished amongst them as the only one in which economists have no organ of their own.'[21] Nevertheless, discussions proceeded at a leisurely pace until the end of 1889. No one seems to have been eager to take the initiative, or it was assumed that Marshall should do so. Marshall had indeed taken an interest and had urged J. N. Keynes to accept the editorship.[22] But Marshall was increasingly preoccupied with completing his *Principles*, and he seems to have hoped that any association would be the result of slow natural evolution from a Cambridge base – 'a private assemblage of persons who know one another and afterwards gradually expand into an organisation'.[23] It took the combined efforts of Foxwell and Gonner, and the threat of the society being founded along lines that were unacceptable to him, to force Marshall into action.

In June 1889 Gonner wrote to Marshall once more, restating the need for a journal and offering 'to do all that I can do to assist in making such an undertaking successful'.[24] Once again, Marshall deflected the plea to Foxwell, leading Gonner to conclude that as far as Marshall was concerned, 'for the next two years or so the matter must rest in abeyance unless active measures be taken. Of course I know he will be glad if such be done and I am sure he will render assistance but he will not take an initiative.'[25] Gonner therefore suggested that they proceed without Marshall, and several steps were taken in preparation for launching the society, the most important and enduring of them being Foxwell's successful recruitment of Edgeworth as editor.[26]

Gonner may well have been right about Marshall's passivity had his plan not differed in one fundamental respect from that favoured by Marshall. Gonner was anxious to make fellowship 'something of an honour' to be conferred 'not for an interest in economics but for work'. He agreed with Foxwell 'as to the absolute necessity of some scientific qualification' for fellowship, though any subscriber could pay for the right to receive publications and general reports.[27] Without such an exclusive clause, he argued:

> Everything would be a wrangle about 'first principles' – and necessarily so for what else could we expect from people ignorant of what the first principles are supposed to be. They may differ about them. Economists do differ about them, but the scientific economist has the advantage of knowing which are the results of the principle. He had read what others have written.... I do not doubt that we can arrive at an agreement.[28]

Gonner soon discovered otherwise. Marshall, he complained to Foxwell,

Foundation and Early Years

is prepared to go through fire and water in order to include the blind and the maim and the bold, he must be in a positively truculent mood. The real matter at stake is the authoritative position of the Society. If catholic in M's sense it cannot be authoritative in any true sense. But this is what we both aim at of course. Of course I want it to be catholic, including all shades of economic opinion and ability, but the opinion and the ability must be economic; and to show that it is so we require something more than the annual payment of one guinea.[29]

As Marshall explained to Foxwell: 'I don't want to include "mere" business men. But I don't want to exclude Bank Directors and others of the class who are for me at least the most interesting members of the Political Economy Club.... It is the men of affairs from whom I learn. Poor Edgeworth would not waste his *great* strength as much as he does if he would study the minds of men of affairs and learn from them to get a sense of proportion.'[30]

Marshall did not find it difficult to have his way. He was to serve his term as President of Section F of the British Association in 1890, when it had been decided to discuss the proposals for a society and a journal. At first he was cautious: 'I should be inclined in favour of the proposal,' he wrote to Foxwell, 'if it had the support of all those interested, but not otherwise.'[31] But he must have realized that he could use the mixed audience attracted to the British Association's meeting to circumvent Gonner's exclusionist designs. Shortly afterwards he suggested that a circular be produced announcing that a proposal to form a society and publish a journal would be discussed after Section F's formal business had been concluded.[32]

In his presidential address to Section F on 'Some Aspects of Competition' Marshall mapped out the future of economic investigation, placing it firmly in the middle ground between the narrow dogmatism of the classical theorists and the hasty wholesale condemnation of competition by socialists.

> Every year economic problems become more complex; every year the necessity of studying them from many different points of view and in many different connexions becomes more urgent. Every year it is more manifest that we need to have more knowledge and to get it in order to escape, on the one hand, from the cruelty and waste of irresponsible competition

and the licentious use of wealth, and on the other from the tyranny and the spiritual death of an ironbound socialism.[33]

Once his conception of the role of the society had been accepted Marshall was keen to avert unnecessary controversy. His circular convening the inaugural meeting of the BEA was emphatically neutral and dealt almost entirely with the need for a journal as a means of producing 'thorough scientific work by persons who have not the time, or are unwilling, to write a formal treatise' – work that was 'too technical for the ordinary magazines, and too short for a book'. The circular further stressed the lesson of the Millar episode by arguing that an association was the best means of ensuring that the journal would 'represent all shades of economic opinion, and be the organ not of one school of English economists, but of all schools'.[34] In the same spirit, Marshall was determined that 'room must be made for Cunningham' – his chief Cambridge critic – on the Council of the new society, as well as for L. R. Phelps, one of the editors of the Oxford-inspired rival *Economic Review*.[35]

The *Economic Review* had originated in the Oxford branch of the Christian Social Union (CSU) during the first half of 1890, and without any knowledge of the Cambridge discussions that led to the BEA.[36] The Oxford CSU, founded in 1889, was dominated by the High Church *Lux Mundi* group who sought to combine Christian ends with practical means of dealing with economic and social problems. While collecting material for the *Review*'s first number, John Carter approached L. R. Phelps, a popular Oxford college lecturer in economics, with the offer of joining its editorial board. At around the same time (June 1890), the Oxford men caught wind of Cambridge developments. They were eager to assure Marshall, Foxwell and others that no competition was intended and were clearly taken aback by Marshall's cool response to their appeals for collaboration. Although Marshall did not relish publication of a rival periodical, he tolerated the inevitable once the BEA was in being.[37] The first number of the *Review* appeared before the *Journal* and at a lower price. Its inception may well have been the final stimulus needed by the founders of the BEA.

The Association's inaugural meeting was prepared by a group that met in the house of John Biddulph Martin, Chairman of Martin's Bank and Honorary Treasurer to the Institute of Bankers. An audience of some 200 attended the actual inauguration held at

University College on 20th November, with invitations having been sent to all lecturers on economics in any university or 'public college', the members of the Councils of the London, Dublin and Manchester Statistical Societies, the members of the Political Economy Club and of the committee of Section F of the BAAS plus a few others.[38] The circular convening this meeting emphasized the now agreed aims of the Association in producing a journal, and Marshall took the opportunity to denounce controversy concerning the interpretation of past economists as counterproductive. He hoped that the journal's reviewers would 'take the writings of ...others in the best possible sense'. In the interests of harmony, he also opposed the organization of public meetings along the lines of those held by the BAAS. Progress could best be secured by all schools working 'amicably together, interpreting each other in the fairest and most generous manner'. More frankly, he added that meetings could easily be dominated 'by people whose time was not very valuable'. The question of public meetings was left in abeyance.

The criterion for membership was raised once more at this meeting by L. H. Courtney, who moved that 'any person who desires to further the aims of the Association, and is approved by the Council, be admitted to membership'. He apologized for saddling the Council with the responsibility for refusing applicants, but felt that there 'were some things which must be taken to be finally fixed'. In the same way that a mathematical journal could not fail to reject a contribution affecting to square the circle, so an economic association could not support patently false views such as that 'an unlimited supply of paper [currency] would cover all the difficulties of the world'. Henry Sidgwick supported some exclusiveness in dealing with 'any obviously objectionable applicant', but Edgeworth argued 'that it was impossible to find any satisfactory test of orthodoxy in economic doctrine', and that any attempt to apply a test would reduce membership to unacceptable levels. The power to exclude was included in the bye-laws, but the criteria for acceptance were left unspecified.

The first Council was created at this meeting with powers to draft rules and add to their number, should they so wish. Viscount Goschen became the first President, despite the mild protests registered by Bernard Shaw against having a party politician occupy this role – an argument with which Goschen himself modestly agreed, though the objection was answered by Marshall, who prefaced his reply by making it clear that he was 'not a political supporter' of Goschen. Indeed, so unmoved were the members of the Council by Shaw's argument that all four of the first Vice Presidents were politicians: A. J. Balfour, a Conservative MP; H. C. E. Childers, a Gladstonian Liberal MP; Leonard H. Courtney, a Liberal Unionist MP; and John Morley, a Gladstonian Liberal, MP.

The composition of the Council underwent little change during the first ten years. Goschen remained President throughout. The Duke of Argyll and Marshall were appointed Vice Presidents in 1893 and 1896 respectively. As some members died their places were taken by a younger generation, including Edwin Cannan, Henry Higgs, A. W. Flux, W. A. S. Hewins, William Smart and Sydney Webb. Most of the Council took little part in the BEA's affairs, the most active members being Bonar, Edgeworth, Higgs, Price, Martin, Elliott and, in the first years, Foxwell. Marshall, although a member of the first Executive Committee created in 1896, attended only four meetings, and only one after April 1891.[39] Having secured the channels of communication and possible lines of influence between academic economists and politicians, the civil service and the business community, while at the same time bolstering an image of the profession's unity, he could safely return to his efforts to reshape the Cambridge curriculum – the efforts which led to the establishment of the Economics Tripos in 1903. The running of the *Journal* and the Association could safely be left in the hands of its various subcommittees.

The most important early tasks were to complete the organization, recruit members and produce the journal. On 24th November, Bonar, Edgeworth and Foxwell were asked by the Executive to prepare circulars canvassing members; Foxwell, Giffen and Martin were charged with seeking a publisher; and Edgeworth 'was instructed to ascertain what eminent writers might be expected immediately to contribute'.[40] At a later meeting Edgeworth was given the freedom to select the articles for the first issue. By 6 December, the circular to prospective members was approved and some 5,000 copies were issued.[41] It was agreed that Macmillan should publish the journal, and it was later determined that it would be a quarterly, with the first issue to appear by the end of

March.[42] Giffen and Foxwell were entrusted with drafting the contract with Macmillan which was approved by the Council on 11 February 1891, less than seven weeks before the first number was published.

The affairs of the journal were delegated to a publications subcommittee (a full committee from March 1891), whose original members appear to have been Foxwell, Giffen, Martin and, from January 1891, Elliott, with Edgeworth attending meetings as a non-member. In addition to publishing the *Journal*, the BEA had intended to translate and publish important foreign works in economics and to reprint early English tracts, an objective that was later to become an important function of the Royal Economic Society. In April 1891, the publications committee was asked to look into the cost of translating, editing and publishing Wilhelm Roscher's *Zum Geschichte der Englischen Volkswirtschaftslehre*. The committee's view was that the BEA's finances were not sound enough to bear the cost. Nevertheless, Foxwell was asked to submit a report on the general issue, and following a discussion of Foxwell's report the Council created an enlarged committee to examine the likely burden on the Association's finances of this kind of scholarly publication. The recommendations of this committee were rejected in April 1893 on grounds of cost. Although £50 was made available as the nucleus for a publications fund, by 1895 this was exhausted without producing any reprints. The only other recorded venture was the reprint of William Petty's *Treatises on Taxes and Contributions*. From its publication in 1895 until after 1901 the publications committee remained inactive while the BEA's finances suffered from falling membership.

During the BEA's inaugural meeting Goschen had complained that 'there was a general idea that economists had finished their proper work in the education of the nation'. In 1895, addressing the Association's annual dinner, Goschen was unable to report any perceptible change in the popular image. The science, he complained, 'was not treated with the respect accorded to other sciences. It received scant courtesy at the hands of politicians and of the practical man, who never reads, never writes, and seldom thinks.'[43] He took offence especially at the decision by the Foreign Office to replace political economy with shorthand in its examinations. A drop in the demand for economics courses within the extension movement gave further cause for concern. In 1894 the

BEA had made some unsuccessful attempts to enhance the status of economics by, for example, urging the Council of Legal Education to add economics to its subjects of instruction. Failures on this front resulted in inaction. Any success in raising the status of economics during this period must be attributed to academic institutionalization at Cambridge, the London School of Economics, Birmingham, Manchester and elsewhere.

The policy of holding regular public meetings, left open at the inaugural meeting, was finally resolved after a long discussion at the annual meeting of 29 July 1892. After seven years the BEA could boast that five public meetings had been organized, though divisiveness was minimized by inviting eminent economists to address meetings rather than allow a general free-for-all.[44] In 1906 a more ambitious departure was announced, namely the decision to emulate the meetings of the American Economic Association by holding an annual 'economic congress' in London, the first of which was devoted to a two-day discussion of 'Small Holdings and the Taxation of Ground Values'.[45] Having got into this business, enthusiasm seems to have grown: in addition to the annual congress, quarterly or termly meetings were started in 1907 and both types of meeting continued until the outbreak of the First World War.

Throughout its first ten years the Council and Executive Committee were greatly preoccupied with finance. This probably accounts for the Council's instruction to Edgeworth in April 1892 that 'in future the size of the Journal should not exceed on an average 12 sheets'.[46] Again in 1896 the editors were asked to try to reduce the length of the *Journal* to 160 pages and to limit the number of copies printed. Shortage of funds also frustrated the founders' plans to promote 'economic investigations' and, as we have seen, it also held back the work of the publications committee.

The BEA had got off to a good start with some 570 journal subscriptions at 1 guinea each within its first year, as well as 100 life compositions at 10 guineas each and a relatively high income from advertising. By the end of 1891 it had invested £450 18s 1d in 3 per cent India Stocks, while reporting a cash balance of £19 50s 5d and net assets of £47 0s 0d. In addition the Association had guarantees for over £700, well above the £300 which in January 1891 the Council had regarded as the minimum necessary for publishing a 208 page journal.[47] However, from 1891 income began to fall, resulting in the cuts in costs shown in table 2.1. In order to cover the costs in 1892 and purchase more India Stocks the guarantors were asked to pay 10s in the pound, thereby raising £251.[48] Even so, the BEA was little better off than it had been in 1891.

Official membership had peaked in 1893–4 at about 750 and by 1895 it had fallen to around 700, of whom 100 were from overseas. Furthermore, subscription accounts were well below official membership figures and, as shown in table 2.2, subscriptions fell by nearly 40 per cent between 1892 and 1900. The fall in membership remained a cause for concern, so much so that in October 1897 the Council agreed to reward the BEA clerk 1s for each new member. In reviewing its work up to 1897 the Council appealed 'earnestly to members to do all they can to induce suitable persons to join the Association', and stated that 'the Association's situation would be still more satisfactory if all Members of the Association would feel it their duty to take an active part in its work, and especially in the enlistment of new Members'.[49]

The fall in subscriptions was at first partly offset by rising non-subscriptions sales of the *Journal* at 5s a copy. But after 1894 advertising diminished and after 1896 there were no further life compositions. Consequently, investments were cashed for two years before they were restored in 1900, when the BEA's net assets reached £1,451 6s 11d (about £50,000 in 1990 values).

The Council's decision to reduce the size and print-run of the *Journal* served to reduce printing and distribution costs, as shown in table 2.1. A major expenditure item was payment to contributors who received 10s per page for original articles and 5s per page for reviews and translations unless the work was of 'exceptional difficulty', in which case Edgeworth could pay up to 7s 6d per page. Authors of notes and memoranda received up to 10s per page at the editor's discretion. Such was the accepted practice, and with the relatively low academic salaries of the period these payments provided an important source of supplementary income. As both editor of the *Journal* and the Association's secretary Edgeworth's initial salary was £100 per annum. The clerk or assistant secretary who assisted both Edgeworth and the Treasurer received £25 per annum.

Table 2.1 British Economic Association Finances

	1892	1894	1896	1898	1900
Income					
Subscriptions	687.3.3	615.16.5	546.8.2	517.7.2	424.19.10
Journal sales	20.2.2	179.16.2	161.18.8	199.3.4	201.10.8
Advertisements	75.0.0	100.0.0	21.7.10	12.12.0	9.14.8
Other income[a]	464.6.4	76.0.6	99.3.3	27.15.2	29.12.0
Total	1246.11.8	971.13.1	846.17.7	756.17.8	665.13.2
Payments					
EJ print	464.11.0	641.16.5	371.14.6	307.12.3	306.7.9
Contributors	225.12.4		203.9.8	187.3.4	170.7.6
Salaries	191.14.3	135.0.0	145.0.0	145.0.0	150.0.0
India Stock (3%)	189.0.0	52.10.0	62.18.6	–	–
Other expenses	112.7.5	137.3.1	63.14.11	54.18.9	51.11.6
Total	1183.5.8	966.9.6	848.18.7	694.13.4	678.6.9
Assets					
India Stock (3%)	630.10.8	900.12.0	1016.12.0	922.7.8	1048.7.4
EJ in stock	100.0.0	100.0.0	100.0.0	100.0.0	100.0.0
Cash	81.4.6	3.8.3	32.14.5	124.8.5	69.7.0
Net assets	781.6.7	1107.3.10	1105.17.11	1123.1.8	1451.6.11

[a] Other income in 1892 reflects £251 received from guarantors plus £199 10s 0d from life compositions of £10 0s 0d repaid at death. In 1894 and 1896, £52 10s 0d and £62 18s 6d respectively were received from life compositions, the balance being dividends from the India Stock.

The BEA's one unqualified success was the *Journal*. As has been shown earlier, it was not intended to be a specialist publication catering solely for the interests of academic or quasi-academic economists. Rather it was meant to serve as a means of disseminat-

Table 2.2 Paying members

1892	1893	1894	1896	1897	1898	1899	1900
650	585	565	505	485	460	460	390

Based on BEA Accounts.

ing economic truth amongst readers from all walks of life, while setting new standards of economic investigation. According to the *Journal of the Institute of Bankers* it was likely to succeed in this aim.

> [T]here is little doubt that the editor [of the *Economic Journal*] is fully aware of the undesirability of letting professors and theorists occupy the whole field, to the exclusion of those who have practical experience in the conduct of business affairs. A great and useful work is before the Economic Association, if they will endeavour to bridge the gulf that yawns between these two classes, and mitigate that somewhat contemptuous attitude which each class is apt to adopt towards the other.[50]

The *Journal* was meant to be catholic, topical and comprehensive, covering home and international affairs, and offering extensive book reviews as well as lists of new books and the contents of current periodicals. The first issue contained ten articles, six Notes and Memoranda and six book reviews. Later numbers usually had no more than four or five articles, more than ten notes, and double the number of book reviews, with the Notes and Memoranda placed after the reviews rather than before them as in the first number. They were also shorter, and a section on Current Topics was added, possibly in an attempt to compete with Edwin Cannan's quarterly report on legislation and parliamentary inquiries in the *Economic Review*.

The changes in the *Journal* reflected financial and practical constraints as well as Edgeworth's perception of his editorial duties. There were always enough Notes and Memoranda, but after the first two numbers, articles were in short supply.[51] As for the order of the *Journal*'s sections, Edgeworth had the articles and reviews printed first to allow him to update Notes and Memoranda and Current Topics, which formed nearly a quarter of the early numbers, until the very last deadline, some two or three weeks before going to print. In catering for a non-specialist readership Edgeworth, with Foxwell and Bonar's support, felt that short analytical reports on current developments possessed wider appeal and greater instructive value than the longer articles. Since periodicals such as the *Journal of the Royal Statistical Society* and the *Journal of the Institute of Bankers* did not provide satisfactory in-depth coverage of relevant current affairs, it was up to the *Journal* to fill the gap.

It was generally agreed that the *Journal* should cover international events and developments in economic theory. This was largely done by the foreign Corresponding Members who sent in reports on whatever subject they deemed suitable, with little interference from Edgeworth.[52] The *Journal* also took particular care to review foreign works, theoretical and descriptive. These were reviewed partly by British scholars and increasingly by foreign correspondents, including Charles Gide, Maffeo Pantaleoni, F. W. Taussig, John B. Clark and Irving Fisher. Notes on English subjects were decided upon by Edgeworth and Higgs, who asked experts for specific reports. These included the work of the Labour Commission, the Trades Union Congress, major strikes, the report by the Commission on Old-Age Pauperism, and various other parliamentary reports and papers. Under Current Topics Edgeworth included meetings of various organizations, sources of statistics, academic and civil service appointments, new legislation and reports on foreign economists' association. Notes and Memoranda were largely descriptive or applied, and the choice of subjects offers a convenient guide to current economic issues.

By far the most frequent subject, over 120 out of the nearly 300 notes in the first ten volumes, was labour, including industrial relations, trade unions and co-operatives, income distribution, and the living conditions of the working classes. Another common theme was socialism. Thus the Notes reflected the prevalent concern aroused by the militancy and growth of new unionism and the increase in the incidence of strikes in England and abroad. It was generally assumed that the state should create conditions favorable to industrial peace and greater social harmony, matters frequently dealt with by contributors.[53] *Journal* contributors tended to support unionism for a variety of reasons, one of which was that unions served as a means of raising wages and reducing poverty. By the 1890s the strict individualism of the Poor Law and the Charity Organization Society was gradually being replaced by a more 'social' view of the nature of poverty. Studies of 'unemployment' also came to replace works on the 'unemployed'.

Other prominent subjects were money and banking with 45 entries, and India (mainly currency) with 60. For the first six years the debate on bimetallism featured prominently, but with an end to falling prices in the mid-1890s monetary issues lost some of their urgency. During the early 1890s the fall in agricultural prices led to frequent notes on agriculture, to be replaced later in the decade by an emphasis on international trade – the result of growing concern over the balance of trade. Railway questions, including that of nationalization, proved a hardy annual with 12 entries. Political economy, economic history and history of economic thought mustered only 20 entries between them, and on a strict classification only one or two notes were theoretical. To summarize, the relative importance of subjects was determined by current concerns, with a strong tendency towards a descriptive rather than a theoretical approach.[54]

Similar observations may be made on the articles and reviews. Bimetallism was a common subject during the early 1890s, with articles strongly in favour of adopting a bimetallic standard, while the reviews remained sympathetic but guarded. This was an area in which Edgeworth found it necessary to exercise considerable caution so as not to antagonize either Foxwell and the bimetallists or Giffen and the monometallists.[55] There were 11 articles on Indian monetary affairs, mainly dealing with the silver question, and six articles on institutional aspects of banking. The one exception here was William Smart's 1891 article on a 'New Theory of Interest' which was an exposition of Böhm-Bawerk's views on the subject.

Concern about the new US tariffs and protectionism in continental Europe and the colonies led to a spate of articles and reviews dealing with books on international trade. The articles again were mainly descriptive, with the exception of Edgeworth's well-known 1894 trilogy on 'The Pure Theory of International Values'. The reviewers tended on the whole to defend free trade (but not untrammelled competition) and were wary of imperial federation or tariff reform.[56] L. L. Price, however, having denounced protection in early issues as 'a policy difficult to reconcile with an intelligent appreciation of the chief results of economic study',[57] underwent a change of heart and later began to express doubts on the universal applicability of free trade.[58]

During the mid-1890s there was also a noticeable increased interest in public finance. Several of the 20 articles in this category were on international subjects, including taxation in the United States and progressive taxation in Holland. There were articles on the incidence of local government rates and their relationship to overall taxation. Again, the most important theoretical work on taxation came from Edgeworth in his three articles on the pure theory of taxation in 1900 and 1901. Other subjects included agriculture, where interest was stimulated by low prices, and railways, mainly from the hand of W. M. Acworth.[59]

Economic history and history of economic thought accounted for some 23 articles. The articles on economic history were on a variety of subjects from the cloth trade in the north of England in the sixteenth and seventeenth centuries to the history of wage movements in France, the United States and the United Kingdom from 1840 to 1891. More is revealed by the reviews on works in economic history. An ecumenical policy towards method is evident from the first number in which the first two reviews, by F. W. Maitland, were of works in economic history. Indeed, in some reviews 'economist' and 'economic historian' were used interchangeably.[60] Economic history was still considered as part of economics although there was some disagreement concerning its state and status. Economic historians and historians regarded economic history as a semi-autonomous discipline, the existence of which was too obvious to require justification. It dealt with some issues which had little to do with mainstream economic theory, such as the relevance of 'wars and political combinations and literature' to the understanding of economic history,[61] or the relation of economic history to constitutional or legal history.[62] The subject even had its own methodological controversies.[63] Some economists, such as L. L. Price, believed that it had reached a sufficiently advanced stage to allow some generalization.[64] Others, such as E. Jenks, were far more sceptical.[65] L. L. Price was representative of most economists, however, in maintaining that the main value of economic history to economics theory lay in supplying useful examples.[66] In view of the intellectual independence already evident in works (and reviews) by economic historians it is not difficult to see in Price's position some of the rationale for the institutional separation of economic history from economic theory.

On the whole reviewers tended to emphasize harmony in the methodological division of labour, especially when both history and theory were used.[67] 'A complete divorce', C. F. Bastable wrote, 'between fact and theory is impossible.'[68] Hence overdependence on, or absence of, facts was criticized.[69] In one instance, however, Edgeworth pronounced it 'refreshing to find in these days a first-rate economist who had the courage to say that deduction is the only effective method'.[70] A similarly tolerant attitude prevailed regarding the relation between current and classical theory.[71]

The relativist view of theory was seldom even hinted at in the reviews, although Bonar suggested that economic doctrine may 'progress by a succession of systems rather than by a uniform evolution'.[72] Yet it sometimes reappeared, as in Cannan's 1892 article on 'The Origin of the Law of Diminishing Returns 1813–1815', in which he demonstrated what he saw as the impossibility of linear continuity in the development of economic theory due to the changing nature of circumstances.[73] Traces of the controversy concerning relativity can also be found in Cannan's 1894 articles on 'The Growth of Manchester and Liverpool 1801–1891', and 'Ricardo in Parliament', and – representing the non-relativists – Price's 1893 article on 'Adam Smith and Recent Economics'.

Marshall was frequently cited as the benchmark of excellence and the final authority on a wide range of issues.[74] His books, including each new edition of the *Principles*, were reviewed at length, and always enthusiastically, by either Edgeworth or Price. Thus Edgeworth in his review of the third edition of the *Principles* wrote:

> The author, unlike so many of that irritable genus instead of deriding those who have misinterpreted him, instead of standing out for every jot and tittle which he had written, has complacently altered expressions which experience had proved to be liable to misconstruction. Like the artist in the well-known story, he has silently listened to and profited by the remarks of experts about details; but meeker than the ancient

master, he has refrained from breaking out against the criticisms which have been *ultra crepidam*.[75]

Marshall was also cited as having achieved the ideal balance between science and practice. In discussing the chapter on trade unions in Marshall's *Elements of Economics of Industry*, Price stated that: 'Few, if any, recent writers on the subject have, we think, combined such originality in theory with such a firm and sensible grasp of practical exigency.'[76] Scientific worth and practical applicability served jointly as the most common criteria of excellence.[77] No work was any good without either, and very good ones offered both. Thus Price praised G. Shaw Lefevre's *Agrarian Tenures* (1893) because 'it will reward the attention alike of the student and of the practical man of affairs'.[78] 'The thirst for knowledge in the sciences', wrote Clara E. Collet, one of Foxwell's London students and, at the time, labour correspondent of the Board of Trade, 'is allowed to be the primary motive of research; a useful end to be attained is in the majority of cases the principal incentive to the economist. The expostulation of the late Professor Rowe to a utilitarian student of mathematics – "For heaven's sake, don't let us do anything useful here!" – finds no echo in the economist's class-room.'[79] Hence sound popular books were approved of, whereas the use of technical terminology incomprehensible to the general reader was criticized.[80]

Of the total number of articles only 13 or 6 per cent can be classified as theoretical, of which more than half were by Edgeworth. Beyond the founders' policy, and in the light of the underdeveloped nature of academic specialization, it is difficult to see how Britain's minute academic community could have supported a predominantly theoretical journal. Accordingly, only about half the articles in the first ten volumes came from academics, some from overseas. Edgeworth with 11 articles was the most prolific, followed by Price (seven), Bastable (five) and Nicholson (five). Sidney Webb wrote four, two with Beatrice as co-author, Marshall three and Sidgwick one. Surprisingly, perhaps, Foxwell, one of the leading advocates of the need for a *Journal*, did not publish a single article, although he plied Edgeworth with advice on articles, reviews and the *Journal*'s layout. A quarter of the articles came from businessmen and bankers, though their share fell in the latter part of the decade. Civil servants were responsible for over 30 articles, while politicians, clergymen and others provided 11 articles.

The catholic approach to the study of economics reflected in the *Journal*'s editorial policy and list of contributors also meant that among the wide variety of books reviewed were some decidedly inferior ones.[81] Edgeworth did more than his fair share of the reviewing, partly to supplement his income but also as a way of filling issues when insufficient material was available from outside contributors. Already by September 1892 he had asked to be relieved of his responsibility as secretary of the BEA. It was eventually agreed at a Council meeting in November 1892 that the Association should appoint 'an officer, resident in London [Edgeworth had to reside for part of the year in Oxford], who would be able to give attention to the organization and development of the association, and who would in the same time be competent to give assistance to the Editor'.[82] In this way Higgs was appointed Secretary and Assistant Editor, to be promoted in 1896 to Joint Editor, while Edgeworth as the senior editor retained the final say on all editorial matters.[83]

Whatever the difficulties the BEA had encountered in the course of its first ten years, the survival of the *Journal* justified the Association's existence. A further step in the promotion of the status of economics was taken with the decision to apply for a royal charter. On the basis of the Executive Committee's recommendation, the Council adopted on 21 June 1901 Higgs's resolution 'that the 10 volumes of the *Journal* and the Index be offered to the King and that his majesty be requested to become Patron of the Society; that the Secretary be empowered to make enquiries with a view to the incorporation of the Association by Royal Charter'. The BEA was about to become the Royal Economic Society.

NOTES

1 See two articles by A W. Coats and Sonia Coats on the social composition of the Royal Economic Society in the *British Journal of Sociology*, 21 (March 1970), 75–85; 24 (June 1973), 165.
2 Both *Mind* and the *English Historical Review* are mentioned as relevant models in the correspondence relating to the founding of the BEA preserved in the Foxwell Papers; see J. N. Keynes to Foxwell, 24 February 1887, and Gonner to Foxwell, 15 February 1890. All letters cited here are from this collection unless otherwise stated. See also Gonner to Giffen, 18 June 1889, Giffen Papers, British Library of Political Science. On the *English Historical Review* more generally see A. Kadish, 'Scholarly Exclusiveness and the Foundation of the *English Historical Review*', *Historical Research*, 61 (June 1988).
3 Foxwell to Phelps, 29 October 1890, Phelps Papers, Oriel College, Oxford; see also A. Kadish, *The Oxford Economists in the Late Nineteenth Century* (Oxford: Oxford University Press, 1982), pp. 141–2.
4 'The Economic Movement in England', *Quarterly Journal of Economics*, 2 (1887), 103.
5 See the entry under 'Palgrave's Dictionary' by Murray Milgate in *The New Palgrave Dictionary of Economics* (London: Macmillan, 1987). See also Foxwell to Phelps, 29 October 1890, Phelps Papers, Oriel College, Oxford, and Edgeworth's review in *Economic Journal* (*EJ*), 2 (September 1892).
6 See Foxwell to Palgrave, 28 October, 10 November, 25 November and 13 December 1885, Palgrave Papers, and Hyde Clarke to Foxwell, 10 April and 14 August 1886.
7 Foxwell to Palgrave, 25 October 1885, Palgrave Papers: '[T]he publication of a monthly Econ. Review... was on the point of starting six months ago; and negotiations are still going on in certain quarters.' See also Foxwell to Palgrave, 10 November 1885, Palgrave Papers: 'A year ago we discussed it at Cambridge.'
8 Gonner to Marshall, 6 November 1885, appended to Marshall to Foxwell, 8 November 1885. Gonner's is probably the Oxford proposal referred to in Foxwell to Palgrave, 10 November 1885, Palgrave Papers.
9 See E. C. K. Gonner, *Political Economy; An Elementary Textbook of the Economics of Commerce* (London, 1888), pp. 5–6.
10 Marshall to Foxwell, 8 November 1885.
11 [H. S. Foxwell], 'Notes on Recent Additions to the Library', *Journal of the Institute of Bankers* (March 1887). For Foxwell's authorship, see W. Talbot Agar to Foxwell, 8 December 1886.
12 Ibid.
13 Foxwell to Palgrave, no date, Palgrave Papers.
14 See Keynes Diaries, University of Cambridge Library, entries for 22 January, 15 February and 13 March 1887; and page opposite entries for 7–10 February 1889.

Foundation and Early Years 45

15 F. Harrison to Foxwell, 1 February 1886. See also James Oliphant's Preface to John Burnett et al., *The Claims of Labour* (Edinburgh, 1886).
16 Marshall to Foxwell, 26 July 1886. More specifically Marshall feared that Millar 'might want more room for people like [A. R.] Wallace – to say nothing of Hyndman'. Wallace was the co-discoverer with Darwin of the theory of natural selection and a prominent advocate of land nationalization. H. M. Hyndman was leader of the Marxist Social Democratic Federation.
17 Foxwell to Palgrave, 21 November 1885, Palgrave Papers.
18 Giffen to Foxwell, 24 March 1887.
19 Bonar to Foxwell, 10 April 1890.
20 Gonner to Foxwell, 16 January 1890.
21 *Journal of the Institute of Bankers* (March 1887); see note 11 above.
22 See Marshall to Keynes, 17 March 1888 and 7 February 1889, Keynes Papers, Marshall Library, Cambridge.
23 Marshall to Keynes, no date, Keynes Papers.
24 Gonner to Marshall, June 1889.
25 Gonner to Foxwell, 11 June 1889.
26 Gonner to Foxwell, 15 February 1890.
27 Gonner to Foxwell, 19 January 1890.
28 Gonner to Foxwell, 13 March 1890.
29 Gonner to Foxwell, 21 March 1890.
30 Marshall to Foxwell, no date, 1890. In similar vein he had advised the Junior Economic Club at University College London 'not to be careful about exclusions'; see Higgs to Foxwell, 18 July 1890.
31 Marshall to Foxwell, 19 March 1890.
32 Marshall to Foxwell and to Palgrave, 22 March 1890.
33 As reprinted in A. C. Pigou (ed.), *Memorials of Alfred Marshall* (London: Macmillan, 1925), p. 291. Also printed in *The Times*, 5 September 1890, the *Journal of the Royal Statistical Society* (December 1890) and the *Journal of the Institute of Bankers* (October 1890).
34 The circular was reproduced in the *Journal of the Institute of Bankers*, November 1891.
35 Marshall to Foxwell, 10 November 1890. On the foundation of the *Economic Review* see Kadish, *Oxford Economists*, pp. 185–92.
36 See Phelps to Foxwell, 27 October 1890.
37 At the inaugural meeting of the BEA he said that if the *Economic Journal* had 'been started a little time ago, the announcement that the Oxford branch of the Christian Union was going to bring out an *Economic Review* would have caused them some dismay. But, as things now were, he thought they were strong enough to support both journals'; see report in *Economic Journal* (March 1891), 4.
38 See Martin's obituary in the *Economic Journal* (June 1897). Reports on the inaugural meeting were published in *The Times*, and the *Manchester Guardian*, 21 November 1890.
39 The Executive Committee consisted of Marshall, Bonar, Booth, Cunningham,

Foxwell, Elliott, Hewins, Palgrave, Sidgwick, Higgs, Edgeworth, Price and Martin.
40 BEA Minute Books, 24 November 1890.
41 The circulars were sent to 'The members of both houses of Parliament, the officials of the Chambers of Commerce in this country, the members of the Employers' Association, the members of the Statistical Society, the higher permanent officials in government offices, and such other classes as the Secretaries should determine' (Minutes, 6 December 1890). Later, an additional 500 circulars were distributed.
42 Minutes, 14 January 1891.
43 *EJ* (June 1895).
44 See 'After Seven Years', *EJ* (March 1898).
45 See Current Topics, *EJ* (March 1906), with the results being reported in March 1907.
46 Minutes, 12 April 1892.
47 Minutes, 21 January 1891.
48 Minutes, 12 April 1892.
49 See 'After Seven Years', *EJ* (March 1898).
50 'The British Economic Association', *Journal of the Institute of Bankers* (November 1891); see also the opinions of Sir Rawson Rawson *The Times*, 26 June 1891.
51 Edgeworth to Foxwell, 16 November 1892, mentions a 'superabundance of material', but their later correspondence deals with Notes and Memoranda rather than articles.
52 On the Corresponding Members see Minutes, 5 September 1891 and 29 June 1892. In 1891 there were 11 such correspondents covering Calcutta (F.C. Harrison), Canada (W. J. Ashley), New South Wales (A. Duckworth), Austria–Hungary (Stephen Bauer), Belgium (Dr Mahaim), France (Charles Gide), Germany (Gustav Cohn), Holland (H. B. Greven), Paris (E. Castelot), Turkey (Rashid Bey) and the USA (F. W. Taussig). By 1899 their number had increased to 17. By foreign Edgeworth also meant American, see Edgeworth to Foxwell, 1 March 1892: 'The foreign books are *selected* by our correspondents. American books *are* foreign I think.'
53 See Narmadeshwar Jha, *The Age of Marshall. Aspects of British Economic Thought* (Patna, 1963), pp. 87–9.
54 This is in keeping with Jha's conclusions based on a survey of the *EJ* articles during the period 1891–1915, dividing them under the headings of Labour, Economic History and Descriptive Economics, History of Economic Thought and Economic Theory, Money, International Trade, Industrial Relations, Public Finance, and Miscellaneous.
55 See Edgeworth to Foxwell, 18 March 1893 and 11 March 1895.
56 For example, F. C. Montagu on Maurice H. Harvey, *The Trade Policy of Imperial Federation* (1892), in *EJ*, 2 (5) (March 1892), David S. Schloss on J. Schoenhof, *The Economy of High Wages*, in *EJ*, 3 (9) (March 1893) and

Foundation and Early Years

C. F. Bastable on Dr C. J. Fuchs, *Die Handelspolitik England und seiner Kolonien*, in *EJ*, 3 (11) (September 1893).

57 Review of B. R. Wise, *Industrial Freedom: a Study in Politics* (1892), in *EJ*, 2 (8) (December 1892). See also his review of C. F. Bastable, *The Commerce of Nations* (1892), in *EJ*, 2 (6) (June 1892).

58 Review of G. Armitage-Smith, *The Free Trade Movement and its Results* (1898), in *EJ*, 8 (31) (September 1898).

59 See Edgeworth to Foxwell, 26 September 1893: 'Acworth cannot understand why we aren't all working on the Economics of *Railways*!'

60 *EJ*, 5 (20) (December 1895). See also F. Seebohm's review of Dr August Meitzen, *Siedelung und Agrarwesen der Westgermanen und Ostgermanen, der Kelten, Romer, Finnen, und Slaven* (1895), in *EJ*, 7 (25) (March 1897), and S. Ball's review of J. S. Leadam (ed.), *The Domesday of Inclosures 1517–1518* (1897), in *EJ*, 8 (29) (March 1898).

61 H. A. L. Fisher's review of H. de B. Gibbins, *Industry in England* (1896), in *EJ*, 7 (25) (March 1898).

62 W. J. Ashley's review of Dr Georg von Below, *Der Ursprung der deutschen Stadtverfassung* (1892) and Dr Alfred Doven, *Untersuchungen zur Geschichte der Kaufmannsgilden des Mittelalters* (1893), in *EJ*, 4 (14) (June 1894).

63 For example W. A. S. Hewins' review of W. Cunningham, *The Growth of English Industry and Commerce in Modern Times* (1892), in *EJ*, 2 (8) (December 1892).

64 See his review of W. Cunningham and Ellen A. McArthur's *Outlines of English Industrial History* (1895), in *EJ*, 5 (19) (September 1895).

65 Review of W. J. Ashley, *An Introduction to English Economic History and Theory*, Part II (1893), in *EJ*, 3 (12) (December 1893).

66 Review of J. S. Nicholson, *Principles of Economics*, vol. 1 (1893), in *EJ*, 3 (12) (December 1893).

67 For example J. Bonar's review of A. von Miaskowski, *Die Aufange der Nationalokonomie* (1891), in *EJ*, 2 (5) (March 1892), and F. Y. Edgeworth's review of Luigi Cossa, *Introduzione allo Studio dell'Economica Politica* (1892), in *EJ*, 2 (8) (December 1892).

68 Review of Giuseppe Ricca-Salerno, *Storia delle Dottrine finanziere in Italia* (1896), in *EJ*, 6 (21) (March 1896).

69 For example L. L. Price on Arthur Twining Hadley, *Economics: An Account of the Relations between Private Property and Public Welfare* (1896), in *EJ*, 6 (24) (December 1896), and C. P. Sanger on Knut Wicksell, *Geldzins und Guterpreise* (1898), in *EJ*, 8 (31) (September 1898).

70 Review of N. G. Pierson, *Leerkoek der Staathuis – houdlunde* (1896), in *EJ*, 6 (23) (September 1896).

71 See Edgeworth's review of J. N. Keynes, *The Scope and Method of Political Economy*, in *EJ*, 1 (2) (June 1891), and Price's review of Marshall's *Element of Economics of Industry*, in *EJ*, 2 (6) (June 1892). See also Price on C. Gide, *Principles of Political Economy* (1891), in *EJ*, 2 (5) (March 1892), on J. S.

Nicholson, *Principles of Political Economy*, vol. II, Book III (1897), in *EJ*, 8 (29) (March 1898) and on W. Smart, *Studies in Economics* (1895), in *EJ*, 6 (21) (March 1896).

72 Review of Camillo Supino, *Il Metodo Induttivo nell'economia politica* (1894) and *Storia della Circolazione Bancaria in Italia 1860-94* (1895), in *EJ*, 5 (20) (December 1895).

73 See Kadish, *Oxford Economists*, pp. 226–7.

74 For example C. F. Bastable on Knut Wicksell, *Finanztheoretische Untersuchungen nebst Darstellung und Kritik des Steuerwesens Schwerdens* (1896) and A. von Matlekovitz, *Geschichte des Ungarischen Staatshaushalts 1867–93*, in *EJ*, 6 (24) (December 1896), and on Carl C. Plehn, *Introduction to Public Finance* (1896), in *EJ*, 7 (26) (June 1897); F. Y. Edgeworth on Augusto Graziani, *Instituzioni di scienza delle Finanze* (1897), in *EJ*, 7 (27) (September 1897), and on Major Leonard Darwin, *Bimetallism* (1897), in *EJ*, 8 (29) (March 1898).

75 *EJ*, 5 (20) (December 1895). See also C. P. Sanger's review of Knut Wicksell, *Geldzins und Guterpreise* (1898), in *EJ*, 8 (31) (September 1898).

76 *EJ*, 2 (6) (June 1892).

77 See H. M. Thompson's review of R. A. Hatfield and H. de B. Gibbins, *A Shorter Working Day* (1892), in *EJ*, 3 (10) (June 1893).

78 *EJ*, 3 (11) (September 1893).

79 Review of *Family Budgets* (1896), in *EJ*, 4 (24) (December 1896).

80 For example Price on R. W. Cooke-Taylor, *The Factory System and the Factory Acts* (1894) and J. Stephen Jeans, *Trusts, Pools, and Corners, as affecting Commerce and Industry* (1894), in *EJ*, 4 (16) (December 1894), and A. W. Flux on Vilfredo Pareto, *Cours d'Economie Politique. Tome Premier* (1896), in *EJ*, 6 (22) (June 1896).

81 'This forenoon', Bonar complained to Foxwell on one occasion, 'has been spent or misspent over a review of a 2nd rate book for Edgeworth. I think I must bar this reviewing even tho' it saves money. Herewith another scrap from the fanatical auto-didakt (hardly didakt at all)!'; see Bonar to Foxwell, 7 August 1893.

82 Minutes, 8 November 1894.

83 Minutes, 14 October 1895.

3
Gentlemen versus Players, 1891–1914

John Maloney

The *Economic Journal* got off to an uninspiring start, with a flood of second-hand inaugural lectures and uninterpreted tables of statistics. Initially it fulfilled, with unreserved success, the expectation of the then president of the Royal Statistical Society that it would be a half-way house between the popular press and the arcane mysteries of his own subject.[1] On the basis of the issues published from 1891 to 1893 it must have been difficult to see what need there was for a new journal. Anything unsuited to, say, the *Contemporary Review* would have jarred there on grounds of dullness, not difficulty. The only exception, and a promise of happier days to come, was Henry Cunynghame's 'Some Improvements in Simple Geometrical Methods of Treating Exchange Value, Monopoly and Rent' (March 1892), where interdependent consumer demands made their first appearance in formal dress.

And, to be fair, the very first article of all not only rises above the general level of the first three years but initiates one of the *Journal*'s most successful features, the colonial comparative study. 'The Eight Hours Day in Victoria' is good rhetoric, good methodology and useful policy advice. After a somewhat lurid opening section ('Feed on our flesh and blood, ye capitalist hyena; it is your funeral feast' concludes the first paragraph, admittedly as a quote from someone else) the author, John Rae, asks why the demands for an eight-hour day became so insistent so suddenly.

Have higher wages put workers onto the backward-bending part of the labour supply curve? In that case why have the even better paid Californians *resisted* limits on the working day? Has tariff protection given workers the security needed to indulge themselves? But on the whole it is the least protected industries that have been most insistent about shorter hours. After concluding that a shorter day is becoming part of workers' 'habitual subsistence wage', Rae goes on to study its effects by comparing those industries which do or do not come within the eight-hours law.

Rae was a journalist, but such articles were as likely to come from professors with advanced mathematical training as from journalists or MPs. The *Journal* in its first quarter-century relied heavily on its empire correspondents, whose numbers grew as Marshall's pupils, in particular, went to spread the word abroad. Thus A. W. Flux, whose mathematical contributions will be noticed in a moment, used his chair at Montreal to cover Canadian policy questions in a way that would lead no one to guess that a theorist of the first order was writing.

But this is to overleap the watershed of 1894 when, with Edgeworth vs Nicholson on utility[2] and Edgeworth vs Böhm-Bawerk on opportunity cost,[3] the *Journal* took off as the forum for argument between professionals that it was meant to have been from the start.[4] Edgeworth's Oxford colleagues may have thought of him as 'The Edger', never prepared to commit himself to an opinion and glacially remote from policy questions. That is not the impression which comes out of the *Journal*. Edgeworth won neither of his 1894 fights. The exchange with Nicholson petered out into agreement to disagree,[5] while on the cost question it was Böhm-Bawerk who saw, and Edgeworth who failed to see, that real and opportunity cost theories of value ultimately come to the same thing.[6] Nor was Edgeworth necessarily victorious in the years to come – his record resembles nothing as much as a chess grandmaster who scores two wins and a loss to every five draws. But there is no mistaking the combative spirit under the courteous style.

Yet Edgeworth's most important contribution in 1894 was his series of articles on 'The Theory of International Values'. (Like many of his novelist contemporaries, Edgeworth preferred serial form for the publication of most of his major work, becoming the first major economist whose articles count for more than his books.) The 1894 trilogy prefigures optimal tariff analysis. Edgeworth discusses the possible benefits to a protectionist country in terms of tax incidence, taking the US duties against Canadian food as an instance. The fact that the importer must be a 'large country' falls out of the analysis without much effort, but is never made explicit by Edgeworth. The March 1894 article ends with an endorsement of the infant industry argument; its sequels (September and December) translate its findings into mathematical language.

Add to all this Flux's demonstration (June 1894), in the course of a mere book review, that payment according to marginal product would exhaust total product if and only if returns to scale were constant, and 1894 can fairly be called the journal's (first) *annus mirabilis*. It also set and confirmed the tone of the professionals' rather complicated attitude towards the amateurs. The latter had to be respected, where appropriate, for their first-hand knowledge of business; engaged in argument when their perspective was close enough to the professional one for discussion to be useful; admonished as politely as possible when they were leading audiences into error; and instructed as part of the economist's audience. The next two sections will explore these themes.

Three names dominate the Journal in its first decade: Edgeworth, L. L. Price[7] and Edwin Cannan.[8] Edgeworth as editor practised assiduous division of labour. Upon himself he took the niceties of theoretical infighting with the mathematically inclined, or those whom he felt could have been mathematically inclined, and had made mistakes because they were not. Price contributed dull, polite reviews of whatever was worthy but theoretically unsophisticated; Cannan was put to work slaughtering the out-and-out cranks. Hovering above the scene, ceaselessly cited as the embodiment of living authority, but rarely descending in person into the journal's pages, Marshall, omnipresent but invisible, may have provoked some blasphemous thoughts among less reverent readers.

Price, at least, made it clear that he saw many of the authors he reviewed less as students of economics than as part of the object of study. Thus George Howell MP, whose *Trade Unionism, New and Old* Price reviewed in September 1891, found his views were important only 'because of their representative character'.[9] How much attention Price gave to error depended on the personal influence of the errant. Thus the Duke of Argyll's[10] book *The*

Unseen Foundation of Society, advertised as a refutation both of Ricardo's theory of rent and of Marshall's efforts to generalize it, was singled out by Price for special attention, first because the Duke wrote so well and secondly because he was a Duke. The public, warned Price, 'will eagerly read his pages, while it may not be disposed to consult the duller authorities whom he assails'.[11] The Duke's knowledge of economic literature, Price went on condescendingly, 'is confined to limits which might with advantage have been enlarged'.[12] Even Marshall (presumably one of the 'duller authorities') was galvanized into defending himself and Ricardo against the Duke in a full-length article.[13] Marshall did no reviewing, though Mrs Marshall was allowed to review the occasional book, always provided that it was by another woman. Bankers, similarly, would be reviewed by other bankers.

Such segregation is unfortunate for the historian – the more that opposite reviews opposite, the fuller the self-portrait of economics that emerges. Nonetheless the reviews provide a fuller account of how the players saw the gentlemen and each other than any other part of the journal. Cannan, as mentioned, was cast in the matador's role. 'Lord Farrer's procedure is exactly like that of the man who tries to find out whether it is raining by a careful inspection of the clouds and the barometer, instead of looking in the puddles and putting his head out of the window.'[14] (Farrer had eschewed measuring the changing value of gold by its price in favour of estimating the respective growth rates of supply and demand and executing some ingenious statistical analysis thereon.) Cannan aside, however, the frankest comments were often in the obituaries. Sometimes these were double-edged. (Price, in a charming obituary of General Walker, confessed that years ago he had reviewed the general's military memoirs and accused him of conducting battles like an economics professor. He was now glad to make amends by confirming that Walker had practised economics like a true soldier.) But Engel, pace Harald Westergaard's obituary, 'had not strictly speaking a scientific mind. His ideas are often vague and unclear, and his results precipitate.'[15] As for Engel's near-namesake, 'he had long been our guest, and we had treated him well; we had allowed him to carry out his work unmolested, in the ways he liked best.'[16] Doubtless Engels would have seen the fairness of that; but how the shrewd capitalist would have resented the tribute that he '*played* the cotton manufacturer'![17]

Inevitably the *Journal* in its early days (or any other days for that matter) reveals much more of how the professionals saw the rest than vice versa. The punishment of error was itself far from unerring. Some of the rank outsiders were simply brushed off: those cranks who indulged in wishful thinking that the role of the state might radically be reduced were patronized rather than confronted. But, even on more technical questions, reviewers could fumble where a decisive hit might have been scored. Cannan is characteristically caustic about Hobson's underconsumptionist doctrine as revealed in *The Problem of the Unemployed* (1896),[18] but, by neither expounding the saving/hoarding distinction nor invoking Say's law, Cannan falls between every possible stool and Hobson comes out more or less unscathed. Even Edgeworth, and in his editorial capacity at that, allows some surprising items to go through without comment. In 1897 he prevailed upon W. M. Acworth, a prolific writer on railway matters, to lecture at Oxford on 'The Theory of Railway Rates'. Edgeworth, Acworth publicly surmised, had invited him out of concern that economics at Oxford was becoming too 'abstract and theoretic' (the standard Oxford complaint about Edgeworth himself). The lecture, printed in that September's *Journal*, is a good instance of the way that 'practical economists – i.e. men with little theoretical training who nonetheless assumed an economist's perspective as one of the standpoints from which they surveyed some practical question – were coming to terms with marginalism. Acworth consistently reveals its influence on him as a generalized way of thinking, without showing any knowledge of specific neoclassical doctrines. Thus in discussing fixed and running costs he derives the short- and long-run criteria for closing an enterprise without any kind of hint that by now this was a standard commonplace of microeconomics. Later in the article something very like the kinked demand curve makes its appearance. Such moments, however, coexist with arithmetical mindbenders (never mind the economic implications) such as the following:

> Of working expenses fully one half, according to estimates made by experts in different countries which largely agree, remain constant. The remaining half are taken to increase proportionately to the increase of traffic.[19]

With Edgeworth letting this kind of comment through, losing almost as many theoretical duels as he won, and relying on a team of regular reviewers circumscribed in scope and often erratic in critical effectiveness, the *Journal* in its first decade could hardly be further from the neoclassical, or Marshallian, steamroller that it has sometimes been made out to be.[20] Most eclectic of all were the miscellaneous notes and memoranda which fill many pages of every issue. Thus in 1895 it was possible to read about 'The Trade Depression in Maine, U.S.A.', 'The Late Boot War', 'The Slums of Great Cities' and 'The Overproduction of Greek Currants'. But the reviews and articles proper, compared with their counterparts today, are almost as good at calling to mind David Cecil's comparison of nineteenth- and twentieth-century literature:

> A book like David Copperfield is a sort of vast schoolboy hamper of fiction: with sweets and sandwiches, pots of jam in their greased paper cups, cream and nuts and glossy apples, all packed together in a heterogeneous deliciousness. And as a result it fills and stimulates the reader as the filtered vitamin B of contemporary genius hardly ever does.[21]

Certainly one is unlikely to learn from today's *Journal* that 11.25 per cent of Jews marry their first cousins,[22] or that a French chain of restaurants for the poor forbids customers to consume more than half a litre of wine with their meal,[23] or even that 'the average Englishman is a very bad judge of tea. His sole criterion of its quality is its colour and strength; its delicate flavour he drowns in sugar and milk.'[24] Also missing from the modern *Journal* is not so much an ethical tone as the distinctive variability of the ethical tone of the 1890s. One writer can furnish an entirely positivistic analysis of the opium industry (the only value judgement comes at the very end and is that Indians should carry on eating it for health reasons).[25] Another sees free trade as eliminating 'strong-limbed and honest-hearted country girls, living in the pure air of the open land, well and usefully employed with their dairy, their pigs and their poultry and the stay of their parents and husbands', and substituting 'town girls with sallow faces and dubious morals, selling short weight of adulterated goods in a foul and smoke-laden town, themselves anaemic, nervous, hysterical, making indifferent daughters and worse wives. Such and such-like are the offerings – sacrifices of flesh and blood – that you heap in blind fanaticism on the altar of free trade.'[26]

However doubtful this particular argument for protectionism might be, the issue was to revitalize the *Journal* at a time when it was fast sliding into dullness. On taking up, for example, the volume for 1901, the two points that first strike the reader are the extreme difficulty of distinguishing the contributions of the trained economists, and the obsession with municipal affairs in general and the rating system in particular. Both features were swept away when the Conservative party adopted imperial preference as a policy in 1903. The protectionists did not have to wait long for the attentions of Edgeworth, Price and Cannan. Cannan enjoyed himself at the expense of an anonymous writer of a series of articles in the *Daily Telegraph*, published as a book with a foreword by Joseph Chamberlain. Its key argument for imperial preference was that 'those who would supply our food import as cheaply as America supplies it now would take in return, on the average, twenty times per head as much of our products as America takes'.[27] A. J. Balfour, despite being put down by Nicholson as 'the popular philosopher who is now prime minister of England', had his collected speeches on the subject respectfully reviewed by Price, himself an advocate of imperial preference. Price disagreed with those critics who accused Balfour of not knowing enough economics. Balfour had 'exposed more effectively than could be done by many dreary pages of formal economic writing the weak places in the armour of Free Trade as a theory applicable to the practice of any time or place'.[28]

Also in the December 1903 issue, the free-trading Edgeworth gave W. J. Ashley's[29] *The Tariff Problem* a notably friendly review. Ashley had firmly grasped the nettle of comparative advantage, using it to justify imperial preference: 'England, with a lessening hold on the industries which require skill and cultivate independence, is turning apparently more and more to occupations in which it has had a "differential advantage" over America and her colonies in the mass of cheap, low-grade and docile labour ... .'[30] Edgeworth quotes this without either obvious enthusiasm or clear antagonism. He does, however, praise Ashley as the representative of 'intelligent protectionism', far too intelligent to tolerate the 'crude popular fallacy' that 'imports are paid for by money which might otherwise be spent at home'.

The opening positions taken up by Edgeworth, Price and Cannan are representative of the way the *Journal* was to handle protectionism in the years to come. No attempt was made to put either protectionists or politicians, *qua* protectionists and politicians, on the side of an insider–outsider distinction. Rather the distinction was between those who understood economics and those who echoed 'popular fallacies', the latter being as likely to be on the free-trade side as on the protectionist. Thus the March 1904 issue opens with Ashley's 'The Argument for Preference' and continues with an early essay on the economics of politics, as W. H. Dawson examines the sectional economic interests which pushed Bismarck into protection in 1879. There follows a curious little article from the 26-year-old Pigou in which a series of theoretical propositions are put forward with explanations which must have been far too cryptic for any but a handful of readers:

> *Problem 2* –
> To ascertain the effect upon price of taxing the supply from one source and expending the proceeds in a bounty upon that from the other, when both supplies obey the laws of diminishing returns. If the elasticities of the two supplies are the same, the price necessarily rises. If the elasticity of the taxed supply is the smaller of the two it may fall. In any event it will rise less than it would do if the proceeds of the tax were not expended in a bounty.[31]

In general, however, contributions to the protectionist controversy – and indeed the articles of the *Journal*'s second decade in general – read as if theorists were taking more care as to what their readers would be likely or unlikely to understand. The main analytical advance that came out of the debate – C. F. Bickerdike's pioneering article on optimal tariff theory[32] – was couched in such terms that laymen could, and did, take up its arguments immediately. Bickerdike's analysis must have looked simple and elegant in 1906 because it still looks simple and elegant today (though it is hard to imagine a modern editor accepting unlabelled axes and an airy invitation to the reader to look for a key diagram by digging out a 12-year-old article by someone else). Bickerdike takes the case where the proceeds from a tariff are handed back to the buyers of the imported good. Their gain, a rectangle in the crucial diagram, dwindles to a line as the tariff approaches zero. But their loss, a triangle of forgone consumer surplus, collapses to a point. There must therefore be some tariff small enough to give them a net gain.

Bickerdike's two limiting cases were where the supply curve

for the import was flat (i.e. where the importing country was insignificantly small) and where the demand curve was vertical. Dogmatic free traders therefore tried to persuade themselves and their listeners that one or other of these situations obtained. Thus a Liberal MP, Russell Rea, in the course of his book *Free Trade in Being* (1908) understood Bickerdike's arguments thoroughly enough to seize the bull by the horns and declare wheat to be a Giffen good. (So strident is the book's tone that there can be little doubt that he would have designated Hispano-Suizas and vintage port Giffen goods had his case required it.) Edgeworth, reviewing the book, contented himself with declaring that, notwithstanding Rea's status as 'a practical man of great sagacity', he thought such a contingency improbable.[33] He had given Bickerdike's analysis a longer examination in 'Appreciations of Mathematical Theories' (*Economic Journal*, September 1908), and his comments here show the feelings of a free trader unexpectedly overtaken in the analytical fast lane by a protectionist. It would be too conspiratorial – and wholly unperceptive of Edgeworth's character – to suggest that his translation of Bickerdike's neat diagram into impenetrable arithmetic was designed to emasculate the optimal tariff argument as a public force. On the contrary, Edgeworth accepted Bickerdike's estimate that the elasticities involved justified duties of $2\frac{1}{2}$–5 per cent on a great number of articles. 'On the platform of pure theory', Edgeworth concluded, 'the free trader must abandon his hectoring tone with respect to the defence of a protectionist tax on the ground that it is a little one.'[34] Nonetheless he feared the consequences of so lavish a gift to 'unscrupulous advocates of vulgar Protection'.

> Mr Bickerdike may be compared to a scientist who, by a new analysis, has discovered that strychnine may be administered in small doses with prospect of advantage in one or two more cases than was previously known .... Let us admire the skill of the analyst but label the subject of his investigation POISON.[35]

Edgeworth loved the homely metaphor. Doubtless it was only the mischance that the article was written two years too early that prevented a reference to Dr Crippen.

Turning economics into a professional discipline involved bringing economic analysis both to questions not previously seen as a matter for economists and to already legitimized areas which had as yet failed to rise above the level of casual empiricism. Pigou was to the fore in both processes, and the *Journal* in its second decade fully records the fact. 'The Unity of Political and Economic Science' (September 1906) is in the best 'Towards the Economics of ...' vein. Pigou does not get beyond analogies, albeit arresting ones – what other economist of the day would have compared a speculator timing a coffee sale with a prime minister timing a general election? Joint production is likened to a party manifesto (the supply of mutton is the less responsive to the demand because of the wool involved; the supply of protectionist governments is similarly constrained by the multi-issue nature of politics), and the government of the day is designated a temporary monopolist earning a quasi-rent.

As for the second form of professionalization – applying marginalism to areas already accepted within the economic canon but not yet wrested from lay control – perhaps the biggest step in this direction was Pigou's *Principles and Methods of Industrial Peace*, where labour economics received a more mathematical treatment than any economics had had from Marshall. And perhaps the most revealing review in the *Journal* between 1900 and 1914 is L. L. Price's assessment of this book. First, it shows the decline in Price's professional status. From an insider kindly but firmly turning the erroneous around to face the light, he has slipped to the station of an outsider looking in on the mathematical redoubt. 'We acknowledge ... that our own unfortunate ignorance of mathematics precludes us from appreciating the technical apparatus used in the appendices.'[36] But, secondly, it shows that a reviewer could confess this and still not be inhibited from making some hard-hitting criticisms. For all Pigou's dialectical ingenuity, said Price, it was doubtful whether the results were worth the effort. Pigou had attacked the outskirts and not the centre of the problem, embarking on 'the fruitless or impossible enterprise of using the "economic organon" in circumstances to which it is hardly applicable'. The mathematics, moreover, was likely to 'cause mischief' by conferring a spurious importance and dignity on Pigou's approach.

What Price meant was that Pigou had focused on mathematically tractable questions (such as whether industrial arbitrators ought to try to influence the distribution of wealth) and avoided, because unable to solve, the crucial problem of how wages were determined under bilateral monopoly. The latter – Price does not mention it here – happened to be the subject of Price's one theoretical contribution. Certainly Pigou handles it less well than Price.

But this is only to emphasize that, within the context of the *Journal* at least, the 1900s were no more Pigou's decade than the 1890s had been Edgeworth's. In 1908 Pigou was to be elevated to the Cambridge chair, aged only 30, on the strength of his promise, and to some extent performance, as an outstanding new leader for the analytical camp in economics. It hardly shows in the *Journal*. Neither of his 'neoclassical' articles does much to advance the subject: the 'economics of politics' article, as already implied, is no more than a series of signposts, while 'Some Remarks on Utility' (March 1903) is almost entirely about the indispensability or otherwise of Benthamism to marginal utility theory. On bilateral monopoly he is inferior to Price, and on the optimal tariff problem far less precise than Bickerdike, as the latter none too subtly hinted when he reviewed Pigou's *Protective and Preferential Import Duties* in the March 1907 *Journal*. Nor were the older generation of 'players' especially impressive. Marshall's only contribution (apart from a brief note on 'An Export Duty on Coal' in 1901) was his celebrated piece on economic chivalry. Foxwell had nothing to say. After 1897 all Edgeworth's articles (two pieces on the rating system excepted) were reviews of other people's articles, and all from the *Journal* at that.

Certainly by 1910 'proper' articles were on the decline. December 1908's issue had but four of them, totalling 56 pages out of 183. In June 1909, reviews for the first time took up more space than articles. And even this was not because there was more serious work needing to be reviewed. It was the extensive margin of cultivation that was shifting out. What Edgeworth could review with a straight face never fails to surprise (though Nicholson permitted himself the flicker of a smile at a startling comparison between Adam Smith and a tapeworm).[37] *Journal* readers were also treated to a long review of William Bell Robertson's *Foundations of Political Economy*: much longer than Robertson's own two-sentence account of value theory.

> The more pronounced the presence of the conditions of value – desire and possession – in the case of any commodity, the more pronounced is the value of the commodity. Let pos-

session be signified by P and desire by D; the value varies as PD.[38]

September 1906 saw a 'review' of an early hydraulic simulation of the banking system, complete with building instructions. As for *Economics for Irishmen*, by 'Pat', the present writer has been unable to discover a copy, but its reviewer of March 1907, H. L. Murphy, expresses regret that 'what promises at the outset to be a scientific investigation of the subject should too soon adopt the somewhat noisy tone which characterises the greater part of it'.[39]

But the *Economic Journal*, perhaps, was determined to demonstrate the principle of diminishing returns. For, while the reviews became more numerous and trivial, the general standard of the diminished article section rose. The 'players' might be batting disappointingly but the 'gentlemen' had perfected some interesting new strokes. With compulsory national insurance, pensions, unemployment benefit and steeply progressive taxation on the British political agenda, the *Journal* took on new life as contributors ranged around the globe investigating how such measures had worked elsewhere. The issue most intensively studied – surprisingly in the light of its relatively low topical profile – was railway nationalization. But here contributors could find little theory upon which to draw, and when Edgeworth chose the railways for his next review article, 'Contributions to the Theory of Railway Rates', he broke with his own tradition and for the most part covered work published outside the *Journal*'s pages. Indeed, with the first two instalments of the four-part article devoted to the general theory of increasing and diminishing returns, readers must have wondered whether the railways were going to be reached at all.

British economics in the Marshallian era was notably weak on monetary theory. Nowhere did this show up in harsher relief than in the journal that unveiled the Fisher equation and Wicksell's doctrine of the natural rate of interest. The *Journal*'s pages are in fact an intensely accurate reflection of British neoclassicists' bored attitude to monetary questions. But the situation was to change quite suddenly between 1909 and 1912 with the arrival on the scene of Frederick Lavington and John Maynard Keynes. The latter's debut, 'Recent Economic Events in India' (March 1909) was another of those successful explanation-by-elimination pieces that the *Journal* seemed able to manage only in a colonial context.

The popular candidates for India's rising food prices – falling productivity, higher demand due to better terms of trade, increased world gold supply and bad harvests – are knocked down one after the other, and Keynes ends up with a straightforward 'overactive printing press' explanation. The theoretical novelty is his demonstration that a price-inelastic demand for exports will jam the specie-flow mechanism and lead to an explosive process whereby domestic credit creation compounds itself by bringing a capital inflow in its train.

On succeeding Edgeworth as editor in 1911, Keynes appropriated much of the reviewing of monetary works for himself. Abrasive though his style may have been, he remained very much within the prevailing professional ethic: academic economists should seek what marked them off from erroneous outsiders, rather than dispute to death every policy question that divided them. Reviewing Fisher's *The Purchasing Power of Money* (1911) Keynes quotes with approval Fisher's distaste for the 'scandal that academic economists have, through outside clamour, been led into disagreements over the fundamental propositions concerning money'.[40] The treatment that Keynes deemed appropriate for monetary cranks was felt in full force the following year by J. A. Hobson:

> One comes to a new book of Mr Hobson with mixed feelings, in hope of stimulating ideas and of some fruitful criticisms of orthodoxy from an independent and individual standpoint, but expectant also of much sophistry, misunderstanding, and perverse thought. In some of his books the first elements greatly predominate. In his latest book now before us, the latter prevail almost throughout. The book is a very bad one, made much worse than a really stupid book could be, by exactly those characteristics of cleverness and intermittent reasonableness which have borne good fruit in the past.[41]

Lavington, reviewing *Monetary Economics* by W. W. Carlile, had even fewer problems – Carlile believed that Marshall had said that 'the marginal utility of eight apples' was less than that of 'five of their number'.[42] Lavington's first actual article appeared in September 1912 and is generally unexciting, although his praise of the banks for pooling risks and thus, uniquely providing insurance without moral hazard must have seemed ingenious to the readers of the day.

On the eve of the Great War, the standard of theoretical contributions, and not only on monetary questions, was rising. The March 1913 issue was especially strong with Pigou on 'The Interdependence of Different Sources of Demand and Supply in a Market' followed by Sydney Chapman's 'The Utility of Income and Progressive Taxation' and a most original piece by Lavington on 'The Social Interest in Speculation on the Stock Exchange'. The *Journal* was soon to go to war, with many of its contributors in the forces and a general preponderance of war articles in its columns. But March 1913 is the pointer to the success of the post-war *Journal* as the most indispensable and exciting market-place for the exchange of economic ideas anywhere in the world.

NOTES

1 The comment, and other speeches greeting the new journal, are to be found in 'The British Economic Association', *Economic Journal (EJ)* (March 1891), 1–14.
2 F. Y. Edgeworth, 'Professor J. S. Nicholson on "Consumers' Rent"', *EJ* (March 1894); J. S. Nicholson, 'The Measurement of Utility by Money' (June 1894); F. Y. Edgeworth, 'The Measurement of Utility by Money' (June 1894).
3 F. Y. Edgeworth, 'Professor Böhm-Bawerk on the Ultimate Standard of Value', *EJ* (September 1894); E. von Böhm-Bawerk, 'One More Word on the Ultimate Standard of Value' (December 1894); F. Y. Edgeworth, 'Professor Böhm-Bawerk on the Ultimate Standard of Value' (December 1894).
4 J. S. Nicholson, at the meeting at which both the British Economic Association and the *Economic Journal* were founded, hoped the latter would be 'an organised market for the exchange of ideas and if in the course of time it also serves to introduce to one another the persons in whom the ideas originate, so much the better. What a deal of controversy might have been spared by a little personal contact!' (*EJ*, March 1891, p. 11).
5 See John Maloney, *Marshall, Orthodoxy and the Professionalisation of Economics* (Cambridge: Cambridge University Press, 1985), pp. 77–9.
6 See John Maloney, 'Real Cost Theory', in *The New Palgrave Dictionary of Economics* (London: Macmillan, 1987), vol. 4.
7 Langford Lovell Frederick Rice Price (1862–1950). Fellow of Oriel College, Oxford, 1888–1923; University Reader in Economic History, 1909–21. Works include *Economic Science and Practice* (1896); *A Short History of Political*

Economy in England from Adam Smith to Alfred Marshall (1st edn, 1891; 14th edn, 1937). Price leaned towards the historical school, but had a greater respect for, and proficiency in, neoclassical economics than did the school's more dogmatic members.
8 Edwin Cannan (1861–1935). Lecturer, London School of Economics, 1897–1907; Professor 1907–26. A neoclassical theorist whose lifelong impatience with mathematics and with Marshall occasionally conceals the fact. Works include *A History of the Theories of Production and Distribution in English Political Economy from 1776 to 1848* (1893); *Wealth* (1914); *An Economist's Protest* (1927).
9 *EJ* (September 1891), 570–2.
10 The 8th Duke of Argyll (1823–1900) was elected Vice President of the British Economic Association in 1893.
11 *EJ* (June 1893), 265.
12 Ibid., p. 265.
13 A. Marshall, 'On Rent', *EJ* (March 1893).
14 E. Cannan, Review of Lord Farrer, 'The Quantitative Theory of Money and Prices', in *EJ* (March 1898), 82.
15 *EJ* (March 1897), 147.
16 Obituary of Engels by 'J.B.' (probably James Bonar), *EJ* (September 1895), 490.
17 Ibid., p.491. Emphasis added.
18 Review is in *EJ* (March 1897).
19 W. M. Acworth, 'The Theory of Railway Rates', *EJ* (September 1897), 323.
20 See, for example, N.Jha, *The Age of Marshall* (London, 1963).
21 Lord David Cecil, *Early Victorian Novelists* (London, 1948) p.12.
22 F. Y. Edgeworth, review of Joseph Jacobs, *Studies in Jewish Statistics*, in *EJ* (March 1892).
23 A. P. MacIlvaine, 'Economical Kitchens in France and Switzerland', *EJ* (June 1896).
24 C. H. Denyer, 'The Consumption of Tea and other Staple Drinks', *EJ* (March 1893), 38.
25 E. N. Baker, 'The Opium Industry', *EJ* (June 1896).
26 C. S. Devas, 'Lessons from Ruskin', *EJ* (March 1898), 34.
27 *EJ* (December 1903), 575.
28 L. L. Price, review of A. J. Balfour, *Economic Notes on Insular Free Trade* (London, 1903), in *EJ* (December 1903), 596. In his obituary of Balfour (*EJ*, June 1930) Keynes went even further, praising *Economic Notes on Insular Free Trade* as 'one of the most remarkable scientific deliverances ever made by a Prime Minister in office', and siding with the book against Marshall's critical marginalia of it in his personal copy (p. 537).
29 Sir William Ashley (1860–1927). Fellow, Lincoln College, Oxford, 1885–8; Professor of Political Economy, Toronto, 1888-92; Professor of Economic History, Harvard, 1892–1901; Professor of Commerce, Birmingham, 1901–25. Works include *An Introduction to English Economic History and Theory*

(1888); *The Tariff Problem* (1903). The most respected and, with interruptions, the mildest methodologist of the English historical school.
30 W. J. Ashley, *The Tariff Problem*, quoted in the *EJ* (December 1903), 573.
31 A. C. Pigou, 'Pure Theory and the Fiscal Controversy', *EJ* (March 1904), 30.
32 'The Theory of Incipient Taxes', *EJ* (December 1906). C. F. Bickerdike (1876–1961) was a protégé of Edgeworth's. Lecturer in Economics and Commerce, University of Manchester, 1910–12; Board of Trade 1912–41.
33 *EJ* (March 1909).
34 F. Y. Edgeworth, ibid., p. 554.
35 Ibid., pp. 555–6.
36 L. L. Price, review of Pigou, *Principles and Methods of Industrial Peace*, *EJ* (September 1905), 383.
37 J. S. Nicholson, review of John Beattie Crozier, *The Wheel of Wealth* (London, 1907), in *EJ* (March 1907), 67.
38 Review of C. P. Sanger in *EJ* (December 1906), p. 577.
39 *EJ* (March 1907), 109.
40 *EJ* (September 1911), 393.
41 J. M. Keynes, review of J. A. Hobson, *Gold, Prices and Wages*, in *EJ* (September 1913), 393.
42 *EJ* (June 1912).

4
The *Economic Journal* and Socialism, 1890–1920

Ian Steedman

> The British Economic Association is open to all schools and parties; no person is excluded because of his opinions. The Economic Journal, issued under the authority of the Association, will be conducted in a similar spirit of toleration. It will be open to writers of different schools. The most opposite doctrines may meet here as on a fair field. Thus the difficulties of Socialism will be considered in the first number; the difficulties of Individualism in the second.

Thus wrote Edgeworth on the very first page of the *Journal*. If the *Journal* was 'to represent all shades of opinion', it was inevitable that discussion of socialism would find a place within its pages.[1] The reader will only need to be reminded that the 1880s had seen the 'revival of socialism' in Britain and will bear in mind the existence, for example, of the Social Democratic Federation, the Socialist League, the Fabians and the 'New Unionism', in Britain alone. On a world scale, it need hardly be added, the period 1890–1920 saw dramatic socialist developments.

The term 'socialism' was – perhaps still is – a protean one and I shall deliberately refrain from proposing an explicit definition for the purposes of this essay. It must be noted, however, that the *Journal* contained discussions of many issues – the eight hours movement, wages, trade unionism, municipal enterprises, the Poor Law, pensions, housing, progressive taxation and railway nationalization, for example – which have been excluded here but could quite properly have been included in a discussion of the *Journal* and socialism. Even so, one still finds far more discussion of socialism in the first three decades of the *Journal* than can be considered in this essay.[2]

A leitmotiv that will be encountered frequently is a combination of sympathy for certain aims and aspects of socialism – not least for cooperation – and a pronounced scepticism towards the viability of the overall socialist project. Socialist values are often endorsed, even if some authors are quick to add that individualists too have their ideals, and it is often accepted that wealth is produced more satisfactorily than it is distributed. In these pre-Robbinsian years, it was frequently supposed that marginal-utility-based arguments could link happiness directly to income equality. The socialist aim was not reduced to that of income equality, however, and the 'democratic control of industry', for example, was discussed both at the beginning and end of our period. The running counterpoint of scepticism was not rooted in arguments relating to the rights of property in land, or even in familiar considerations on 'waiting' and the supply of capital. Rather, there is a recurring emphasis on the centrality of change in economic life, on the importance of invention and of entrepreneurship, it being strongly suggested that a socialist society could not provide the equivalent of business leadership and would result in a stagnant unprogressive economy. Thus, the 'fourth agent of production', Marshall's 'Organization', was made central to the criticism of socialist proposals and to the defence of individualism. 'Human nature' also played its predictable role in that criticism–defence.

Eschewing further generalities, we turn first to consider four major papers – by Courtney, Webb, Sidgwick and Marshall – and then to introduce the *Journal*'s treatment of three major themes – Marxism, cooperation and syndicalism/guild socialism. Our discussion of the four papers should give the reader some feel for the style of the relevant discussion in the *Journal*'s early years, while our treatment of the three major themes will have to serve as indications, no more, of the breadth and depth of the *Journal*'s concern with Socialism.[3]

The Difficulties of Socialism and of Individualism

As promised by Edgeworth, the first issue in March 1891 carried Leonard Courtney's 'The Difficulties of Socialism', while the June issue presented Sidney Webb's fierce reply, 'The Difficulties of Individualism'. Courtney's starting point was the ill-defined nature of 'Socialism'. He suggested that 'every Socialist is in some fashion or other struggling after a new society, organized in a different manner from that to which we are accustomed – not a modification of it, resting on the same principles as before, but a re-formation out of which may commence a new career and a new fulfilment of humanity'. The endless succession of visions and failures, in Courtney's view, 'affords room for satire, but also for sympathy', for there is one permanent element of vision, that 'of a perfect order' without waste, conflict or jealousy.

Courtney was concerned to discuss large-scale socialist societies in which community of goods is far more likely to result from confiscation than from renunciation. He considered first the case of land in a country in which, wisely or unwisely, land ownership has long been allowed to adhere in and to be transferred between individuals: 'it will be very difficult indeed to affirm the right of the community to resume without full recompense such ownership, except upon principles which would justify the confiscation by the community of all possessions'.[4] The moral difficulty is yet greater, Courtney urges, with respect to justifying the confiscation of produced means of production, the creation of which has involved 'the strength, craft and patience' of the creator, qualities 'inseparable from himself'. The socialist doctrine confessedly involves 'the confiscation of all the superior results arising from the differentiated superiorities of different men; or, to use the technical phrase, the rent of ability'.

What of the milder forms of socialism, in which various industries are gradually acquired – and paid for – by the nation or by municipalities: is this not merely a development of existing trends – one that simply changes, wisely or unwisely, the structure of property ownership? But if it be proposed that taxation 'shall take away all the income derived from the use of industrial capital' then the moral difficulty indeed reappears, 'for it need not be pointed out that the morality or immorality of such an appropriation cannot depend upon whether it is done in half-a-dozen instalments instead of one cut'.

How well would a socialist society function if it were once established? Courtney's central concern in this regard relates to invention, innovation and new products. The 'progress of industrial improvement has depended, and must depend, upon the continuous unceasing introduction of alterations, many of them apparently minute'; the 'socialized community would be a slowly moving, if not stagnant, organism'. Change, including locational change, appears in fact to be the major challenge to socialist organization. After drawing attention to the vast and ever-changing role of foreign trade, which might baffle a 'bureau of foreign commerce', Courtney declares that, while Newton might be able to 'foretell the movements of the spheres', not even his intellect could keep track of the constantly evolving, world-wide 'living organism' of industry and commerce.

Courtney concluded, however, on a more optimistic note, insisting that the 'Socialist promise' must be compared 'not merely with the society that exists, but with society as it too might become, though remaining based on the principles that now underlie it, as its units grew in morality and wisdom'. 'Consider what might be accomplished through a growth in temperance, prudence, and the gift of sympathy. The world would be transformed without any invasion of personal liberty ... . The individualist has his ideal.'

Sidney Webb was not impressed. He complained that Courtney had made little or no explicit reference to historical developments, to Owen, Comte and Marx, or to the modern cooperative movement; that he had said little of the growth of factory and other legislation, of trade unionism and of municipal socialism. Webb's own *Socialism in England* (1987 [1890]) had of course been centred on just those historical and institutional developments of which Courtney made light; the two men approached the study of socialism in quite different ways.

According to Webb, 'one of the initial "difficulties" to be overcome by Individualists [is] that so many of them received their economic and historical training before we had learnt to think of social institutions and economic relations as being as much the subjects of constant change and evolution as any biological organism'. A man of his time, Webb insisted on the 'appreciation of historical evolution', deducing that: 'It is therefore not a question of whether the existing social order shall be changed, but of how this inevitable change shall be made.' Webb proceeded to what is almost a 'definition' (for him) of modern socialism. It is 'not a faith in an artificial Utopia' but a conviction that 'social health' is something 'apart from and above the separate interests of individuals' that must be consciously pursued. The 'lesson of evolution' is that competition must be replaced by conscious coordination. The 'best government is accordingly that which can safely and successfully administer most'.

Conversely, 'the main "difficulties" of the existing social order ... are those immediately connected with the administration of industry and the distribution of wealth'. In brief, private property produces an extreme income inequality and hence a bad pattern of output, senseless luxuries being produced when there is not enough bread. Turning to consider these matters in greater detail, Webb takes up Courtney's closing remarks – to the effect that socialist proposals should be compared not only with the existing state of affairs but also with what an improved individualist society might become – and turns them to his advantage. 'For to-day it is the Individualist who is offering us ... an untried and nebulous Utopia,' while the Socialist seeks merely to extend the principles 'to which the stern logic of facts has already driven the practical man. ...Factory-Acts and municipal gas-works we know, but the voice of Mr Auberon Herbert, advocating "voluntary taxation", is as the voice of one crying in the wilderness' – not the only point at which Webb employs biblical language.

No advance in the worker's thrift and sobriety 'would remove the fundamental inequality arising from the phenomenon of rent'. Nor is industrial capital fundamentally different from land in this respect, according to Webb: 'The whole differential advantage of all but the worst industrial capital, like the whole differential advantage of all but the worst land, necessarily goes to him who legally owns it.'[5] Perhaps under the influence of this alleged similarity between interest and rent, Webb proceeds to discuss land and produced means of production without even raising the question whether there is an important distinction to be made between their conditions of supply. Even in replying to Courtney's argument that confiscation is immoral, Webb refrains from distinguishing land from capital, even though Courtney had himself made much of the distinction in that very context. Webb claims that 'against the permanent welfare of the community the unborn have no rights'. While present owners, and even their children, should be treated generously, their later descendants have no claim on currently existing assets.

In objecting to the income inequality arising from private property, Webb argues, socialists have no need to appeal to abstract principles: facts suffice. It 'obviously results in a flagrant "wrong production" of commodities'. Because of great discrepancies in the marginal utilities of expenditures, 'The last glass of wine at a plutocratic orgy ... is economically as urgently "demanded" as the whole day's maintenance of the dock labourer for which its cost would suffice'. Webb then takes up what he describes as being 'in many respects the most serious "difficulty" of Individualism – namely, its inconsistency with democratic self-government'. He develops at length Marx's famous argument about the 'double freedom' of the worker (with no explicit reference to Marx) and argues that the growing scale of capitalist production has rendered obsolete the idea that personal freedom is greatest where collective rule is minimized. Hence, it is in the factory and the mine 'that irresponsible personal authority over the actions of others' is to be found in a politically democratic society. The captains of industry should be and gradually are being 'turned into salaried servants of the public'; and Webb cited railways, public bakeries, schools, waterworks, gasworks and housing as examples. 'And there is no contrary movement. No community which has once "municipalized" any public service has ever retraced its steps or reversed into action.'[6]

Webb's peroration was forward looking and sharply focused: 'whatever Socialism may have meant in the past its real significance now is in the steady expansion of representative self-government into the industrial sphere'. The Socialist 'urges that personal freedom can be obtained by the great mass of the people only by their substituting democratic self-government in the industrial world for that personal power which the Industrial Revolution has placed in the hands of the proprietary class'. The main difficulty for the Individualists, Webb proclaims, 'is the advance of democracy, ever more and more claiming to extend itself into the field of industry'. Not that that advance is to be precipitate: 'Industrial democracy must ... necessarily be gradual in its development; and cannot for long ages be absolutely complete. The progress of Socialism may be compared, indeed, to the approximation of the hyperbola to its asymptote.'[7] And if the asymptote keeps moving away ...?

Webb makes absolutely no reply to Courtney's doubts about the difficulties of running a fully socialized economy, unless it be, by implication, in his remarks to the effect that each step towards socialism is taken only when experience has already shown that step to be practicable. Certainly, he makes no attempt at a theoretical reply to Courtney's questions.

The Economic Lessons of Socialism

Sidgwick's delightful essay on 'The Economic Lessons of Socialism' (1895), by contrast, was firmly theoretical. 'By "Socialism" I mean the practical doctrine, that it is desirable to abolish private property completely or to a great extent, with a view to increasing the ordinary remuneration of labour, and thus increasing happiness by producing a greater equality of incomes.' Sidgwick was concerned with the relations between socialism, on the one hand, and political economy, on the other. He took it for granted that there was an 'unmistakable drift towards Socialism in Western Europe', adding that this was 'a reasonable source of alarm to some, and perhaps of hope to others'. As for this aspect of the matter, Sidgwick suggested, 'probably most educated persons are now as well acquainted as they desire to be with the arguments on both sides'.[8] His purpose, rather, is to examine 'what Political Economy has learnt from Socialism'. The converse question is implied to be less interesting because socialism's 'leading ideas are indeed few and comparatively simple'.

After seeking to deflate the pretensions of 'Teutons' and of 'scientific' socialism in general, and of Marx in particular, Sidgwick considers first the lessons learnt 'from the earlier Socialism'. After Smith, political economy 'was a body of doctrine consisting of two distinct parts', the one showing how wealth was produced, distributed and exchanged under liberty, and the other showing that this was the best possible system. Distributional questions were not stressed. 'The first effect, then, of the collision with Socialism, and of the Socialistic criticism of the actual distribution of incomes, was to bring Political Economy to a clearer consciousness of the essential difference, from a scientific point of view, between the two parts of its teaching.' This led to an emphasis on the first part of the doctrine and to a justification of the outcome of economic liberty only 'in a more limited and guarded way', at least in English political economy. Indeed, 'the problem of ameliorating distribution was more distinctly recognised as important' and J. S. Mill 'was actually – at any rate when he revised the third and later editions [of his *Principles*] – completely Socialistic in his ideal of ultimate social improvement'. Sidgwick had been surprised to learn from Mill's *Autobiography* how socialist Mill's views had become: 'But though Mill had concealed from us the extent of his Socialism, we were, I think, conscious of having received from him a certain impulse in the Socialistic direction', not least in his ceasing to regard political economy as implacably opposed to socialism.

More specifically, Sidgwick suggested that, while both Smith and Ricardo had cast the landlord in a less than wholly flattering light, 'it was left for Mill to emphasise the claim of society to the "unearned increment" of value'. If Mill did not definitely advocate land nationalization in his *Principles*, 'it looms, if I may so say, on the horizon'. By contrast, Mill, following Senior, explained 'the main part of the capitalist's share of the produce in terms of the capitalist's "remuneration for abstinence"'. Labour's claim to the whole product was thus rejected. The clash with Marxian socialism, Sidgwick suggests, had helped to clarify this muddled argument. Thereupon he gives a beautifully clear explanation of the distinction between (a) the labour required to produce the instruments which aid labour and (b) the labour done to produce 'the commodities on which the owner of capital spends *that part of his interest which he does not save*' (emphasis added); only the latter could be avoided in a socialistic state. If Sidgwick had only mentioned steady growth explicitly, he would here have propounded proleptically the 'Samuelson–Weizsäcker' theorem.

The older stress on saving, however, in Sidgwick's view, failed to capture fully the role of the capitalist, for *invention*, as well as abstinence is central to the accumulation process. The greater attention paid to invention 'in more recent treatises is partly', he suggests, 'due to the influence exercised by the controversy with Socialism'. This leads him 'to another shortcoming in the older view of the capitalist's function ... the inadequate recognition by the older writers of the importance of business ability'. 'This completer analysis of the process of accumulating and employing capital, bringing into prominence inventive and industrial skill, is, I conceive, the latest lesson for which Political Economy has been in some measure indebted to the controversy with Socialism.'

Sidgwick concludes by remarking that there has been little socialist experiment. If there is to be socialist experiment at the level of the state, 'One nation will probably be found sufficient: and I trust that we shall all agree to yield the post of honour to Germany, in this branch of the pursuit of knowledge.'

The Social Possibilities of Economic Chivalry

Alfred Marshall made few contributions to the *Journal* of direct relevance to our theme, but his March 1907 paper on 'The Social Possibilities of Economic Chivalry' was indeed a major contribution. Echoing, without referring to, some of the central themes of both Courtney and Sidgwick, Marshall presents an ethical view of economic activity which permits him simultaneously to welcome the activity of the state for social amelioration and to oppose collectivism.

Marshall's starting point is the 'common saying that we have more reason to be proud of our ways of making wealth than of our ways of using it' and the claim that a large part of output is merely wasteful. He refers to, without dismissing, 'the belief that a vast increase of happiness and elevation of life might be attained if those forms of expenditure which serve no high purpose could be curtailed, and the resources thus set free could be applied for the welfare of the less prosperous members of the working classes'. Nevertheless, the reasonable dissatisfaction, with which every thoughtful person must regard the existing distribution of wealth, 'is in danger of being perverted towards ill-considered measures of reform by Utopian reformers'.

If business has its sordid sides and some men 'become rich by foul means', it remains the case, Marshall argues, that 'a chivalrous desire to master difficulties and obtain recognised leadership' is the chief motive to success in business. Since the growth of bureaucracy, both in state enterprises and in very large joint stock companies, is hostile to the 'constructive business faculty', it is necessary to increase the honour and esteem awarded to successful business leaders. This leads Marshall to the watershed which divides the large majority of economists from collectivists. It is not that economists reject the belief that much work for social amelioration 'can be better performed by the State than by individual effort'. On the contrary, 'In this sense nearly every economist of the present generation is a Socialist. In this sense I was a Socialist before I knew anything of economics.' What divides economists (or Marshall at least) from the collectivists is, rather, the conviction that, 'so soon as collectivist control had spread so far as to considerably narrow the field left for free enterprise, the pressure of bureaucratic methods would impair not only the springs of material wealth, but also many of those higher qualities of human nature, the strengthening of which should be the chief aim of social endeavour'. Nevertheless, there was much that government could and should do – 'So I cry, "*Laissez faire*: Let the State be up and doing"; let it not imitate those people who have time and energy enough to manage their neighbours' households, while their own is always in disorder.' It need hardly be said that both sides of this *cri de coeur* were important for Marshall. The state should specialize; it should do – and do well – those things best done by it and it should refrain from interfering 'in matters where the private hand is competent for action'.

More sweepingly, Marshall then permits himself the sub-heading: 'Social disaster would probably result from the full development of the collectivist programme, unless the nature of man has first been saturated with economic chivalry'. Collectivist failures, Marshall argues, have proved that, 'in the common man jealousy is a more potent force than chivalry'. Hence, 'the all-pervading bureaucratic discipline' of complete collectivism either would lead people to flee abroad or, if this were impossible, would lead to tyranny. 'The world under free enterprise will fall far short of the finest ideals until economic chivalry is developed. But until it is developed, every great step in the direction of collectivism is a grave menace to the maintenance even of our present moderate rate of progress,' because of its stifling effect on improvements. Thus socialism as the proper use of wealth, through the state where appropriate, is to be welcomed; but it is better combined with free enterprise than with collectivism, for the latter threatens the production of wealth.

Marxism

During its first 30 years the *Journal* paid relatively little attention to Marx's political economy, and that little appeared almost exclusively in the form of book reviews and was focused largely on *Capital*, volume III.[10] This is hardly surprising, perhaps, not least because Edgeworth agreed with Cassel 'as to the distortion of Ricardo's doctrine by Marx; and as to "the ridiculously exaggerated importance which has been attached to this Socialist theory of value", not only by the apostles of Socialism, but by its opponents. A science which makes concessions to a scholastic like that of Marx does not know what is due to itself.'

Capital, volume III, and the notorious 'transformation problem', were heralded in Current Topics for September 1894, when it was noted (by the sardonic Edgeworth?) that 'A third volume (Book iii) of Karl Marx's *Kapital* is expected to appear before the end of the year. It will contain the solution of problems left unsettled in the earlier portions of the work if we may believe the editor, Friedrich Engels.' The third volume did so appear and was reviewed by F. Butlin, one of the *Journal*'s leading reviewers of matters socialist at that time, Butlin's sentence is severe:

> It is not ... probable that the contents of the present volume will affect the judgement already passed by economists on the results arrived at in the earlier ones. It would seem rather to show that a theory based on the assumption that value is determined exclusively by labour, could not be further developed without being brought into conflict with facts too familiar to be overlooked. Marx does not succeed in reconciling his theory with the facts of industrial life, without, at the same time, sacrificing its consistency.

Butlin then provides a clear statement of the 'transformation problem' left over from volumes I and II (though he does not use the term) before returning to volume III. 'Here Marx arrives at the singular conclusion that the rate at which goods are exchanged for each other, is not determined by the amount of labour expended on them', this because profit rates have to be equalized. Now in the first volume, Butlin writes, Marx asserted that 'the rate at which goods exchange for one another' is 'determined exclusively by labour. It is difficult to see how this assertion can be reconciled with the conclusion arrived at in the third volume.' Stressing the importance of a proper understanding of demand, supply and value, Butlin concludes by suggesting that 'the greatest stumbling-block to the success of the cause Marx had so much at heart lies in his own theory of value'.

Be that as it may – and we have noted the Cassel/Edgeworth view which suggests otherwise – Butlin had further opportunities to return, in effect, to the same issues. Thus in September 1898 he reviewed the English translation of Böhm-Bawerk's famous *Karl Marx and the Close of his System: A Criticism*. As might be expected, Butlin first draws out Böhm-Bawerk's view of the relations between *Capital*, volumes I and III: in Butlin's own words, that 'the theory of value, as it is stated in the first volume of *Das Kapital*, is contradicted by the theory of profits in the third volume'. He goes on, however, to suggest that Böhm-Bawerk's book is more wide ranging in its scope,[11] this being important because, while the 'unsatisfactory character of the third volume has been very generally acknowledged', this 'is not sufficient in itself to condemn the whole system'. Butlin accepts the rather damning view that 'Marx did not set out to find the true law of value, but having, as he thought, found it, he set out to convince others of the truth of this law – on the acceptance of which he thought so much depended – by logical arguments where possible, and when these failed by "dialectical tricks"'.[12]

Marxism was not, of course, reducible to the 'transformation problem' even in the pages of the *Journal*. The very first volume contained, for example, a note by John Rae on 'The German Socialist Party' (September 1891), which discussed the Sozialist Partei Deutschland (SPD) draft programme for the Erfurt Congress to be held in October. The role of 'the veteran Friedrich Engels' is referred to and a detailed list of the draft programme's demands is given. In December 1891, Rae reported on the Erfurt Congress itself; the new programme was adopted 'in a lump without a word of discussion'. The general mood of the SDP congress was, in Rae's view, even more moderate than it had been a year before. Four years later, Friedrich Engels was treated, *post mortem*, to a long and scholarly obituary, in September 1895, by 'J. B.' (presumably James Bonar). In a little over two pages, Bonar presented a wide-ranging and generally flattering account of Engels's life and work.[13]

Attention to German Marxism in the pages of the *Journal* was by no means confined to the Erfurt Congress and to the veteran Engels, however. In the December 1899 issue the lead review was James Bonar's long account of Eduard Bernstein's highly significant *Die Voraussetzungen des Sozialismus und die Aufgaben der Sozialdemocratie* (later to be known in English as *Evolutionary Socialism*). Bonar was in no doubt as to the importance of Bernstein's book. The 'Social Democratic party has always contained men willing to do good economical work and place it before the world to be tested on its merits. There is much in the writings of Marx and Engels that the world will not willingly let die; and we are not unduly magnifying the work of Mr. Bernstein when we say that it has something in it of the quality of the elder men's, together with a moral or intellectual courage even greater than theirs ... . He will need all his courage, for the Congress of the party, held a few weeks ago, has declared his views to be heresy.' In Bonar's judgement, 'Mr. Bernstein's Socialism is not irreconcilable with ordinary Radicalism. He might join hands with Mr. Sidney Ball, who writes (*Economic Review*, October, 1899) in a similar strain about general principles.' 'The principles of Mr. Bernstein, in fact, seem to give us not Social Democracy, but Democracy without Socialism.'[14]

If Sidgwick was somewhat dismissive of Marx's contribution to political economy at the beginning of our period, at its close Edgeworth was positively scathing. 'We have much sympathy with those who hold that the theories of Marx are beneath the notice of a scientific writer,' he opined, in opening his March 1921 joint review of J.S. Nicholson's *The Revival of Marxism* and Achille Loria's *Karl Marx* (in English translation). Nevertheless, 'the refutation of prevailing fallacies has always been recognised as part of the economist's province ... . Accordingly, gratitude is due to Professor Nicholson for having performed the heavy task of reexamining *Das Kapital* and other writings of Marx.' But Nicholson, it seems, was not well rewarded for his efforts; '"the more I read of Marx ... the more hopeless and depressing was the effect"'. Marx's theory of value was a retrogression, ignoring contemporary analysis of demand. And Edgeworth agrees with Nicholson that the mathematical apparatus in *Das Kapital* '"is on a par with the maps and charts and ciphers put into the novels about the treasures hidden by pirates"', that '"what was original in Marx was wrong"'. Nor can Marx be saved by any neat counterposing of the professor from Turin to the professor from Edinburgh: 'Any shred of authority that Professor Nicholson may have left to the author of *Das Kapital* disappears in Professor Loria's treatment of the subject.' Marx's claims concerning the concentration of capital, the theory of surplus value and the solution of the 'transformation problem' are all to be rejected. Marx was also found guilty of being acerbic and deplorably ungrateful. At this point Edgeworth's review of Loria's work suddenly becomes more interesting, for Loria 'is an enthusiastic admirer of the man whose defects he candidly admits. The countervailing merits attributed to Marx are extolled in encomiums of almost lyrical profusion ... . Space fails us to transcribe all the eloquent eulogies of the "sage" and "martyr" "who struggled and suffered and died for the Supreme Redemption".' Not surprisingly, perhaps, Edgeworth at once raises the 'psychological question, of some practical importance, how the same mind could hold at the same time with respect to the same person judgements so different as those which we have cited'. Referring to Clough's *Dipsychus*, to the history of religious rationalism and to 'the worshippers at the shrine of Marx', Edgeworth's implied answer is that the 'importance of Marx's theories is, indeed, as Professor Nicholson shows, wholly *emotional*'.[15]

With respect to developments in the German Marxist movement, then, the early readers of the *Journal* were kept much better informed than the modern economist might be inclined to suppose. At the same time – and without inconsistency – Marx's theories of value, price and profit were treated with persistent rejection and even scorn, little relieved by any more positive assessment of other aspects of his work.

Cooperation

If Marxism was not dear to the hearts of most *Journal* contributors, 'there has always, from the days of Mill, been at least a Platonic sympathy of economists with Cooperation. In Mr. Price's case it is much more than Platonic, as his Preface shows': thus James Bonar (1905). Whatever the justice of Bonar's wider claim, it is certainly the case that cooperation received substantial and often sympathetic treatment in the early years of the *Journal*. It was Bonar himself who, in December 1891, reviewed at some length both *The Cooperative Movement To-day* by George Jacob Holyoake and *The Cooperative Movement in Great Britain* by Beatrice Potter. The latter was immediately put in her place in Bonar's opening word: 'Miss Potter seems to regret that the British public gains its impressions about the Cooperative Movement from "littérateurs and orators" of the middle and upper classes who have hitherto "voiced" the movement ... . The two volumes before us are voices from the same undesirable quarter; and we must listen to them under protest.' Having delivered his gibe, however, Bonar moved straight to a central issue – the controversy within the cooperative movement over whether profits should be distributed to cooperative workers (*qua* workers and not simply as cooperative shoppers receiving a dividend). 'Mr. Holyoake's new book ... presents the Individualist's ideal of cooperation' and 'Mr. Holyoake [like] Mr. Vansittart Neale and Mr. Thomas Hughes' holds that part of profits should be so distributed. By contrast, 'Miss Potter supports the official view, as presented by Mr. Benjamin Jones (Manager of the London branch of the Wholesale Society), and his companions in office, – that the division of profits among consumers is enough, and any attempts to make the workers share therein are necessarily vain.' Far from being an individualist cooperator, Miss Potter pleads 'for an Industrial Concern between Cooperation and Trades Unions' and many readers 'may be stumbled by her frank alliance of Cooperation and State Socialism'. Bonar declines to side with Potter in respect of her suggestion that the cooperative movement cannot stop short of removing ownership of the land and the other means of production from private hands. Quoting her to the effect that, 'before we can have a fully developed democracy, the nation at large must possess those moral characteristics which have enabled Cooperators to introduce democratic self-government into a certain portion of the industry, commerce and finance of the nation', he sardonically observes that, 'It may occur to some of us that, if these qualities were universally developed, we might be able to dispense with the benevolent despotism of a State Socialism.'

In September 1892, L. L. Price (he of the 'much more than Platonic' sympathy for cooperation, who had been taught by Marshall in Oxford) argued in 'Profit-Sharing and Cooperative Production' that J. S. Mill's confident prophecy seemed unlikely to be fulfilled. Benjamin Jones (1847–1941, London Manager of the Co-operative Wholesale Society) was not impressed and his 'Co-operation and Profit-Sharing' of December 1892 provided a substantial account of the history of the cooperative movement designed to correct 'the current mystification of the public as to what are the aims and principles of co-operators'. We cannot trace here Jones's account of the historical development of the cooperative movement but we must certainly note his optimistic prognosis. Confident both that there is an 'economic law which ensures the triumph of the most efficient machinery' and that the most just system is the most efficient one, Jones proclaims that all conflict will disappear and democratic organization become ubiquitous in all spheres of life, 'from the family to the international relations of the world'. Just two years later, in December 1894, Price was able to comment on Jones's views in his review of the latter's *Co-operative Production*. Price endorses Jones's objections to profit-sharing in cooperative enterprises; amongst other things, 'the system of imparting a share in the profits to the consumer is democratic in its tendencies and liberal in its aims, while profit-sharing on the contrary is prone to engender a spirit of narrow exclusive aristocracy'. Price accepts Jones's historical account of the failures of cooperative production 'in the stricter sense of the term' (i.e. as involving some self-management and profit-sharing), though only, it would seem, with some sadness and with the hope that those failures will provide useful lessons for the future.[16]

The members of the British Economic Association (BEA), it need hardly be said, did not confine their interest in cooperation to the pages of the *Journal*. As is well known, Alfred Marshall delivered the inaugural address to the Co-operative Congress at Ipswich in June 1889, as Beatrice Potter, also present, noted in her diary entry for 7th June 1889. She also took the occasion to add some further negative references to Edgeworth – further, that is, to those in her entry for 4 June, where she referred to him as 'an old admirer and a present lover! Even if I had not my work, the prospect of a matrimonial engagement and the preliminary receipt of addresses, bores me intolerably ... . Poor fellow! He bores me.'[17] It would take us too far afield, however, to follow all of the extra-*Journal* efforts of BEA members in favour of – or against – cooperation of various kinds.

A consistent, and consistently graceful, advocate of cooperation in the pages of the *Journal* was Charles Gide, whose contributions naturally helped to balance any undue emphasis on cooperation in Britain. As Edgeworth put it in his amusing review of Gide's *La Co-opération*, in March 1902, 'Co-operation, indeed, is for Professor Gide not only a business, but a faith. The zeal of an earlier generation glows in his pages. But he is not blinded by his ardour to the difficulties that have to be contended with. He more than once pauses to enumerate the hostile forces.' (Those hostile forces are perceived to include ladies in general, cooks in particular, the French people, orthodox Catholics and orthodox political economists; see Edgeworth's review for further details.) Gide's most substantial contribution was his 'Has Co-operation introduced a New Principle into Economics?' (December 1898), a direct reply to Pantaleoni's critique of cooperation in the March, April and May 1898 issues of the *Giornale degli Economisti*. Gide first attempts to turn the tables on Pantaleoni by arguing that it is only a cooperative system which can make a reality of free competition, drive profits down to zero and render the consumer 'King'; how then can the *libéral* Pantaleoni be an opponent of cooperation? The parting of the ways between liberalism and cooperation lies, for Gide, at the crux of distributional justice, since only the former maintains that (according to Gide) free exchange produces justice. Taking as his text the 'celebrated bargain between Esau and Jacob', Gide concedes that, 'At the moment when the bargain was concluded, the birthright was assuredly of less value [to Esau] than the dish of lentils. Where simple souls – like ourselves – are scandalised, is at the thought of Jacob's ill-gotten gains at Esau's expense, of his acquiring something a million times more valuable than what he gave!' All those 'who do as Jacob did are absolved by the hedonist. But co-operation absolves them not. Far from it!' 'Well then, says M. Pantaleoni ... confess ... that you would have the hedonistic principle superseded by the charity principle.' At this point Gide is less self-assured than usual, for cooperators repudiate the giving and receiving of charity as a central principle, yet he is not clear where to draw the line between charity, on the one hand, and altruism or mutualism, on the other.[18]

Syndicalism and Guild Socialism

If cooperation sometimes evoked the quiet sympathy, or more, of some early writers in the *Journal*, sharp hostility more often marked their responses towards two major objects of discussion in the later part of our period: the syndicalist and the guild socialist movements. The fact that the period from summer 1911 to 1914 was a turbulent one, with the dockers, railwaymen and miners engaging in the 'greatest series of industrial disputes in Britain since 1889–90', naturally gave a sharper edge to that discussion.[19] In the following years, syndicalism was the subject of several book reviews, of which we can only consider two.[20]

Not every economist today will at once associate D. H. Robertson with any interest in socialist revolution but his blend of analysis and fantasy was in fact directed in September 1913 to the discussion of Syndicalism (and later, to Guild Socialism). His review of *Syndicalism and the Co-operative Commonwealth; How we shall bring about the Revolution,* by Emile Pataud and Emile Pouget, opened with a flourish: 'To those fatigued with the mythologies of M. Sorel, this is in many ways a refreshing book. At last we are told with some approach to definiteness what two, at least, of those who profess and call themselves Syndicalists really do want, and how they propose to get it.' However, Robertson is critical. 'The authors, indeed, are at some pains to conceal the suicidal effects of the general strike *per se*: from the description of the "spiking" of the ovens on p. 22 one would suppose that only the capitalist class consumed bread.' Robertson notes that 'the instruments of production, though managed, are not apparently in any sense to be owned by the workers in the trade'. Although necessities are to be free, there will be 'labour-notes' for luxuries and 'It is left entirely to the syndicates in the luxurious trades to change their occupations in accordance with movements of demand as evidenced by the use of these notes. It is gratifying to learn that the goldsmiths and the jewellers set a good example in this respect, but one looks in vain for a guarantee that it will be followed.' Moreover, although Pataud and Pouget are said to propose various coordinating bodies, 'they wield no power in the interests of consumers against a refractory syndicate. One cannot repress a vision of a distracted Labour Exchange telephoning to Mr. Sidney Webb to send over a competent bureaucrat to put an end to the reign of industrial anarchy.' Robertson's criticism is by no means all light-hearted or merely witty, however. If each trade 'is to be allowed a blank order on the trades making the instruments of production', he observes, this is 'a system which seems hardly likely to conduce to economy of management'. Most fundamentally, while this is a 'refreshing' book, it is also a 'disappointing' one, for 'It is redolent of the central fallacy of Syndicalism – that oblivion of the standpoint of the consumer which is at the bottom of the worst excesses alike of trade unionism and of capitalism.' In the end, then, 'We are left with a *réchauffé* of the visions of early English Socialism, exhilarating, like all fine visions, to the imagination, but leaving the reason distrustful and unconvinced.' Other reviewers of works on Syndicalism (see n. 20) were no more impressed by its claims.

It was only eight years after the original publication of George Sorel's *Reflections on Violence* that Sidney Ball reviewed an English translation in September 1916. 'This is not a book that one would naturally expect to find exposed in what M. Sorel would call the "drawing-rooms" of economists – or for the matter of that in any well-regulated drawing-room.' But it may be expected to interest economists, even if *'the classic of Syndicalism'* is not a guide to syndicalism but rather 'a philosophical interpretation of the Syndicalist movement'. Sorel considers the class war, direct action etc., 'But the idea which really attracts our author ... is the significance of proletarian violence [and] the "function" of violence as an (or even the) ethical agent in progress.' Indeed, 'M. Sorel has, in fact, a new beatitude – blessed are the violent for they shall inherit the earth – and his criticism of contemporary Socialism is in effect that it is not violent enough.' Any element of paradox results, in Ball's view, from Sorel's 'continually passing from a popular to an unpopular and even esoteric use of the conception' of violence. 'It is to M. Sorel a real energy of the soul, "a striving after perfection" ... . He attributes to violence, in fact, the *rôle* of what Keats calls "making souls".' 'But regarded as a philosophy of Syndicalism [Sorel's] thesis may be reduced to the proposition that the essential doctrine of Marx can only be fulfilled through the idea of the general strike ... the idea of a general strike has all the revealing and compelling power of an apocalyptic vision – of a second coming.' Ball's overall assessment of Sorel's *Reflections* is by no means wholly negative. They carry 'a protest against facile optimism and the false prophets who cry peace when there is no peace'; they constitute 'a challenge of an unusually uncompromising kind to much in our modern thoughts and practice that seems to have become divorced from realities'. If it 'is a synthesis of the extremes that we miss in these Reflections on Violence ... this need not affect our appreciation of the extreme which M. Sorel has given us – and in such full and exuberant measure'.[21]

If syndicalism was mirrored in the pages of the *Journal* as primarily a French or American movement, with only pale reflections inside Britain, guild socialism naturally appeared as a domestic product. Indeed, although works by A. R. Orage and by S. G. Hobson were reviewed, guild socialism was largely represented for the *Journal* by the figure of G.D.H. Cole. It was not with any great implied approval, one imagines, that the author of Current Topics for June 1917 wrote: 'It is not an easy task to satisfy one who can say with Mr. Cole, "I do not think the relations of Labour and Capital will be improved after the war, and I hope they will not, because I believe in the class-struggle and regard their interests as irreconcilable. Any system which supposes co-operation betweeen Capital and Labour will break down".' Despite this – or because of it – Cole's work received much attention in the pages of the *Journal* towards the end of our period.

The *Journal*'s first really substantial treatment of guild socialism took the form of L. L. Price's June 1919 review article of three books by G.D.H. Cole.[22] This opened with the words: 'These three small books unfold a large and, we must add, a sinister design.' Nor did the tone of the article immediately soften for, after recognizing Cole's wide knowledge and skill as an author, Price at once insisted that, 'the language used sometimes degenerates into the vulgar scream of coarse vituperation, and the tone and temper shown are marred by an assertive arrogance and petty caprice which are not the less provoking because they may seem to be forced, or are calculated to offend ... . He poses in the character, and is, we gather, highly pleased with the unlovely rôle, of a brazen apostle of revolution; and, according to his repugnant but authoritative dictum, the conception of a perpetual "class-struggle" is "fundamental" to his reasoning.' Moreover, 'we should be dishonest if we did not say at the outset that [the spirit of Cole's argument] seems to us not merely mischievous, but detestable'.

Price's displeasure was not so much provoked by the first two of the books reviewed – *An Introduction to Trade Unionism* and *The Payment of Wages* – but by the third book under review – *Labour in the Commonwealth*. There, in Price's judgement, Cole appeals 'not so much to broad, disinterested hopes for the peaceful, united advance of the whole community as to the limited selfishness and stormy passions of one particular class, however large it be'. Price admits a 'certain ingenuity' in Cole's 'attempted reconciliation of the continued influence of the Organising State, representing the interests and meeting the wants of the public as consumers, with the independence of producers, controlling their own work'. 'The doctrine thus outlined of National Guilds has, [Cole] confidently maintains, the merits, without the defects, of Marxian Industrial Unionism. It tries to meet satisfactorily the revolt of Syndicalists disgusted with State Socialism. It is based, we are told, on the conception that political freedom can be properly found only in a combination of ideas of democracy and function.' Price expresses some sympathy with Cole's thought at this point – but, 'Still, we are unable to rid ourselves of an uneasy reservation that, to the public specially addressed, all this dextrous fencing will appear mere intellectual gymnastic ... . His speculative theorising is not, as we judge, safe from the impeachment of being "academic" in the meaning that it is in truth fantastic ... . He cannot, it would appear, resist the fascination of *châteaux en Espagne*.'[23]

With D.H. Robertson's help we may conclude this section on a lighter note. In December 1920 he wrote of G.D.H. Cole's *Chaos and Order in Industry*, 'in his latest book (we write in July) he promises to relate the actual with the ideal, and to develop in separate detail, for a number of leading industries, what he regards as immediately practicable steps towards the establishment of democratic control. This promise comes as a great refreshment to the *bourgeois* reader, to whom the mutual polemics of Coleite and Hobsonite are apt to bear a faint flavour of Big and Little Endianism, and who finds the record of the competitive body-snatching of Craft and Industrial Unions more palpable indeed, but even less exhilarating. On this occasion Mr. Cole has made a gallant attempt to pitch his tent somewhee between the Trade Union Lodge and Cloud-cuckoo-land; but now and again a sand-storm blows it away.' Robertson expresses his approval of some of Cole's criticisms of contemporary capitalism and endorses Cole's distinction between the actual *negative* powers of trade unions and the *positive* powers that Cole would like them to possess. And Cole is quoted to the effect that '"no successful enterprise is ever really managed by a Committee, and none ever will be; but the Committee is ... necessary for the giving of general directions and for the criticism of methods and results"'. Nevertheless, a series of quips leads Robertson to a more serious probing. 'Mr. Cole's work is so full of knowledge and power that it is of interest to inquire rather closely why it does not carry instant and overwhelming conviction. Eloquent, industrious, imaginative and sincere – how is it that he still leaves us unregenerate?' Robertson finds the answer in two aspects of 'a certain naïveté of mind, at once disarming and irritating'. The first is that, for all his appreciation of 'brain-work', Cole fails to take seriously the role of the *entrepreneur* – 'his passing will leave a gap to be filled. Yet is any real provision made for filling it? That seems to be the fatal limitation of Mr. Cole's policy of dyarchy or "encroaching control" ... will the most complete control of workshop conditions fit the Trade Union for control of the broader issues of business policy unless it sits at the feet of those who know their job, profit-mongers though they be?' 'And this brings us to a second manifestation of Mr. Cole's ingenuousness – a certain prudishness, born perhaps of defective analysis, on the subject of Profit.' The production of 'relatively unnecessary or even pernicious things' is not peculiar to capitalism but is rooted partly in human wastefulness and partly in income inequality. Nor is the sphere of profit 'co-extensive with the sphere of personal greed'. 'And will not the price of those "collective contracts" in the engineering trade depend upon demand and conjuncture, and partake of the essence, if not of the name, of profits? Yet it would be absurd, of course, to suppose that a shop-committee could be greedy.'[24]

Concluding Remarks

A striking feature of the *Economic Journal* in its first 30 years is the frequency with which socialism, broadly interpreted, was considered – not least in the Notes and Memoranda, Book Reviews and Current Topics sections. We have noted the *Journal*'s concern, in its earliest years, for openness and for academic freedom, which meant (given the general climate of the times) that some attention to Socialism was only to be expected.[25] But the amount of space devoted to reports of Trades Union Congresses, trade union journals, reports of international Socialist and Co-operative congresses, for example, might well surprise the modern economist. To report is not necessarily to express support, of course, but overt sympathy for some aspects of trade unionism and for many aspects of cooperation was in fact expressed quite frequently. Arguments for reduced income inequality and for at least some forms of expanded state activity were also at home in the ethos of the *Journal*'s early years. Support for the 'class war' or for 'class hatred', whether expressed by G.D.H. Cole or anyone else, was quite another matter and was referred to with deep hostility. Those aspects of Marxism, syndicalism and guild socialism which were treated in the *Journal* were often considered in some detail and the judgements pronounced were not favourable, as was often made very plain. Amongst the various criticisms made both of specific forms of socialism and of the more amorphous British 'collectivism' of the time, there was a persistent emphasis on the importance of change, on the need for invention, for innovation and hence, it was argued, for entrepreneurs and for their rewards. This perception of the economic process supported simultaneously a criticism of various socialist proposals, a defence of the market system and the upholding of a qualified civilized version of individualism which some at least would have been ready to call socialism.

NOTES

Earlier versions of this paper were presented to seminars at the Universities of Leeds, Manchester and Naples and a conference at the University of Gronigen. I am grateful to Hillel Steiner and Donald Winch for encouragement and criticism.

1 Coats would seem to imply (1967, p. 715; 1968 p. 356) that the *Journal*'s openness was limited to the early years, but unfortunately the point is not developed.

2 As a *very* crude index, we may note that, even after excluding municipal enterprises, the Poor Law etc., we listed almost 400 items bearing on socialism in the *Economic Journal* (*EJ*), 1890–1920.

3 Thus we cannot touch on the extensive treatment in the *Journal* of the relations between socialism and the churches. Nor on the discussions of 'trade interest', concerning the attempts of capitalists and workers in a given industry to make *common* cause against the interests of all those deriving their incomes from other industries. Nor, again, can we discuss here the considerable space devoted in the *Journal*'s pages to reporting the activities, conferences, publications etc. of trade union and socialist organizations – and of anti-socialist organizations. (To give just one example, 'the first circular of "The Independent Labour Party"' was reproduced, apparently in full, over $2\frac{1}{2}$ pages of small type (1894, pp. 368–71) and denounced both 'the exploiting plutocracy of Liberalism' and 'the confiscating aristocracy of Toryism'. Both sexes were called upon 'to enrol under the banner of the I.L.P., and to at once engage in the great and glorious crusade' etc.) Material on socialism and the churches, on trade interest and on socialist and labour affairs is available from the author.

4 It need hardly be said that the 'land question', the writings and lecture tours of Henry George, explicit proposals for land nationalization, the concern with agricultural and urban rent etc. all formed a *major* part of British discussions about socialism in our period. In the view of L.L. Price (*EJ*, 1891, p. 123), 'It can scarcely be questioned that the only part of the propaganda of modern socialism, which has as yet obtained any wide currency in England, is that known as the "nationalization of land".' See, for example, McBriar (1966) and Wolfe (1975) for discussion of these matters. Further relevant material is available from the author.

5 Webb here refers (p. 369, n. 1) to his own article on interest (*Quarterly Journal of Economics*, January 1888), reproduced with some additions in the *Proceedings of the National Liberal Club Political Economy Circle*, vol i, 1891. Later that year F.C. Montague wrote, in his review of these *Proceedings*, that, 'Mr Sidney Webb's essay on the rate of interest seems to us to teem with disputable matter. It tries to develop a definition of economic interest parallel to the definition of economic rent' (*EJ*, pp. 600–1).

6 Webb's discussion of evolution develops into a consideration of 'the race struggle' (p. 378). Socialism, it seems, must replace competition inside the nation but is, for Webb, a necessary condition for success in the international 'race struggle'! A man of his time indeed.

7 See, for example, McBriar (1966) and Wolfe (1975) for detailed discussion of the Fabians, of Webb's relations with Marshall etc.

8 Sidgwick's paper may usefully be seen as a development of his address to the British Association, nine years earlier; see his 'On the Economic Exceptions to Laissez Faire', in Smyth (ed.) (1964).

9 Both the general thrust of Marshall's paper and some of his parallels between Germany and Russia clearly irritated Gustav Cohen considerably; his 'Govern-

ment and Laissez Faire' (*EJ* 1907) never mentioned Marshall's paper by name but there is no doubt that it provides one of Cohen's central targets.
10 As background, see Hobsbawm's 'Dr. Marx and the Victorian Critics' (Hobsbawm, 1979, ch. 13).
11 C.F. Wicksteed's 1884 critique of Marx's value theory, which turned entirely on the early chapters of *Capital*, vol. I.
12 In March 1899 Butlin reviewed both Marx's *Value, Price and Profit* (the pamphlet against Citizen Weston) and a work by Dr Karl Diehl on Marx's value theory.
13 A less attractive glimpse of Engels, however was, given by C. Violet Butler in her September 1907 review of an American edition of *Landmarks of Scientific Socialism (Anti-Duehring)*.
14 See also *EJ* (June 1909) and *EJ* (March 1910) for reviews of works by Sombart and by Hammacher respectively on Marx's system of thought.
15 In June 1921 Nicholson accused the author of *Karl Marx and Modern Socialism*, F. R. Salter, of vacillating rapidly between eulogies of Marx and demonstrations of his errors. Nicholson prefers Sir Thomas More's *Utopia* to the work of 'the class-hatredists' (p. 227).
16 The arguments over the producer and consumer orientations for the cooperative movement were pursued in the pages of the *Journal* by 'X' in March 1902, by Henry Vivian in June 1902 and by Catherine Webb in her December 1908 review of Fay's *Co-operation at Home and Abroad*. (Vivian (1868–1930) was a Liberal MP and editor of *Co-partnership*.) Two leading cooperators, J.T.W. Mitchell and G.J. Holyoake, received substantial obituaries in the *Journal*, in June 1895 and March 1906 respectively.
17 See N. and J. MacKenzie (eds), 1892, volume 1, pp. 283–7; in an editorial note to volume 2, the MacKenzies refer, more discreetly, to 'F.Y. Edgeworth (1845–1926) ... professor of political economy at King's College, London; he had formed a forlorn attachment to Beatrice shortly before she met Sidney' (p. 73).
18 Early in 1898 Gide lectured on cooperation in Lausanne; Pareto was not impressed. See his letters to Pantaleoni (then in Geneva), both 1898 and, earlier, 1897 on Pantaleoni's own three-part article on cooperation (Pareto, 1960). Gide's involvement in and knowledge of the cooperative movement was by no means purely theoretical; nor was he unaware of its possible wider ramifications. In his June 1895 contribution, 'The Union between Agricultural Syndicates and Co-operative Societies in France', for example, he noted that 'in France at this moment the collectivist socialists are making a great effort to win over the rural districts' (p. 206) and then observed that, 'If it can be worked, this alliance between agricultural syndicates and co-operative societies will serve to strengthen [resistance to the collectivist socialist tactics] by uniting the country dwellers with a part of the urban population in one and the same defensive league' (p. 207). Gide's later reports on the International Co-operative Alliance Congresses at Cremona (1907) and Hamburg (1910) were no less sensitive to wider political issues.

19 See Winter, 1974, p. 2. See also, for example, Current Topics for December 1910 and for June 1912. In the latter the writer notes, with reference to a coal strike, that 'the Labour Party were in difficulties throughout' in knowing how to respond to the openly sectional approach of the Syndicalists (pp. 346–7).
20 See too the reviews of works on syndicalism in December 1912, March 1914, June 1914 and December 1914. Also Edgeworth's remarks on the Webbs and syndicalism (1920, pp. 220–1).
21 It may be noted that Sidney Ball (St John's College, Oxford), a Christian and a socialist, was tutor to both Tawney and G.D.H. Cole.
22 In June 1915 Orage's *National Guilds* had been reviewed, by P. Sargent Florence, and in March 1919 Cole and Mellor's *The Meaning of Industrial Freedom*, by Henry W. Macrosty (the civil servant and member of the Fabian Executive, 1895–1907, who published a number of Fabian Tracts).
23 See also D.H. Robertson's June 1920 review of Cole's *Social Theory*, Henry Vivian's review of S.G. Hobson's *National Guilds and the State* (June 1920) and Hélène Reynard's 'The Guild Socialists' (September 1920, pp. 321–30). Reynard is sharply critical of the Guild Socialists on the grounds that their assumptions about human nature are even more of a caricature than are those embodied in the 'economic man' (pp. 328–9). A guild system, she argues, could be exploitative and oppressive (p. 329).
24 By 1922 Cole had abandoned Guild Socialism and was being sharply attacked by his former colleague, Mellor, who had himself joined the Communist Party (Winter, 1974, p. 281).
25 The *Journal*'s concern for freedom of expression was not confined to the British Isles. See, for example, 1894, p. 474 on Russian censorship of Loria's work; 1897, pp. 459, 546 on Pantaleoni's being driven from Naples to Geneva; 1897, pp. 645–6 on allegations that President Andrews had been forced to resign the presidency of Brown University because of his views on the silver question and on trusts.

References

Coats, A.W. (1967): 'Sociological Aspects of British Economic Thought (ca. 1880–1930)', *Journal of Political Economy*, 75, 706–29.
Coats, A.W. (1968): 'The Origins and Early Development of the Royal Economic Society', *Economic Journal*, 78, 349–71.
Hobsbawm, E.J. (1979 [1964]): *Labouring Men. Studies in the History of Labour* (London: Weidenfeld and Nicolson).

McBriar, A.M. (1966): *Fabian Socialism and English Politics, 1884–1918* (Cambridge: Cambridge University Press).
Pareto, V. (1960): *Lettere à Maffeo Pantaleoni*, Volume Secondo (ed. by G. de Rosa) (Rome: Banca Nazionale del Lavoro).
Smyth, R.L. (ed.) (1964): *Essays in the Economics of Socialism and Capitalism* (London: Duckworth).
Webb, S. (1987 [1890, 1893]): *Socialism in England* (Aldershot: Gower).
Winter, J.M. (1974): *Socialism and the Challenge of War. Ideas and Politics in Britain 1912–18* (London and Boston: Routledge and Kegan Paul).
Wolfe, W. (1975): *From Radicalism to Socialism* (New Haven, CT: Yale University Press).

5
The Attitudes of the Economics Professions in Britain and the United States to the Trust Movement, 1890–1914

Philip L. Williams

In 1892 Marshall wrote that 'there are few more pressing studies than those of the relative gains and losses which would accrue to monopolists and the public generally from different courses of action'.[1] These sentiments could have been expressed by Marshall's friend and contemporary on the other side of the Atlantic, John Bates Clark. In their responses to the trust movement, the differences and similarities between these two are, in some ways, indicative of the professions they led. At the outset of their careers they were influenced by the writings of the German historical school: both came to see the growth in the size of the representative firm from a teleological or evolutionary perspective. They shared a mode of analysis of trusts and adopted a set of policy prescriptions that (until Clark's conversion to trust-busting in 1912) were broadly consistent. The principal difference between the two lay in the extent of their participation in public debate and their influence over policy.

Each of the leading American economists to write on antitrust policy prior to 1890 (J.B. Clark, Henry Carter Adams, Richard T. Ely and Arthur T. Hadley) had undertaken postgraduate study in Germany.² They were representative of those American postgraduates who in the 1870s and 1880s familiarized themselves with the German historical school from close quarters and then proceeded to proclaim with fervour their peculiarly American version.³ Whereas contemporary German writers on trusts devoted their energies to the production of scientific tomes on the inevitability of the emergence of combinations, their younger American colleagues followed the lead of masters such as Johannes Conrad, Ernst Engel and Adolf Wagner in developing theories of state intervention – in particular, the state intervention considered appropriate as a response to the combination movement being discussed in the popular journals.

Each of the four young turks mentioned above took his first teaching position in the period 1879–81; each was embroiled in the famous controversy over method and policy that surrounded the founding of the American Economic Association (AEA) in 1885; and each felt compelled to offer the public the benefit of trained economic analysis on the key public issue of the day: the causes and consequences of what we know as the first merger movement, 1870–90. Although the British Economic Association was modelled on the American Economic Association, the British body showed none of the commitment to policy of its American forebear. Indeed, the surviving documents reveal a quiet orderliness and a marked openness to disparate views.

Ely was the acknowledged leader of the founders of the AEA. In his autobiography he stresses the evangelical spirit of the enterprise. 'Two aspects of the early history of the American Economic Association should be stressed: first, it represented a protest against the system of laissez faire, as expounded by writers of the older school of "orthodox" American economics... the second...was the necessity of uniting in order to secure complete freedom of discussion; a freedom untrammeled by any restrictions whatsoever.'⁴ Controversy focused on the first clause of the Statement of Objects and Platform which Ely had drafted for discussion by the Association. It read: 'We regard the state as an educational and ethical agency whose positive aid is an indispensable condition of human progress. While we recognize the necessity of individual initiative in industrial life, we hold that the doctrine of laissez-faire is unsafe in politics and unsound in morals; and that it suggests an inadequate explanation of the relations between the state and its citizens.'[5]

Not only did this lead to vigorous debate (and subsequent redrafting) at meetings of potential members, but the argument spilled over into the weekly journal *Science*, for which Henry Carter Adams wrote an excellent explanation of the historical school's view on the relation of jurisprudence and economics: '...public opinion considers the social interest; and with this the individual interest does not always harmonize. The one holds in mind the ultimate, the other the immediate, results; and the only way in which the social purpose can influence the practice of individuals is for law to establish uniformity of action. This is the most important use of law as an agency of reform.'[6] These sentiments might have been expressed by any of the young German-trained Americans or, indeed, by J.S. Mill. Ely tells us that Mill exercised some considerable influence on the 'new economics' of 1885. 'We found that, in spite of Mill's half-hearted defence of the "let alone" system, he really justified pretty much of everything that those of the younger group stood for.'

The Trust Movements and their Interpretation

In contrast with popular agitators, the young German-trained professionals stressed that much of the growth in the size of the representative firm could be attributed to real efficiencies of large-scale production: the trust movement was an inevitable consequence of changing technologies.

The theoretical underpinning of the idea of natural monopoly was provided by John Stuart Mill's *Principles of Political Economy*.[8] In Book I, chapter IX, Mill presented what Stigler has taught us to call the survivor principle:[9] that the number of firms in any freely competitive industry will tend towards industry output divided by that scale of production at which long-run average cost is minimized. Following his presentation of the survivor principle, Mill noted that in certain industries – such as gas, water and railways – economies of scale accrue over such a large range of scales that only one firm could survive the rigours of free competition.[10] Mill obliged further by providing a label for this class of industry: the natural monopoly.

> All the natural monopolies (meaning thereby those which are created by circumstances, and not by law) which produce or aggravate the disparities in the remuneration of different kinds of labour, operate similarly between different employments of capital. If a business can only be advantageously carried on by a large capital, this in most countries limits so narrowly the class of persons who can enter the employment, that they are enabled to keep their rate of profit above the general level.[11]

Mill's analysis of natural monopoly was repeated by many of the American professional economists examining the trust movement – and, frequently, with a flavour provided by the German historical school. This German influence is evident in their presentation of industrial concentration as a natural evolutionary development. Even in the writing of the young J.B. Clark (when still allied to the Christian Socialists) one can find language that, by combining Mill with the German sources, sounds like that of Marx, Blanc or Fourier.[12] In an article entitled 'The Limits of Competition', J.B. Clark claimed that the assumption by the English classical economists (such as Ricardo and Cairnes) that capital is free to move among activities was valid for their time; but this principle had '...apparently ceased to operate in very extensive fields. ...The new era is distinctively one of consolidated forces; rival establishments are forming combinations, and the principle of union is extending itself to the labour and the capital in each of them.'[13]

Henry Carter Adams's monograph, *The Relation of the State to Industrial Action*, was highly influential in explaining the trust movement by means of Mill's analysis of natural monopoly.[14] Even before Adams's monograph was published by the AEA it was being favourably quoted by Hadley and James.[15] Ely and Wells were quick to follow, with articles in the non-specialist press.[16]

Adams classified industries into three types according to the shapes of the long-run marginal cost curves of their constituent firms.

> All industries, as it appears to me, fall into three classes, according to the relation that exists between the increment of product which results from a given increment of capital or

labour. These may be termed industries of constant returns, industries of diminishing returns, and industries of increasing returns. The first two classes of industries are adequately controlled by competitive action; the third class, on the other hand, requires the superior control of state power.[17]

In the 1880s and 1890s American professional economists were provoked into print by populist opposition to the formation and activity of trusts. They were concerned not so much with setting out the optimal policy towards trusts as to argue that much of the increase in concentration was the inevitable result of changing technologies which favoured a growth in the size of the representative firm.

The British economics profession did not embrace the strongly historicist analysis of their American counterparts. The explanation for this difference must refer both to academic background and to the facts of industry. In the first place, the British economics profession was much less influenced by the German historical approach. Secondly, because the trust movement was much less apparent in Britain than in the United States or Germany, British economists were stimulated to explain the trust movement by factors that were specific to German or US industry rather than by some supranational teleology. The favourite country-specific explanator was the tariff.

The leader of the historical school of economics in Britain, W.J. Ashley, argued that, although protection may have some influence, there were deeper forces behind the trust movement centring on what he called 'the economic atmosphere' of the United States.[18] He proceeded to argue that, by 1899, America had assumed the position formerly occupied by England as 'the classic home of the great industry'.

> The home market is far larger; it is constituted by a population living on the whole more comfortably, and able to furnish a stronger 'effective' demand; both capital and labour are more mobile; and, finally, but quite as important as any other consideration, the individualist spirit is more generally diffused and more deeply penetrating. No country ever before offered such opportunities for making a fortune to those who can manage to attract towards themselves the purchasing power of the public. Accordingly, all the phenomena resulting from competitive production on a large scale have been exhibited in America with an intensity and a reverberating publicity

such as was never known before. And the Trusts are, in main, simply an attempt to lessen and, if it may be, avert altogether the disastrous and harassing effects of cut-throat competition, after a completer experience of what that competition means than any country has ever been through before.[19]

One century later, economists have difficulty appreciating the weight given to the force of custom by professional economists at the end of the nineteenth century. Custom was defined by the 1894 edition of Palgrave's *Dictionary* as 'the doing a thing because others have done it'. It states: 'Early in the century it was taken for granted that the only serious hindrance in the way of perfect competition was custom.'[20]

Ashley was not alone among the English historical economists in developing this relationship between the decline of custom and the trust movement. When Foxwell wrote that 'everything which is most characteristic of our age, from the consolidation of Empires down to the quackeries of advertisement, is favourable to the growth of these monopolies of efficiency',[21] he had in mind the disintegration of the influence of custom and the consequent ability of the lower-cost producer to eliminate the smaller-scale producer with higher unit costs.

The point is argued most eloquently by J.A. Hobson.

> Under old business conditions custom held considerable sway; the personal element played a larger part alike in determining quality of goods and good faith; purchasers did not so closely compare prices; they were not guided exclusively by figures, they did not systematically beat down prices, nor did they devote so large a proportion of their time, thought, and money to devices for taking away one another's customers. From the new business this personal element and these customary scruples have almost entirely vanished, and as the net advantages of large-scale production grow, more and more attention is devoted to the direct work of competition. Hence we find that it is precisely in those trades which are most highly organised, provided with the most advanced machinery, and composed of the largest units of capital, that the fiercest and most unscrupulous competition has shown itself.[22]

Marshall was notoriously reticent in acknowledging his indebtedness to other economists, so it is not surprising that he acknowledged no indebtedness to the historical school. Despite some recent work touching on the topic, J.R. Whitaker's judgement remains apt: '...the question of Marshall's indebtedness, to the Historical School – both its major German stem and its minor English branch – is a large one deserving detailed treatment. I am inclined to think the debt was small, and that similarities were more a matter of a common starting point.'[23] Although the extent and immediacy of the influence may be debated, the fact is that Marshall's *Industry and Trade* was influenced by an evolutionary view of history and an historicist type of nation-centred analysis.[24] Book II of *Industry and Trade* explores reasons for the growth in the size of the representative firm. These reasons are not restricted to changing technology. They include the growing size and complexity of markets, new legal structures (the joint-stock form) and new techniques of management.[25]

Why was Britain Different?

Contemporary writers were unanimous in their verdict that industrial concentration had increased much more in the United States over the period 1870–1914 than did industrial concentration in England. Unfortunately, the collection of industry concentration statistics was almost non-existent in England during the period.[26] The evidence relied upon by contemporary commentators was impressionistic and depended principally on comparisons of the extent to which a few firms (or a cohesive combination) accounted for a substantial proportion of industry output. Even less reliable were the stories of the formation of new trusts. As D.H. Macgregor pointed out, the stories ignored the subsequent lives of the trusts. He argued that the analysis of the lives of trusts made one optimistic about the virility of competitive processes.

> Over the period 1903 to 1912, for instance, the statistics of liquidations of Joint Stock Companies in England were on the average as follows:
>
> | Companies on the Register | Paid-up Capital (1,000's) | New Companies | Liquidations | Capital involved in liquidations (1,000's) |
> |---|---|---|---|---|
> | 40,101 | 1,862,107 | 5,028 | 1,860 | 54,531 |
>
> This was an average rate of liquidation of 4½ per cent of companies, *involving* 3 per cent of the capital. It is not an

unqualified record of competitive results, because no country was without some extent of combination. But it is the record of prevalently competitive conditions including those which obtained under partial forms of combination.[27]

Although most contemporary writers accepted the proposition that the trust movement had progressed further in the United States than in England, the real debate was over the reasons for the difference and the weight that should be given to each reason. The principal reasons were the tariff, a low level of concentration in mining, government regulation of mergers between railway companies, and the independent spirit of the British entrepreneur.

In the first few decades of its existence, the *Economic Journal* served as the vehicle by which British economists were informed of developments in the economic policy of other countries. In a series of articles on US tariff policy, F.W. Taussig wrote of the influence of tariffs on the trust movement. Britain did not participate in the move of many of its key trading partners after 1873 to impose protective import duties. The McKinley Act of 1890 presented the manufacturers of the United States with far higher levels of tariff protection than they had enjoyed before the Civil War of 1861–5.[28] The Tariff Act of 1894 revised some of the duties contained in the legislation of 1890. The reasons for the revision were due, at least in part, to public outrage at the protection the tariff was seen to provide for the trusts.[29] In drawing this connection between the tariff and the trust movement, popular opinion was supported by the expert view of the economics profession on both sides of the Atlantic. The tariff was seen as increasing the price of imported product which set a ceiling on the prices a trust or combination was able to charge. For example, Jenks argued that the effect of the McKinley Act's lowering of tariffs on raw and refined sugar was to reduce the profit margin of the Sugar Trust from one cent a pound or more to three-eighths of one cent.[30]

Richard T. Ely wrote extensively on the link between the tariff and the formation of trusts.[31] Like D.H. Macgregor in England,[32] Ely argued that the tariff should be removed over time.

> Its design was to shut off foreign competition altogether or to weaken its force, but not to prevent competition among domestic producers. Within a few years, however, home manufac-

turers, seeing foreign competition excluded, have availed themselves of this circumstance to form trusts and combinations, whereby all competition has been excluded, all producers have been placed at the mercy of a ring, and those who have dared oppose them have been crushed by a tyranny in comparison with which the alleged tyranny of trades-unions sinks into insignificance.[33]

In contrast with the experience of the United States, Britain provided many examples of combinations that had collapsed as a result of competition from imports. A much-cited example was the collapse in 1900 of the Birmingham Bedstead Makers' Alliance. It doubled the price of bedsteads between 1891 and 1900, but this stimulated imports and the demise of the cartel in 1900. It was not re-activated until 1912. Under the protection from imports provided by the war it was able to operate with safety.[34] Many similar examples can be given. Even the Salt Union discovered that natural protection was insufficient to keep out imports at the prices it attempted to set.[35]

Natural protection was sufficient for the formation of a coal trust in Britain in this period – but none was formed. Even when the Boer War led to very high prices for coal in Britain in 1900, costs of transport from Germany and the United States meant that no coal was imported into Britain. Despite this protection, British coal producers were unable to emulate their German and American counterparts in forming a cartel. The reason was the same as that which ruined the old Coal Vend: the multiplicity of sources of production whose ability to collude was weakened by the improvement of communications in the period after the collapse of the Vend.[36]

A third reason given for the weakness of Britain's trust movement was government regulation of mergers among enterprises based on government licence, in particular, railway companies. In the United States, popular outrage against trust in the 1880s had been directed most notably at the manner in which Rockefeller's Standard Oil Company had been able to secure secrete rebates for its shipments on railroads. Not only were these rebates not given to its rivals, but the rebates were also paid to Standard Oil on the oil shipped by its rivals. Indeed, the Industrial Commission concluded: 'There can be no doubt that in earlier times special favours from railroads were a prominent factor, probably the most important factor, in building up some of the largest combinations.'[37]

The Parliament at Westminster initially granted concessions to railway companies in a 'casual and arbitrary manner'.[38] As a consequence many small companies had to be merged to form the great 'through lines'. 'But while Parliament allowed each company the sole right of tapping the resources of the districts immediately adjacent to its line, it always carefully refrained from allowing such an amalgamation as that would leave a large section of the country entirely at the mercy of one company.'[39] This rule was not always followed, because Parliament was deflected from its course by the railway interest.[40] Nevertheless, arrangements of the type arranged by the free-wheeling Rockefeller were much more difficult to secure in England.

The final reason given by contemporary commentators for the comparative difference in the power of the trusts was the relative independence of spirit of the British entrepreneurs. The chief exponent of this theory was Robert Liefmann who maintained that 'the chief reason for the absence of cartels in many branches of English industry lies in the fact that the doctrines of extreme individualism still retain a firm hold over English manufacturers'.[41] This view was adopted by the US Industrial Commission in its *Report on Trusts and Combinations* of 1902. The *Report* (largely written by Jeremiah Jenks) was impressed that trusts were less prevalent in England than in the United States, but it argued against the removal of the tariff. The reason for Britain's relative freedom from trusts was the independent spirit of the British entrepreneurs, rather than the tariff.[42]

Policy Prescriptions

As can be seen from the above discussion, professional economists did not follow the element of populist literature which equated largeness of size with monopoly power. In the 1880s professional economists in the United States (led by Ely) argued that size (of itself) was of no concern; rather, public concern should be directed at monopoly power. By the late 1880s the idea of limit pricing was well established in the literature. Henry Sidgwick's *Principles* contained a particularly clear exposition.[43] Those who maintained that entry is free as a general rule (apart from natural monopolies) drew the conclusion that so-called artificial monopolies were of no concern to the state.[44]

Until the great wave of merger activity beginning in 1895 neither economists in the United States nor their colleagues in Britain had proposed detailed schemes for the control of monopoly. By and large, they placed much faith in the competitive pressure of imports and potential entrants. However, by 1899 J.B. Clark had become convinced that trusts could erect what are now known as 'strategic' barriers, i.e. those purposely erected to reduce the possibility of entry.[45]

> There is often a considerable range within which trusts can raise prices without calling potential competition into positive activity. The possible competitor does not, by any means, become a real one as promptly as he should. The trouble is, that he has not a fair chance for his life when he actually appears on the scene. He is in very great danger of being crushed by the trust, by virtue of certain abnormal things that the trust is now allowed to do.[46]

Clark identified three classes of strategy by which barriers could be erected: creating false information, price discrimination and exclusive dealing. He argued that antitrust policy should be directed against such strategies.

It was commonplace among American economists at the turn of the century that asymmetries of information could constitute a barrier to entry. The treatises on antitrust by Clark, Ely and Jenks all advocated compulsory disclosure of profitability according to state-prescribed accounting standards. The 1902 report of the Industrial Commission of the House of Representatives endorsed this proposal.

The acknowledged leader among economists in the call for publicity was Henry Adams. A firm in a competitive industry would only be able to sustain super-normal profits if potential entrants were unaware of that profitability. By forcing the publication of profits, potential competition would be strengthened. By creating misleading information about their profitability certain firms had been able to safeguard excess rates of return. Because the misleading information was a deadweight loss, firms should not be able to gain by its dissemination.[47]

Clark's second strategy by which barriers to entry could be

erected was price discrimination. Such a use of price discrimination would be an 'unfair' practice – by which Clark meant it would damage economic efficiency. (Marshall uses the term in the same context in *Industry and Trade*.) The extent to which conduct could be regarded as unfair is, for Clark, a matter of some delicacy of judgement. For this reason, expert members of a Commission, similar to the Interstate Commerce Commission, would be more appropriate decision-makers than members of the judiciary.[48] Marshall expresses a similar attitude, and, indeed, his *Industry and Trade* contains many messages of congratulation for the work of the fledgling Federal Trade Commission.

By far the most detailed contemporary British analysis of government policy on monopoly was the fellowship dissertation of D.H. Macgregor (written under Marshall), published as *Industrial Combination*. Macgregor was opposed to the strengthening of the law on price discrimination on the ground that discrimination is merely a symptom of monopoly power and that the latter should be the target of the legislature (and the lowering of tariffs the instrument). Clark disagreed. Although he was in favour of attacking the sources of monopoly power, he was aware that (particularly in the cases of natural monopoly) this was difficult to achieve. Furthermore, he regarded unfair practices (such as price discrimination) as the means whereby monopoly power that was otherwise contained in small pockets of industry became ubiquitous: 'What economic law clearly shows is that monopoly will not come if the practices on which it depends shall be suppressed, and the people may be trusted to determine whether the suppression is or is not possible.'[49]

The third strategy that Clark considered needed to be regulated was exclusive dealing, for example 'factors agreements' by which a company only offers to sell or only offers rebates to those merchants who refuse to handle the products of competing suppliers. Like Clark, Macgregor did not approve of exclusive dealing contracts. They 'are regarded most generally, boycotts; they prevent access of third parties to the market, or impede their operation therein. They do not permit the criterion of efficiency to operate freely.'[50] Such boycotts are particularly 'formidable' in services (transport, banking and the press) in which 'the principle of substitution acts less freely', i.e. if undertaken by a firm with substantial monopoly power. But, as with price discrimination, Macgregor agreed that much of the unfair behaviour Clark saw as producing monopoly was merely the manifestation of power granted by the state. Macgregor argued that by removing state franchises many monopolies would be abolished.

Conclusion and Coda

The trust movement was a transatlantic phenomenon, but one that was much more pronounced in the United States. One of the key reasons for this difference was the degree of tariff protection. Contemporary observers pointed, in addition, to other influences: the fragmented nature of mining in Britain, the regulation of mergers among railway companies in Britain and the individualistic spirit of the British entrepreneur.

The trust movements of each country led to two types of analysis. On the one hand professional economists (particularly those with a sympathy for the German historical school) engaged in positive analysis – trying to understand why the size of the representative firm was increasing. On the other hand (and this was more common in the United States) there was normative analysis of whether the problem was real and, to the extent that it was, how the state ought to respond. Such normative analysis was not well developed in the United States until the turn of the century. British economists never embraced detailed regulation to the extent advocated by the Americans. Generally, the British position was that a lowering of tariffs and a reduction in government meddling would largely solve the problem of trusts. By 1912 Clark, the leading writer on trusts in the United States, had become convinced that his earlier position (that the state should ensure adequate information and regulate price discrimination and exclusive dealing) was inadequate. His faith in exclusive reliance on potential competition was shaken; and he began to advocate controls over industry concentration.[51]

Mainstream professional writers in Britain did not consider the problem to be nearly so urgent – until the intervention of the First World War. The experience of war did much to stimulate collusion among British enterprises.[52] Anxiety about the likely prevalence of collusion in the post-war period led to the formation of a Committee on Trusts by the Ministry of Reconstruction.[53] In an addendum to the Report, Ernest Bevin, J.A. Hobson, W.H. Watkins and Sidney Webb argued that the Report did not go far enough. Stricter controls were necessary. These controls were not of the type advocated by J.B. Clark and his colleagues in the United States. Rather they were of the type advocated by Pigou in Cambridge:[54] control of prices. Pigou's analysis was a direct extension of Marshall's proposal in the *Principles* for a tax on goods which obey the law of diminishing return and a bounty on the production of goods with sharply increasing returns.[55]

In the 1920s the US profession continued to analyse the problem of trusts very much within the framework established by J.B. Clark at the turn of the century. In Britain, the tradition of Marshall remained powerful. By 1920, both the United States and the British profession were more prominent and influential than they had been three decades earlier. Nevertheless, in the field of antitrust, the US profession was both more prominent and more influential than its British counterpart.

NOTES

1 Alfred Marshall, *Elements of Economics of Industry*, 1st edn (London: Macmillan, 1892), p. 257.
2 Adams studied under Wagner and Held (see Joseph Dorfman, 'Henry Carter Adams: The Harmonizer of Liberty and Reform', in Henry Carter Adams, *Relation of the State to Industrial Action and Economics of Jurisprudence* (ed. with an introduction by Joseph Dorfman) (New York: Columbia University Press, 1954), p. 11. Ely studied at the Universities of Halle and Heidelberg (see Obituary by H.C. Taylor, *Economic Journal* (1944), 132–8). Clark studied at Heidelberg and Zurich (see Obituary in *New York Times* 22 March 1938, p. 21). Hadley studied at Berlin under Wagner among others (see Morris Hadley, *Arthur Twining Hadley* (New Haven, CT: Yale University Press, 1948)).
3 For a general review of this movement see Jurgen Herbst, *The German Historical School in American Scholarship* (Ithaca, NY: Cornell University Press, 1965). For an impression of the Wagner seminar see H.R. Seager, 'Economics at Berlin and Vienna', *Journal of Political Economy*, 1 (1893), 236–62.

4 Richard T. Ely, *Ground Under Our Feet* (New York: Macmillan, 1938), p. 132.
5 Richard T. Ely, 'Report of the Organization of the American Economic Association', *Publications of the American Economic Association*, 1 (1886), 6–7.
6 Henry Carter Adams, 'Economics and Jurisprudence', *Science*, Supplement, 8 (2 July 1886), 15–19.
7 Ely, *Ground Under Our Feet*, p. 157.
8 John Stuart Mill, *Principles of Political Economy*, 9th edn, 1885 (ed. by W.J. Ashley) (London: Longmans, Green, 1909), pp. 132–42.
9 George J. Stigler, 'The Economies of Scale', *Journal of Law and Economics*, 1 (1958); reprinted in *The Organisation of Industry* (Homewood, IL: Irwin, 1968), pp. 71–94.
10 Mill, *Principles*, p. 143.
11 Mill, *Principles*, p. 410.
12 For a discussion of Marx's analysis, see Philip L. Williams, 'Monopoly and Centralisation in Marx', *History of Political Economy*, 14 (1982), 228–41. For the views of Blanc and Fourier see the extracts in Mill's chapters on socialism, reprinted in *Collected Works* (Toronto: University of Toronto Press, 1967), pp. 703–53.
13 John Bates Clark, 'The Limits of Competition', *Political Science Quarterly*, 2 (1887), 47.
14 See William Letwin, *Law and Economic Policy in America* (Edinburgh: Edinburgh University Press, 1967), p. 75. Henry Carter Adams, *Relation of the State to Industrial Action*; reprinted from *Publications of the American Economic Association*, 1 (1887), in *Relation of the State to Industrial Action and Economics of Jurisprudence* (ed. with an introduction by Joseph Dorfman) (New York: Columbia University Press, 1954).
13 Arthur T. Hadley, 'Private Monopolies and Public Rights', *Quarterly Journal of Economics*, 1 (1886), 37; Edmund J. James, 'The Relation of the Modern Municipality to the Gas Supply', *Publications of the American Economics Association*, 1 (2, 3) (1886).
16 Richard T. Ely, *Problems of Today*, 3rd edn (New York: Thomas Y. Crowell, 1890), p. 123. The volume comprises papers which were written for the *Baltimore Sun*. See also David A. Wells, *Recent Economic Changes* (New York: D. Appleton, 1889), p. 74. This volume comprises papers which were originally published by the (New York) *Popular Science Monthly* and, in part, by the (London) *Contemporary Review*.
17 Adams, *Relation of the State*, p. 105. Dorfman shows in a footnote to this passage that Adams's marginalist language is modelled on Jevons's *Theory of Political Economy*.
18 Sir William Ashley, 'American Trusts', *Economic Journal*, 9 (1899), 162–72, at pp. 166–7.
19 Ashley, 'American Trusts', p. 168.
20 R. L. Phelps, 'Competition and Custom', in Sir Robert Harry Inglis Palgrave

(ed.), *Dictionary of Political Economy* (London: Macmillan, 1919), vol. I, p. 377.

21 H. S. Foxwell, 'The Growth of Monopoly, and its Bearing on the Functions of the State', in *Papers on Current Finance* (London: Macmillan, 1919), p. 266.

22 John A. Hobson, *The Evolution of Modern Capitalism* (London: Walter Scott, 1919), p. 168.

23 John R. Whitaker, 'Some Neglected Aspects of Alfred Marshall's Economic and Social Thought', *History of Political Economy*, 9 (1977) 192–3. For the recent secondary literature, see Alon Kadish, *The Oxford Economists in the Late Nineteenth Century* (Oxford: Clarendon, 1982), and John Maloney, *Marshall, Orthodoxy and the Professionalisation of Economics* (Cambridge: Cambridge University Press, 1985).

24 See Philip L. Williams, 'The Place of *Industry and Trade* in the Analysis of Alfred Marshall', in K. Tucker and C. Baden Fuller (eds), *Firms and Markets, Essays in Honour of Basil Yamey* (London: Croom Helm, 1986).

25 Alfred Marshall, *Industry and Trade* (London: Macmillan, 1920).

26 See Alex Hunter, 'The Measurement of Monopoly Power', in Alex Hunter (ed.), *Monopoly and Competition* (Harmondsworth: Penguin, 1969).

27 D.H. Macgregor, 'Rationalisation of Industry', *Economic Journal*, 37 (1927), 522.

28 F.W. Taussig, 'The McKinley Tariff Act', *Economic Journal*, 1 (1891), 326–50.

29 F.W. Taussig, 'The New United States Tariff', *Economic Journal*, 4 (1894), 573–94, especially p. 590.

30 Jeremiah W. Jenks, 'Trusts in the United States', *Economic Journal*, 2 (1892), 70–99, at p. 86.

31 These writings included a monograph: Richard T. Ely, *The Tariff and Trusts* (Chicago, 1888).

32 D.H. Macgregor, *Industrial Combination* (London: George Bell, 1906), p. 236.

33 Richard T. Ely, 'The Tariff and Trusts – Expenditures for Internal Improvements', in Albert Shaw (ed.), *The National Revenues* (Chicago, IL: A. C. McClurg, 1888), pp. 56–7.

34 See Herman Levy, *Monopolies, Cartels and Trusts in British Industry* (London: Macmillan, 1927), p. 200.

35 Patrick Fitzgerald, *Industrial Combination in England* (London: Pitman, 1927), p. 78.

36 Levy, *Monopolies, Cartels and Trusts*, pp. 182–4. See also Fitzgerald, *Industrial Combination*, pp. 26–35.

37 57th Congress of the United States, 1st Session, House of Representatives, Doc. No. 380, *Final Report of the Industrial Commission*, p. 615. See also Jenks, 'Trusts in the United States', pp. 74–6.

38 Gustav Cohn, 'On the Nationalisation of Railways', *Economic Journal*, 18 (1908), 524.

39 Henry W. Macrosty, *Trusts and the State* (London: Grant Richards, 1901), p. 154.
40 Francis W. Hirst, *Monopolies, Trusts and Kartells* (London: Methuen, 1905), p. 63.
41 Liefmann, *Schutzzoll und Kartelle* (1903), pp. 8–9; quoted in Levy, *Monopolies, Cartels and Trusts*, p. 174.
42 *Report of the Industrial Commission*, pp. 627–30.
43 Henry Sidgwick, *The Principles of Political Economy*, 1st edn (London: Macmillan, 1883), pp. 351–2.
44 George Gunton was the most famous exponent of this position; see his 'The Economic and Social Aspect of Trusts', *Political Science Quarterly*, 3 (1888), 403 (his emphasis). In his early years Gunton seems to have published in the more respectable journals.
45 Steven C. Salop, 'Strategic Entry Deterrence', *American Economic Review (Papers and Proceedings)*, 69 (1979), 335–8.
46 J.B. Clark, *The Control of Trusts* (New York: Macmillan, 1901), p. 14.
47 See, for example, Henry C. Adams, 'What is Publicity?', *North American Review*, 175 (1902), 895–904.
48 J.B. Clark (with J.M. Clark), *The Control of Trusts* (New York: Macmillan, 1912), pp. 110–17.
49 J.B. Clark, *Essentials of Economic Theory* (New York: Macmillan, 1907), p. 395.
50 Macgregor, *Industrial Combination*, p. 77.
51 See John Maurice Clark, 'J.M. Clark on J.B. Clark', in Henry W. Spiegel (ed.), *The Development of Economic Thought* (New York: Wiley, 1952), pp. 592–612.
52 See A.C. Pigou, 'Government Control in War and Peace', *Economic Journal*, 28 (1918), 363–73, and Macgregor, 'Rationalisation of Industry'.
53 See Ministry of Reconstruction, *Report of the Committee on Trusts*, 1919.
54 See Pigou, 'Government Control in War and Peace'.
55 Alfred Marshall, *Principles of Economics* (London: Macmillan for the Royal Economic Society, Variorum Edition, 1961), pp. 472–3.

6
Reviews by Edgeworth

Peter Newman

When Pigou came to review Edgeworth's *Papers Relating to Political Economy* his brief discussion of volume III, which consists entirely of reviews, contained the remark: 'I shall not, naturally, attempt to review reviews' (Pigou, 1925b, 182). That word 'naturally', thrown away in such masterly fashion, is a deep comfort to anyone who contemplates undertaking a complete analysis of Edgeworth's reviews, for such a project would require the reading of over 200 works in seven languages. Moreover, fairness to both the authors and Edgeworth would also require knowledge of the state of play in each topic at the time of each review. This essay has a more modest aim, being simply a general discussion that among other things tries to discover why so sharp an intellect should have spent so much time and energy on reviewing, an activity that most present-day economists would regard as at best of secondary importance.

Edgeworth was a prolific writer. No complete bibliography exists, but gathering together what is available and counting his multipart works separately (e.g. treating 1911a, b, 1912b and 1913b as four papers) produces a total of more than 500 books, essays, articles and reviews written over the half-century 1876–1926.[1] Other economists have written more, of course, but their output often includes works with the label 'popular', which by no stretch of the

Francis Ysidro Edgeworth, 1845–1926
(By courtesy of the Warden and Fellows of All Souls College, Oxford)

imagination could ever be pinned on Edgeworth. His production looks even more stupendous – one of his favourite words – when one realizes that less than a fifth of it had appeared before he edited the first issue of the *Economic Journal*, at the age of 46. What proportion consisted of reviews is a question more easily asked than answered, since (as so often with Edgeworth) surface appearances are deceptive; an attempt to answer it will be found in the appendix to this chapter.

There is an important sense, however, in which *any* count of the books and articles that Edgeworth reviewed, no matter how carefully done, will always be an underestimate of his true reviewing activity. The brilliantly original and constructive analysis of *Mathematical Psychics* had gone largely unappreciated and misunderstood by his contemporaries, even by its two great reviewers Jevons (1881) and Marshall (1881), and perhaps as a result Edgeworth confined most of his subsequent work in economics to the rigorous scrutiny of a host of past and current literature, both national and international, putting to good use 'all the polyglot graces of his unique style' (Robertson, 1916, 66; 1931, 219).[2]

This observation is not new. Many years ago George Stigler remarked that

> Edgeworth did not write exhaustively on general theoretical problems. His notable article, 'The Theory of Distribution,' [1904a] is thoroughly typical; in it he presents not so much a theory of distribution as a commentary on the views of a large number of contemporaries and predecessors. (1941, 109)

More recently, Hicks has justly pointed out that

> his later writings on economics . . . are not often constructive like [*Mathematical Psychics*]. They are mostly of the nature of reviews; even the longest are mainly review-articles. There was no other economist, of his period, who read so much of what was appearing, in many countries and in many languages . . . So Edgeworth's reviews, and review-articles, which are brought together in the three volumes of his *Papers*, are invaluable to the student of the economics of that period. One can read him on Marshall, on Walras, on Pareto, on Böhm-Bawerk, on Fisher, on Cassel; and since it is the same mind that is reflecting on each of them, he ties them together. (1984, 164)

Edgeworth himself painted a similar though typically metaphorical picture of his approach, at least as he employed it in one of his papers: 'I do not attempt here to cultivate the fields which have been indicated; but as I pass in the course of a rapid survey, I may sometimes root up a weed which has proved noxious, or drop a seed which may germinate' (1910, 83; quoted in part by Stigler, 1941, 108). Pleasingly rural though this image is, a more appropriate simile for the arch-reviewer Edgeworth would seem to be that of a classic jazz musician who takes another's song as an occasion for his own improvisation around and above and beyond the melody, shifting keys as he goes, until the dizzied and delighted audience neither recalls nor cares where it all began. 'In private talks . . . he dived where he chose and one could not always tell where he would come up again' (Bonar, 1926, 647).

Taken as a whole, Edgeworth's reviewing covered an immense range, not only of languages but also of content. His extraordinary competence in foreign languages enabled him to review works in Dutch, French, German, modern Greek, Italian and Spanish, as well as to quote freely from classical Greek and Latin. However, his known reviews before 1891, most of which were in *The Academy*, had a relatively limited range, being concentrated in economic analysis (Bastable, Böhm-Bawerk, Jevons, Marshall, Nicholson, Walras and Wicksteed) and economic method (Sidgwick and Thorold Rogers). He reviewed little in applied economics, the notable exceptions being Jevons's *Investigations in Currency and Finance*, Giffen's *Growth of Capital* and Booth's *Labour and Life of the People*.

Since he was 'halfheartedly' courting Beatrice Potter at the time (MacKenzie and MacKenzie, 1977, 134), Edgeworth's review of volume I of Booth's survey may have come about because of the three impressive chapters she contributed to the enterprise, these being 'the monographs which we have selected for especial commendation' (1889b, 440). Certainly, he was effusive in his praise for the 'picturesque description and piquant detail' she provided, judging her to be Booth's 'ablest coadjutor', and commending 'the brilliancy of . . . [her] . . . style', whose 'purple patches do not appear to us out of place in a work of scientific research' (ibid.). At much the same time, in his first Presidential Address to Section F of the British Association, Edgeworth had scathing words for an article by Sidney Webb, whose 'search for the "keystone" among the factors of distribution is nearly as hopeless as the speculation of the ancients about the real *up* or *down*' (1889d, 507). Miss Potter, who unlike Edgeworth never did care for 'the abstract economics of Ricardo and Marshall' (Webb, 1926, 442), first met Mr Webb a few months later, in February 1890. They married in June 1892 and lived busily ever after.

Edgeworth had a lifelong concern for the problems of women's work and wages, beginning with 1879, pp. 406–7, and 1881, pp. 78–9,[3] and resulting in a few articles, several reviews, and his only preface to someone else's book (1904b). Perhaps this concern also owed something of its persistence to a continuing interest in the work of 'Mrs. Sidney Webb', for as late as 1922 he gave prominent and favourable notice of her contributions to the subject in his second Presidential Address to Section F of the British Association, on the topic 'Equal Pay to Men and Women for Equal Work' (1922b).

From 1891 onwards Edgeworth spread his reviewing much further afield, helped no doubt by his relatively free hand as editor of the *Journal*.[4] Bowley observed that

> In the reviews written by himself and republished [in 1925a], his encyclopaedic knowledge is as evident as the acuteness of his critical powers; but even these reviews are selective, for he appears to have looked critically at every book that reached the *Journal's* office. A request for a review would be accompanied by some apposite remarks on particular points in the text. . . . an erroneous impression that his sole interest was in refinements and exceptions, in mathematical curiosa . . . is completely dispelled by reading his volume of reviews . . . it is to be hoped that a just view of his range has now been reached by all competent judges. (Bowley, 1934, 123)

The breadth of Edgeworth's interests is shown by the list below, which divides his 162 reviews for the *Journal* into ten broad categories. To sort them all into neat discrete compartments is of course impossible. Where, for example, does one put the review (1893a) of a work by a learned divine on the bearing of bimetallism on the Irish Land Question? (Answer: in 'Ireland'.) In particular, the splitting of four of the ten categories into components labelled 'theory' and 'empirical' is necessarily rather arbitrary, especially for those works principally concerned with policy. Nevertheless, rough as it is, the classification serves the useful purpose of indicating how Edgeworth spread his efforts over an extraordinarily wide range.

Economic theory, including mathematical economics 32
Economics relating to war 26
Money, including index numbers
   theory 15
   empirical 6
International trade
   theory 5
   empirical 10
Labour economics, including industrial relations
   theory 5
   empirical 10
Demography 9
History of thought 7
Public finance
   theory 4
   empirical 3
Ireland 4
Others 26

This collection is much too diverse for detailed review. One can point only to a few salient features, such as his sustained interest in several perennial questions of economic policy. Thus in the 1890s he reviewed books on bimetallism, and in the next decade works on the 'tariff question'. Such problems of current economic policy came to be a preoccupation for him in the decade that began in 1914, since the war and its aftermath raised a host of new issues. During this period he reviewed no less than 26 books and pamphlets relating to the war, variously published in English, French, German, Italian or Spanish; the reviews of all but six of them were reprinted in *Papers Relating to Political Economy* (1925a, vol. III). Indeed, the war affected Edgeworth deeply, sometimes in rather strange ways, as when at about the age of 70 he posed for his photograph while wearing a wholly unidentifiable khaki uniform, and sometimes in rather touching ways, as when in *On the Relations of Political Economy to War* (1915a, 28-9) 'the principle of utility [i.e. joint utility maximization] is offered as the regulative idea or norm appropriate to negotiations . . . [when] . . . a selection has to be made from the wide range of terms which either party would rather accept than go to war'.[5]

One category conspicuously missing from the list above is 'methodology'. Although – or perhaps because – he had earlier reviewed several books on economic method, which at that time was principally concerned with debating historical versus theoretical approaches to economics, Edgeworth lost no time in turning firmly away from it in the *Journal*. At the end of his very first review in June 1891 (a generally favourable discussion of J.N. Keynes's *Scope and Method*), he testily observed that 'we cannot conceal a certain impatience at the continual reopening of a question on which authorities appear to be substantially, if not in phrase, agreed' (1891b, 423). After this pronouncement he reviewed no more books on that subject and his editorial policy was always set steadily 'against tedious expositions of methodology and the like (which often, in his opinion, rendered German Journals unuseful)' (Keynes, 1926, 151).

That Edgeworth reviewed seven books on the history of thought should come as no surprise to anyone, but the four reviews on Ireland might have surprised Hicks, who – perhaps dismissing appendix VII of *Mathematical Psychics* (1881) as an Irish bull[6] – wrote that Edgeworth 'rarely speaks of Ireland in his works' (1984, 157). Perhaps the nine reviews on demographic subjects would also surprise those who, like most economists, know Edgeworth only from *Mathematical Psychics* and the *Papers*, and not his demographic-cum-statistical work in the *Journal of the Royal Statistical Society* (e.g. 1885, 1898a).

Sometimes he uses a review to ride a particular hobby-horse, such as his well-known belief expressed in his Inaugural Lecture at Oxford in 1891 that, since 'the path of applied economics is so slippery', one should 'combine an enthusiastic admiration of theory with the coldest hesitation in practice' (1925a, vol.I, 8; see also Hutchison, 1953, 107–8). At other times we are startled to find him referring to himself in the third person, like many modern professional athletes. Thus he says (1905, 70; 1925a, vol.III, 136), apropos Marshall's foreign trade curves, '[a]s it has been said by one who used this sort of curve, a movement along a supply-and-demand curve of international trade should be considered as attended with rearrangements of internal trade; as the movement of the hand of a clock corresponds to considerable unseen movements of the machinery'.

The 'one' here is of course Edgeworth himself, for everything placed after the comma is a word-for-word reprise of a celebrated passage in 'Theory of International Values – II' (1894b, 424–5; 1925a, 32). This strange way of proceeding probably had its origins in his genuine modesty, but the impression it leaves is quite the opposite. Edgeworth was neither so abstract nor so modest, however, that he could not on occasion command a lapidary wit. The following small selection shows him as a master of the well-timed literary left hook:

> It appears to us that Jevons here goes to the very edge of a certain pitfall, and that Mr. Wicksteed goes one step further. (1889a, 71)

> It is given to few to unite like Mr. Cunynghame the powers of popular exposition and scientific investigation. Apparently it is not given even to him to apply both powers at the same point. (1905, 63; 1925a, vol.III, 136)

> Irish butter, which in the earlier 'eighties could be described as principally used for adulterating margarine, now rivals the products of Denmark. (1918, 199; 1925a, vol.III, 245)

The list also shows that after 1891 Edgeworth retained his primary interest in reviewing economic theory. In the first decade of the *Journal* his notices accounted for about a third of the works in theory which were reviewed, most of the rest being tackled by Flux and Price.[7] Although the following 20 years were not very productive of books in general economic theory, still Edgeworth reviewed much of what did appear, including works by Pareto and Pigou. With the appearance of Cassel's *Theoretische Sozialökonomie* in 1919, however, both economic theory and Edgeworth's reviewing of it picked up steam. In the next five years he wrote long reviews not only of Cassel (1920) but also of Amoroso's *Economia Mathematica* (1922a), Bowley's *Mathematical Groundwork* (1924), J.M. Clark's *Overhead Costs* (1925c), Marshall's *Money, Credit and Commerce* (1923), and the second edition of Pigou's *Economics of Welfare* (1925b) – not a bad performance for someone who turned 75 in February 1920.

As Hicks implied in the passage above, Edgeworth passed under review almost all the major – and a good many of the minor – figures in the neoclassical pantheon. A striking exception was the great Wicksell. Although it was at Edgeworth's invitation that Wicksell published in 1907 his expository address on cumulative processes to the British Association (Gårdlund, 1958, 230), and

Edgeworth joined in the discussion of the paper, there appears to be no other evidence that he knew or appreciated Wicksell's work. There being limits to even Edgeworth's cosmopolitanism, this was probably due in part to the zariba of Swedish that surrounded most of Wicksell's publications. But that does not explain why he left an attractive work like *Über Wert, Kapital und Rente* to Flux for review, nor why he reviewed none of Wicksell's other great books in German, *Finanztheoretische Untersuchungen* (1896), *Geldzins und Güterpreise* (1898) and *Vorlesungen über National-ökonomie* (1913). A more plausible possibility is that Wicksell's strength was in precisely those areas of economic analysis – capital theory and monetary theory – in which Edgeworth was weak, so that the former's work had little intrinsic appeal for him.[8] But even that argument, persuasive as it is, fails to account for Edgeworth's neglect of Wicksell's original work in public finance. Perhaps, like the innovations in *Mathematical Psychics*, the contributions to be found in *Finanztheoretische Untersuchungen* were just too original.

Edgeworth often used reviews to call attention to questions of technical importance that were of interest to him at the time. Thus, as Stephen Stigler has pointed out, in his very early review of Jevons's *Investigations in Currency and Finance* (1884) he posed the question, 'one of the most delicate in statistics – namely, under what cirucmstances does a difference in figures correspond to a difference of fact' (1884, 38). Simultaneously with this comment, in his work on statistical theory: 'Edgeworth's plan . . . was to do at last what had been talked about and assumed possible for over a century, but had never been accomplished: adapt the statistical methods of the theory of errors to the quantification of uncertainty in the social, particularly economic, sciences' (S. Stigler, 1978, 295).

Again, in his review of Bickerdike (1906), Edgeworth pointed out 'an important principle in . . . mathematics', whose 'economic application . . . takes the following form: A *small* change of an economic variable quantity at the margin commonly causes a *very small* change in the corresponding surplus' (1908, 399–400, his italics). A footnote provided an exact definition of this 'principle', which was an inequality between certain finite differences of functional values evaluated in the neighbourhood of a maximum. The derivation of this inequality is not given, but it seems to depend upon the reasonable assumption that any point which yields a strict maximum of the function concerned is surrounded by a neighbourhood, at all points of which the function can be taken to be locally strictly concave; similarly for a minimum, and for functions involving several variables.[9]

Sometimes, Edgeworth should have flagged a technical difficulty in the work under review but did not. A rather embarrassing example of such failure occurred with Pigou's *Wealth and Welfare*, not only in the inability of Edgeworth's review (1913a) to spot the errors in the concept of rising marginal supply price, but also in the perpetuation of those errors in his article 'Contributions to the Theory of Railway Rates – IV' (1913b), which played variations on Pigou's themes. These gaffes did not go unnoticed. One can almost hear the aged Wicksell's chortles as he writes: 'Unfortunately, he [Pigou] seems to have got hold of the wrong end of the stick to some extent, and with him, *mirabile dictu*, Edgeworth' (1958, 214; from a review article on Bowley's *Mathematical Groundwork*, dated 1925).

Pigou had claimed that 'in industries of diminishing returns the supply price is less than the marginal supply price . . . . It follows that, other things being equal, . . . the marginal net product of investment tends . . . in industries of diminishing returns to fall short of . . . the marginal net product yielded in industries in general' (1912, 176–7). The basic flaw in this argument was caught very quickly in their reviews by both J.M. Clark (1913) and Allyn Young (1913). Clark's criticism is less well known: 'But there seems to be a *non sequitur* in the argument, so far as competitive businesses of diminishing returns are concerned, since the extra cost, which the author claims the competitive price ought to cover, consists of increases in rental values of lands already under cultivation, and hence is a mere transference of income and not an outlay of labor or capital by society as a whole' (1913, 624).

Young's comments generalize these increases in land rents to increases in all rents and quasi-rents, which 'do not represent an increased *using up* of resources in the work of production. They merely represent *transferences* of purchasing power' (1913, 683, his italics). While Pigou's response to these criticisms (1920) is of no concern here, Edgeworth's own rueful response may be found in the preface to the reprint (1925a, vol. II, 429) of his paper (1913b), and more especially in his review (1925b) of the second edition of Pigou's book, where he admitted that, in constructing the curve of marginal supply prices,

> it is an error to treat the rents paid as a cost in the sense with which we are here concerned; an error acutely pointed out both by Professor Alleyn [sic] Young and Professor Maurice Clark, and candidly acknowledged by Professor Pigou. . . . The truth might have been suggested by the classic formula, 'Rent does not enter into the cost of production,' as accepted by Marshall. . . . But we do not seek to extenuate an error into which we ourselves have fallen. We only hope that it is not unpardonable to have erred with and through Professor Pigou. (1925b, 39)[10]

Given that Edgeworth reviewed so many books, it was only to be expected that several of his reviewees must have felt sufficiently victimized to fight back, either privately or publicly. Although in the nature of things we could hardly hope to learn much about the private protests, in fact we do know a good deal about one of them. Moreover, it provides the entertaining spectacle of the two best theorists in England fighting over the empirical validity of the Giffen Paradox.[11]

The trouble began in March 1909 with Edgeworth's review of Russell Rea's *Free Trade in Being* (1908), a collection of occasional pieces by an intelligent ship-owning Member of Parliament. Rea had reprinted from the *Westminster Gazette* his recent correspondence with Pigou on the subject 'Is it possible to tax the foreigner?', and in the course of this he suggested that 'a rise in the price of wheat would increase rather than decrease the consumption in this country' (1908, 126). Pigou, in reply, said that 'This certainly *used* to be the case; but I doubt if it is appreciably the case now' (ibid., 131, his italics). Edgeworth's review also was 'disposed to question' Rea's conjecture, and even went so far as to assert that: 'Even the milder statement that the elasticity of the demand for wheat *may* be positive, though I know that it is countenanced by high authority, appears to me so contrary to *a priori* probability as to require very strong evidence' (1909, 105, his italics).

As Stigler remarked (1947, 153), 'There could be little doubt of the identity of the "high authority"' who was being so gratuitously challenged, and the carping Marshall soon rose to the bait. His letter of 21 April 1909 (Pigou, 1925a, 438) began with the words:

'I have just noticed your review of Rae [sic] in the Ec. J.. I don't want to argue', and then proceeded to do just that, vehemently reaffirming his earlier assertions of the empirical relevance of the Paradox. These had appeared both in the third edition of the *Principles* (1895, 208) and in a House of Commons *Memorandum* published only five months before (although written in 1903; see Marshall, 1926, 382–3). Giving Edgeworth no rest, Marshall returned to the fray the very next day with a second and much longer letter (Pigou, 1925a, 439–42), concerned chiefly with problems of wheat supply rather than demand.[12] But in its last paragraph he resumed his earlier defence of the reasonableness of the Paradox, this time using a theoretical example rather than casual empiricism.

> I believe that people in Holland travel by canal boat instead of railway sometimes on account of its cheapness. Suppose a man was in a hurry to make a journey of 150 kilos [km]. He had two florins for it, and no more. The fare by boat was one cent a kilo, by third class train two cents. So he decided to go 100 kilos by boat, and fifty by train: total cost two florins. On arriving at the boat he found the charge had been raised to $1\frac{1}{4}$ cents per kilo. 'Oh: then I will travel $133\frac{1}{3}$ kilos (or as near as may be) by boat, I can't afford more than $16\frac{2}{3}$ kilos by train.' Why not? Where is the paradox? (Pigou, 1925a, 441)

Let b be the distance in kilometres travelled by boat, r that by railway, and let p_b, p_r be the prices in cents per kilometre for the two modes of travel. Let h be the number of minutes needed to travel 1 km by boat, and k be the corresponding figure for rail travel; presumably, $h > k$. Then Marshall's phrase 'a man was in a hurry' can be taken to mean that he chooses b and r so as to minimize total time elapsed $bh + rk$, subject to both a budget and a distance constraint. This can be formulated as a linear programming problem:

Choose $b^* \geq 0$, $r^* \geq 0$ to min $bh + rk$

subject to

$$bp_b + rp_r \leq 200 \qquad (6.1)$$

and

$$b + r \geq 150 \qquad (6.2)$$

Measuring r on the abscissa and b on the ordinate, a diagrammatic treatment of the constraints (6.1) and (6.2) when $p_b = 1$

and $p_r = 2$ would show the feasible region to be the triangle whose vertices are (50, 100), (150, 0) and (200, 0). Since $h > k$, the straight line $bh + rk$ must reach this region first (i.e. minimize total time) at the vertex (50, 100), which is Marshall's suggested solution. When p_b changes to 5/4 the feasible region shrinks to the triangle with vertices ($16\frac{2}{3}$, $133\frac{1}{3}$), (150, 0), (160, 0), and the (unchanged) line $bh + rk$ meets this new region first at the vertex ($16\frac{2}{3}$, $133\frac{1}{3}$) which again is Marshall's suggested solution.

Thus Marshall's example formulated and solved a simple linear programming problem of minimizing time costs. This is quite interesting but irrelevant to the question of Giffen's Paradox, which involves maximization of utility. For why should maximization of the traveller's total utility subject to his budget constraint imply that he also minimize his time costs? Given the non-standardness of Marshall's formulation, it should come as no surprise that it yields a non-standard 'paradoxical' conclusion.

It is puzzling that Marshall should have thought this linear programming example at all relevant to Giffen's alleged tale of the English poor who live (or lived) mostly on bread. Perhaps, at the back of his mind, he thought to take a least-cost diet approach to the formulation of the poor's problem of getting enough to eat; or perhaps, as he pathetically remarked in a third letter to Edgeworth written on 27 April, 'on subtle points . . . my mind is now of little use' (Pigou, 1925a, 442). The content of Edgeworth's response to the first two letters from Marshall is not known, but the fact of such a response is attested by Marshall's third letter. This begins by thanking Edgeworth for his 'all too kind letter', and then goes on to announce his desire to withdraw from the debate he himself had started, pleading as usual his incapacity for controversy and urging as usual the need to see the 'One in the Many and the Many in the One' (ibid.).

Public protest against Edgeworth's reviews took several forms, one of which might be called the *protest direct*, as in the case of Henry Ludwell Moore. Edgeworth's review (1912a) was generally full of praise for the *Laws of Wages* but was sharply critical of Moore's chapter IV, which had (a) assumed that the 'industrial ability' of workers is normally distributed, (b) estimated, using data from France and Massachusetts, that wage rates are normally distributed and (c) inferred from (a) and (b) the further proposition that differences in wage rates are causally connected with differences in ability, so that 'a doctrine of pure economics is statistically verified' (Moore, 1911, 93; for a recent discussion see Christ, 1985, 42–4).

Edgeworth had a field day with this glaring *non sequitur*, gleefully pointing out that because human weights are distributed normally one might just as well infer that wages depend upon how heavy you are. Moore was understandably miffed at such merriment and submitted a stolid reply to the *Journal* in which he argued that Edgeworth 'fails to see the economic relevancy of the Galton–Pearson theorem' (1912, 317) on which Moore's statistical derivations were based, and so does not realize that there was indeed economic content to the inferences drawn in chapter IV.

Edgeworth's rejoinder was unrepentant. 'Let it be examined whether Professor Moore has shown, or even attempted to show, the existence of *correlation* in a technical sense between the compared phenomena' (1912c, 317, his italics). Indeed, it was precisely because Moore had (in the words of the original reviews) 'overlaid a simple matter with useless and cumbrous technicalities' (1912a, 70) that he had hidden even from himself the fact that 'So thin an argument could not have passed muster' (1912c, 318).[13]

The *protest indirect* was exemplified by the case of Professor Graziani. Edgeworth's review (1897) of Graziani's book on public finance first complimented the author on his scholarship and then showed that his analysis of tax shifting under monopoly was irretrievably incorrect. Graziani did not protest these criticisms directly to the *Journal*, but instead published the next year in Turin a brochure aimed entirely at Edgeworth's review. He continued to insist that a specific tax on a monopolized product need not raise its price, and took the occasion to criticize the mathematical methods which had been used to deny this proposition.

By way of response, the editor of the *Journal* then devoted an entire review article (1898b) to the brochure, giving a simple and patient restatement of his original analysis that made brilliant use of one of his most striking pedagogic 'parables'. He assumes first that the monopolist has no costs, and likens the resulting diagram of total cost and revenue curves to a prison cell with a low concave ceiling in which the prisoner tries to stand upright as far as possible (parable: tried to maximize profits). A specific tax is then introduced and added to the zero costs. The effect of this

'Inquisitorial ingenuity makes the floor of the cell [parable: the total cost curve] an inclined plane' (1898b, 235–6), and as a consequence the prisoner, still trying to stand upright, necessarily chooses a part of the floor to the *left* of his original position (parable: chooses a lower output and therefore a higher post-tax price).

Even this elegant fable failed to convince the stubborn Graziani, who in yet another book seized on an earlier admission by Edgeworth, of the existence of 'peculiar cases in which the second differential (as well as the first) vanishes at the point of maximum or becomes infinite' (1898b, 235, n.2), to reaffirm his original position. But, protested Edgeworth in his review of this third work, the earlier neglect of such cases was not 'arbitrary' but simply 'one of the postulates with respect to the form of a "function", employed in abstract reasoning, which are justified by a sort of common sense founded on wide experience' (1904c, 607).[14] As Edgeworth had earlier said of Graziani's warnings against the mathematical method: 'The inability to use it is not a qualification for appreciating its usefulness' (1898b, 239).

A third form of protest of Edgeworth's reviews was *protest by principal and agent*, illustrated by the case of Walras and von Bortkiewicz. Both the manner and the matter of their protest are worth examination, the former because it was so absurdly elaborate, the latter because it included serious issues concerning the role of the entrepreneur in general equilibrium theory – issues that even now are not generally understood.

The manner will be discussed first. The story begins in late 1887 when the 19 year old Ladislaus von Bortkiewicz, then a student at the University of St Petersburg, wrote to Lausanne to express his admiration for Walras's work in mathematical economics (Jaffé, 1965, 229–31). This began a correspondence which soon convinced the 52 year old Walras of the ability and loyalty of his young disciple. Then there appeared Edgeworth's review (1889c) of the second edition of the *Eléments*, in which among other things he criticized the Walrasian entrepreneur who makes neither profit nor loss, '*ni bénéfice, ni perte*'. Suspicious as always of the good intentions of the English, and sometimes with reason, Walras loathed this review and soon hit upon a good way to respond. Why not commission his student friend to write a second review of the *Eléments*, have him devote most of it to criticism of

Edgeworth's review, and then arrange for its publication in the *Revue d'Economie Politique*, where Walras had influence with one of its editors, Charles Gide?

No sooner said than done. Edgeworth's review appeared in early September 1889, Walras's letter of invitation to von Bortkiewicz was sent in mid-October, the immensely flattered young student responded with a draft to Walras in late November, Walras vetted it in December, the resulting 'review' was published in January, and in February an offprint went off to Edgeworth.[15] The note by Walras which accompanied this offprint was of truly breathtaking hypocrisy: 'Here is the reply to your criticisms. I congratulate myself on having followed, in this instance, my usual rule of conduct in waiting [!] in case a third person felt like undertaking the job. Done by me, it would have been suspect; and I genuinely believe that it would not have been done so well' (Jaffé, 1965, 390; my translation, as elsewhere in this section). Whether Edgeworth knew about all the stage management is not clear. In any event he replied to Bortkiewicz with a long well-reasoned article (1891a) in the *Revue* early the following year and this, as will be seen, put paid to the controversy.

The substance of the debate covered most of the points raised in Edgeworth's review of the *Eléments*. Apart from questions of the book's style, and the problem of the entrepreneur to be discussed below, these were (a) the theory of capitalization, (b) *tâtonnement*, and (c) the offering of *simpliste* theoretical answers to such difficult practical questions as the 'Anglo-Indian monetary problem'.[16] Items (a) and (c) have been touched upon already, while (b) is discussed in Newman (1990). Regarding (c), it is hard to imagine a better brief statement of the use and limitations of abstract economic theory than Edgeworth's comment: 'There is a discipline adapted to the schools, and which it is profitable to have studied, but which has no direct bearing upon action' (1889c, 435).

The present discussion will focus only on that part of the debate which concerned the modelling of the entrepreneur in general equilibrium theory. It begins with an apparent digression on two of the ways in which that problem has been handled in recent theory, the description following the perspicacious account in McKenzie (1987, 499–502).

One such way is to generalize Walras's original linear system of single output firms to a system based on linear activities with joint outputs. This was the route taken by Cassel, von Neumann, Koopmans and McKenzie himself. When prices and activities are at their equilibrium levels, no activity that is used makes a profit and no activity that makes a loss is used, these being two rules that together constitute von Neumann's law. In the modern activities model this law plays the logical role which, in the original Walrasian model, was occupied by the entrepreneurial rule *ni bénéfice, ni perte*. However, the essential emphasis in both these versions is placed on activities rather than firms, precisely because (a) they *are* linear models and (b) competitive markets are assumed to exist for *all* factors and products. In exactly the same way that, in elementary partial equilibrium price theory, the distribution of firms in a competitive industry with constant unit costs is indeterminate, so in these constant returns to scale models the identity and size of individual firms is of no interest, compared with the levels of individual activities.

Such formulations contrast with the role of the firm in the general equilibrium model found in Hicks (1939), where

> a firm is associated with each economic agent who is a consumer and who may be a worker and owner of resources, but who also may be an entrepreneur. As an entrepreneur he owns a possible production set based on his personal characteristics and perhaps some other non-marketed resources. Of course, most of these individual enterprises will be inactive. (McKenzie, 1987, 500)

Such a Hicksian entrepreneur should aim to maximize utility rather than profit, since the latter makes no sense as a primary goal unless all the resources which the entrepreneur supplies are marketable; but in that case we are back to systems of Walrasian type. Which of these two ways of modelling general equilibrium is appropriate depends of course on the aims of the underlying theory. McKenzie's persuasive view, held by him for many years and restated in 'General Equilibrium' (1987, 502), is that the activities model is appropriate to a perfectly competitive economy in which individual agents are of negligible importance and free entry is allowed.

In contrast, the Hicksian formulation has some appeal in that it appears to preserve the individual identity of firms. This individuality will be illusory, however, unless there is some degree of increasing returns to scale for each firm, or some amount of positive interaction between firms, sufficient in either case for the firm's equilibrium production levels to be large enough for it to be a non-negligible 'atom'. But then there supervene all the well-known difficulties of trying to prove existence of competitive equilibrium with non-convex production sets. So the Hicksian approach, in so far as it differs significantly from the Walrasian approach, is much more difficult than it looks.

But what, to paraphrase *Mathematical Psychics* (1881, 138), is all this to Edgeworth and Walras–Bortkiewicz? Simply that the role of the entrepreneur as envisaged by Walras–Bortkiewicz is basically that appropriate to the linear activities model, while the role as envisaged by Edgeworth is that appropriate to the Hicksian model. No wonder that the debate on this issue was so full of mutual misunderstanding, for the two sides were living in quite different theoretical worlds.

Such a claim needs justification. This is easy enough for Walras–Bortkiewicz, since after all the linear activities model descends directly from Walras. It is much less easy for Edgeworth. In note h to his brilliant Presidential Address (1889d) which formed the intellectual basis for his review (1889c), although published two weeks later, Edgeworth described the nature of his economic agents in almost precisely Hicksian terms, as those were given in the quotation above from McKenzie. The only – but important – difference was that Edgeworth allowed also for the possibility that, 'since his indulgences may vary with the nature of his employment', the utility function of each rth agent might well vary in form with each of his possible occupations s, so that 'it' (i.e. they) must be written ϕ_{rs} rather than in the simpler form ϕ_r.

This description of economic agents is essential to Edgeworth's development of some embryonic ideas of Cairnes and Sidgwick into a sharp and typically subtle contrast between industrial competition and commercial competition. In the model of general equilibrium envisaged by industrial competition, there is a finite collection of such agents who own all the resources and who, on the basis of expected prices for all traded commodities, must decide not only how much to produce and consume but also what occupation to follow, i.e. what products to produce. It is a crucial and explicit assumption of industrial competition that each agent can choose only *one* occupation. The reason for this restriction is not argued in detail, but it appears to depend upon an implicit appeal to the Smithian economies induced by division of labour. Although this presumably leads to (as we would now say) non-convex production sets, Edgeworth does not explicitly consider the analytical difficulties that that implies for general equilibrium theory.[17]

In industrial competition, therefore, the optimization problem of each agent is not the usual one: given his utility and production functions, choose the vector of demands and supplies that will maximize his utility. Instead, because both the production *and* the utility functions of each agent vary with occupation, it is the much more complicated problem: choose the right pair of utility and production *functions* (i.e. the right occupation), thence the right vectors of demand and supplies, to maximize 'net advantages' over all occupations. This is what Edgeworth meant when he referred, in the text of his address, to 'the complexities introduced by division of labour [where] it is seen to be no longer a straightforward problem in algebra or geometry, given the nature of all the parties, to find the terms to which they will come' (1889d, 498).

These individual optimization problems are thus problems in the calculus of variations rather than in differential calculus; and rather nasty ones at that, being akin to some problems in what we would now call optimal control theory.[18] Edgeworth, who in *New and Old Methods of Ethics* (1876) had 'already showed a confident and creative mastery of the calculus of variations' (S. Stigler, 1978, 290), was quite aware of that. 'The equation of net advantages imports that the advantage, ϕ_{rr}, of the occupation which the individual chooses is not less than ϕ_{rs}, the advantage of any other occupation open to him' (1889d, 504, note h). Moreover, 'in the calculus of variations there is all the difference in the world between problems where one has to find a maximum, and those where one has to find the greatest possible value' (1891a, 24).

Like everyone since, Edgeworth made no attempt to solve these individual problems of optimization nor, still less, the equilibrium model of industrial competition itself. Instead, 'I do not attempt here to discuss any matter fully, but only to illustrate the suitability of the subtle language of mathematics to economical discussion' (1889d, 504, note h).

After the subtleties of industrial competition, commercial competition was easy and non-controversial. In some ways analogous, on the side of human capital, to the Marshallian short run on the side of physical capital, it refers to the situation where each agent

r has already chosen an occupation s and, for some unexamined reason, is *committed* to that line of action. Hence he has just one utility function ϕ_r rather than several ϕ_{rs}, and his decision becomes an optimizing problem of the usual kind, choosing demands and supplies to maximize that function ϕ_r. 'Regarding commercial competition', said Edgeworth (1891a, 24) 'we are in accord with M. Walras.'

Edgeworth's distinction between industrial and commercial competition was first made in his Presidential Address (1889d), and was not explicitly used as a basis for his criticism of Walras's profit-and-loss-less entrepreneur in his review (1889c). However, Walras saw a copy of the Presidential Address (1889d) in late October and drew Bortkiewicz's attention to it, in time for the latter to incorporate his understanding of it into the final draft of his 'review' (1890). It is doubtful whether Walras himself even began to understand the mathematics of industrial competition, for in 1877 Amstein's use of a simple Lagrange multiplier technique to derive the least-cost choice of factors 'was . . . far beyond Walras's ken' (Jaffé, 1964, 97); and it was only after 1900 that he returned to study and understand that derivation.[19] Perhaps in part because of such difficulties, Edgeworth's Address provoked in Walras a more than usually choleric reaction to 'théorie anglaise'. A letter to Charles Gide contained the bitter lament that

> I had thought that the introduction of the mathematical method into political economy would have had for its first result the banishing of empty phrases and charlatanism and the reign of precision and conscience. But I see with sadness that there are also mathematical empty phrases and charlatanism; and Edgeworth is a past-master at them. (Jaffé, 1965, 370)

The 'review' by von Bortkiewicz sadly misunderstood industrial competition. Quoting the passage from the text of Edgeworth's Address (1889d) that has been cited above, beginning 'the complexities introduced by the division of labour . . . ', he says in mock sorrow: 'It is to be regretted that Mr Edgeworth has not made this idea more explicit' (1890, 82). But, replied Edgeworth, that was exactly what I did do in note h of the appendix to the Address (1889d), which was explicitly addressed to serious students of the subject (1891a, 25–26, n.2).

After reading Edgeworth's article, von Bortkiewicz wrote to Walras suggesting that perhaps he should withdraw from the controversy with 'this man of talent and of science', adding with commendable candour,

> I believe that one must concede to Edgeworth that there really is no complete analogy between industrial and commerical competition. . . . I ought to admit that I had not fully grasped what he meant by that phrase [division of labour], and the reproach that he addresses to me in note 2 on p. 25 appears to have merit; in truth, I did not take into account Note h on p. 504 of *Nature*. The reason was that I understood by "division of labour" something quite different from what Edgeworth meant. (Jaffé, 1965, 430)

Walras had earlier and rather rashly opened an Eastern Front against the two redoubtable Viennese bankers Auspitz and Lieben. Now, with some reluctance, he agreed with his young disciple that there should be a general cease-fire: 'I have had, exactly like you, the impression that direct polemics ought to be abandoned against both Edgeworth and Auspitz and Lieben' (Jaffé, 1965, 434).

Bortkiewicz was not the only one who misunderstood Edgeworth over division of labour, and this misunderstanding grew over the years as the latter said less and less about industrial competition and more and more about the 'oddity' of Walras's entrepreneur who made neither profit nor loss. In time, he became merely tiresome on the subject. So it is no surprise that historians of thought, taking him at his later words rather than his earlier symbols, have severely criticized his treatment of the Walrasian entrepreneur. George Stigler's dismissal is typical: 'Edgeworth's view of the entrepreneur has been shown to be definitely inferior to that of Walras for the purposes of economic analysis' (1941, 128). Not true of course, but Edgeworth had only himself to blame.

At the start of this essay the question was raised: Why did so able an economist as Edgeworth spend so much energy on reviewing so many books and articles? Although only Edgeworth himself could have answered that question satisfactorily, the following speculations may not come amiss.

Mathematical Psychics was a powerful bolt of theoretical lightning shot at the economics profession, but it seems to have been terrified rather than electrified by Edgeworth's brilliant display. Thus paralysed rather than stimulated, for many years economists felt unable or unwilling to follow the path he had blazed. Sanguine by nature, however, Edgeworth made the best of this non-response by choosing to devote most of his future constructive efforts to the theory of statistics. In economics, he seems to have been willing to settle under the umbrella of Marshall's *Principles* and cast himself in the role of chief running commentator, over many years, on the work of his distinguished contemporaries. His position as editor of the *Journal* fitted neatly into this scheme of things.

Sometimes, his comments were expressed in long formal set-pieces on such subjects as the theory of distribution, of international trade, of monopoly, of returns to scale, of taxation. At other times he chose the more informal route of review articles to make his points, while at still others mere reviews sufficed. There never was any sharp division in his mind between these various forms of expression; they simply merged one with another to form a seamless whole. The lasting impression left by this marathon commentary, of which the vast collection of reviews forms but a part, is of a mind possessed of acute analytical power, great intellectual curiosity and a phenomenal memory, allowed to ramble at will – his will – throughout the whole of economics.

In settling for this role of commentator after his high but unfulfilled hopes for *Mathematical Psychics* Edgeworth must have experienced disappointment, just as in settling for the life of a bachelor 'He did not have as much happiness as he might have had' (Keynes, 1926, 153). But just as 'in many ways a bachelor life suited his character', so the job of universal reviewer could not have been entirely uncongenial. As a boy in Ireland, Edgeworth 'would read Homer seated aloft in a heron's nest'. As a man, he would 'let a train pass at a junction when he was deep in a book' (Bonar, 1926, 647). The same source reports that once, high in the Swiss Alps, he could not be persuaded to raise his eyes from a novel by Bulwer Lytton in order to watch 'a brilliant display of lightning' in the Grindelwald far below. Anybody who could do *that* was a born reviewer.

APPENDIX: How many reviews did Edgeworth write?

Johnson lists 132 book reviews from the *Journal*, covering 144 titles, plus 17 more reviews in *The Academy*.[20] The addition of information from various other sources, such as Bowley's partial list (1928, 139) of Edgeworth's book reviews in the *Journal of the Royal Statistical Society*, and some unpublished discoveries by Stephen Stigler, amends *Johnson's* list to 173 reviews of 187 books. This is probably a serious undercount on several grounds. First, for those general periodicals to which we know he contributed – *The Academy, Journal of Education, Mind, Nature* – it is doubtful that the list of his known book reviews is complete. Secondly, although firm evidence is lacking it seems likely that he also reviewed for other publications of the same kind. So a bibliography for Edgeworth that would include all his reviews, as well as all his other writings, would require a careful trawl through the crowded seas of contemporary intellectual magazines (see for example Sullivan, 1984). Some of the difficulties confronting such an endeavour are the now brittle pages of several of those magazines, the tradition of anonymous reviewing in many, and the quite inadequate indexing of most.[21] Thirdly, *Johnson* does not include review articles in its category 'reviews' but instead assigns them to 'articles'. This raises the difficult question: When is a review article more a review than an article? Conservatively, only nine of Edgeworth's review articles are counted here as book reviews (1893b, 1898b, 1901, 1915b, c, 1916, 1917a, b, 1922a), and together these account for 19 more titles, bringing the total to 206.

These revisions imply that 140 of Edgeworth's reviews, comprising 162 books, appeared in the *Journal*. The reviews are not merely numerous in themselves but constituted a significant fraction of all its reviews. Jha (1963, 7) gave the number of books it reviewed between 1891 and 1915 as 1,084, and the above estimates imply that Edgeworth handled 112 (6.2 per cent) of them. Of course many reviewers came and went over this quarter-century, but only a relatively small group – Ashley, Bastable, Bickerdike, Bonar, Cannan, Dearle, Flux, Higgs, Nicholson, Pigou, Price, Sanger among them – were called upon frequently over many years.[22] Of these, it was only his younger colleague at Oxford, L. L. Price, who approached at all closely to Edgeworth's performance, with a record of 155 books reviewed in the *Journal* between 1891 and 1928.[23]

Many of Edgeworth's *Journal* book reviews were reprinted to form almost all of volume III of *Papers Relating to Political Economy* (1925a), whose table of contents apparently indicates that reviews of some 76 books were collected in this fashion. But that table is deceptive on several counts: (a) the item listed at p. 152 reviews not one but two books, while that at p. 194 (nicely called 'Economists at War') reviews four books in all; (b) the review articles of (1916 and 1917a, b) appear in the table as only three items, but together they cover 12 books; (c) chapters by Mrs Fawcett and by Marshall, from the book reviewed in 'After-War Problems' (1917b), are listed as if they were separate additional books; (d) one entry (the reprint of 1894a) reviews an article, not a book. Moreover, the order of appearance of the book reviews in the table frequently varies, without explanation, from their chronological order. The net result is a peculiar list which actually contains 68 separate reviews of 86 books, corresponding to 49 per cent of the actual reviews and 53 per cent of the titles.

It is not easy to fathom why Edgeworth selected only about half of his *Journal* reviews for inclusion in volume III. Its modest length – it is roughly half as long as each of the others – implies that it could probably have been expanded to accommodate more, if he had judged that desirable. Nor is it easy to discover his criteria for selecting which reviews to reproduce. The only hint about this offered in the Preface to the *Papers* (1925a, vol. I, viii) is his elimination of 'reviews, which are merely declaratory of a book's contents, and perhaps of the critic's summary opinion as to the worth of the book', i.e. reviews like most of those we read now. There must have been more to it than that.

So far, the count has been limited to Edgeworth's reviews of books. But in a move that was quite unusual for his time, and which probably only the editor of a major journal could have risked, he went beyond mere books into the reviewing of recent articles, both those in his own journal (e.g. 1907a, b, 1908), and those in other periodicals (e.g. 1894a, 1895). This development achieved a synthesis of sorts, a kind of prototype of today's ubiquitous 'literature survey', in the extraordinary two-part article (1915b, c) that simultaneously reviewed three books and three articles. This followed an earlier review elsewhere (1914) of one of the books, which he now judged the best of the three.[24]

NOTES

1 Although rather inaccurate and quite incomplete, still the most useful bibliography of Edgeworth is that assembled under Harry Johnson's supervision at Cambridge in 1953–4 (see S. Stigler, 1978, 318). A mimeographed version of this was circulated from Chicago under the auspices of George Stigler sometime around 1960, but the original remains unpublished; it is referred to in the appendix as *Johnson*.

2 Edgeworth's work in statistics was quite different in character. Beginning in 1883 and continuing for the rest of his life, he made many constructive and important contributions to the theory of statistical inference; see Stephen Stigler (1978; 1986, ch. 9; 1987).

3 Apparently using only the 1881 reprint in quoting this passage on women's wages, Keynes went rather astray in the rhetorical flourish which introduced it: 'but who in space and time but Edgeworth in the 'eighties, whose sly chuckles one can almost hear as one reads, would treat it thus' (1926, 146).

To be fair, Edgeworth had died only in mid-February and Keynes must have put himself under pressure to publish this obituary of his fellow-editor in the March issue of the *Journal*. The result was extraordinary, an affectionate and sparkling memoir that bore few traces of the speed with which, presumably, it was written.

4 In other respects this free hand may have hurt him, by enabling him often to avoid 'having to respond to editors' and referees' comments' (Creedy, 1986, 20).

5 '[S]o far-reaching and not confined to material objects are the principles of economic negotiation or exchange without competition' (1915a, 25) that it was quite natural for Edgeworth to apply the contract theory of *Mathematical Psychics* (which book he nowhere mentions) to problems of pre- and post-war negotiations. What was less reasonable was his persistence, throughout a wide variety of applications such as this one, in focusing attention only on that allocation in the core which yields 'the principle of utility'. His stubborn insistence on this narrowly utilitarian solution probably helped to mislead his readers, not only into the false belief that his contract theory depends on interpersonal measurability of utility, but also into underrating its naturalness as a framework for analysing most problems of bargaining.

The lyrical peroration to *On the Relations of Political Economy to War* (1915a, 35–6) found Edgeworth in the novel role of prophet:

> Personally, and not countenanced by the physicists, I dare to hope that access would be won to the stupendous store of energy which lies hid in the world of atoms. Innumerable particles rushing at rates of many thousand miles per second will be harnessed to the service of man – inexhaustible sources of energy, immeasurably surpassing Niagara and Victoria Falls. In unexpected ways the wonders prophesied in *Locksley Hall* will come to pass; 'And the kindly earth shall slumber lapped in universal law'.

Well, hardly.

6 In a passage that dates from 1802, but whose style is very like that of her nephew Ysidro Francis, the Introduction to Maria Edgeworth's *Essay on Irish Bulls* conjectures that '*a laughable confusion of ideas* constitutes a bull' (her italics). This designation certainly seems appropriate to the long (126–48) appendix VII to (1881), which is actually entitled 'On the Present Crisis in Ireland' but is almost entirely concerned with Edgeworth's pure theory of contract. Half-way through even he feels constrained to ask, rather sheepishly, 'But what is all this to *landlords* and *tenants*?' (138, his italics).

7 Witness Flux's well-known double-barrelled review (1894) of Wicksell's *Über Wert, Kapital und Rente* and Wicksteed's *Co-ordination* . . . , a review which cast a bright light on the latter work but a dim one on the former (cf. Stigler, 1941, 262, n.1).

8 A hint of this lack of a theory of capital may be found in the index to Stigler (1941), which has a chapter on each of ten major neoclassical theorists. Under the heading 'capital concept', p. 389 of this index refers to the contributions of nine of them, the lone exception being Edgeworth. His lack of understand-

ing further shows up in, for example the curt dismissal of Walras's theory of capitalization in his review of *Eléments* (1889c), a theory which although deeply flawed deserves much more careful examination than Edgeworth gave it. But in a sense Edgeworth was in good company, since after Jevons's pioneer efforts there was no substantial British tradition in capital theory until the 1930s. Apart from his work on index-numbers, which occupies most of the section III on 'Money' in volume I of the *Papers*, and his much more original work on probability theory applied to banking (e.g. 1888), which inexplicably was not reprinted in *Papers Relating to Political Economy* (1925a), Edgeworth made no major contributions to monetary theory.

9 Edgeworth himself does not mention this dependence on local concavity. That is scarcely surprising, however, since an explicit general theory of convex functions was only just coming into being with the work of Jensen (1906).

10 The scansion and internal rhyme of the last half of this sentence are surely deliberate. They recall irresistibly some lines about Elinor Glyn, a steamy novelist of the 1920s, which circulated (and maybe even originated) in Oxford academic circles at the time:

> Would you like to sin/With Glyn/Upon a tiger skin?
> Or perhaps to err/With her/Upon some other fur?

11 Stigler's classic article (1947; 1965) contains much fuller details of this episode than are given here, although he does not comment on Marshall's canal–railway example. A survey of current thought on the Giffen Paradox may be found in Walker (1987).

12 Regarding Marshall's letter of 21 April, Stigler observes that: 'We do not know Edgeworth's reply; in his rejoinder [the letter of 22 April] Marshall merely reaffirms what is not in dispute – that a positively sloping demand curve can exist' (1947, 153). But scrutiny of this 'rejoinder' reveals no indication that Marshall had received any reply from Edgeworth, since it appears simply as a continuation of the vigorous counterattack on Edgeworth's review that the first letter had begun. In those faxless days it would in any case have been 'contrary to *a priori* probability' for letters to have made the round trip Cambridge–Oxford–Cambridge in just one day; not even the efficient postman Trollope aspired to that.

13 It is odd that Edgeworth did not see fit to reprint either of these salutary contributions in his *Papers*, especially since Moore's basic error is sometimes seen even today, almost concealed by much more subtle disguises than those which deceived him.

14 In modern language such exceptional cases are *of measure zero* or *nowhere dense*, depending on whether measure or category is being used to capture the idea of 'negligibility'.

15 This episode may be traced through most of the letters appearing on pp. 363–435 of *Correspondence of Léon Walras and Related Papers* (Jaffé, 1965); it is a nice example of the speed of controversy in nineteenth-century academic journals. Of course nowadays, with our high speed communications, we often

manage to do in just three years what then, with their stodgy technology, used to take all of three months.

16 Unfortunately, in this review Edgeworth also fell into the error of presuming that the Walrasian model neither did nor could allow for Jevonian disutility of labour. This bee in his bonnet, continuing to buzz in several of his subsequent writings, not only justifiably annoyed Walras–Bortkiewicz but also fuzzed his subtle analysis of industrial competition.

When Edgeworth came to reprint (1889d) he made a handsome apology for this misunderstanding, and formally withdrew any passage in which his bee had buzzed (1925a, vol. II, 310); but that was rather late in the day, especially for the long-gone Walras.

17 Although Roy's brilliantly stimulating work on self-selection (1951) is not concerned with formal general equilibrium theory, in several respects it has much in common with Edgeworth's industrial competition; for a discussion of modern econometric developments of Roy's theory, see Heckman (1987).

18 Edgeworth referred the readers of 'La théorie mathématique . . . ' (1891a) to the 'beautiful investigations' of Todhunter (1871) for instruction on the appropriate part of the calculus of variations. This remarkable book was in part an early attempt to investigate what are now known as 'chattering controls' in the theory of optimal control; for an interesting discussion, see L.C. Young (1969).

19 Jaffé (1964, 96) has suggested that Amstein's never-published letter of 1877 was 'probably the first instance of the use of the Lagrange method in economics'. But Edgeworth himself had earlier used Lagrange multipliers quite freely in *New and Old Methods of Ethics* (1876), not only in the ordinary differential calculus but also in the calculus of variations. Indeed, his use of that method in the variational context occurred earlier in the book (p. 38) than his first use of it in the usual finite-dimensional context (p. 43).

20 Actually *Johnson* lists just 142 titles, but that is because it omits two books, one by Guyot which Edgeworth reviewed together with a book by de Foville (1925a, 152–7), and another by George Russell ('A.E.') which he reviewed together with a book by Smith-Gordon (1925a, 243–8).

21 Given the importance of club life in late Victorian London, clues as to which magazines Edgeworth wrote for might well be provided by which of their editors were members of one or both of his London clubs, the Athenaeum and the Savile, the latter founded in 1868 by Auberon Herbert. Thus James Sutherland Cotton, editor of *The Academy* from January 1881 to November 1896, joined the Savile in the same year (1871) as Edgeworth, and both apparently remained active members 52 years later (Savile, 1923, 109–10). For each of the four years (1878–9 to 1881–2) in which Edgeworth served as Secretary or Committee Member of the Savile, the club records his name as Ysidro Francis Edgeworth (ibid., 75–7), thus confirming that he changed the order of his baptismal names relatively late in life (see Newman, 1987, 85).

22 In the light of Edgeworth's interest in women's work and wages, it is worth observing that more women reviewed books for the early issues of the *Journal*

than might have been expected. Thus, in the period 1901–10 there were 154 reviewers, of whom 18 were women. Several of these, such as Helen Bosanquet (12 reviews in the decade), Lilian (Tomn) Knowles (11) and Hélène Reinherz (17), appeared quite often in the review pages. In 1987 there were 91 reviewers for the *Journal*, of whom three were women.

23 Price started very strongly out of the gate, reviewing 50 books for the *Journal* in its first five years. But his pace slowed to a trot thereafter, possibly because his increasing disenchantment with formal economic theory and his increasingly protectionist leanings (on which see Petridis, 1987) led to intellectual disagreement with the free-trading theorist Edgeworth. After 1928 his reviewing for the *Journal* ceased altogether. Edgeworth and Price apparently remained on good personal terms throughout, for 30 years taking country walks together every week during the Oxford term. Prince's two interesting memoirs (1926, 1949–50) portray Edgeworth as an affectionate if at times exasperating colleague and friend, given to various enthusiasms such as the early cinema. It is fascinating to trace the evolution of Price's prose style, from quite straightforward narratives (1891a, b) to the convoluted sentences of his memoirs. These, to adapt a remark of Stephen Stigler (1978, 294), rival the later manner of Henry James in all but literary merit.

24 This writing of two reviews of the same edition of the same work was nothing new for Edgeworth. He did it also for the first edition of Marshall's *Principles* (1890a, b), which was of course a much more important book.

REFERENCES

Works by F.Y. Edgeworth

An asterisk after the year means that the work in question is reprinted in *Papers Relating to Political Economy* (1925a), in whole or in part, and possibly under another title. The location of this reprint in (1925a) is indicated after each work by the notation [volume no, page no.]

(1876)   *New and Old Methods of Ethics* (Oxford: James Parker).
(1879)   'The Hedonical Calculus', *Mind*, 4, 394–404.
(1881)   *Mathematical Psychics* (London: Kegan Paul), 150 pp.
(1884)   Review of 'W.S. Jevons: *Investigations in Currency and Finance* (ed. H.S. Foxwell)', *The Academy*, No. 627 (19 July), 38–9.
(1885)   'On Methods of Ascertaining Variations in the Rate of Births, Deaths and Marriages', *Journal of the Royal Statistical Society*, 48, 628–9.
(1888)   'The Mathematical Theory of Banking', *Journal of the Royal Statistical Society*, 51, 113–27.

(1889a)	Review of 'P.H. Wicksteed: *The Alphabet of Economic Science*', *The Academy*, No. 874 (2 February), 71.
(1889b)	Review of 'Charles Booth (ed.): *Life and Labour of the People*, Vol. 1', *The Academy*, No. 895 (29 June), 439–40.
(1889c)	Review of 'Léon Walras: *Eléments d'Economie Politique pure* ... deux-ième édition', *Nature*, 40 (5 September), 434–46. [Not in (1925a) as such, but relevant parts may be found in II, 310–12.]
(1889d)*	'Points at which Mathematical Reasoning is Applicable to Political Economy', being the Opening Address to Section F of the British Association, *Nature*, 40 (19 September), 496–508 [II, 273–310].
(1890a)	Review of 'Alfred Marshall: *Principles of Economics*', *Nature*, 42 (14 August), 362–4.
(1890b)	Review of 'Alfred Marshall: *Principles of Economics*', *The Academy*, No. 956 (30 August), 165–6.
(1891a)	'La théorie mathématique de l'offre et de la demande et la côut de production', *Revue d'Économie Politique*, 5, 10–28.
(1891b)*	Review of 'J.N. Keynes: *The Scope and Method of Political Economy*', *Economic Journal*, 1, 420–3 [III, 3–7].
(1893a)	Review of the 'Most Rev. Dr. Walsh: *Bimetallism and Monometallism: what they are and how they bear upon the Irish Land Question*', *Economic Journal*, 3, 286.
(1893b)	Review of 'James Bonar: *Philosophy and Political Economy in some of their Historical Relations*', *Mind, New Series*, II, 520–5.
(1894a)*	'Professor Böhm-Bawerk on the Ultimate Standard of Value', *Economic Journal*, 4, 518–21, 724 [III, 59–64].
(1894b)*	'Theory of International Values – II,' *Economic Journal*, 4, 424–43 [II, 31–47].
(1895)*	'Pierson on Scarcity of Gold,' *Economic Journal*, 5, 109–14 [II, 351–5].
(1897)*	Review of 'A. Graziani: *Istituzioni di Scienza delle Finanze*', *Economic Journal*, 7, 403–8 [III, 80–5].
(1898a)	'Miscellaneous Applications of the Calculus of Probabilities – II', *Journal of the Royal Statistical Society*, 51, 119–31.
(1898b)	'Professor Graziani on the Mathematical Theory of Monopoly', *Economic Journal*, 8, 234–9 [III, 89–95].
(1901)*	'Mr Walsh on the Measurement of General Exchange Value', *Economic Journal*, 11, 404–16 [I, 369–83].
(1904a)*	'The Theory of Distribution', *Quarterly Journal of Economics*, 18, 159–219 [I, 13–60].
(1904b)	Preface to J. Ramsay McDonald (ed.): *Women in the Printing Trades* (London: P.S. King).
(1904c)*	Review of 'A. Graziani: *Istituzioni di Economia Politica*', *Economic Journal*, 14, 605–7 [III, 130–2].
(1905)*	Review of 'H. Cunynghame: *A Geometrical Political Economy*', *Economic Journal*, 15, 62–71 [III, 136–44].

(1907a)* 'Appreciations of Mathematical Theories – I', *Economic Journal*, 17, 221–31 [II, 320–31].
(1907b)* 'Appreciations of Mathematical Theories – II', *Economic Journal*, 17, 524–31 [II, 331–9].
(1908)* 'Appreciations of Mathematical Theories – III', *Economic Journal*, 18, 392–403, 541–56 [II, 340–66].
(1909*) Review of 'R. Rea: *Free Trade in Being*', *Economic Journal*, 19, 102–6 [III, 164–8].
(1910)* 'On the Use of the Differential Calculus in Economics to Determine Conditions of Maximum Advantage', *Scientia*, 7, 80–103 [II, 367–86].
(1911a)* 'Contributions to the Theory of Railway Rates', *Economic Journal*, 21, 346–70 [I, 61–79].
(1911b)* 'Contributions to the Theory of Railway Rates – II', *Economic Journal*, 21, 551–71 [I, 79–99].
(1912a) Review of 'H.L. Moore: *Laws of Wages*', *Economic Journal*, 22, 66–71.
(1912b)* 'Contributions to the Theory of Railway Rates – III', *Economic Journal*, 22, 198–218 [I, 172–91].
(1912c) 'Professor Moore's "Laws of Wages"', *Economic Journal*, 22, 317–23.
(1913a)* Review of 'A.C. Pigou: *Wealth and Welfare*', *Economic Journal*, 23, 62–70 [III, 181–9].
(1913b)* 'Contributions to the Theory of Railway Rates – IV', *Economic Journal*, 23, 206–26 [II, 429–49].
(1914) Review of 'W.E. Zawadski: *Les mathématiques appliquées à l'Economie Politique*', *Journal of the Royal Statistical Society*, 77, 754–7.
(1915a) *On the Relations of Political Economy to War* (Oxford: Oxford University Press), 36 pp.
(1915b)* 'Recent Contributions to Mathematical Economics – I', *Economic Journal*, 25, 36–63 [II, 450–77].
(1915c)* 'Recent Contributions to Mathematical Economics – II', *Economic Journal*, 25, 189–203 [II, 478–91].
(1916)* 'British Incomes and Property' (a review article of J.C. Stamp: *The Application of Official Statistics to Economic Problems*), *Economic Journal*, 26, 328–36 [III, 204–12].
(1917a)* 'Some German Economic Writings about the War', *Economic Journal*, 27, 238–50 [III, 215–28].
(1917b)* 'After-War Problems', *Economic Journal*, 27, 402–10 [III, 228–37].
(1918)* Review of 'L. Smith-Gordon: *Rural Reconstruction in Ireland*' and 'A.E. (George Russell): *The National Being*', *Economic Journal*, 27, 198–202 [III, 243–8].
(1920)* Review of 'G. Cassel: *Theoretische Sozialökonomie*', *Economic Journal*, 30, 530–6 [III, 266–72].
(1922a) 'The Mathematical Economics of Professor Amoroso' (a review article of L. Amoroso: *Lezioni di Economia Mathematica*), *Economic Journal*, 32, 400–7.

(1922b) 'Equal Pay to Men and Women for Equal Work', *Economic Journal*, 32, 431–57.
(1923) Review of 'A. Marshall: *Money, Credit and Commerce*', *Economic Journal*, 33, 198–204.
(1924) Review of 'A.L. Bowley: *The Mathematical Groundwork of Economics*', *Economic Journal*, 34, 430–4.
(1925a) *Papers Relating to Political Economy* (three volumes, London: Macmillan on behalf of the Royal Economic Society).
(1925b) 'The Revised Doctrine of Marginal Social Product' (a review of the second edition of A.C. Pigou: *The Economics of Welfare*), *Economic Journal*, 35, 30–9.
(1925c) Review of 'J.M. Clark; *Studies in the Economics of Overhead Costs*', *Economic Journal*, 35, 245–51.

Other Works

Bickerdike, C.F. (1906): 'The Theory of Incipient Taxes', *Economic Journal*, 16, 529–35.
Bonar, J.B. (1926): 'Memories of F.Y. Edgeworth', *Economic Journal*, 36, 647–53.
Bortkiewicz, L. von (Bortkévitch) (1890): Review of 'Léon Walras: *Eléments d-Economie Politique pure . . . deuxiéme édition*', *Revue d'Économie Politique*, 4, 80–6.
Bowley, A.L. (1928): *F.Y. Edgeworth's Contributions to Mathematical Statistics* (London: Royal Statistical Society).
Bowley, A.L. (1934): 'Francis Ysidro Edgeworth', *Econometrica*, 2, 113–24.
Christ, C.F. (1985): 'Early Progress in Estimating Quantitative Economic Relationships in America', *American Economic Review*, 75–6 (December), 39–52.
Clark, J.M. (1913): Review of 'A.C. Pigou: *Wealth and Welfare*', *American Economic Review*, 3, 623–5.
Creedy, J. (1986): *Edgeworth and the Development of Neoclassical Economics* (Oxford: Basil Blackwell).
Flux, A.W. (1894): Review of 'K. Wicksell: *Über Wert, Kapital und Rente nach der neuern nationalökonomischen Theorien*' and of 'P.H. Wicksteed: *An Essay on the Co-ordination of the Laws of Distribution*', *Economic Journal*, 4, 305–13.
Gårdlund, T. (1958): *The Life of Knut Wicksell* (Stockholm: Almqvist and Wicksell).
Heckman, J.J. (1987): 'Selection Bias and Self-selection', in J. Eatwell, M. Milgate and P. Newman (eds), *The New Palgrave: A Dictionary of Economics* (London: Macmillan), vol. 4, pp. 287–97.
Hicks, J.R. (1939): *Value and Capital* (Oxford: Clarendon Press).
Hicks, J.R. (1984): 'Francis Ysidro Edgeworth', in A.E. Murphy (ed.), *Economists and the Irish Economy: from the Eighteenth Century to the Present Day*

(Dublin: Irish Academic Press in association with Hermathena, Trinity College, Dublin), pp. 157–74.
Hutchison, T.W. (1953): *A Review of Economic Doctrines 1870–1929* (Oxford: Clarendon Press).
Jaffé, W. (1964): 'New Light on an Old Quarrel', *Cahiers Vilfredo Pareto*, 3, 61–102.
Jaffé, W. (ed.) (1965): *Correspondence of Léon Walras and Related Papers* (Amsterdam: North-Holland), vol. II.
Jensen, J.L.W.V. (1906): 'Sur les fonctions convexes et les inégalités entre les valeurs moyennes', *Acta Mathematica*, 30, 175–93.
Jevons, W.S. (1881): Review of *Mathematical Psychics*', *Mind*, VI, 581–3.
Jha, N. (1963): *The Age of Marshall; Aspects of British Economic Thought 1890–1915* (Patna, India: Novelty). A second edition of this work was published in London in 1973 by Frank Cass.
Keynes, J.M. (1926): 'Obituary: Francis Ysidro Edgeworth, 1845–1926', *Economic Journal*, 36, 140–53.
MacKenzie, N. & J. (1977): *The Fabians* (New York: Simon and Schuster).
Marshall, A (1881): Review of '*Mathematical Psychics*', *The Academy*, No. 476 (18 June), 457.
Marshall, A. (1895): *Principles of Economics*, 3rd edn (London: Macmillan).
Marshall, A. (1926): *Official Papers* (London: Macmillan).
McKenzie, L.W. (1987): 'General Equilibrium', in J. Eatwell, M. Milgate and P. Newman (eds), *The New Palgrave: A Dictionary of Economics* (London: Macmillan), vol. 2, pp. 498–512.
Moore, H.L. (1911): *The Laws of Wages* (New York: Macmillan).
Moore, H.L. (1912): 'A Reply to Professor Edgeworth's Review of Professor H.L. Moore's "Laws of Wages"', *Economic Journal*, 22, 314–17.
Newman, P. (1987): 'Edgeworth, Francis Ysidro', in J. Eatwell, M. Milgate and P. Newman (eds), *The New Palgrave: A Dictionary of Economics* (London: Macmillan), vol. 2, pp. 84–98.
Newman, P. (1990): 'The Great Barter Controversy', to appear in J.K. Whitaker (ed.), *Centenary Essays on Alfred Marshall* (Cambridge: Cambridge University Press).
Petridis, A. (1987): 'Price, Langford Lovell Frederick Rice', in J. Eatwell, M. Milgate and P. Newman (eds), *The New Palgrave: A Dictionary of Economics* (London: Macmillan), vol. 3, pp. 950–1.
Pigou, A.C. (1912): *Wealth and Welfare* (London: Macmillan).
Pigou, A.C. (1920): *The Economics of Welfare* (London: Macmillan).
Pigou, A.C. (ed.) (1925a): *Memorials of Alfred Marshall* (London: Macmillan).
Pigou, A.C. (1925b): 'Professor Edgeworth's Collected Papers', *Economic Journal*, 35, 177–85.
Price, L.L. (1891a): *A Short History of Political Economy in England* (London: Methuen).
Price, L.L. (1891b): '*West Barbary*', or *Notes on the System of Work and Wages in the Cornish Tin Mines* (London: Henry Frowde).

Price, L.L. (1926): 'Obituary: Francis Ysidro Edgeworth', *Journal of the Royal Statistical Society*, 89, 371–6.
Price, L.L. (1949–50): *Memories and Notes on British Economists 1881–1947*, 106 pp, deposited in Brotherton Library, University of Leeds. (The date 1949–50 is assigned here to this undated manuscript, which on p. 1 refers to the death of J.N. Keynes, occurring in 1949. Price himself died in 1950.)
Rea, R. (1908): *Free Trade in Being* (London: Macmillan).
Robertson, D.H. (1916): Review of 'Edgeworth: *On the Relations of Political Economy to War*', *Economic Journal*, 26, 66–7.
Robertson, D. H. (1931): *Economic Fragments* (London: P.S. King).
Roy, A.D. (1951): 'Some Thoughts on the Distribution of Earnings', *Oxford Economic Papers, N.S.*, 3, 135–46.
Savile Club (1923): *The Savile Club 1868 to 1923* (London: privately printed for the Committee of the Club).
Stigler, G.J. (1941): *Production and Distribution Theories* (New York: Macmillan).
Stigler, G.J. (1947): 'Notes on the History of the Giffen Paradox', *Journal of Political Economy*, 55, 152–6.
Stigler, G. J. (1965): *Essays in the History of Economics* (Chicago, IL: University of Chicago Press).
Stigler, S.M. (1978): 'Francis Ysidro Edgeworth, Statistician', *Journal of the Royal Statistical Society, Series A (General)*, 141, 287–322.
Stigler, S.M. (1986): *The History of Statistics* (Cambridge, MA: Harvard University Press).
Stigler, S.M. (1987): 'Edgeworth as a Statistician', in J. Eatwell, M. Milgate and P. Newman (eds), *The New Palgrave: A Dictionary of Economics* (London: Macmillan), vol. 2, pp. 98–9.
Sullivan, A. (ed.) (1984): *British Literary Magazines; The Victorian and Edwardian Age, 1837–1913* (Westport, CT: Greenwood Press).
Todhunter, I. (1871): *Researches in the Calculus of Variations* (London: Macmillan).
Walker, D.A. (1987): 'Giffen's Paradox', in J. Eatwell, M. Milgate and P. Newman (eds), *The New Palgrave: A Dictionary of Economics* (London: Macmillan), vol. 2, pp. 523–4.
Webb, B. (1926): *My Apprenticeship* (London: Longmans, Green).
Wicksell, K. (1958): *Selected Papers on Economic Theory* (ed. by E. Lindahl) (London: Allen and Unwin).
Young, A.A. (1913): 'Pigou's Wealth and Welfare', *Quarterly Journal of Economics*, 27, 672–86.
Young, L.C. (1969): *Lectures on the Calculus of Variations and Optimal Control* (Philadelphia, PA: W.B. Saunders).

John Maynard Keynes, 1883–1945
(By courtesy of Dr Milo Keynes)

7
Keynes as Editor

Donald E. Moggridge

On 17 October 1911 at a special meeting with Alfred Marshall in the chair, on the motion of Edwin Cannan, seconded by F.Y. Edgeworth, the Council of the Royal Economic Society appointed the 28 year old Cambridge economist Maynard Keynes editor of the *Economic Journal* at a salary of £60 a year[1] in succession to Edgeworth. The only other person considered was Professor W.J. Ashley of Birmingham, who, according to the minutes of the meeting, was 'quite unable to find the time to undertake the work'. Keynes's duties were to begin at the year end. (He actually started the week before Christmas, his first editorial act being the rejection of a submission by Archdeacon Cunningham.)[2] He remained editor until the April 1945 issue had gone to press, when he was succeeded by Roy Harrod and Austin Robinson as Joint Editors. At the same time Austin Robinson succeeded him as Secretary of the Society, a job Keynes had taken on in 1913. Although, probably because of his youth, he had an advisory editorial board (1912–19),[3] and after 1919 had joint or assistant editors – Edgeworth (1919–26),[4] D.H. Macgregor (1926–34) and Austin Robinson (1934–45) – for 33 years and one issue Keynes played the central role in the development of the *Journal*'s character and reputation. Throughout the period, he was responsible for the 'front' part of the *Journal* – for the articles, notes and memoranda, as well as the make-up of each issue and seeing it through the press. His editorial colleagues after 1919 were responsible for reviews, official publications and the noting and listing of new books. While the editors, of course, consulted over individual articles and shared the 'Current Topics' section, the main editorial responsibility was Keynes's.

My discussion will concentrate on Keynes's career as editor, paying particular attention to the editorial practices he followed and the decisions he made. The evidence underlying the discussion will be the published issues of the *Journal*, the surviving editorial papers in the Keynes Papers in King's College, Cambridge, and the Minute Books of the Society.

When Keynes took over the *Journal* it was running to about 650 pages per annum and publishing about 20 articles a year. By the mid-1920s, it was averaging about 675 pages and the number of articles had grown to 25. In March 1925 the Council agreed that from 1926 the *Journal* would add an annual *Economic History* supplement including ten articles in 125 pages. At the same time it agreed that the size of the *Journal* should not exceed an average of 168 pages per issue. To keep to this limit it agreed that 'the editors be requested to exercise at their discretion some discrimination against the insertion of articles from foreign contributors except in the case of special interest or importance'.[5] A decade later the number of articles in the *Journal* was up by another two to three, and each issue was normally 75 pages longer. (*Economic History*, which contained reviews from 1934, still ran about ten articles an issue but with reviews had risen to 175 pages.)[6] The paper restrictions of the Second World War, which reduced the number of issues each year from four to three and ended the life of the *Economic History* supplement,[7] make comparisons for the 1940s unhelpful. Thus, in the course of his career as editor, Keynes published 143 issues of the *Journal* and its supplements which contained something of the order of 1,100 articles, plus several thousand more notes, memoranda, review articles and reviews.

Unlike some modern editors, Keynes himself had few inhibitions about placing his own articles in his own journal. While he was editor, his only publications in other English language professional journals, other than seven replies to critics of which only two were over a page in length, number two: his November 1914 invited contribution to the *Quarterly Journal of Economics*, 'The City of London and the Bank of England, August 1914' (*JMK*, XI, 278–98), and his 1936 Jevons centenary allocation to the Royal

Statistical Society which appeared in that Society's *Journal* (*JMK*, X, 109–50). He was not even inhibited from using his position as editor to reply to articles by others in the same issue in which they appeared, going so far as to place his own comments immediately after the piece that had irked him.[8] However, in later years he became slightly more restrained in this, informing one contributor with whom he was in dispute over some points prior to publication that: 'It is a mistake for an editor to quarrel with contributors.'[9] As far as I can tell from the records, he submitted none of his own contributions to an external referee. Nor could he have done so in some cases, for the articles themselves were only finished at the last possible date. His 'War and the Financial System, August 1914', which appeared in the September 1914 issue, was not finished until 3 September.[10] The *Journal* normally appeared on the 15th of the month. Printers were accommodating in those days: they still were in the 1930s, if we are to judge from the editorial correspondence and Keynes' own submission of a book note for the September 1939 issue of the *Journal* on 28 August (*JMK*, XXIX, 273).

As far as contributors other than himself were concerned, Keynes was generally sparing in his use of external referees. He did, of course, use them, particularly in cases where he had doubts about the submission. On several occasions, however, he sent the submission to the referee with a copy of his own draft letter of rejection[11] or at the least a strong hint of his own views. Thus he wrote to J.R.N. Stone on 4 April 1944 on a national accounting submission:

> May I have your comment on the enclosed? It seems to me to be a very difficult and complicated discussion of a controversy which ought not to exist. The only reason for printing anything is that it has a distinguished history of balminess. But this particular article does not seem to bring all that out with the necessary clarity.
>
> Bowley's treatment of the subject is obviously balmy, as I think he himself now admits. Colin Clark's not less, though whether he admits it I am not so sure. If I really said in 1940 what is attributed to me, I also was balmy.

On another occasion, this time with a Kalecki submission, 'A Theorem on Technical Progress', he left the first referee, Joan Robinson, in no doubt about his views. When she did not fall into line, he sent the submission to Nicholas Kaldor, again with an indication of his views. Kaldor agreed with Keynes and the submission eventually appeared in *The Review of Economic Studies* for May 1941. His referees also let him down in the case of Frank Ramsay over Roy Harrod's invention of the marginal revenue curve (Harrod, 1951, 159–60),[12] but they rarely seem to have convinced Keynes that he had made a mistake. For the *Economic History* supplement there is more correspondence with referees than in the general *Journal* files, although here Keynes depended more often than not on a single referee, J.H. Clapham.

From the time of publication of *A Treatise on Money* (1930) until the outbreak of war in 1939, Keynes as editor faced particular difficulties with submissions dealing with his own published work. He was caught in three ways. First, he did not wish to be unfair to his critics – and for that matter to the profession. Second, he also did not wish to turn the *Journal* into 'a propagandist organ' (*JMK*, XIV, 88). Finally, he did not wish to distort the coverage of the *Journal* by concentrating overly on one area of economics (ibid., 187; XXIX, 248).[13] In this situation he consulted extensively, initially with Dennis Robertson and subsequently with A.C. Pigou.[14]

Ultimately, however, Keynes made the overwhelming majority of editorial decisions himself. He did not regard the job as onerous: indeed, by the 1930s it was one of those activities classed as 'non-work' and done after dinner (Kahn, 1984, 176). As in other areas of his life, he made decisions quickly. To take one example: Lionel Robbins submitted his 'Interpersonal Comparisons of Utility: A Comment' on 31 October 1938; Keynes accepted it on 3 November and the article appeared in the December issue. Nor was this treatment only accorded to the established. After an initial contact on 8 July 1940, A.R. Green, whose notepaper described himself as a 'Designer, Woodworker & Boatbuilder, Fair hulls produced by geometrical methods', and who had been trained in mathematics at Cambridge before being influenced by the arts and crafts movement, sent Keynes a draft of a letter he was sending to *The Times*. On 15 July, Keynes suggested that Green turn the idea into something for the *Journal*. The resulting draft came in on 31 July, was accepted on 7 September and appeared under the title 'The Tax Curve' in the December 1940 issue. In fact, in most cases a month was the maximum time between initial submission and final acceptance, and this was exceptional, unless the article was to be subjected to substantial revisions and the whole process then became dependent on the time available to the author. He did not keep a backlog of articles in reserve: at worst an author might see only one issue of the *Journal* appear between the acceptance and the appearance of his article. Only with the Second World War and Keynes's many lengthy visits abroad did matters slip somewhat.

When it came to getting an article into shape for the *Journal*, Keynes could take immense pains and trouble. The longest surviving exchange of correspondence concerns R.F. Harrod's 'An Essay on Dynamic Theory' which appeared in March 1939. Keynes remarked to Pigou, 'I do not think there has ever been an article about which I have corresponded with the author at such enormous length in an effort to make him clear up doubtful and obscure points and reduce its length' (*JMK*, XIV, 320).[15] The actual correspondence covers 30 pages of the *Collected Writings* (XIV, 321–50). Yet the long constructive editorial suggestion was not uncommon. Keynes had done it from the beginning of his editorship: the first surviving case, a letter of five and a half pages, concerned J.C. Wedgwood's 'The Principles of Land Value Taxation' which appeared in the *Journal* for September 1912.[16] And they were to continue. They could sometimes turn a rejected article into an acceptable one. A good example is Hans Singer's 'Price Dispersion in Periods of Change' which appeared in December 1938. It was originally submitted in March under the title 'Prices under the Blum Experiment', and Keynes had rejected it for two reasons. First, it covered the same themes as Kalecki's 'The Lessons of the Blum Experiment' which had appeared in March. Second, and more important, Keynes told Singer that he was rejecting it because 'it seems to me that you have got hold of a very good idea which could be expounded to better advantage after a little more work'.[17] Singer returned to the piece and resubmitted it on 17 June with the comment that 'the article is entirely due to the way your suggestions have started me thinking'. More often, it would involve a substantial re-shaping of something that Keynes had already accepted, even though his suggestions might involve a two-thirds reduction in length.[18]

Thus far, we have only dealt with articles submitted to the *Journal*. However, it was always open to Keynes to solicit articles. He did this throughout his career, starting with D.H. Robertson's

'A Narrative of the Coal Strike', announced in the June issue (p. 343) and published in September 1912, continuing through Irving Fisher's 'A More Stable Gold Standard' of December 1913 and Luigi Einaudi's 'The Growth and Present Situation of the Public Finances of Italy' of December 1915, through to Samuel Courtauld's April 1942 'An Industrialist's Reflections on the Future Relations of Government and Industry'. Most of these commissions, like the experimental discussions on 'Monetary Reform', 'The National Debt' and 'Problems of Rationalisation' of June 1924, September 1925 and September 1930, represented the editor's attempts to open his columns to contemporary problems and issues, as he had done with several articles of his own, most notably 'The German Transfer Problem' of March 1929 (*JMK*, XI, 451–9) and 'The Income and Fiscal Potential of Great Britain' of December 1939 (*JMK*, XXII, 52–66). (The latter was also part of the orchestration of his campaign for compulsory saving which culminated in *How to Pay for the War* and the 1941 Budget.) During the Second World War he went further and successfully 'liberated' internal civil service discussions for the columns of the *Journal*, the most quoted being the J.E. Meade/J.M. Fleming 'symposium' on 'Price and Output Policy of State Enterprise' of December 1944, which had started life as an internal discussion in the Economic Section of the War Cabinet Offices.[19]

On one occasion, Keynes went even further in his efforts to obtain material for the *Journal*. In the case of the opinion surveys of Charles Madge on 'Civilian Consumption and War Savings', Keynes met Madge, helped him raise finance for the project from the National Institute for Economic and Social Research, provided him with interim finance to get the project started and then – as well as advising on the shape of questionnaires and publishing the results in three successive issues of the *Journal* – fed the early results into the discussions leading up to the 1941 Budget.[20] This was the first occasion in British history that public opinion surveys had played a role in the making of budgetary policy.

I have so far largely devoted my attention to submissions that ultimately found their way into the *Journal*. At the end of his career, Keynes claimed that he had 'Never rejected what deserved publishing; have published much that wasn't'.[21] Earlier, he had reported to Edwin Cannan on 5 January 1934:

> Of course, I print quite a number of articles which in my personal opinion are not up to much, but I have to compromise as best I can between those which I fancy myself on their merits and those which, on one ground or another, have some sort of claim to appear. I feel much clearer, however, about the de-merit of the articles I reject than I do about the merit of most of those which are included. I have always tried to find space for anything which seemed to have a claim of any substantial sort and the somewhat numerous articles which I reject would, I declare, make a shocking show on any standard, if they were to be assembled.

The simplest reason was that there were serious problems with the submission. Keynes could be blunt, as when he remarked of a Kalecki piece (*JMK*, XII, 836)

> I am inclined to return to the opinion that the article is pretentious, misleading, inconclusive and perhaps wrong. I would rather have cheese to a weight equal to the paper it would occupy in 5,000 copies of the *Journal*.

That was to a referee. He could be equally blunt to an author. He told W.E. Armstrong on 4 April 1944:

> I do not doubt that a serious problem will arise as to how wages are to be restrained when we have a combination of collective bargaining and full employment. But I am not sure how much light the kind of analytical method you apply can throw on this essentially political problem.
>
> However this may be, it seems to me clear that your article, in its present shape, is half-baked and not fit for publication. I have not been able to spare time to read it carefully enough to know whether there is anything in it at the bottom. But I find it a bit of a rigmarole, of which I fear the reader would make little or nothing. It is neither clear what you are driving at nor where you arrive. And behind all that lies my doubt as to whether the method you are employing is capable of helping much with this particular problem. Also do you not in many cases use symbols where words would do as well and be much clearer?
>
> Sorry to be so critical. But I felt I owed it to you to explain why it is I cannot take it for the *Journal*.

At perhaps the other extreme, if only in its being uncharacteristic of Keynes, was the rejection of a submission by C.F. Bickerdike on 9 February 1921 (after Keynes had taken the advice of Sir

Charles Addis, a director of the Bank of England and a member of the Council of the Society) on the grounds of his 'deprecating [a piece] which might possibly weaken their [the Bank of England's] position at a time when they are likely to need all the strength they can get'. In other cases, space was cited as a constraint. In at least two cases, one an outright rejection and the other a deferral in publication, the constraint invoked was that the author had already had more than his share of recent issues (*JMK*, XIV, 187, 302). In other cases, the space constraint was called into play in a different way. With Milton Friedman on 4 February 1938 it was[22]

> The pressure on our space is, however, so great that we have to distinguish between material which is of primarily statistical and that which is of primarily economic interest, and I am afraid that the claims of what you sent me are not quite strong enough for me to accept it.

The previous November, with a submission by J.M. Fleming on liquidity preference, it was that the *Journal* had been 'deluged by articles on this and cognate subjects', thus forcing Keynes 'to make a somewhat strict selection'. For Paul Douglas, with a discussion of Gustav Cassel's criticisms of marginal productivity theory and Douglas's own methods of attack in *On Quantitative Thinking in Economics* (1935), Keynes claimed in his rejection letter of 23 September 1937 that the article would produce a rejoinder and a reply, and that

> I think it is safe to say that no-one who matters has paid the slightest attention to Cassel's book . . . . To 99 economists out of 100 you are merely preaching to the already converted. For the hundredth, or Cassel himself, there is no chance of salvation.

Alternatively, the article might be better suited to another journal, the *Economic History Review, Political Quarterly* or *Review of Economic Studies* (or 'Children's Magazine' owing to its founding by a group of younger dons and graduate students). Finally, a submission might be quite acceptable but Keynes would still reject it. As he told his Assistant Editor on 22 August 1941 in a comment reflecting both contemporary paper rationing and the occasional xenophobia to which he was subject:[23]

It strikes me as a competent academic exercise which any competent analytical economist could accomplish if he wanted to. I did not find it interesting or really relevant to anything that matters. I do not see any ground for an American economist to occupy a large number of pages in the *Journal* with it. Why should he not publish it in America? I did not find myself making any criticisms, but felt, as I have said, that it is just an academic exercise.

Over the years Keynes had become quite used to devising grounds for saying no.

Inevitably, some rejected contributors felt aggrieved.[24] More than one had to be reminded that 'I am afraid that the question of articles accepted for the *Economic Journal* must rest with the editor, and not the contributors'.[25] In another case, C.F. Bickerdike, writing on monetary theory, wanted to use material from his article 'Paying for War by Loans' which Keynes had edited out before its appearance in September 1915 and which Bickerdike claimed would have given him priority over Pigou and Hollander for its treatment of inflation. Keynes on 20 October 1920 was prepared to allow him a brief footnote but continued, 'I do not think it would be possible for me to admit into the columns of the *Journal* questions as to who would have had priority if rejected communications had not been rejected'. Nor would he give space to printing material not in the originally printed article. Bickerdike's proposed piece never appeared.

Having selected his articles, Keynes does not seem to have followed any consistent pattern of placement, except for the Presidential Address to Section F of the British Association for the Advancement of Science, which normally featured as the lead article in Keynes's time and for several decades after. Royal Economic Society Presidential Addresses normally also appeared first. Otherwise, some important articles appeared first, but so too did some odd ones. Authors of lead articles could be economists or non-economists (Millicent Fawcett, Malinowski, Courtauld); old or young, famous or unknown, friends of Keynes or not. There seems to be no pattern at work, although one presumes that Keynes was operating on some principle.

Thus Keynes put the *Journal* together. Such an account leaves open the question of how good a job he did. Contemporaries were generally satisfied. Even a critic such as Edwin Cannan could remark in a memorandum of 1 February 1934 to a committee looking for a successor to D.H. Macgregor as Joint Editor:

> He may not be exactly the ideal editor, who is, I suppose, one who has no ideas of his own and a great respect for those of other people, but his most hostile critic cannot say that the Society has not prospered during his editorship.

When he retired in 1945, Keynes received further tributes, both private and public. Sir John Clapham, calling it 'a great editorship', commented on the fact that the *Journal* 'has always been catholically open to all the sects'.[26] His successors went further on the first page of the April 1945 issue of the *Journal*:

> That editing has been far more than a nominal control of what was to be published. A whole generation of economists would testify to the influence which he exercised with his meticulous, but always constructive, criticism. None but the authors in the secrecy of their own hearts (and perhaps not even they) can know how much of what was ultimately printed was their own, and how much had sprung from the lively ingenuities of his mind. It was to the young and promising that he was particularly lavish with his help, and today (no longer so young) they remember that aid with gratitude.

Certainly membership in the Society soared. At the end of 1911 it had been 563. By 1915 it had risen to 747. By 1939 it was 4,502. Domestic individual memberships rose fivefold; foreign individual memberships eightfold; and institutional memberships, perhaps helped by the introduction of special terms for libraries in October 1913, tenfold (Coats and Coats, 1973, 166). The profession at large also recognized the quality of his choices (Schumpeter, 1946, 490). Articles from his editorship were a significant part of the more theoretical volumes of the American Economic Association's series of *Readings*[27] with the selections well distributed across the subject areas of the discipline.[28] The two volumes of *A Survey of Contemporary Economics* (1948 and 1952) saw contributions from the *Journal* well represented in the more theoretical sections. By the 1960s, many of these, now classics, appeared in the footnote references to the three-volume American Economic Association/Royal Economic Society *Surveys of Economic Theory* (1965–6).[29]

Thus did Keynes shape the *Journal*. Edgeworth had given him a good start and an example. As Keynes put it in his first issue as editor:[30]

> The *Journal* in its present form is virtually his [Edgeworth's] creation; and its present position among economists his achievement. The new editor wishes to take this opportunity of saying that it is his intention to follow so far as he can the existing tradition. It is laid down in the preamble to the constitution of the Society that the *Journal* is intended to represent all shades of economic opinion and to be the organ of all schools. The new editor will seek to pursue not only Professor Edgeworth's impartiality, but also the method by which he has happily blended the work of academic economists with contributions from non-academic sources.

He certainly maintained the blend of different schools and academic and non-academic sources, even though, during his career as editor, economics – if not necessarily the British subscribers to the *Journal* (Coats and Coats, 1973) – became more professionalized. His successors, faced with both more rapid professional expansion and increasing technicality, had more of a problem. But that is another story.

NOTES

All references to *The Collected Writings of John Maynard Keynes* (ed. by E. Johnson and D.E. Moggridge), 30 volumes, London: Macmillan, 1971–89, take the form *JMK*, volume number (Roman numerals), page number(s). All references to documents, unless otherwise indicated, are to Keynes's own editorial files, previously labelled EJ/1–4, in the Keynes Papers in the Library of King's College, Cambridge, supplemented by Austin Robinson's editorial correspondence with Keynes which has been deposited with them. (All these papers are now being re-sorted and re-catalogued.) I should like to thank Susan Howson, Donald Winch and Sir Austin Robinson for helpful comments on earlier drafts.

1 At current retail prices, that sum would be the equivalent of £1,750. Indexed by male earnings in manufacturing, the sum would be £7,500. During Keynes's career, the editor's salary increased to £100 in 1917, £160 in 1920, £200 in 1923, £250 in 1926 and £350 in 1929. From 1919, the Joint or Assistant Editor received the same stipend.

2 King's College, Keynes Papers, Keynes to F.A. Keynes, 23 December 1911.
3 Throughout its life the editorial board was chaired by Edgeworth. Its members were 'expected to advise the Editor, so far as they conveniently can, on matters which he refers to them, and to make to him from time to time any suggestions which they think might be helpful to him' (Royal Economic Society Minutes, 17 October 1911; also reprinted on page 665 of the December 1911 *Economic Journal*). In the surviving material in the Keynes Papers, there is no correspondence besides that relating to the rotation of the membership of the board other than Edgeworth. When the Council abolished the Board on 2 February 1919, its disappearance was not accompanied by any note in Current Topics.
4 As a result of the demands of Keynes's Treasury service, Edgeworth had been acting as *de facto* Joint Editor from late 1915. This had been recognized in February 1917, when the increased editor's stipend of £100 was divided equally between Keynes and Edgeworth, and again on 2 July 1919 when the latter was appointed Joint Editor, 'this decision', according to the minute, in fact regularising the arrangements which have been informally in place for some time'.
5 Minutes, 3 March 1925.
6 During the 1930s, owing to pressures on space, Keynes on at least two occasions contemplated increasing the number of ordinary issues of the *Journal* from four to six per annum. No change was made, although in 1933 and again in 1936 the average size of each issue was increased, first to 176 and then to 200 pages. (Keynes to Macgregor, 20 August 1930 and 8 February 1933; Council Minutes, 4 October 1930, 17 March 1933 and 13 December 1934.)
7 After the war, the *Journal* returned to four issues annually, but the *Economic History* supplement was not revived. Instead, the Society agreed to provide the Economic History Society with a subvention which allowed it to raise the number of issues of the *Economic History Review* from two to three per annum. It did impose the requirement, however, that members of the Royal Economic Society receive preferential subscription rates for the *Review* (Minutes, 6 December 1945 and 10 February 1947; Barker, 1977, 2).
8 Good examples here are his 'A Reply to Sir William Beveridge' (*JMK*, XIX, 125–37) which immediately follows the author's 'Population Policy and Unemployment' (December 1923) and his 'A Comment on Professor Cannan's Article' (*JMK*, XI, 414–19) which immediately follows the author's ' Limitation of Currency or Limitation of Credit' (March 1924). However, the habit continued into the 1930s, the last example being 'Alternative Theories of the Rate of Interest' (*JMK*, XIV, 201–15) which appeared in the June 1937 issue immediately after Bertil Ohlin's 'Some Notes on the Stockholm Theory of Savings and Investments, II' to which it was, in part, a reply.
9 Keynes to Paul Einzig, 30 April 1938.
10 Keynes to John Neville Keynes, 25 August and 3 September 1914. (When the September issue appeared it referred in Current Topics (p. 508) to financial data appearing as late as 10 September.)

11 See, for example, Keynes to A.L. Bowley, 25 March 1938, concerning Milton Friedman's submission 'The Assumptions of Linearity and Normality in the Analysis of Family Expenditure Data'. Bowley agreed with Keynes's editorial decision but suggested alterations to the rejection letter (Bowley to Keynes, 28 March 1938). For an *Economic History* example see Keynes to Clapham, 14 June 1930.
12 The correspondence (two letters from Keynes to Harrod and three from Harrod to Keynes, all dated between 7 July and 1 August 1928) survives in the editorial files.
13 The question of balance had arisen before. On 14 March 1928, when he accepted Lionel Robbins's 'The Representative Firm' (September 1928), he remarked:

> It is by no means a coincidence that I should be accepting so many articles at the same time on this group of topics, since this happens at the moment to be a part of the subject where progress is really being made by the medium of reasonable controversy. *But all the same I must not overload the Economic Journal with too large a proportion of such matter in a single issue.* (Emphasis added)

The June 1928 issue contained Pigou's 'An Analysis of Supply' and G.F. Shove's 'Varying Costs and Marginal Net Products'.
14 See Keynes to Robertson, 26 October 1933, concerning E.F.M. Durbin's discussion of the *Treatise on Money*; the Keynes–Pigou exchanges in *JMK*, XIV, 320, and XXIX, 173–8, on post-*General Theory* discussions of his work; and Keynes to Oskar Lange, 10 April 1940, on a Lange–Marschak reply to Keynes's review of Tinbergen. In this last case, Keynes did offer the authors the chance of resubmission if, after reading Tinbergen's own reply to Keynes, 'there are some points not dealt with by him which you would like to pick out for special emphasis, and would let me have something running to, say, four or five of your MS pages I would like to have the chance of considering again whether we could find room for that.' The authors did not take up the offer.
15 He continued, 'I produced a little effect, but not perhaps very much in proportion to the effort.'
16 Keynes to Wedgwood, 1 July 1912.
17 Keynes to Singer, 4 April 1938.
18 See, for example, T. Balogh to Keynes, 5 March 1941, and Keynes's reply of 7 March on Balogh's submission on compensation. When Balogh submitted the article, he accepted that it was too long and that 'the first 18 pages could be safely left out, except perhaps the first introductory paragraph'. Keynes agreed on the need for shortening, but thought the first 18 pages 'definitely required'. Probably this disagreement over its shaping, plus the fact that Keynes would not print it until the June–September issue, meant that it never appeared.
19 The process of 'liberation' had been protracted, for the discussions had started in the spring of 1944 (L. Robbins to Keynes, 4 April 1944). For the original

Economic Section discussions, see Public Record Office, T230/16. See also Howson, 1988, ch. 3.

20 The three articles were 'War Time Saving and Spending: A District Survey' (June–September 1940); 'The Propensity to Save in Blackburn and Bristol' (December 1940); and 'Public Opinion and Paying for the War' (March 1941). For Keynes's injection of the results of these surveys into policy-making, including the official distribution of 20 galley proofs of the December article, see *JMK*, XXII, 215, 254, 274–6, 302; XII, 821, 822. For the surrounding correspondence see *JMK*, XII, 810–29.

21 Keynes's notes for his remarks at the dinner marking his retirement from the editorship, 21 June 1945.

22 The piece was 'The Assumptions of Linearity and Normality in the Analysis of Family Expenditure Data'. When he submitted it on 4 February 1938, he admitted that it had already been rejected by the *Quarterly Journal of Economics*. The referee or, more accurately, the reviser of Keynes's draft letter of rejection was A.L. Bowley. (See Keynes to Bowley, 25 March 1938, and Bowley to Keynes, 28 March 1938.) To judge from the American Economic Association's *Index of Economic Journals* the paper was never published.

23 But see above, p. 144.

24 Keynes's rejection of Wicksell's 'Ricardo on Machinery and the Present Unemployment' in January 1924 certainly rankled (Gardlund, 1958, 323). The article eventually appeared in the *Journal* almost 55 years after Wicksell's death (Jonung, 1981).

25 Keynes to E. van Dorp, 13 April 1938.

26 Clapham to Keynes, 30 January 1945.

27 The more applied volumes had no contributions from the *Journal*, presumably because it was less likely than contemporary American journals to publish applied work on American conditions.

28 *Readings in Price Theory* had contributions originally published during Keynes's editorship from Wicksteed, Clapham, Pigou, Robertson, Sraffa and Hotelling; *Readings in the Theory of International Trade* contributions from Keynes, Ohlin, Williams and Robertson; *Readings in Welfare Economics* contributions from Young, Meade and Fleming, Kaldor and Ramsey; *Readings in the Economics of Taxation* contributions from Chapman, Young and Robertson; *Readings in Monetary Theory* contributions from Cannan and Meade; and *Readings in the Theory of Income Distribution* and *Readings in Business Cycle Theory* contributions from Tarshis and Ohlin respectively.

29 Only three pieces appeared in all these three sources; 15 appeared in two and the remaining 31 in one only. An average of one and a half 'classic' articles per year, if one uses this standard for 'classics', is probably not too bad for an editor.

30 March 1914, 156.

REFERENCES

Barker, T. C. (1977): 'The Beginnings of the Economic History Society', *Economic History Review, 2nd Series*, 30, 1–19.
Cassel, G. (1935): *On Quantitative Thinking in Economics* (Oxford: Clarendon Press).
Coats, A.W. and Coats, S.E. (1973): 'The Changing Social Composition of the Royal Economic Society 1890–1960 and the Professionalisation of Economics', *British Journal of Sociology*, 24, 165–87.
Gårdlund, T. (1958): *The Life of Knut Wicksell* (Stockholm: Almqvist and Wicksell).
Harrod, R.F. (1951): *The Life of John Maynard Keynes* (London: Macmillan).
Howson, Susan (ed.) (1988): *The Collected Papers of James Meade, II, Value Distribution and Growth* (London: Unwin Hyman).
Kahn, (Lord) R.F. (1984): *The Making of Keynes' General Theory* (Cambridge: Cambridge University Press).
Jonung, L. (1981): 'Richardo on Machinery and the Present Unemployment: An Unpublished Manuscript by Knut Wicksell', *Economic Journal*, 91, 195–205.
Schumpeter, J. (1946): 'John Maynard Keynes, 1883–1945', *American Economic Review*, 36, 495–518.

Part II

Recollection

8
Fifty-five Years on the Royal Economic Society Council

Austin Robinson

The first meeting of the Council of the Royal Economic Society (RES) that I attended was held on 5 July 1934. The RES was then only 44 years on the way to its centenary. Edwin Cannan was in the chair. The others present, of the total membership of 37, were no more than seven – Alfred Hoare (then Treasurer), Sir Charles Addis, James Bonar, Henry Higgs, D.H. Macgregor (my predecessor as Assistant Editor of the *Journal*), Maynard Keynes and myself. We met, as usual, in the attractive room of the Royal Statistical Society in Adelphi Terrace, with its lovely view across the river.

When, towards the end of the meeting, Macgregor had gone off to catch his train back to Oxford and we were deciding 'on the proposal of Mr. Higgs . . . to affix a new description plate to the Portrait of Viscount Goschen, First President of the Society . . . the present plate having become illegible', Maynard Keynes passed over to me a scribble reminding me that Bonar, Higgs and Hoare all went back to the earliest beginnings of the Society and that I was the only person present who had not been a member of the Council for more than 20 years. Continuity was the outstanding characteristic of the Council. Ten of its 30 ordinary members retired each year. Unless one of them had signified his desire to

Austin Robinson

resign, the ten were duly re-elected and so on indefinitely.

One had at once a feeling that Bonar, Higgs and Foxwell regarded the RES as their Society. In a sense this was justified. They, together with Edgeworth until his death in 1926, attended almost all the meetings and were frequently a majority of those present. A meeting of seven was typical. There was little to decide. Until 1964 we solemnly elected 'Fellows' to the Society and published their names in the *Journal*. But we seldom had any adequate evidence of their qualifications. I cannot remember that any applicant was ever rejected. And since election was necessary, fairly frequent meetings had to be held. In 1934 there were four meetings. In 1900–2 there were six meetings attended only by the Editor and the Secretary. On 7 April 1905, Henry Higgs, then Secretary, conducted a meeting alone and recorded its decisions. That meeting not only elected new Fellows; it also elected a new Treasurer and moved the Society's account from one bank to another.

Cannan, in the chair at my first meeting in 1934, was only the second academic economist to be President of the Society. Goschen held the Presidency from 1890 until he resigned in 1906. The office was next offered to Alfred Marshall, but he wrote 'regretting his inability to accept the office through stress of work'. Thereupon, on the motion of Mr Schloss and seconded by Mr Cannan, 'it was agreed that the Council considered it advisable that as a rule the President should not hold office for more than three years'. That decided, they unanimously agreed to offer the Presidency to the Right Honourable R.B. Haldane. Despite the resolution, he held office for 22 years, until his death in 1928.

A meeting on 13 December 1928 again passed a resolution in almost the same words as in 1906. But after 38 years of distinguished but inactive politicians they added the rider 'that the President should be a person distinguished in economic study or administration'. They not only passed this resolution, but they did something about giving effect to it. They made Foxwell the first economist to be President. The situation had hitherto been further complicated by the fact that the office of Vice President was also an honorific rather than a working office, held in the earliest years by four Right Honourables – Balfour, Childers, Courtney and Morley.

In the earliest years Edgeworth had doubled in the offices of

Secretary of the British Economic Association and Editor of the *Journal*. The early pages of the first Minute Book are in his untidy and almost illegible handwriting. After the well-attended inaugural meeting the detailed planning and decisions quickly devolved onto a small number of people prepared to do the work. The major decisions were made at a meeting held on the same day as the public meeting at University College London, with an attendance of some 17 of those elected to the Council by the inaugural meeting. It was their first Council meeting that in turn elected the first officers of the Association. Some of those who attended, including Palgrave and Neville Keynes, were seldom, if ever, seen again at any subsequent meeting.

It soon became apparent that Edgeworth could not carry the entire load of editing the *Journal* and running the Association. This involved, of course, not only the tasks of editorship but also those of admitting Fellows, collecting subscriptions, despatching the *Journal*, keeping the books, running the meetings, and all the rest. After a couple of years, at meetings in July and November 1892, it was decided to appoint someone who should be both Secretary with responsibility for the organization and development of the Association and at the same time Assistant Editor to Edgeworth. The division of the editorial responsibilities is not defined. One wonders whether the responsibility of the Assistant Editor for all reviewing, which I inherited from Macgregor, goes back to this time.

The first Secretary and Assistant Editor was Henry Higgs. Edgeworth, the great economist, Anglo-Irishman, professor of economics at Oxford, author of papers that every educated economist still reads, is still a familiar name. Higgs is now almost forgotten. But in his time and in the early history of the Association and its transition to the Royal Economic Society in December 1902, Higgs played a major part and deserves a place in our memories.

The office of Chairman of the Council had been included in the earliest Bye-laws (it was recorded in 1903 that the Charter empowers us to make 'Bye-laws' and that 'by-laws' are unauthorized). Leonard Courtney was duly elected in 1893. But since he seldom attended, the actual chairman might on any given occasion be almost anyone of suitable seniority. And when Courtney surrendered the office to Bonar a few years later, it was not always Bonar who took the chair. It was not until 1929, with

Foxwell's Presidency, and a few years before I came onto the Council, that there was any real consistency, with the President regularly in the chair. In 1926 Alfred Hoare, the Treasurer, sometimes presided with Bonar present; sometimes Bonar presided with Hoare present.

Alfred Marshall, who had played so large a part in the initial foundation of the British Economic Association (BEA), was content to have brought the *Journal* into existence and played almost no part in the subsequent administration of the Association itself. He was made a Vice President in 1896. But he very seldom attended a meeting, and then only (as when the young Maynard Keynes was first made Editor) in order to achieve some specific objective of his own. This curiously ambivalent system with its inevitable consequence of putting all real power in those earlier years into the hands of the Editor and Secretary had persisted, as I have said, down to 1928 – long after Keynes had succeeded Edgeworth as Editor in 1911 and Hamilton as Secretary in 1913.

Of Hamilton I have been able to find out little. He had been a Cambridge graduate in 1902 in the Moral Sciences Tripos, which at that time included economics. He had been ordained at Durham, presumably by Bishop Westcott, before he became an undergraduate to a curacy in that diocese; he was a curate at Trumpington while taking the tripos and after graduating became, for a period, a lecturer in the University of South Wales at Cardiff. It was while there that he took over in 1906 from Higgs. In 1910 he returned to Cambridge with authorization to lecture for the pass-degree. Whatever his other qualifications may have been, he was not a very good Secretary for the RES. He held office from 1906 to 1912 without distinction, and not infrequently alone with Edgeworth. His period was almost certainly the nadir of the Society. In 1912 he ran into trouble with a rather larger meeting of the Council. The Minute Book records that 'Sir Thomas Elliott expressed the displeasure of the Council at the serious delay occurring in the arrangements made by the Secretary for holding the Annual Meeting. The general conduct of the business of the Society during the current year was discussed and in the course of the discussion the Secretary asked to be allowed to tender his resignation.' Whatever the explanation of this, Hamilton is recorded as having become Minto Professor of Economics at Calcutta in 1913 and as having moved later to Patna. Keynes's take-over of the Secretaryship in

1913 was recommended by a Committee of the Council of which he had been a member since 1912.

When I became Assistant Editor in 1934 I knew nothing of this earlier history. Cannan was a regular chairman of our meetings, and one had a sense of continuity. But there was no question about how the Society ran. Keynes ran it, and reported what he had done and what he proposed to do. The meetings served to validate his actions.

In Cambridge I was responsible for the review section of the *Journal*. I was given a ration of pages. We settled anything that needed to be settled on a Sunday morning, myself seated among the Sunday papers and the proofs of the *Journal* at the foot of Keynes's bed in his room at King's. He would tell me whom he was trying to get to write what. I, of course, proof read the articles, but they were wholly his concern. He would occasionally ask me whom I was trying to get to review some book in which he was interested. But he was content to delegate the reviewing to me. I remember telling him that I proposed to ask John Hicks to review the *General Theory*. I thought that he was sufficiently detached from its genesis, though he was by then in Cambridge. He thought it a good idea.

The change to an academic President did little at first to change the traditions of the Council. A typical meeting continued to be seven or eight. One could still be sure that Higgs, Bonar and Hoare would be there. Occasionally Beveridge or Hawtrey would attend. Gradually a few of the younger generation were added to the Council, and very occasionally Lionel Robbins or Roy Harrod might be there. And when in 1936 the Royal Statistical Society lost the use of Adelphi Terrace and moved to Portugal Street, the London School of Economics Council members, especially Robbins and Arnold Plant, became more regular attenders.

But by 1934 the links with the past were all too rapidly disappearing. Edgeworth had died in February 1926. Cannan died in harness early in 1935, while still President. Foxwell lived on until 1936. Hoare died in 1938, Higgs in 1940 and Bonar in 1941. But by then it was war-time. For the moment we were scarcely conscious of what this would mean after the war.

Of Foxwell and Cannan on the Council I have no very vivid memories. By 1934 Foxwell seldom attended a meeting. Cannan I can still visualize in the chair in the room in Adelphi Terrace. I remember myself anxiously looking at his collar-stud. I had been brought up on the story of how Cannan demolished Marshall's consumer's surplus by arguing that he would gladly pay a guinea any day than appear in public without a collar-stud, but this did not mean that he derived 365 guineas a year of consumer's surplus from having one. He was a good chairman. But I have no recollection of him trying to control or modify Keynes's policies or activities.

The main concern of the earliest meetings that I attended in 1934 as member of the Council and Assistant Editor of the *Journal* was with the future extent of the accommodation of the RES in Adelphi Terrace. The Royal Statistical Society had asked us to surrender a room which had hitherto been ours and used by Macgregor for handling the books sent to the *Journal* for review and their dispatch to reviewers. The final agreement was that we should continue to use their Council Room for our Council meetings, and that one of their staff should at intervals pack all the books and journals addressed to the RES into a large box which shuttled backwards and forwards to Cambridge, where I rented a room for myself and a secretary in what were then some of the university offices. In practice, I frequently short-circuited this process by driving up to Adelphi Terrace and loading the accumulation of books and journals into the back of my car. In a year or two the problem disappeared as publishers were persuaded to send books to our new address.

Another concern at this time was with the raising of funds to help one or two Jewish economists who were refugees from Nazi Germany. This was in those years a matter of great concern to many universities; with Keynes and Clapham I was heavily involved in this in Cambridge, and it was inevitable that the RES should share in this general involvement.

When Cannan's Presidency came to an end in 1935, he was succeeded by W.R. Scott, great personality and great student in all that concerned Adam Smith. He, only the third of our new-type more academic Presidents, like his two predecessors, went back to the early days of the Society. While I do not remember him as ever standing in the way of change, with Bonar, Higgs and Hoare still the loquacious regulars at most meetings, it was difficult to escape the feeling that one was attending a performance devoted to the propagation of the gospel according to Adam Smith.

I am not certain that I was ever as conscious as I ought to have been in 1934 of the astonishing contrast between the economics of Cambridge and that of the actual working minority of the RES Council. In Cambridge we were in the last stages of the gestation of Keynes's *General Theory*. The *Journal*, issue by issue, was rewriting or creating employment theory or imperfect competition; economics was beginning its transition into a quantitative science. The Council of the Society even in the 1930s was happily dominated by the traditions of the great nineteenth-century classics; it took little or no active interest in what Keynes was publishing in its *Journal*. Those economists of Keynes's generation or a still younger generation who were members of the Council – Pigou, Robertson, Robbins, Harrod for example – while contributing frequently to the *Journal*, played no significant and continuous part in the administration of the Society; they left it to Keynes. Occasional suggestions of possible publications came from others – from Gregory for example – but the principal publication proposals came also from Keynes. Merely by exercising his responsibilities he quietly controlled the Society.

Higgs and Bonar, it must be borne in mind, were both in their old age by 1934 when I first knew them, and it is as such that inevitably I remember them. Higgs, born in 1864 in Cornwall, was by then 70. He was, I am sorry to say, unquestionably senile and very deaf and could contribute nothing worthwhile to our discussions. Maynard Keynes's amusing but cruel account of him, and of Cannan's efforts to restrain his ramblings, as reprinted in *Essays in Biography*, needs to be read in its proper context as a postscript to Clara Collet's much fuller and friendly obituary in the *Journal* in 1940. Higgs, who in his younger days had been a Treasury official and for some years Private Secretary to Campbell-Bannerman as Prime Minister, had played a very active part in the creation of the BEA and the RES. This is no place to evaluate his work on Cantillon, his re-editing of Palgrave under impossible conditions of minimal change, and his other contributions to scholarship. What matters is that, as I said earlier, he carried on his shoulders in the early critical years much of the burden of keeping the Society and its *Journal* alive at a time when others failed to do so. It is perhaps forgivable if in old age he did not know when to let go.

Bonar was very different. Born a Scot near Perth in 1852, he must have been 82 when I first knew him. Much older than Higgs, he showed few signs of age. My own very vivid memories of him are of his participation in the Malthus Celebration, held in Cambridge in March 1935, when Bonar received a very well-earned LL.D. from Cambridge University and Keynes made me responsible for looking after him throughout the day. He contributed one of three allocutions to the afternoon's commemoration of Malthus in the hall of King's and also replied at a great dinner in the evening at Jesus, Malthus's college, to the Master's proposal of the toast '*in piam memoriam* of Malthus'. (In parenthesis, a glance at the menu of that dinner reminds one vividly of the decline in the academic standard of life since 1935.) Like many Scots before him, born in a manse, Bonar had gravitated through Glasgow University to Balliol College at Oxford, and thence with a First in Lit.Hum. to a variety of civil service jobs including that of Senior Examiner of the Civil Service Commission and later that of Deputy Governor of the Mint in Canada. What I find interesting is that neither of these two stalwarts of the first 50 years of our existence was a normal university teacher, though both were great contributors to the study of classical economics.

As the years went on the number of economists of the younger generation who were elected to the Council increased. For 1939–40 there were seven of my generation elected. But the war made London meetings difficult and Keynes's heart trouble led to meetings of three or four people in his house in Gordon Square, or in his room in the Treasury to transact formal business. A meeting in March 1940 was attended by only three members of the Council – Fay, Keynes and myself – but we decided a number of matters of importance, some of them dictated by war conditions: shortage of paper required that we should publish only three issues a year of the *Journal*; we changed the terms of life membership; we approved the accounts for the previous year; we agreed to propose Beveridge as the next President; the other two extended my tenure as Assistant Editor.

And so we muddled through the early war years. Keynes and I edited the *Journal* as best we could and wherever we happened to be. I have memories of writing short notes on unimportant books in the cellars of the Cabinet Office where I slept, and on the train to Cambridge if I had a rare weekend. My RES secretary, Helen Oman, coordinated the proof reading and dealt with the printers and publishers.

As the war went on and more economists became absorbed into Whitehall, the attendances at a Council meeting explicably began to increase. And with the deaths of Cannan, Foxwell, Hoare, Higgs and Bonar the whole character of the Council began to change. We were no longer dominated by the founding fathers. More important, perhaps, by 1944 after five years of war many of the younger members of the Council, who in 1938 had been content to leave the running of the RES to Keynes, were holding senior posts of responsibility in the civil service and very naturally expected to share in the making of policy in the Society.

The dramatic change in the administration came in 1944. Keynes decided that the time had come when he should hand over the heavy work of the editorship of the *Journal* and the secretaryship of the Society to someone younger. The Council, when it learned of his intention at a meeting in May 1944, appointed a committee composed of Beveridge as President, Lionel Robbins, John Jewkes and Keynes himself to consider the editorial implications. At the same time it made me Joint Editor rather than Assistant Editor. The next Council meeting made Roy Harrod Joint Editor from the beginning of 1945 and made me Secretary as well as Joint Editor. It was understood that Harrod should succeed Keynes as editor of the articles and that I should continue as review editor.

It was an important element in the transition, though not immediately minuted, that Keynes should for three years continue to keep a controlling eye on my running of the Society by becoming President. He was duly proposed and elected at the annual meeting in June 1945. Thus when he died in 1946 he was President and no longer Secretary. At the next meeting we elected Hawtrey, then Treasurer, to fill the vacancy and Humphrey Mynors to take over from Hawtrey the office of Treasurer.

Thus by mid-1946 the administration of the RES had in a few years come down not just a generation but, in effect, half a century. We had our long traditions, however, and what we actually did continued to be dominated by what Keynes had done and was intending to do. Those who attended Council meetings were, nonetheless, increasingly members of my own generation. More important, Roy Harrod's interests were very similar to those of Keynes and the *Journal* continued to be primarily a journal of applied political economy, concerned to solve the intellectual problems of eliminating the nation's current practical economic difficulties. The initial post-war problems of the Society and its Council were inevitably those of adjusting pre-war subscription rates and life compositions to the printing and administration costs of the post-war world.

Hawtrey was succeeded as President by Dennis Robertson. It was under the latter's leadership that a delegation of four members of the Council – Robertson, Robbins, Hawtrey and myself – represented the Society at the meeting in 1949 that formally brought into existence the International Economic Association, in the running of which the Society, and I as its representative, have played a major part throughout the subsequent 40 years.

Robertson was followed by Hubert Henderson. Once again the Society suffered the sad experience of the death of its President during his tenure of office. Hubert Henderson died in February 1962 after election as Warden of All Souls College, Oxford, but before actual admission to that office. On this occasion it was Lord Brand who was elected to take his place.

It was during these tenures of the office of President that the Council was largely concerned with the form in which it should commemorate Keynes and the 33 years of service that he had given to the Society as Editor and Secretary. Over the years between his death in 1946 and the final decision in May 1954, innumerable alternatives were considered and discussed formally and informally. There was initial uncertainty as to whether there was likely to be a national memorial or whether American funds might be forthcoming. The earliest suggestion of an annual memorial lecture was rejected as inadequate; the British Academy adopted it many years later at Lionel Robbins's suggestion. A proposal for the acquisition of a building in London to become the Society's headquarters quickly proved to be beyond any possibly available resources and the more humble proposal of a reading room was unattractive; it was one of the proposals considered and rejected at a meeting in May 1951. The Council, unable to reach any decision, then appointed a small committee 'to consider the matter further'. One of the proposals we put to the Council was that we should create and endow a travelling fellowship which would enable a chosen economist to travel round the world and see at first hand many of the cultures and economic systems of the world actually at work; this was temporarily accepted but later referred back to an enlarged committee as concentrating the benefits on a very small number of fortunate people. Finally, in May 1954, the Council accepted a proposal from its committee that the memorial should take the form, considered on a number of earlier occasions, of 'a series of fine editions of the great economists', starting with 'an edition of Lord Keynes's writings published and unpublished'. The same meeting made Richard Kahn, Roy Harrod and myself responsible for this and authorized the appointment of Elizabeth Johnson to begin the work. So began the task which proved immensely greater than we then envisaged and of which the final stages are being completed as I write this more than 30 years later.

During these years other publications initiated by Keynes were progressively reaching completion. The greatest of these – Sraffa's edition of Ricardo – had been authorized as early as February 1930. By October 1938 Keynes had been reporting to the Council that the eight or nine volumes 'would soon be ready for publication', again in October 1939 that eight volumes would soon be ready for publication, and in March 1940 that he could assure us that he had already bought enough paper for the edition. The story of the subsequent discovery of the letters of Ricardo to Mill and the heroic achievement of the Cambridge University Press in interleaving the new letters into the initial setting belongs to the 1950s and my own period as Secretary. The series was not finally published until 1951–5.

But Ricardo was by no means the only major publication of the Society during those years. They saw Guillebaud's great variorum edition of Marshall's *Principles*, Richard Kahn's translation of Wicksell's *Interest and Prices*, William Jaffé's translation of Walras's *Elements of Pure Economics* and his edition of Walras's *Correspondence*, Denis O'Brien's three-volume edition of *The Correspondence of Lord Overstone*, Werner Stark's edition of *Bentham's Economic Writings*, and the beginnings of our cooperation with the American Economic Association on the production of the series of surveys of recent work in different branches of economics which were first published in the two journals and ultimately in three collected volumes. The opportunity to buy these on special terms was a considerable inducement to join the Society.

These years also saw other breaks with the past. Almost from Keynes's earliest taking over of the Secretaryship of the Society he had entrusted the detailed responsibility of collecting subscriptions, keeping the list of members and their addresses up to date, keeping the accounts, recovering income tax, preparing the list of new 'Fellows' for printing in the *Journal*, and the writing up of the Minute Book to S.J. Buttress, who initially was head clerk of King's College, Cambridge, where he worked under Keynes as Bursar. He, with his son to help him, was an immensely loyal and meticulous servant of the servant of the Soceity for 42 years between 1913 and 1955. He was, I must confess, not always the easiest of colleagues. He could not believe that anyone other than Keynes, with himself as repository of the tradition, could be entrusted to run the Society. Of his complete devotion to the Society there is no possible question. When he died in 1955 it was necessary to organize an entirely new administration with Arthur Fuller, head clerk of St Catharine's College, in charge of finances and book-keeping, and Mrs Baird in charge of subscriptions, addresses and the rest. The Treasurer at this time was exclusively concerned with investment policy. I can only say that, from the Secretary's point of view, it was a very much more relaxed and happy arrangement and I could always get from Fuller the information that I needed.

Inevitably during the war years and early post-war years the Society could undertake no major innovations. We were content to keep things going and to restore the fourth annual issue of the *Journal* from 1946. We began rather inadequately the task of adjusting subscriptions and expenditures to the price levels of the post-war world. But I have always regarded 1954 as the turning point in the Society's history. Lionel Robbins in that year succeeded Lord Brand as President. The actual participating and working membership of the Council was now of his generation and my own. More important, the attendance at meetings of the Council, now held in the London School of Economics, was usually of the order of 20 members and the attendance at the annual meetings, held in the theatre of the School, could be measured in hundreds. The RES had grown up and had become democratic. Its membership, which had been 694 in 1914 and 4,578 in 1938, was 6,356 in 1954 and was growing rapidly as a war-time generation graduated and began professional work.

Sadly in 1954 we lost Humphrey Mynors as Treasurer when his increasing responsibilities as Deputy-Governor of the Bank of England made his continued tenure of the office impossible. We elected as his successor Denny Marris and through him maintained our close relationship with Lazards, begun through Lord Brand and continued down to the 1980s.

During Robbins's Presidency we made no great changes of policy and introduced no major new activities. But in distant retrospect I can now see that something rather important was happening. Keynes had been, if not by intention but because he had to be, the whole administration of the Society. When he died we continued for a time to execute policies he had inaugurated. But that could not continue indefinitely – I myself was no Keynes. I wanted to be assured that there was general agreement that any policy changes were sensible and in the interest of the Society. I had known Robbins well in war-time and had worked closely with him in the Economic Section of the Cabinet Office. Thus as Secretary I worked more closely with him than I had with his immediate predecessors. And rather than report what had been done, we began to involve the now young and active Council in discussing what should be done.

Even after he had been succeeded by Carr-Saunders in 1956 and by Robert Hall in 1959, I continued to consult Robbins as well as my current President when some major decision had to be made at short notice before the next meeting of the Council. I did not always agree with him politically. But I knew that I would always get good and wise advice. He never attempted to dominate the Society in the way that Keynes had done. But he exercised nonetheless a considerable influence over our policies in the 1950s and 1960s.

During these years, and for a considerable period ahead, the principal activities of the Society remained what they had been from the beginning: the publication of the still very influential *Journal* and the publication of books of scholarship in the field of economics which were unlikely to pay their way but which, in the broader interest of economics, deserved publication.

It was during this period that it became necessary to strengthen the team responsible for the editing and proof reading of the *Journal* as it became both larger and more complex. From 1951 Robin Matthews, then a young Fellow of St John's College, Cambridge, recently recruited from Oxford, joined Joyce Baird and myself at the Cambridge end of the operation as Associate Editor. I still remember his singular capacity for finding misprints that the author, my fellow Editor and I myself had all failed to discover. He held this office until he moved back to Oxford as Drummond Professor in 1965.

The Society was not rich. The problems of the level of the subscription and of the adequacy and treatment of the life composition and of the adjustment of the small stipends of our three or four staff came before almost every Council meeting. But down to the stock exchange crises of 1973–4 we could afford to maintain a relatively active publication policy, cooperating sometimes with the British Academy, sometimes with the Economic History Society, sometimes with the American Economic Association, but in almost all cases expecting and incurring no more than a manageable loss. We were living within our income and building up a very considerable reserve.

It was at its meeting on 24 November 1960 that the Council 'received with very great regret the resignation of Sir Roy Harrod from the office of Editor, to take effect from a date convenient to the Council'. Roy Harrod, like Maynard Keynes, had carried the whole responsibility for the articles and notes sections of the *Journal*, leaving the final make-up and further proof reading to Matthews and myself and my secretary in Cambridge. It is not my task to discuss the *Journal* as I saw it over the 35 years or so that I was one of its Editors. I shall confine myself to saying that I think that Roy Harrod, with his double interest in real economic policy and in the development of economic theory, continued very ably and vividly the very similar qualities of the *Journal* under Keynes's editorship. He was a rapid and immensely thorough worker. But it was a gruelling task. Harrod wrote to me, and I think to the many contributors to the *Journal*, long and detailed letters in his own very recognizable handwriting. How many hours he gave to the editing of the *Journal*, as well as to all else that he did, I do not know. He quite certainly overworked himself. The Council appointed a small committee to discuss with me how some relief might in future be provided to his successor. At the next meeting Charles Carter was appointed in Harrod's place with agreement that he should be provided with generous secretarial support.

The organization was also changing in other ways. It was during Robert Hall's Presidency that he and I first discussed between ourselves and then brought to the Council in February 1960 the possibility of some rotation of the Council. From the earliest beginnings membership of the Council had been virtually a life appointment. The number of university professorships was then small. A Council of 30 included a large majority of the senior economists in the country. That was by 1960 no longer true. The number of students of economics was rising fast, the number of economists was rising correspondingly, the number of universities was increasing, the number of senior economists in government service, in banks, in businesses and industries was growing rapidly. It was obvious that an almost static Council of the RES could not be properly representative of all these groups.

We brought the question to the Council. We were very naturally reminded of the advantages of continuity and the importance of doing nothing to penalize those who lived at a considerable distance from London. But the Council, after appointing a small committee to develop the idea, and discussions that spread over several meetings, accepted the general argument and adopted a scheme by which members should be elected for a period of five years, six members of the Council of 30 to retire each year. It would be for the Council to propose that one or two (office holders for example) might be nominated for re-election. To make the introduction of the scheme possible, the existing Council very generously put their resignations in the hands of the small committee, which drew by lot the names of those members of the existing Council who should retire in each of the first five years.

In this way some assurance was obtained that a majority of the then existing number of senior economists should serve on the Council at some time and that few of the increasing number of new universities would be permanently unrepresented. On the whole the scheme has worked well. But it has meant that the Council is not, and cannot be to the extent that the older Council was, a group including the heads of economic departments in most universities. Recently the need to supplement the Council by such a body has become apparent and the RES has taken the initiative in organizing it to make possible fully representative and fully authoritative discussion of university teaching problems.

The re-organization of the Council began to take effect at the annual meeting of the Society in June 1961. It was quickly followed by a further re-organization. At its meeting in November 1962 I had to report the receipt of a letter from the Clerk to the Privy Council telling us that his Council was concerned by the multiplicity of 'designatory letters' and their desire that their use should be confined to 'denoting a full professional qualification'. Under its Charter and Bye-laws a member of the RES had, at least from the grant of its Charter, always been known as 'Fellow of the Royal Economic Society' (F.R.Econ.S) and there was little doubt that a few Fellows of the Society did in fact use the designatory letters to suggest the possession of qualifications which they may have possessed but which certainly had never been verified.

The Council had decided, as early as 1891, that individual tests of qualifications were both undesirable and for some 5,000 current members or even the 600 who join each year, many of them in foreign countries, impracticable with the resources we possessed. When the Privy Council letter was considered in 1962 the contemporary Council reaffirmed the earlier decision. We decided that it was better to surrender the title of 'Fellow' and describe those who belonged personally to the Society as 'Members'. But, as the Privy Council recognized, this was a very considerable task. The title of 'Fellow' was embodied not only in the Bye-laws but also in the Charter. The Bye-laws were out of date and contained transitional provisions for the change of the Society from the BEA to the RES in 1902 which were irrelevant 60 years later. If the Bye-laws had to be revised they needed to be revised completely.

The revision inevitably brought difficulties to the surface. This was the period in which the freedom of universities and colleges to invest in equities and similar safeguards against inflation was under discussion and freedom was being secured by them. It was natural that our Treasurer (Denny Marris) should wish to clarify his powers. Keynes had assumed that we possessed the same powers as had been conceded to academic bodies. Was this in fact true? We obtained a legal opinion from Mr Brunyate QC, which indicated that in his view we possessed the necessary freedom to safeguard ourself against inflation. Thus on 19 October 1966, Sir Sydney Caine (now RES President), Marris and I had a meeting with the Clerk of the Privy Council in which we tried to clarify the position. Sir Godfrey Agnew left us not much clearer. He told us, as was to be expected, that the Privy Council could not be bound by Brunyate's opinion, but he would do nothing to prevent the Society exercising the powers of investment which, on the basis of the opinion, it believed itself to possess. When, perhaps foolishly, I inquired whether 'if the Society asked for a formal widening of its powers of investment to be written into the Charter and Bye-laws' it was likely to be granted, he made it plain (again to quote my record) that 'he would not expect the Privy Council to be prepared to concede as wide powers as had been given to universities and colleges'. Thinking about the problems of living in a world of inflation has moved on a long way since 1966.

The questions of nomenclature and investment were no more than a couple of the things which had to be discussed and settled by our committee to revise the Bye-laws – Robert Hall, the current President, John Hicks, Arnold Plant and myself. We had to decide what needed change, how to change it, agree a rough draft, then get a final draft from Linklater and Paines (our lawyers), and finally get it through the Council before presentation at the Annual Meeting. With 60 years of obsolescence to clear up, it does not surprise me that it took us four years and three RES Presidencies to complete the work. It changed the conduct of our business surprisingly little. It legalized what we were in fact already doing. The Council no longer concerned itself with the nominal election of individual Fellows; they were no longer enshrined in the pages of the *Journal*.

The rewriting of Bye-laws was not the only activity of the Presidencies of Roy Harrod, James Meade and Sydney Caine. By far the greatest other concern was with the great publications of the Society mentioned earlier and some new ones: Patricia James's edition of *The Travel Diaries of T.R. Malthus*, our edition of Quesnay's *Tableau Economique*, and the early thinking about the Jevons papers (later to appear under the editorship of R.D. Collison Black), Marshall's unpublished writings (later to appear under the editorship of J.R. Whitaker), and the *Surveys of Economic Theory*. All of these were going along at this period. We regarded publications as a very important element in the Society's work.

The next problem with which the Council had to deal was, I regret to say, caused by myself. During a period in 1967 when Sydney

Caine, the President, was abroad and Robert Hall was standing in for him, I raised with him the question of my retirement or at least the lightening of my load (I was now 70 and retired from my Cambridge teaching). Since 1945 I had held the offices of both Secretary and Joint Editor (in practice Review Editor) first with Roy Harrod and more recently with Charles Carter. Robert Hall consulted Lionel Robbins, James Meade, Harry Johnson and others. When they brought it to the Council, the Council asked me to remain Secretary while they considered the future pattern of administration. They made Phyllis Deane Review Editor and responsible for the collection of subscriptions, so that the existing Cambridge office could continue for a few more years.

The previous concentration of the administration in Cambridge had given the impression, wrongly in my view, that the Society was Oxbridge dominated. The Council, by deliberate policy, was, designed to cover the whole country; only about one-eighth of it were currently working in Oxford or Cambridge. No President since Keynes in 1946 had come from Cambridge. Policy was in practice greatly influenced by Robbins and others at the London School of Economics and by economists working in Whitehall and the City. But whatever the truth, it had become important that the Society should be seen to be national and not parochial.

This naturally meant breaking up the administration, keeping much of the expenditure and distribution of the *Journal* with the editing, thus separating it from the policy-making activity of the Secretary, and leaving publication policy temporarily with review editing, again remote from financial policy. As a political solution this was inevitable and unquestionably right. From the point of view of efficiency and the relation of other activities to the major activity of publishing the *Journal*, it has never worked quite as easily as when Keynes was responsible for everything. And with the need for coordination and correspondence it has been more expensive.

It took several years to work out the new widely distributed system. It was several years before a separate Publications Secretary was appointed. For a period Donald Winch was responsible for both review editing of the *Journal* and our publications policy. The difficulty was that we could not plan a new divided administration until we knew what future policy would be. We could not visualize what the Society would be doing in the future until we had decided what the subscription, long overdue for increase, might be. And obviously the new Secretary should have a say in all this. And equally clearly the retiring Secretary should not determine future policy. Thus a much heavier load than usual fell upon Alec Cairncross who had succeeded Sydney Caine as President in 1968. A small committee of ex-Presidents was appointed to help him.

After discussion of possible alternatives it was decided to invite Charles Carter to move from the office of Joint Editor to that of Secretary, now to be entitled Secretary-General. When he agreed, it was necessary to find a new Editor. It was finally decided to appoint Brian Reddaway for a period of five years, 1971–6. His request to have associated with him a mathematical economist (in practice David Champernowne) was accepted. Miss Deane continued, of course, to be Review Editor and Managing Editor. The committee of the Council also proposed the creation of an Editorial Board of 12 economists who might meet, say, once a year to advise on editorial policy. The new regime began from 1 January 1971. It was disbanded in 1976 when the editorship was taken over by John Flemming at Oxford and the review editorship by Donald Winch at Sussex. These two roles have continued to be separate and they make it possible for two distinct viewpoints to be brought to bear on *Journal* policy.

Under Charles Carter's editorship the practice of referring articles to referees had become more usual than it had been under Keynes or Harrod, but was, I think, limited to articles which he took seriously or on which he wanted advice. Reddaway made rather greater use of referees and referred many promising articles to Champernowne. It is only in recent years that the practice of referring almost all articles to a referee has become normal practice.

It was a necessary part of the rethinking of the Society's activities that the subscription should be raised – something that for several years I had been unsuccessful in persuading the Council to agree. It was finally agreed in my last meeting as Secretary to propose to the next Annual Meeting that the normal subscription should be raised from £2 10s to £5, with various allowances for special groups. In the very near future this was to prove a very fortunate decision.

It was thus at the end of 1970, after 36 years of editorship and 26 years as Secretary, that I came to the end of my period as an officer of the Society. But it did not end my close involvement in its affairs. As was said earlier, our memorial to Keynes was in the form of a great edition both of his ten published books and of a selection of his more important published and unpublished economic writings. With the advice of Roy Harrod, his biographer, and Richard Kahn, his executor to whom the copyright of any uncollected economic writings had been bequeathed, I was responsible at that time and ever since as Managing Editor for the series of *The Collected Writings of John Maynard Keynes*.

This was a vast task, much bigger than we had visualized when we began it. We had to begin by sorting and cataloguing the papers. We next reprinted some of the existing books. But the most laborious task was that of selecting unpublished papers to be printed – a task that became much greater when the restriction of publication of official papers was reduced to 30 years, thus bringing all his war-time memoranda into consideration – and writing the minimum of background necessary to provide their setting.

The first editor of the volumes containing such papers was Elizabeth Johnson, living in Cambridge while her husband, Harry Johnson, was still a Fellow of King's College. But Harry Johnson's meteoric career carried her to Manchester, London and Chicago and away from the archive of papers. Thus progress was very slow. We had long decided that the first group of four books should contain one volume of the new material. It was only in 1971 that we were able to publish two groups, each of four volumes. My own task had been that of seeing several of Keynes's earlier life-time volumes through the press and giving occasional help, criticism and encouragement to Liz Johnson. But progress was worryingly slow until we were lucky enough to find Don Moggridge with his unusual combination of thorough scholarship, quick decision and good judgement as to what to select for publication. He began the most difficult task of all – Keynes's drafts and correspondence on his way to the *Treatise* and the *General Theory*. He finally filled the gaps between the point reached by Liz Johnson's volumes (XV–XVIII) and the end. Increasingly the editing of the series became his responsibility.

But the problems of editing were by no means the only problems. The problems of its finance were on my lap and have kept me since 1970 still in close and active participation in the affairs of the Society. We designed the edition from the first as our memorial to Keynes and not as a strictly commercial undertaking. We expected to make a loss but not a large loss. It was not an edition which a commercial publisher could be expected to undertake. We could not foresee its scale. Thus like the Ricardo edition we planned to publish it on commission; we chose Keynes's publishers, Macmillan, who alone could solve the problems of copyright. We assumed, unrealistically in a world of rapid inflation, that the income from sales of a group of four books would return after a period to finance the publication of another four. But that apart, while I was still Secretary we had built up our reserves other than in unsold books to about £200,000 with the needs of the edition very much in mind.

I have described the problems of the Keynes edition in some detail because a few years later they complicated a situation which, quite apart from them, would have been difficult. With Charles Carter's take-over and the wider diffusion of the administrative responsibilities the Society ran successfully until 1973, under the Presidencies of Henry Phelps Brown and Donald MacDougall. It was during this period that Marris, our Treasurer, felt obliged to resign after a serious illness. He was succeeded by Alan Prest, then a professor at the London School of Economics.

A sad loss during this period came with the retirement in 1974 of Arthur Fuller who, since the retirement of Buttress in 1955, had been Assistant Secretary and Accountant of the Society. This part-time job had meant that he was constantly available to the editors and myself and could readily be consulted. His more official responsibilities were taken over after an interval by one of the staff of our auditors. This no doubt simplified the tasks of the Treasurer and Secretary-General, but it meant that those of us with delegated responsibilities had no-one other than our auditors to whom to turn for financial help, and in my own case at least it threw a lot more work onto anyone who wished to think about alternative possibilities.

It was the world-wide financial crisis of 1973 that created grave problems for the RES, and particularly for the new Secretary-General and Treasurer. The market value of the Society's investments, which had been £196,056 at end-1972, fell to £138,203 at end-1973 and £81,349 at end-1974. At the same time the investment in work in progress and currently unsold copies of the Keynes edition was rising very rapidly. The two chief officers of the Society very naturally became alarmed and asked that work should stop on the edition. Rightly or wrongly I was very reluctant to do this unless ordered to do so by a formal meeting of the Council. With the help of Don Moggridge we were just beginning to make really satisfactory progress. The two officers, one in Lancaster and one in London, found difficulty in quickly calling an emergency meeting of the Council.

In retrospect I do not know whether I was right or wrong. The editorial work on the Keynes edition continued on its slow course, but for a time we sent nothing to the printers. Perhaps more important, the market value of our investments recovered by end-1975 almost to the value of end-1973. Meanwhile the Council very properly set up a small committee of nine senior members of the Council to hold an inquest into the whole business.

In retrospect what I think we learned from that crisis and the inquest into it were two things. First, that the Society had no effective means of handling a short-term emergency. A Council of 30 elected members and another ten or more members who, after holding the chair, had become honorary Presidents could not be summoned at short notice to decide an urgent problem. I myself, when Secretary, had often consulted informally with three or four ex-Presidents before dealing with some minor matter of urgency. But that was not sufficient with a major problem.

Second, we learned that in the post-1969 re-organization we had created four separate subsidiary activities of the Society – editing the *Journal*, editing the Keynes series, editing other publications, organizing conferences – without giving enough thought to creating any effective coordinating system to achieve a universally accepted overall policy within the means of the Society. Those of us who were responsible for the day-to-day work of these subsidiary activities each needed authority to commit expenditure and were perhaps excessively reluctant to accept without argument unexpected instructions from a Secretary-General and Treasurer that completely upset all our plans.

The misunderstandings could be serious. I give two examples: the two Editors of the *Journal* found themselves greatly overworked with an increasing stream of submissions; they wished to have the assistance of a young Cambridge don well known to both of them for the remainder of their tenure. This arrangement got bogged down on the assumption that it was to be a long-term appointment, potentially affecting the long-term policy of rotating the editorship around alternative universities. In my own case, as Managing Editor of the Keynes edition, there was uncertainty which could have been cleared up as to whether or not it had been the original intention that money should be spent on the memorial to Keynes, and whether our investments were, as I had assumed, an expenditure reserve, built up for that purpose, or an endowment which it was the responsibility of the Treasurer to keep intact.

The committee reached the conclusion that lack of coordination was the chief problem. Its solution was the establishment of an Executive Committee of some ten members, chiefly holders of administrative offices of the Society – the President, Secretary-General, Treasurer, the managing Editor of the *Journal*, the Review Editor, the Publications Secretary and four selected members of the Council. The next President-designate, or until he is nominated, the ex-President, is also now a member. I myself, as Managing Editor of the Keynes edition, have been allowed to attend. This committee as it has developed during the subsequent 15 years, has proved to be a quite invaluable instrument for the coordination of the divided responsibilities, for pre-considering proposals that are to be put to the Council, and for preliminary discussions of possible new activities of the Society. It meets more frequently than the Council, and in an emergency such as that of 1973 could quickly be called together.

Very regrettably Charles Carter and Alan Prest, who had borne the strain of the crisis, were reluctant to devote time and energy to initiating this new system. Ronald Tress and Tad Rybczynski became Secretary-General and Treasurer respectively.

We were not entirely out of the wood. The Society's accounts had for many years been audited by a well-known Cambridge firm which had accepted throughout Keynes's secretaryship the inclusion in the assets of the Society of stocks of its books in hand and work in progress valued at their cost of production. When a book (Guillebaud's Marshall for example) had exhausted its sales we decided what write-off was necessary and voted it. Our new auditors in London, Messrs Thomson, McLintock & Co., were not happy about this traditional process and in the audit of 1976 qualified their approval of our accounts, saying in effect that there was inadequate evidence of the value embodied in the stocks of unsold books. Our new Secretary-General and Treasurer very naturally responded to this by introducing a very severe process of valuation and writing-off which by 1988 had had the curious longer term effect of valuing the entire stock of hard-back copies of the edition of 30 volumes, apart from the preparatory work on the general index, at zero, despite the fact that they continue to bring us in a considerable income.

From 1973 until 1987, first under Ronnie Tress and from 1980 under Aubrey Silberston as Secretary-General, the Society continued to maintain a cautious policy of rebuilding its finances while maintaining its traditional activities. Large annual surpluses have been used principally to create a reserve fund and an investment income sufficient to cover much of the increased administrative costs of the Society. It has enjoyed during this period the Presidencies in succession of Nicholas Kaldor, Arthur Brown, Richard Stone, Phyllis Deane, David Worswick, Robin Matthews and, as I write, Frank Hahn.

These years from 1975 to 1987 under these successive Presidencies were years of consolidation rather than of major innovation. In practice the financial position of the Society very quickly recovered. By 1977 the Society was running at an overall surplus of £42,000, with an £18,000 surplus on the *Journal* and a reserve of investments valued at just under £130,000. We have continued of course to produce the *Journal*, with John Flemming, Charles Feinstein and recently John Hey taking over in turn from Brian Reddaway and David Champernowne. The *Journal* has progressively changed from being, as it had been under Keynes and Harrod, reading matter for those interested in modern applied political economy, to being reading matter for those who enjoy mathematical models, to the benefit of the latter but the slight regret of the former.

We have completed, roughly two each year, all 30 volumes of the huge edition of *The Collected Writings of John Maynard Keynes*. With Donald Winch as Publications Secretary we have restored the long tradition of the publication by the Society of important contributions to scholarship in the field of economics. These include Paul Sturges's *Economists' Papers, 1750–1950: A Guide to Archive Sources* (1975); *The Economic Advisory Council, 1930–1939: A Study in Economic Advice During Depression and Recovery* (1977) by Susan Howson and Donald Winch; and *Statistical Tables of National Income, Expenditure and Output of the*

U.K., 1855–1965 (1977) by Charles Feinstein.

Conferences supported by the RES have given rise to publications on the personal distribution of incomes, the concept and measurement of involuntary unemployment, and Keynes and the modern world. Variorum editions of Malthus's *Essay on the Principle of Population* and of his *Principles of Political Economy*, prepared by Patricia James and John Pullen respectively, have just been published, and John Whitaker's edition of Marshall's correspondence is in its final stages as I write.

We have made during these years a number of minor advances. We have joined with the Association of University Teachers of Economics in the holding of conferences and the publishing, in what is in effect a fifth annual issue of the *Journal*, of the best papers to the conference. We have cooperated with the association representing those teaching economics in schools in making a survey of the content, actual and desirable, of courses and school examinations in economics. We have celebrated with a large conference in Cambridge the centenary of the birth of Maynard Keynes. We have introduced a scheme to send a distinguished visiting lecturer to a university which would welcome his assistance. We have thus been far from inactive.

Perhaps in the long run more important, the income from the large investment fund built up by Tad Rybczynski as Treasurer has given us latitude to think about new activities. In 1987, during Robin Matthews's Presidency, the Executive Committee considered this question During the past three years, under Frank Hahn's Presidency and the continuing administration of Aubrey Silberston and our new Treasurer, Jeremy Hardie, we have considerably extended our traditional activities. Perhaps the most important innovation has been a committee of representatives of most economic departments in universities of the British Isles. Many of these may have been members of our Council in the past, but under our system of rotation are no longer serving. This has quickly become a valuable forum for the exchange of ideas and criticisms.

Thus the RES enters its second century full of vigour and new activity. It has to be borne in mind how different is the world in which the Society now has to work from that of 1890 when we started, or in 1934 when I first became involved. During the early post-war years, as has been said, the number of universities and of departments of economics not only rapidly increased; with larger faculties there has also come much more specialization. Specialists scattered widely between universities now predominate; the general economists of my younger days have become rarities in the universities, though they still remain numerous in the government service and in the working world. Specialist journals now proliferate. Communication has become necessary between specialist and specialist as well as between the specialist and the general economist and the numerous specialist journals that now meet their needs.

At the same time we have been increasingly affected by technical changes. In my early days as an economist the means of communication were predominantly the printed word published in a journal. One subscribed to the two or three journals that published the articles one wished to read. Libraries were few and inadequate. The xerox did not exist. One almost automatically joined the RES because this was the way to get the *Journal*. Now most researchers depend on the large libraries. The journals depend primarily on their sales to libraries. Specialists exchange xeroxes of their drafts.

Moreover the character of research has changed. The full-time economic research worker was almost non-existent in the 1930s. Until the war a considerable proportion of the limited research that then existed took the form of establishing the facts and figures of the more important components of the economy. The contribution of government departments, though immensely important, was relatively small. There was as yet no Central Statistical Office. During the war, in order that we might make the most of inadequate supplies, the government began to collect and organize a greatly increased range of statistics, and since the war has continued to expand its coverage. More important, it has given us the official series of consistently defined national income estimates which form the foundation of so much of modern economics. Thus far less field work of the type of my younger days remains to be covered by the university economist of today. The great growth of the Government Economic Service and of the number of business economists has left the function of the university economist, apart from teaching, increasingly ambiguous, with the making of models of the supposed working of minor fractions of a hypothetical and often a closed economy as the principal current activity.

It has been far from clear what the principal functions of the

RES should be in this changing world. My own view is that it should be that of forming a link between all the various groups of economists, encouraging communication between them, conveying the results of the work of the specialists to the general economists, and also (and more important) conveying in the other direction the problems and uncertainties encountered in practice by the general working economists to the university model makers. The greatest and most persistent danger of the mathematical model maker is irrelevance.

Over the 55 years that I have been on the Council that body and the Society itself have greatly changed. It is now more businesslike, more efficient, more commercially minded, more prosperous. At the same time it is less influential, less central to the whole body of economic thinking in Britain, less concerned with current macroeconomic policy-making, and its *Journal* is less widely read than it was in the 1930s when Keynes was in charge, or in the 1950s when Harrod was in charge. Membership of the Society is now, I fear, less necessary to one's work as an economist. Editorial policy has in recent years, or so it seems to a mathematically illiterate ancient, made the *Journal* a means of communication between specialist and fellow-specialist. And as a corollary the highly skilled model maker is not infrequently ill-informed regarding the problems that it is most urgent to solve.

More serious, I think, the character and outlook of the Society has changed. It started as an alliance of the working economist and the academic economist. Bonar, Higgs, Hoare in my early days had been working economists. Both Bonar and Higgs were civil servants of their day. In the 1930s we were concerned with the total profession of economists. It is only since 1975 or thereabouts that the university economists have predominated on the Council to the extent they do today and that the alliance between the two sectors of the profession has almost disappeared, not, I think, by intention but by inadvertence and because new activities have been primarily concerned with university needs. This I myself deeply regret. I hope that it is only a transient phase and will as quickly disappear. If I regret some of these changes it probably means no more than that, like Bonar and Higgs in my early days, I belong to a world that is past and am reluctant to adapt to the world of the twenty-first century.

Officers 1891–1991

British Economic Association   1891–1902
Royal Economic Society   1902–

Presidents

1891–1906	G.J. Goschen
1906–29	R.B. Haldane
1929–32	H.S. Foxwell
1932–4	E. Cannan
1935–7	W.R. Scott
1937–40	A.C. Pigou
1940–5	W.H. Beveridge
1945–6	J.M. Keynes
1946–8	R.G. Hawtrey
1948–50	D.H. Robertson
1950–2	H.D. Henderson
1952–4	R.H. Brand
1954–6	L.C. Robbins
1956–8	A.M. Carr-Saunders
1958–60	R.L. Hall
1960–2	J.R. Hicks
1962–4	R.F. Harrod
1964–6	J.E. Meade
1966–8	S. Caine
1968–70	A.K. Cairncross
1970–2	E.H. Phelps-Brown
1972–4	G.D.A. MacDougall
1974–6	N. Kaldor
1976–8	A.J. Brown
1978–80	J.R.N. Stone
1980–2	Phyllis Deane
1982–4	G.D.N. Worswick
1984–6	R.C.O. Matthews
1986–9	F.H. Hahn
1989–	J.A. Mirrlees

Editors

1891–2	F.Y. Edgeworth
1892–1906	F.Y. Edgeworth
	H. Higgs
1906–8	F.Y. Edgeworth
1908–12	F.Y. Edgeworth
	H.B. Lees Smith
1912–19	J.M. Keynes
1919–22	J.M. Keynes
	F.Y. Edgeworth
1922–34	J.M. Keynes
	D.H. Macgregor
1934–45	J.M. Keynes
	E.A.G. Robinson
1945–61	R.F. Harrod
	E.A.G. Robinson
1961–70	C.F. Carter
	E.A.G. Robinson
1971–7	W.B. Reddaway
	D.G. Champernowe
	Phyllis Deane
1977–80	J.S. Flemming
	D.N. Winch
1980–3	C.H. Feinstein
	D.N. Winch
1984–6	C.H. Feinstein
	D.A. Collard
1986–9	J.D. Hey
	D.A. Collard
1989–	J.D. Hey
	R. Backhouse

Secretaries or Secretaries-General

1891–2	F.Y. Edgeworth
1892–1906	H. Higgs
1906–12	C.J. Hamilton
1912–45	J.M. Keynes

1945–71	E.A.G. Robinson
1971–6	C.F. Carter
1976–9	R.C. Tress
1979–	Z.A. Silberston

Treasurers

1891–7	J. Biddulph Martin
1897–1905	A.S. Harvey
1905–12	F.W. Buxton
1912–39	A. Hoare
1939–46	R.G. Hawtrey
1946–54	H.C.B. Mynors
1954–69	A.D. Marris
1970	W.M. Allen
1971–5	A.R. Prest
1975–87	T.M. Rybczynski
1987–	J.M. Hardie

Publications Secretary

1971–	D.N. Winch

NOTES

1 The names of Officers are given in the form in which they first became associated with the Society and without the titles or offices which very many of them later acquired.
2 The office of Secretary became that of Secretary-General from 1971.
3 The names recorded as Editors are confined to those of the Senior or Managing Editor and the Review Editor. During various periods of the history of the *Journal* there have been advisory committees or groups of assistant editors. Most but not all of these have been recorded on the annual title page.

4 The appointment of Henry Higgs first as Assistant Editor and subsequently as Joint Editor to Professor Edgeworth are recorded in the Minute Book and he is profusely thanked when he retires. His name never appears on the annual title pages with Edgeworth's.
5 There was also for many years the office of Honorary Secretary of whom there was sometimes one and sometimes two. There were no duties or responsibilities attached and the Office was abolished in the revision of Bye-laws in 1966.

Part III

Reassessment

9
Editorial Introduction

John Hey

This part of our centenary volume is concerned with the second half of the century and with the *Economic Journal*. To many of those who lived through the excitement of the Keynesian revolution, when Keynes himself was editor of the *Journal*, the postwar decades might appear to be anticlimactic. Yet in looking through the *Journal* during the past 50 years, I have been struck by the large number of important papers that have appeared during this period. My task of selection has therefore required considerable strength of mind and a vast amount of pruning.

As a result of this I have selected five significant papers belonging to each of the last five decades, each of which seemed to me to be particularly important, not only in their original context but for their implications for future research. In each instance I asked the authors of these articles to review their earlier contribution from a present-day perspective.

Richard Stone's 1948 review of the influential book by John von Neumann and Oscar Morgenstern on *The Theory of Games* (1944) rightly identified the book as setting an important precedent for work to follow. As the years have since borne witness, the book has been seminal in its implications: numerous publications have arisen from it, and it probably has the highest citation count of all volumes in economics published around that time – indeed, probably since that time. In his paper for this volume, Richard Stone surveys the impact of the book and examines how the Neumann–Morgenstern theory has influenced the way in which economists analyse problems. In an enlightening survey Stone examines numerous applications of the theory of games, as well as summarizing the major contributions to the theory since 1944.

Not only in the theory of games, but elsewhere, expectations have played a crucial role in economics. In 1952 Frank Hahn published an article on 'Expectations and Equilibrium' which set the agenda for much research in the subsequent decade. Now, more than 30 years later, and with the wisdom conferred by many years of research in the area, Frank Hahn looks back on his article and forward to the future of modelling expectations in equilibrium. His essay nicely summarizes the current state of play as far as expectations are concerned and highlights not only the strengths of the present position but also its deficiencies. It is not clear to me what final message emerges from Hahn's paper – whether one should be optimistic or pessimistic about the future. As in other matters, the answer presumably depends on one's own expectations.

When I wrote to Paul Samuelson, inviting him to revisit the subject discussed in his 1962 article on 'The Gains from International Trade Once Again', which, as the title suggests, was itself a reassessment of an earlier paper, he sensibly decided to cast his net somewhat wider, while remaining within a field that has been dear to readers of the *Journal*. In his paper for this volume he discusses the use of consumer surplus in economics – a topic that has exercised the best minds in economics for well over a century. In many ways Samuelson's view of consumers' surplus is like Hahn's view of expectations: cautiously agnostic. Readers should notice the title of Samuelson's piece – carefully designed to avoid offence!

In many respects the 1970s were notable for dramatic changes in econometric methodology, and one particular article in the *Journal* had a profound influence on a subsequent generation of applied econometric models. I am referring, of course, to the paper by J. E. H. Davidson, D. Hendry, F. Srba and S. Yeo on 'Econometric Modelling of the Aggregate Time-Series Relationship between Consumers' Expenditure and Income in the U.K.' (1978). This set the tone for the development through the early part of the 1980s – at least until cointegration burst upon the scene. In this respect a look back at the techniques in DHSY (as it is now known) by the authors themselves is eminently appropriate. In their paper for this volume David Hendry, John Muellbauer and Anthony Murphy put in context their approach to modelling the consumption function in particular, and indeed to modelling in economics generally, by comparing it with alternative approaches. It is still not clear whether a dominant methodology will emerge in econometrics, though it is clear that Hendry and his collaborators have had a profound influence on the way econometrics is practised.

This is also the case with macroeconomics, where one naturally thinks of the work by Martin Weitzman in the early part of the 1980s. Two of the papers he published in the *Journal* were particularly influential: the 1983 paper on profit sharing and the 1982 paper on the implications of increasing returns to scale. It took some persuading to get Martin Weitzman to contribute to this volume because he thought it rather presumptuous for one so young to be looking back from such a near perspective. But many would regard these two Weitzman articles as being seminal, changing the way we think about economics. I find this reappraisal of what he was trying to do and what he has achieved most insightful.

Taken together, these five essays clearly indicate that the *Journal* was involved in some fundamental debates during the second half of its century of existence. That the original authors have been prepared to revisit earlier triumphs and modestly reconsider them here speaks for itself. I now let the authors do so.

10
The Theory of Games Revisited

Richard Stone

The Beginning

In 1944 the *Theory of Games and Economic Behavior* (Neumann and Morgenstern, 1947) burst on the world. It deservedly received a most enthusiastic reception: I have in mind among many others the reviews of Jacob Marschak (1946) and Leonid Hurwicz (1945). By the time I got round to writing a review for this *Journal* (Stone, 1948) a second edition had appeared in 1947. I opened my review with the words 'Unquestionably, for economists, the great work of von Neumann and Morgenstern is the most important contribution that has appeared since J. M. Keynes's *General Theory* was published in 1936', though I pointed out that its field was very different.

It may have seemed strange to many of our profession in 1944 to propose games of strategy such as noughts and crosses, poker or chess as models for microeconomic behaviour. I thought it a brilliant innovation, and that for several reasons. Like these games, economic behaviour depends on decisions made under uncertainty. In economic life as in games, interests may be opposed or coincident. Gaining information about the others while preserving one's own business secrets may be important. Trust, bluffing and intimidation all have a part to play. Altruism and dirty tricks both make their appearance. The thought of modelling all these complications

Table 10.1

	B's strategies			
A's strategies	1	2	3	Row minima
1	9	4	2	2
2	7	5	6	5
3	1	3	8	1
Column maxima	9	5	8	

is daunting. But Neumann and Morgenstern made a good beginning and set a task to their fellow gamesmen which has been worked on avidly since their book appeared.

If a game is to be played rationally the players must have a clear idea of what they are trying to achieve by their play. Whatever their aim, players must have a strategy designed to reach it. Neumann and Morgenstern start off with two-person zero-sum games in which what one player wins the other loses, so that the value of the game, the sum of the payoffs to the two players, is zero. These might be called constant-sum games since the best strategies would not be affected if a given constant were added to each of the payoffs. The minimax strategy recommended by the authors is designed to ensure that each player does the best he can, given that his opponent plays his best (but unknown) strategy. How this works out best can be seen by considering a simple payoff matrix designed to enable each player to choose the best of three strategies (table 10.1).

The nine entries in the body of the table show the payoff to A for any combination of the three strategies available to each player. Each player is supposed to know these numbers but not to know which strategy his opponent will adopt; so, though A would like to make the number as large as possible and B would like to make it as small as possible, each is led to adopt a policy of 'play safe'. To this end, A concentrates on the row minima and chooses their maximum, since in this way he can be sure of getting this amount whatever B may do; and, correspondingly, B chooses the minimum of the column maxima, thereby restricting A's gain to this amount.

Table 10.2

	B's strategies	
A's strategies	1	2
1	5000	4000
2	3000	6000

If these numbers are the same, as in my example, then it is clear what strategies the players should adopt: each player should use his second strategy.

If the maximum of A's minima is equal to the minimum of B's maxima, there is said to be a pass through the payoff matrix at the point of equality, usually termed a saddlepoint. There may be several of these or none. In the first case one (or both) of the players can use some freedom in choosing a best strategy. In the second case it is not immediately apparent what they should do. It may be possible to eliminate some strategies that are dominated by another strategy which would give better results to the player in all circumstances. But it would still be necessary to decide how to use the remaining strategies. Neumann proved that, provided that each player is willing to shift his concern from his gain to the expected value of this gain, it is always possible to find a solution in the form of grand strategies in which the players adopt their individual strategies with appropriate probabilities. These grand strategies are termed mixed strategies.

The use of mixed strategies can be illustrated by an example given by Dorfman, Samuelson and Solow (1958) relating to duopolists A and B who have two strategies each: to offer either 100 units of the product (strategy 1) or 200 units (strategy 2). The demand and cost conditions are such that their combined profit is 10,000 in all circumstances. Suppose A's payoff matrix is as in table 10.2. Write p for the probability that A uses strategy 1. Then if B uses strategy 1, A may expect

$$5000p + 3000(1-p) = 3000 + 2000p \qquad (10.1)$$

and if B uses strategy 2, A may expect

$$4000p + 6000(1-p) = 6000 - 2000p \qquad (10.2)$$

Table 10.3

	A's payoff			B's payoff	
	B's strategies			B's strategies	
A's strategies	*1*	*2*	A's strategies	*1*	*2*
1	5000	4000	1	5000	7000
2	3000	6000	2	6000	2000

Since the first of these equations is an increasing function of p and the second is a diminishing function of p, the value of p which will give A the largest expected profit is at the point of equality of the two equations. Thus $p = 0.75$ and A can expect to get 4,500 whatever B does. A similar analysis for B shows that the corresponding probability for him, say q, is 0.5 and that he can expect to get 5,500 whatever A does.

This neat result depends on the fact that we are dealing with a constant-sum game in which B gets 10,000 minus whatever A gets. So let us extend the example to remove its constant-sum feature. Suppose the payoff matrices for A and B are as in table 10.3.

The joint profits now vary from 8,000 to 11,000 depending on the strategies adopted. We have already worked out the optimal probability of adopting strategy 1 for A and found that $p = 0.75$ and that under the constant-sum assumption the corresponding probability for B is $q = 0.5$. Let us now work out q from the new table. Proceeding as before, we have

$$5000q + 7000(1 - q) = 7000 - 2000q \qquad (10.3)$$

and

$$6000q + 2000(1 - q) = 2000 + 4000q \qquad (10.4)$$

Equating these two equations gives

$$6000q = 5000 \qquad (10.5)$$

or

$$q = \tfrac{5}{6} = 0.83 \qquad (10.6)$$

in place of the 0.5 we found in the constant-sum case.

If in this game both players use their mixed strategy, A will obtain 4,500 and B will obtain 5,333. But if B uses his mixed strategy and A uses strategy 1, then A will obtain 4,833 in place of 4,500; and if A uses his mixed strategy and B uses strategy 2, then B will obtain 5,750 in place of 5,333. So in a variable-sum game the equilibrium we found in the constant-sum game disappears and the duopolists had better act collusively if they can. I shall return to duopoly later.

When we pass to games with more than two players the position becomes much more complicated since the participants can combine in various ways to form different numbers of players. The number of types of game grows with the number of participants. I showed in 1948 (Stone, 1948) that with ten participants, say an industry with ten firms in it, there are 42 types of game depending on how they group themselves, and no less than 115,975 games in all. Clearly it would take an economist a long time to sort out this situation unless he made one of the limiting assumptions of monopoly or perfect competition.

It can be seen from this brief and incomplete account of the beginnings of the theory that the players of an economic game among producers are faced with a number of serious difficulties. First, they must be able to formulate their own strategies and envisage those of the other players. Second, they must be able to evaluate the payoffs that may arise in various circumstances. Third, saddlepoints are rare, and only in the case of constant-sum games, which are unusual in economics, will the use of mixed strategies lead to an equilibrium solution. And fourth, there is typically a large number of players so that the scope for coalitions, mergers and take-overs is immense.

Types of Game and Solution Concepts

As the theory developed, games came to be classified in various ways and a number of different solution concepts were formulated. One of the most interesting distinctions is that between non-cooperative games, in which the players cannot communicate or make binding agreements about the strategies they will adopt, and cooperative games, in which they can. With non-cooperative games (sometimes called contests) there is nothing to do but play, whereas with cooperative games an important feature may be pre-play negotiations and the binding agreements that may emerge from them. These two stages may be divided into negotiations (talk) and the game proper (action). The first stage is usually modelled as a contest and the second as a cooperative game in which the outcome of the first stage is enforceable.

The solution of a game expresses the outcome to be expected if the game is played by rational players. We have already seen an example of this in Neumann and Morgenstern's solution of two-person zero-sum games. The players choose strategies that lead to the saddlepoint, and the outcome is given by the payoff matrix for this pair of strategies. In more complicated cases, the solution may not be confined to a single value.

In extending the concept of a solution two quite different approaches have been employed. The first is the axiomatic method which considers the axioms that ought to be satisfied by an acceptable solution. The second approach is to model explicitly the negotiation stage. Up to about 1980, reliance was mainly placed on the first method but more recently the second has been actively pursued. It seems likely that in the future both methods will be needed.

As a consequence of different choices of axioms and different methods of approach, the resulting solution concepts vary. They are analogous to different forms of average as a summary of the central tendency of distributions. We cannot say that one is right and the others are wrong but only that one may seem more appropriate than the others in dealing with a particular problem.

I shall now give a brief account of some of the more important solution concepts, beginning with Nash's solution for non-cooperative games. This is also known as the Nash equilibrium and is a fundamental building block of game theory.

The Nash Solution for Non-cooperative Games

This concept, introduced by John Nash in 1951, applies to situations in which it is impossible for the players to communicate or collaborate in any way. It is expressed in terms of strategies rather than outcomes and is sometimes referred to as a strategic equilibrium. It can be defined as follows. Let $s_1 \ldots s_n$ be strategies adopted by n players and let $s_1^* \ldots s_n^*$ represent the best strategy of each player if each plays his best strategy. Then

$$s^* = (s_1^* \ldots s_n^*) \tag{10.7}$$

is a Nash equilibrium. If this strategy vector is adopted, then no single player can obtain a higher utility by changing his strategy if the others stick to theirs. Everyone is making a best answer to everyone else's best answer.

Originally the Nash equilibrium was conceived in terms of a static situation in which each player makes a single choice in ignorance of the choices of the other players. It can be extended, however, to a variety of dynamic situations, as in Selten (1965, 1975), Kreps and Wilson (1982a,b) and Rubinstein (1982). An example will be found below.

The Nash Bargaining Solution for Cooperative Games

Following his original paper on the bargaining problem (Nash, 1950), Nash worked out a specific application to a two-person cooperative game (see below), proposing a set of axioms which, if satisfied, yield a unique solution (Nash, 1953). Binmore and Dasgupta (1987, 23) write the solution u^* for n players in the form

$$u^* = \prod_{i=1}^{n} (u_i - c_i)^{b_i} \tag{10.8}$$

This expression is to be maximized subject to $u_i \geq c_i$, where u_i is an element of the feasible set of outcomes, c_i is a reference point below which player i will not allow himself to be pushed and b_i denotes player i's bargaining power.

The Core

The concept of the core stems from Neumann and Morgenstern's stable sets and was developed by Shapley (1952) and Gillies (1953) in the early 1950s. The core of a game is the set of all feasible outcomes that are not dominated. Denote the set of all players by N and a coalition (a subset of N) by S. An outcome y is feasible if it can be achieved by N. Another outcome x is said to dominate y if a coalition S can achieve its part of x and all the members of S prefer x to y.

Consider a game with transferable utility of value v. Feasibility of x means that $x(N) \leq v(N)$, and the domination of y by x via S means that $x(S) \leq v(S)$ and $x_i > y_i$ for all players i in S. The core of v is the set of all feasible y with $y(S) \geq v(S)$ for all S.

As an example take the three-person voting game with

$$y = (\tfrac{1}{3}\ \tfrac{1}{3}\ \tfrac{1}{3}) \qquad (10.9)$$

If players 1 and 2 got together they might be able to exclude player 3 and achieve

$$x = (\tfrac{1}{2}\ \tfrac{1}{2}\ 0) \qquad (10.10)$$

which depends on mutual trust and dominates y. If player 2 is a tough guy he may be able to improve on the last imputations by allying himself with 3 and excluding 1, to give

$$x = (0\ \tfrac{2}{3}\ \tfrac{1}{3}) \qquad (10.11)$$

which again dominates y. Further, player 2 being the kind of person he is might try to make himself dictator by excluding 3 as well as 1, to give the dominant payoff vector

$$x = (0\ 1\ 0) \qquad (10.12)$$

Given the appropriate personalities and circumstances, 1 or 3 could replace 2, so that in this example the core would have plenty of elements; it would therefore provide several solutions though it could not be expected to pinpoint any particular one. It is not difficult, however, to think of games in which the core is empty and can therefore provide no solution.

The Shapley Value

The Shapley value is intended to provide a unique payoff vector in terms of the potential contribution of each participant in the game and was originally developed by Lloyd Shapley (1953). It can be worked out by answering two questions. Can any participant, i say, win on his own? If not, it will require a coalition to win. Can a participant, by joining another participant or a coalition of any of the other participants, convert a losing situation into a winning one? If so, the game can be modelled as follows.

Let us write N for the set of all participants, $v(N)$ for the Shapley value of the game, S for a subset of the players (usually but not necessarily a coalition), n for the number of participants and s for the number of participants in a coalition S. Then

$$v(N) = \sum_i \sum_s \frac{(n-s)!(s-1)!}{n!} [v(S \cup i) - v(S)] \quad (10.13)$$

where $\cup$ denotes the union of S and i and is a coalition even if S is a single participant. The meaning of this expression can be illustrated by a simple example given by Guillermo Owen (1982).

Consider a company with four shareholders owning 10, 20, 30 and 40 shares respectively. If a decision requires the approval of shareholders with a majority of the shares, then a decision can only be taken by a coalition. Since $n = 4$ and $s = 2$ or $s = 3$, the first part of the above expression is simply $\frac{1}{12}$. The term in square brackets is either 1 or 0 depending on whether adding i to S does or does not convert S into a winning coalition.

Shareholder A can score 1 only if he joins B + C; shareholder B can score 1 if he joins D, or A + C or A + D; shareholder C can score 1 if he joins D, or A + D or B + D; and shareholder D can score 1 if he joins B, or C, or A + B, or A + C or B + C. Thus we have finally

$$v(A) = \tfrac{1}{12} \quad (10.4)$$

$$v(B) = \tfrac{3}{12} = \tfrac{1}{4} \quad (10.5)$$

$$v(C) = \tfrac{3}{12} = \tfrac{1}{4} \quad (10.6)$$

$$v(D) = \tfrac{5}{12} \quad (10.7)$$

$$v(N) = 1 \quad (10.8)$$

These numbers can be compared with the shareholdings of A, B, C and D: namely $\tfrac{1}{10}, \tfrac{1}{5}, \tfrac{3}{10}$ and $\tfrac{2}{5}$. Finally, if B held 30 instead of 20 shares, then A could not score at all and we should have $v(i) = (0\, \tfrac{1}{3}\, \tfrac{1}{3}\, \tfrac{1}{3})$.

The calculation of the Shapley value may involve a great deal of arithmetic but methods are available for overcoming this difficulty, and Owen (1982) gives applications to the United Nations Security Council, showing that the bulk of the power lies with the permanent members, and to constitutional amendments, in Canada, showing the relative importance of different provinces and regions.

The Banzhaf–Coleman Index

The Banzhaf–Coleman index, proposed in the late 1960s by Banzhaf (1965) and Coleman (1971), is similar to the Shapley value and is based on an unweighted average of the swings θ_i, for player i, where

$$\theta_i = v(S \cup i) - v(S) \qquad (10.9)$$

and

$$v(i) = \frac{\theta_i}{\sum_{j=1}^{n} \theta_j} \qquad (10.20)$$

If we apply this formula to the shareholder-voting example we obtain the same answer. This is because in that case all the swings had the same weight, which is not usual with the Shapley measure where the size of S usually makes a difference. In the case of the Security Council voting game the index gives the permanent members an advantage by a factor of 10 compared with a factor of 100 in the Shapley value.

Other Solution Concepts

I shall do no more than mention three other solution concepts which can be related to the core, namely to the set of imputations which are not dominated (or to which there is no objection). This set of imputations is in the bargaining set if there is no justified objection to it, i.e. there is no counter objection. Thus the core is included in the bargaining set. Other solution concepts in the core are the kernel, introduced in 1965 by Davis and Maschler, and the nucleolus, a single point in the kernel, introduced in 1969 by Schmeidler.

Thus while we may accept the minimax solution to two-person zero-sum games, in general there are many solutions, depending on which concept is adopted. In this connection Intriligator (1971, 130) makes an interesting point: as the numbers of players approaches infinity the solution tends to an equilibrium point and the various relevant concepts such as the core and the Shapley value converge to this point.

Table 10.4

	1 Bread	2 Cheese	Minimum requirements
Food prices (pence per lb)	$p_1 = 6$	$p_2 = 21$	
1 Calories (thousand)	$a_{11} = 1$	$a_{12} = 2$	$b_1 = 3$
2 Protein (25 grams)	$a_{21} = 1$	$a_{22} = 4$	$b_2 = 4$

Linear Programming and Games

Linear programming and game theory are two different subjects but they are related in a useful way. A linear program and its dual can be converted into a two-person zero-sum game; and a two-person zero-sum game can be converted into a linear program.

I shall illustrate this relationship by means of a very simple example, given by Roy Allen (1956), of a minimum-cost diet which will provide at least given amounts of certain essential nutrients. Suppose there are n foods bought in quantities $x_1 \ldots x_s \ldots x_n$ and m minimum nutrient requirements, $b_1 \ldots b_r \ldots b_m$. The price of a unit of food s is p_s and a unit of food s provides a_{rs} units of nutrient r.

Suppose that in this example $n = m = 2$. The data required are set out in table 10.4.

If we write z for the total cost of food and x_1 and x_2 for the quantities bought, then the problem can be formulated as follows:

minimize

$$z = p_1 x_1 + p_2 x_2 \qquad (10.21)$$

subject to

$$a_{11} x_1 + a_{12} x_2 \geq b_1 \qquad (10.22)$$

$$a_{21} x_1 + a_{22} x_2 \geq b_2 \qquad (10.23)$$

$$x_1 \geq 0 \qquad (10.24)$$

$$x_2 \geq 0 \qquad (10.25)$$

The solution gives $z = 22\frac{1}{2}$ pence, $x_1 = 2$ lb and $x_2 = \frac{1}{2}$ lb.

Questions of this kind give rise to a dual problem in which instead of trying to minimize something we try to maximize something else. Suppose we try to maximize the expenditure on the diet containing the minimum quantities of nutrients so as to get the most varied diet that meets these requirements. Let us write ζ for total expenditure and ξ_1 and ξ_2 for expenditure in pence per unit on the two nutrients. Then the problem becomes:

maximize
$$\zeta = b_1\xi_1 + b_2\xi_2 \qquad (10.26)$$

subject to
$$a_{11}\xi_1 + a_{21}\xi_2 \leq p_1 \qquad (10.27)$$

$$a_{12}\xi_1 + a_{22}\xi_2 \leq p_2 \qquad (10.28)$$

$$\xi_1 \geq 0 \qquad (10.29)$$

$$\xi_2 \geq 0 \qquad (10.30)$$

The solution to this problem gives $\zeta = 22\frac{1}{2}$ pence, $\xi_1 = 1\frac{1}{2}$ pence per unit and $\xi_2 = 4\frac{1}{2}$ pence per unit.

We can put these two problems together and consider a matrix, v say, where

$$v = \begin{bmatrix} 0 & 0 & a_{11} & a_{21} & -p_1 \\ 0 & 0 & a_{12} & a_{22} & -p_1 \\ -a_{11} & -a_{12} & 0 & 0 & b_1 \\ -a_{21} & -a_{22} & 0 & 0 & b_2 \\ p_1 & p_2 & -b_1 & -b_2 & 0 \end{bmatrix} \qquad (10.31)$$

as the payoff matrix of a two-person zero-sum game. Suppose this game is played with the optimal mixed strategy $y = (y_1, y_2, y_3, y_4, y_5)$, the same for each player, with $y_5 \neq 0$. Then $x_1 = y_1/y_5$ and $x_2 = y_2/y_5$ is the solution of the minimum-cost diet problem; and $\xi_1 = y_3/y_5$ and $\xi_2 = y_4/y_5$ is the solution of its dual. If we scale the ys so that they sum to 1 we find that $x_1 = 2$, $x_2 = \frac{1}{2}$, $\xi_1 = 1\frac{1}{2}$, $\xi_2 = 4\frac{1}{2}$ and that $z = \zeta = 22\frac{1}{2}$ as before.

So the solution of the linear program and its dual can be obtained from the solution of a game with the appropriate payoff matrix.

This result depends on $y_5 \neq 0$. If $y_5 = 0$ the game has a solution but the linear program and its dual do not.

It is not difficult to generalize this simple example. In matrix form the payoff matrix of order $n + m + 1$ can be written as

$$v = \begin{bmatrix} 0 & A' & -p \\ -A & 0 & b \\ p' & -b' & 0 \end{bmatrix} \quad (10.32)$$

Thus it can be seen that the methods developed to solve games can be used to solve linear programs and *vice versa*.

Other references which will help to fill out this brief treatment can be found in *Activity Analysis of Production and Allocation*, edited by Tjalling Koopmans (1951) and in *Linear Programming and Economic Analysis* by Dorfman, Samuelson and Solow (1958).

Duopoly and Oligopoly

Duopoly was first studied in 1838 by A. A. Cournot. In his version each seller chooses the quantity he offers so as to maximize his profits but is assumed not to act collusively with the other. In 1883 J. L. F. Bertrand published a critical review of Cournot, proposing a version in which the duopolists choose prices rather than quantities. In 1924 Arthur Bowley introduced the idea of conjectural variation, suggesting that one seller's choice of quantity might be affected by his expectation about his rival's choice. Ten years later H. von Stackelberg (1934) proposed a model in which one seller, the leader, took account of Bowley's conjectural variation, and the other, the follower, responded along a Cournot reaction curve. How all this works out can be seen from a simple example given by Intriligator (1971).

Assume that two producers of an identical product, with outputs q_1 and q_2, have cost functions

$$k_1 = cq_1 + d \quad (10.33)$$

and

$$k_2 = cq_2 + d \quad (10.34)$$

and face an inverse demand curve

$$p = a - bq \quad (10.35)$$

where $q = q_1 + q_2$ and a, b, c and d are positive constants. The profit, or gain, of producer 1 is

$$g_1 = (a - bq)q_1 - cq_1 - d \tag{10.36}$$

and that of producer 2 is

$$g_2 = (a - bq)q_2 - cq_2 - d \tag{10.37}$$

Each producer seeks to choose an output level which will maximize his profit in a static environment, in which case Bowley's conjectural variation does not arise. If g_1 and g_2 are to be maximized with respect to q_1 and q_2, then the first-order conditions for a maximum, namely

$$\frac{\partial g_1}{\partial q_1} = a - 2bq_1 - bq_2 - c = 0 \tag{10.38}$$

and

$$\frac{\partial g_2}{\partial q_2} = a - bq_1 - 2bq_2 - c = 0 \tag{10.39}$$

must be satisfied, giving

$$q_1 = q_2 = \frac{a - c}{3b} \tag{10.40}$$

and

$$p = \frac{a + 2c}{3} \tag{10.41}$$

This is the Cournot equilibrium, often referred to as the Cournot–Nash equilibrium since it can be regarded as the solution to a non-cooperative game.

It is a simple matter to generalize this solution to a larger number of firms. Suppose there are not two but n firms, the typical one being j. Then

$$q_j = \frac{a - c}{(n + 1)b} \tag{10.42}$$

$$q = \frac{n(a - c)}{(n + 1)b} \tag{10.43}$$

and

$$p = \frac{a + nc}{n + 1} \quad (10.44)$$

If, however, there is only one firm, a monopoly, then

$$q_1 = q = \frac{a - c}{2b} \quad (10.45)$$

and

$$p = \frac{a + c}{2} \quad (10.46)$$

At the other extreme, as $n \to \infty$, $q_j \to 0$ and $p \to c$. This is the perfectly competitive equilibrium with individual outputs indefinitely small and price indefinitely close to marginal cost.

At the Cournot equilibrium, the duopolists are not maximizing their joint profits. If they want to do this, and if the law allows it, they must cooperate, produce the monopoly output and sell at the corresponding price. If they share production equally, we shall have

$$q_1 = q_2 = \frac{a - c}{4b} \quad (10.47)$$

and

$$p = \frac{a + c}{2} \quad (10.48)$$

If, however, they are influenced by their expectations about one another's production, then we shall have to add a conjectural variation term $-b(\partial q_2/\partial q_1)$ to the first-order condition for profit maximization by firm 1, and similarly for firm 2. On the assumption that firm 2 makes a Cournot reaction to firm 1, then

$$q_2 = \frac{a - c - bq_1}{2b} \quad (10.49)$$

In this case the conjectural variation is $\partial q_2/\partial q_1 = -\frac{1}{2}$, and if this is taken into account by firm 1, then its reaction curve is

$$q_1 = \frac{2(a - c - bq_2)}{3b} \quad (10.50)$$

This is a Stackelberg reaction curve. In Stackelberg's model of duopoly it is assumed that there is a leader who reacts along this curve and a follower who reacts along a Cournot curve. In this example the equilibrium for the leader, firm 1, would give

$$q_1 = \frac{a-c}{2b} \qquad (10.51)$$

with

$$q_2 = \frac{a-c}{4b} \qquad (10.52)$$

and *vice versa* if firm 2 were the leader.

In Stackelberg's model the order of the moves by the two firms is all important: there can be only one leader. The leader will do better than if they both choose a Cournot curve and the follower will do much worse. But there is another possibility: the firm cast by circumstances in the role of follower might not be aware of it, or might not accept it, and might react along a Stackelberg curve. If it did, each firm would try to produce the monopoly output and the market would be so oversupplied that both firms would do very badly. However, in Intriligator's (1971) example the follower would still do better than if it had reacted along a Cournot curve, and would also have the satisfaction of greatly reducing its rival's profit.

To sum up: the choice of the Stackelberg curve S provides the dominant strategy, but as with the prisoner's dilemma (see below) its inconsistent use by both the duopolists lands them in a much worse position than would the Cournot curve C. So if you are a leader and can use S and at the same time ensure that your rival uses C, do so. If you cannot do this, use C yourself and make sure that your rival does the same. Best of all, enter into a collusive agreement with your rival to share the monopoly output and sell at the monopoly price.

Bargaining

Bargaining is nothing new in economic life and it might be wondered if there is anything to add to accepted ideas. These are based on two postulates reflecting an individual and a joint rationality. A bargainer need not agree to a proposed settlement and a rational

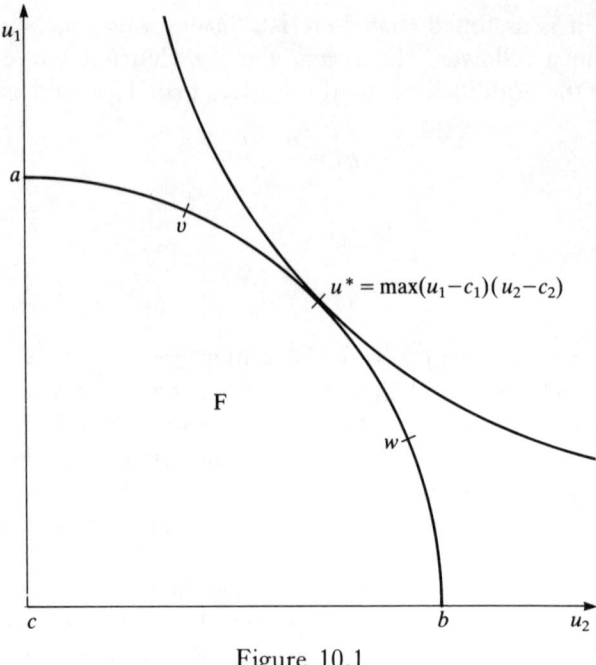

Figure 10.1

bargainer will not do so if it offers him less than his concession limit. If we write u_1 and u_2 for the utility to bargainers 1 and 2 of a proposed settlement, and c_1 and c_2 for the corresponding concession limits expressed in terms of utility, then $u_1 \geq c_1$ and $u_2 \geq c_2$ for all acceptable proposals. Further, the bargainers will not accept the outcome $u = (u_1, u_2)$ if in the set F of feasible bargains there is another outcome (u'_1, u'_2) in which $u'_1 > u_1$ and $u'_2 > u_2$. There is therefore an upper boundary to F between the two concession limits; Edgeworth (1881) termed the points on this boundary 'possible final settlements' and Pigou (1905) termed the whole boundary the 'range of practicable bargains'. The two bargainers will settle for some point on this range, but which one?

This question was answered by John Nash (1950, 1953) by making use of Neumann–Morgenstern cardinal utilities. The Nash solution can be most easily seen from figure 10.1. In the diagram the utilities of bargainers, or players, 1 and 2 are measured respectively along the vertical and the horizontal axes. I have placed the origin of the diagram at the joint concession limit $c = (c_1, c_2)$ since

1 is not prepared to accept anything less than c_1 and 2 is not prepared to accept anything less than c_2. So the set of feasible bargains that need to be considered is given by the area abc, and the range of practicable bargains by the edge ab. The maximum utility to the players is the point at which a rectangular hyperbola drawn between the two axes is tangential to ab. This point, marked u^* in the diagram, is the point on ab at which $(u_1 - c_1)(u_2 - c_2)$ is a maximum.

In 1930 the Danish economist Frederik Zeuthen put forward a bargaining principle which leads to the Nash solution and brings out more clearly the dependence of bargaining on the two players' attitudes to risk. Suppose that 1's last offer is $v = (v_1, v_2)$ and 2's last offer is $w = (w_1, w_2)$, where both v and w are on the boundary ab but $v_1 > w_1$ and $v_2 < w_2$; what should the players do?

If 1 accepts w he will obtain w_1. If he insists on v he will obtain either v_1 or, if 2 does not accept v, his concession limit (or conflict payoff) c_1. If 1 thinks that the probability is p that 2 will refuse to accept v, then 1 can expect to receive $(1-p)v_1 + pc_1$, whereas if he accepts 2's offer he will receive w_1. If 1 is rational he will only stick to his last offer v if

$$(1-p)v_1 + pc_1 \geq w_1 \tag{10.53}$$

i.e. if

$$p \leq \frac{v_1 - w_1}{v_1 - c_1} = r_1 \tag{10.54}$$

say. Similarly, if 2 thinks that the probability is q that 1 will refuse to accept w, then 2 will only stick to w if

$$(1-q)w_2 + qc_2 \geq v_2 \tag{10.55}$$

i.e. if

$$q \leq \frac{w_2 - v_2}{w_2 - c_2} = r_2 \tag{10.56}$$

say. The quantities r_1 and r_2 can be considered to be the highest probability of a conflict that each player would face rather than accept the other player's offer; they are termed risk limits.

Zeuthen thinks that the next concession must always be made by the player with the smaller risk limit, i.e. by the player whose last offer had the higher Nash product $(u_1 - c_1)(u_2 - c_2)$. If the players follow Zeuthen's principle they will tend towards agreement at the Nash solution.

In this section I have confined myself to a brief description of bargaining games without going into details or attempting to give proofs. Anyone wishing to supply these deficiencies should consult Harsanyi (1977, 1982) and Harsanyi and Selten (1987).

Cooperation versus Self-interest

Players may adopt a friendly cooperative attitude to their opponent or a non-cooperative self-centred one. The consequences of adopting these two strategies are brought out clearly in the prisoner's dilemma, a two-person variable-sum game invented by Merrill Flood and Melvin Dresher around 1950 and formalized shortly afterwards by A. W. Tucker.

The set-up is as follows. Two men, caught with stolen goods, are suspected of burglary, but there is not enough evidence to convict them in the absence of a confession. For simplicity I shall assume that, if they both confess, each will be fined £2,000 for burglary; If neither confesses, each will be fined £500 for the possession of stolen goods; if one confesses and the other does not, the one who confesses will get off scot free and the other will be fined £5,000, the heaviest penalty for burglary, on the testimony of the other. This is explained separately to each man.

Thus each man, call them A and B, has two strategies: (a) not to confess, i.e. to cooperate with his partner; (b) to confess, i.e. to play false or defect. In the payoff matrices for the two men (table 10.5), A's strategies are shown in the rows and B's in the columns.

On the face of it the dominant strategy of each man, in ignorance of what his partner will do, is to defect. So each follows his dominant strategy, with the result that they both pay a fine of £2,000.

After they have paid their fines, the two meet at the pub. 'We don't want that to happen again', says A. 'You're quite right', says B, 'we must sign a legally binding agreement to the effect that if either of us confesses on a future occasion he undertakes to give a sum of money, say £4,000, to the dogs' home.' 'But', says A, 'I'm not so fond of dogs that I want to give them all that money every

Table 10.5

	A's payoff			B's payoff	
	B's strategies			B's strategies	
	1	2		1	2
A's strategies	Cooperate	Defect	A's strategies	Cooperate	Defect
1 Cooperate	−500	−5000	1 Cooperate	−500	0
2 Defect	0	−2000	2 Defect	−5000	−2000

Table 10.6

	A's payoff			B's payoff	
	B's strategies			B's strategies	
	1	2		1	2
A's strategies	Cooperate	Defect	A's strategies	Cooperate	Defect
1 Cooperate	−500	−5000	1 Cooperate	−500	−4000
2 Defect	−4000	−6000	2 Defect	−5000	−6000

time we go out together.' 'Don't worry,' says B, 'the dogs will never see a penny from either of us.' He sketches out a new table incorporating the legal agreement (table 10.6).

'So you see,' continues B, 'when we take our binding agreement into account, our dominant strategy is to cooperate and the dogs will never get a penny. Furthermore, the arrangement is highly moral since neither of us is tempted to let down the other for personal advantage.' 'That looks good,' says A.

The only trouble with this idea is that it is hard to see how such an agreement, so clearly against the public interest, could be drawn up in a way that would be legally binding. If this objection is valid, perhaps the best advice to the two men is to read, mark and inwardly digest a good book on the subject such as Robert Axelrod's *The Evolution of Cooperation* (1984). I shall have more to say about this book and its lessons below.

Game Theory in Other Branches of Economics

I have already spoken of the theory in relation to duopoly and bargaining, two topics in which it might be expected to be particularly relevant. But for some years now it has hardly been possible to pick up an economic journal without finding at least one article on games. Indeed the theory seems to have penetrated most fields of economics. In this section I shall give a few more examples to show their diversity.

Keeping Down Costs

Williams (1954) gives a simple example set up as a game against nature. A piece of apparatus depends on the functioning of a certain component which can be bought for $1 but which if defective would involve the firm in an outlay of $10. One strategy for the firm would be to pay its $1 and hope for the best. A second would be to test the component at the cost of another $1, but this procedure will only detect a fault three times out of four. A third would be to employ a sure-fire test which costs virtually nothing but breaks 90 per cent of the sound components. A fourth would be to buy a superior fully guaranteed component for $4. Thus the payoff matrix is as in table 10.7.

By the well-known graphical method, fully described by Williams and many others, it is easy to discover that the only strategies that the firm need consider are 2 and 3 and that their best mix is in the proportions $\frac{4}{5}$ and $\frac{1}{5}$. If for each sound component we weight the cost associated with each strategy by that strategy's relative use, we shall obtain the value of the game to the firm, namely

$$\frac{(4 \times -2) + (1 \times -10)}{5} = -3.6 \qquad (10.57)$$

Thus the firm must expect to spend on average $3.6 per component and in the circumstances of the case cannot reduce this average.

Table 10.7

	Nature's strategies	
Firm's strategies	1 Defective	2 Sound
1 No test	−10	−1
2 $1 test	−4¼	−2
3 Sure-fire test	−1	−10
4 Guarantee	−4	−4

The Allocation of Overhead Costs

A demonstration of how game theory can be applied to the allocation over landing fees of capital costs such as runway and terminal construction in airports is given by Littlechild and Owen (1973). This problem arises in calculating fair landing fees for aircraft of different sizes. The runway costs are mainly dictated by the largest plane that is to land at the airport. The landing fee should be based on the variable cost, which can readily be estimated, plus an apportionment of the capital cost. The authors tried two apportionments, one based on the nucleolus and the other on the Shapley value, for aircraft landing at Birmingham Airport in 1968–9, and by adding each apportionment to the variable cost they calculated two sets of landing fees. Although the fees move in a similar way in the two sets, there are considerable differences between them, particularly for large aircraft, and in both sets the fees calculated for the smallest and the largest types of aircraft are much higher than those actually charged.

The Game of Tariff Wars

John McMillan (1986) gives a comprehensive account of the application of the theory of games to international economics. In the chapters on tariffs he illustrates his analysis with a two-country (A and B) two-commodity (1 and 2) example, but it can be generalized to any number of countries and commodities. His discussion brings out the conflict we have met before between individual and collective rationality. Both countries would be best off under free trade but this is not a Nash equilibrium, which is what countries usually go for. Suppose A's tariff is zero; then B can make itself better off by imposing a tariff on its imports from A; and A can act similarly. Finally they will reach the Nash equilibrium when each country's tariff is optimal with respect to the other's tariff. This will take place with A's tariff equal to the reciprocal of the elasticity of B's demand for A's exports; and with B's tariff equal to the reciprocal of the elasticity of A's demand for B's exports.

Though collectively irrational, the Nash equilibrium is individually rational, so neither country by its own actions can make itself better off by departing from it. However, A and B can both improve their position by agreeing to mutual tariff reductions. It does not follow that in all circumstances both would be better off by reducing all the way to zero.

As there is no international legal system to enforce agreements between countries, tariff policy is essentially a non-cooperative game. Indeed it may be wondered how the General Agreement on Tariffs and Trade (GATT) has been so successful in reducing tariffs after the Second World War. It would appear from Kenneth W. Dam (1970) that GATT's principal weapon is to encourage countries to respond to violations by increasing their own tariffs while at the same time ensuring that in this repeated game the retaliations are not so large as to drive the system back to its static equilibrium.

Trends and Cycles: the Predator–Prey Model

Richard Goodwin presented his paper on a growth cycle to the First World Congress of the Econometric Society in 1965 and it was published in 1967. It is based on the Lotka–Volterra predator–prey model but the principal players are not two types of animal but capitalists and workers opposing one another in a plane with ordinate v (the proportion of the labour force employed) and abscissa u (the workers' share of the product). A point $(\bar{u}, \bar{v})$ in this plane corresponds to the average values of u and v, and the behaviour of the players drives the economy round a limit cycle about this point as boom succeeds slump succeeds boom. The model is extremely ingenious and has given rise to an extensive literature.

One question is whether the cyclical movement is due to the myopic behaviour of the players, which prevents them from realizing the uselessness of fluctuating around $(\bar{u}, \bar{v})$, or whether this movement would take place even if the players behaved rationally. Balducci, Candela and Ricci (1984) answer this question by treating the model as a non-cooperative differential game in which the aim of the players is to reduce the cyclical fluctuations to a minimum. In terms of strategies, the workers can vary the intensity of their demand for higher wages and the capitalists can vary the proportion of profits devoted to investment. It is assumed that the workers do not save. It turns out that the Nash solution implies the maximum increase in the wage rate and the maximum employment rate corresponding to the complete reinvestment of profits. If the players follow optimal Nash strategies the economy will move according to Goodwin's equations, which are thus shown not to reflect myopia on the part of the players but to be consistent with rational behaviour. The authors investigate the application of a leader–follower model to this situation and find that while the centre is changed the cycles remain. I believe that the cycles would be reduced if less extreme, and I think more realistic, assumptions were made about the saving propensities of the players; but that is a different story (Stone, 1984).

Neumann's Growth Model

An extremely interesting book has recently appeared on Neumann's growth model. One of the contributors, Mohammed Dore, has two papers in it (1989a,b) linking the model with game theory. In the first he shows that the model is an interpretation in economic terms of the mathematical result embodied in the minimax theorem, and this leads to a discussion of the bilinearity of prices and quantities and the equality of the interest rate and the growth rate. In the second he gives a numerical example of a multistage variable-sum game played by two firms whose strategies are to invest or not to invest in each of two periods. The optimal strategies and the optimal trajectory are worked out by means of dynamic programming. The results, which include a number of Nash equilibria and Pareto optima, are interesting, if a little mysterious to the simple-minded, and bear out the author's contention that optimality in a dynamic variable-sum game is extremely elusive. The best trajectory, that which provides the largest profit to the two firms combined, arises if both A and B invest at stage 1 and only B invests at stage 2; they do fairly well if neither invests at all; and badly if they both invest at each stage.

International Policy Coordination

It is only in the last few years that game theory has entered the extremely complicated area of international policy coordination. The problems encountered are formidable. In the first place a correct model of the world economy must be constructed. Ideally, in order to do this it is necessary to find out how the various countries or groups of countries view the international scene and what their knowledge is of each other's aims and policies; to decide on the length of the time horizon one wants to consider; and to allow for the effect of uncertainty. Assuming that a 'true' model has been constructed on these lines, it is then possible to work out a choice of strategies.

An attempt to measure the gains from international coordination has been made by Oudiz and Sachs (1984). The authors compare two equilibria: one in which the government of each country pursues optimal policies, taking the policies of other countries as given; and the second in which the governments of the different countries bargain over a coordinated policy package. The first is the outcome of a Nash non-cooperative game and the second of a Nash cooperative bargaining game. The players are the United States, West Germany and Japan, who are assumed to know the 'true' model of the world economy and exactly what actions the others are taking. The authors take the Japanese Economic Planning Agency model and the American Federal Reserve Board's multicountry model as possible true models. This pioneering study leaves many factors out of the picture; nevertheless some gains from cooperation make their appearance, though only on a modest scale. Thus for the three years 1984–6 the gain from cooperation, measured in terms of equivalent gross national product growth and judged by the American model, is 0.17 per cent for the United States, 0.33 per cent for West Germany and 0.99 per cent for Japan. Judged by the Japanese model, however, the gains are smaller.

In a more recent paper Frankel and Rockett (1988) examine the complications that arise if the policy-makers do not agree about the true model. It seems that the gains to a country from finding out how the world really works and adjusting its policy accordingly are likely to be greater than the potential gains from policy coordination. In other words according to these authors what matters is that the model be correct.

In another recent paper Turnovsky, Basar and D'Orey (1988) examine policy coordination in a dynamic setting. Like Oudiz and Sachs, they report small but not unimportant welfare gains, of the order of 6–10 per cent, for cooperation over Nash.

The Use of Experimental Economics to Test Game Theory

Economics is not generally regarded as an experimental science. Unlike the position in astronomy and physics, there has not until recently been collaboration between economists and experimental psychologists which would provide economics with a body of tested behavioural principles applicable to microeconomic behaviour. But in the last 20 years or so things have been changing. Game theory, which is concerned with how a rational player intent on maximizing his gains should behave, is a normative theory and may not tell us much about how people actually do behave. In order to find this out, gamesmen have devised some ingenious experiments, with interesting results. I shall give two examples. Others will be found in Roth (1987) and in Dawes and Thaler (1988).

Sharing the Cake or the Ultimatum Game

The ultimatum game is relevant to bargaining situations, and the results of a number of experiments are described by Thaler (1988).

In the simple one-stage game the position is as follows. The first player, the allocator A, is given a sum of money c and told to offer some of it, x, to the second player B. If B accepts, he receives x and A retains $c - x$; if B refuses, neither receives anything. If A and B were the gain-seeking rationalists that economists like to write about, A would offer B a negligible amount, thus keeping as much as possible for himself, and B would accept this offer because something is better than nothing. Needless to say, people do not behave like this.

The players may have a sense of fairness; even if A's is rather weak, B may be so outraged at being offered a derisory share that he will refuse and so A will get nothing either. In a German experiment reported in 1982 (Güth, Schmittberger and Schwarze, 1982) with 21 pairs of economics students, the modal offer was an even split and the mean offer was $0.37c$. In a replication a week later the mean offer was $0.32c$ and small offers under $0.3c$ tended to be rejected. In a second experiment with 37 new subjects, the players were asked to make offers and indicate the minimum amounts they would accept before playing the game. The mean offer was $0.45c$ and the reservation demand was at least $0.14c$ with a median of $0.36c$. Experiments in Canada and the United States showed a similar concern with fairness.

A two-stage variant of the game, played in England, is reported by Binmore, Shaked and Sutton (1985). It starts as already described, but if the offer is rejected the game goes on to a second stage at which the stake is reduced by a discount factor to $0.25c$; A and B change roles so that B becomes the allocator; and A must accept anything B offers him. It is in A's interest that the game should not proceed to the second stage and so he should offer B at least $0.25c$, since at the second stage B might offer him a derisory sum and keep most of the $0.25c$ for himself.

When the game was first played, the players were not told in advance that there could be a second stage, and the result of stage one was similar to those of the German and American experiments: the modal offer was $0.50c$ and only 10 per cent were in the neighbourhood of $0.25c$. The game was then played again from scratch, with former players B in the role of A. This time the players knew about the second stage, and the result was more in accordance with game theory: the modal offer at stage one was just below $0.25c$. The conclusion was drawn that considerations of fairness 'are easily displaced by calculations of strategic advantage, once players fully appreciate the structure of the game'. There are some unusual features, however, about the way in which this game was presented to the players which would seem to invalidate this conclusion. In any event many other variants of the game and questionnaires relevant to it have been tried and there

The Prisoner's Dilemma

Another game to which the experimental method has been applied is the prisoner's dilemma. This is usually set up in one of three ways: as a single play between a pair of players, as a sequence of plays or as play against a programmed player. In the first form there is no interaction between the players. In the second form it is possible to study their interaction in making successive choices. And in the third form it is possible to see how a player reacts to different strategies played repeatedly; for example, is cooperation (not confessing) typically reciprocated or exploited.

Some of the results of these experiments are not very surprising. For instance, the larger the payoff for reciprocated cooperation or the smaller the payoff the double defection (confessing) the more frequent are cooperative choices, and the smaller the payoff for unreciprocated cooperation the more frequent are defecting choices.

More interesting are the results of repeated play. Averaged over many rounds, the number of cooperative choices at first tends to decrease, due perhaps to lack of success in attempts to establish cooperation. But after a time the proportion of cooperative choices tends to increase, suggesting that the players have come to a tacit agreement. Players tend to agree eventually on both adopting either a cooperative or a defecting strategy.

Play against a programmed player is described in detail by Robert Axelrod (1984). The author organized two computer tournaments in which programs for playing the prisoner's dilemma opposed each other over five sequences of about 200 plays each. The programs were written by economists, mathematicians, political scientists, psychologists and sociologists. In addition there was a program that played at random. Some of the programs were short and simple; others were very long. The tournament was won by the shortest of all, Anatol Rapoport's Tit for Tat, which begins by cooperating and then does whatever the opponent did at his last move. This program is friendly in the sense that it is never the first to defect, a characteristic shared by almost all the other programs at the top of the score. It possesses other desirable features such as being provocable, forgiving and clear.

The fact that Tit for Tat won in this and in a second much larger tournament does not imply that is is necessarily the best of all possible strategies but only that it was the best submitted. The other programmers were worried about the weights of punishment and forgiveness in it: they were inclined to think it was too forgiving. In fact, had any of them been willing to submit the sample program which was sent to them at the outset, Tit for Two Tats, which was even more forgiving, it would have won the tournament; but nobody was.

As things turned out, it was apparent that many of the programs tended to be too competitive, not forgiving enough and too pessimistic about the responsiveness of the other side. Tit for Tat was the most successful in promoting cooperation and brought out the surprising fact that most players were not aware that they were playing against their own mirror image at one remove. Rapoport (1987) suggests that this may account in many cases for the escalation of mutual hostility.

Concluding Remarks

For obvious reasons I have concentrated on game theory in relation to economics; in fact it has spread much wider, to sociology, politics, psychology, biology, statistics and doubtless other fields. But looking only at economics I think it has borne out the hopes of those who received it so enthusiastically nearly 50 years ago.

Although logically rigid and mathematically demanding, game theory seems to me to have played its part in making economics a less dismal science than it once was. Its emphasis on collective and not just individual rationality, though not exactly new, has raised the discussion of what is 'rational' from after dinner conversation to something that serious people can take seriously. Its treatment of cooperation in the prisoner's dilemma deals in different contexts with a problem which turns up everywhere in human affairs. The stimulus it has given to experimental economics has brought to prominence a method which has a lot to offer to the understanding of the physiological aspects of economic behaviour.

It is enlightening to apply some game theory to constructed

examples. It is much harder to apply it to real world problems but some progress is being made even here, as I have tried to show in this paper. It bears out Keynes's contention that it is useless to erect an elegant superstructure on insecure foundations. In my opinion, game theory has done a great deal to alter our view of the foundations of economics.

NOTE

I wish to thank my friend and colleague Partha Dasgupta for several helpful discussions while I was writing this paper and for reading and commenting on my draft. Needless to say, he has no responsibility for any error or confusion that remains.

A LIST OF WORKS CITED

My list is a modest one, so before I give it I shall indicate some sources which provide more extensive references.

Morgenstern (1976), in the paper he wrote in his collaboration with Neumann, mentions a bibliography on game theory prepared in Vienna which goes up to 1970 and contains over 6,200 titles, among them dozens of books in many languages.

The survey by Schotter and Schwödiauer (1980) gives a substantial bibliography and so do some of the books in my list, in particular Axelrod (1984), Binmore and Dasgupta (1986, 1987), Friedman (1986), Maynard Smith (1982) and Owen (1982).

The entries in *The New Palgrave* (Eatwell, Milgate and Newman, 1987) dealing with game theory and with topics such as Nash bargaining and the prisoner's dilemma also provide fairly full references.

My list is as follows.

Allen, R.G.D. (1956): *Mathematical Economics* (London: Macmillan).

Axelrod, Robert (1984): *The Evolution of Cooperation* (New York: Basic Books).

Balducci, R., Candela, G. and Ricci, G. (1984): 'A Generalization of R. Goodwin's Model with Rational Behaviour of Economic Agents', in R.M. Goodwin, M. Krüger and A. Vercelli (eds), *Nonlinear Models of Fluctuating Growth* (Berlin: Springer).

Banzhaf, J.F., III (1965): 'Weighted Voting Doesn't Work: a Mathematical Analysis', *Rutgers Law Review*, 19, 317–43.

Bertrand, Joseph Louis François (1883): 'Review of Cournot's *Recherches sur les principles mathématiques de la théorie des richesses*', *Journal des Savants* (September), 499–508.

Binmore, Ken, and Dasgupta, Partha (eds) (1986): *Economic Organisations as Games* (Oxford: Blackwell).

Binmore, Ken, and Dasgupta, Partha (eds) (1987): *The Economics of Bargaining* (Oxford: Blackwell).

Binmore, Ken, Shaked, Avner and Sutton, John (1985): 'Testing Noncooperative Bargaining Theory: a Preliminary Study', *The American Economic Review*, 75 (5), 1178–80.

Bowley, A.L. (1924): *The Mathematical Groundwork of Economics* (Oxford: Clarendon Press).

Coleman, J.S. (1971): 'Control of Collectivities and the Power of a Collectivity to Act', in B. Lieberman (ed.), *Social Choice* (London: Gordon and Breach).

Cournot, Antoine Augustin (1838): *Recherches sur les principes mathématiques de la théorie des richesses* (Paris: Hachette) (English transl. by N.T. Bacon, New York and London: Macmillan, 1897; reprinted 1927).

Dam, Kenneth W. (1970): *The GATT: Law and International Economic Organization* (Chicago, IL: University of Chicago Press).

Davis, M. and Maschler, M. (1965): 'The Kernel of a Cooperative Game', *Naval Research Logistics Quarterly*, 12, 223–59.

Dawes, Robyn M. and Thaler, Richard H. (1988): 'Cooperation', *Journal of Economic Perspectives*, 2 (3), 187–97.

Dore, Mohammed H.I. (1989a): 'The Legacy of John von Neumann', in M. Dore, S. Chakravarty and R.M. Goodwin (eds), *John von Neumann and Modern Economics* (Oxford: Clarendon Press).

Dore, Mohammed H.I. (1989b): 'Game Theoretic Growth: a Numerical Illustration', in M. Dore, S. Chakravarty and R.M. Goodwin (eds), *John von Neumann and Modern Economics* (Oxford: Clarendon Press).

Dorfman, Robert, Samuelson, Paul A. and Solow, Robert M. (1958): *Linear*

Programming and Economic Analysis (New York: McGraw-Hill).
Eatwell, John, Milgate, Murray and Newman, Peter (eds) (1987): *The New Palgrave* (London: Macmillan).
Edgeworth, F.Y. (1881): *Mathematical Psychics* (London: Kegan Paul).
Frankel, Jeffrey A. and Rockett, Katharine (1988): 'International Macroeconomic Policy Coordination when Policymakers Do Not Agree on the True Model', *American Economic Review*, 78 (3), 318–40.
Friedman, James W. (1986): *Game Theory with Applications to Economics* (Oxford: Oxford University Press).
Gillies, D.B. (1953): 'Some Theorems on n-person Games', Ph. D. Thesis, Department of Mathematics, Princeton University.
Goodwin, Richard M. (1967): 'A growth cycle', in C.H. Feinstein (ed.), *Socialism, Capitalism and Economic Growth* (Cambridge: Cambridge University Press).
Güth, Werner, Schmittberger, Rolf and Schwartze, Bernd (1982): 'An Experimental Analysis of Ultimatum Bargaining', *Journal of Economic Behaviour and Organization*, 3, 367–88.
Harsanyi, John C. (1977): *Rational Behaviour and Bargaining Equilibrium* (Cambridge: Cambridge University Press).
Harsanyi, John C. (1982): 'Solutions for Some Bargaining Games under the Harsanyi–Selten Solution Theory', *Mathematical Social Sciences*, 3, 179–91, 259–79.
Harsanyi, John C. and Selten, Reinhart (1987): *A General Theory of Equilibrium Selection in Games* (Cambridge, MA: MIT Press).
Hurwicz, Leonid (1945): 'The theory of economic behaviour', *American Economic Review*, 35, 909–25.
Intriligator, Michael D. (1971): *Mathematical Optimization and Economic Theory* (Englewood Cliffs, NJ: Prentice Hall).
Koopmans, Tjalling C. (ed.) (1951): *Activity Analysis of Production and Allocation* (New York: Wiley; London: Chapman and Hall).
Kreps, David M. and Wilson, Robert (1982a): 'Sequential Equilibria', *Econometrica*, 50 (4), 863–94.
Kreps, David M. and Wilson, Robert (1982b): 'Reputation and Imperfect Information', *Journal of Economic Theory*, 27, 253–79.
Littlechild, S.C. and Owen, G. (1973): 'A Simple Expression for the Shapley Value in a Special Case', *Management Science*, 20, 370–2.
Marschak, Jacob (1946): 'Neumann's and Morgenstern's New Approach to Static Economics', *Journal of Political Economy*, 54, 97–115.
Maynard Smith, John (1982): *Evolution and the Theory of Games* (Cambridge: Cambridge University Press).
McMillan, John (1986): *Game Theory in International Economics* (Chur: Harwood Academic).
Morgenstern, Oskar (1976): 'The Collaboration between Oskar Morgenstern and John von Neumann on the Theory of Games', *Journal of Economic Literature*, 14 (3), 805–16.

Nash, John F. (1950) 'The Bargaining Problem', *Econometrica*, 18 (2), 155–62.
Nash, John F. (1951): 'Non-Cooperative Games', *Annals of Mathematics*, 54, 286–95.
Nash, John F. (1953): 'Two-person Co-operative Games', *Econometrica*, 21 (1), 128–40.
Neumann, John von, and Morgenstern, Oskar (1947): *Theory of Games and Economic Behavior*, 2nd edn (Princeton, NJ: Princeton University).
Oudiz, Gilles and Sachs, Jeffrey (1984): 'Macroeconomic Policy Coordination among the Industrial Economies', *Brookings Papers on Economic Activity*, 1, 1–75.
Owen, Guillermo (1982): *Game Theory*, 2nd edn (New York: Academic Press).
Pigou, A.C. (1905): *Principles and Methods of Industrial Peace* (London: Macmillan).
Rapoport, Anatol (1987): 'Prisoner's Dilemma', in *The New Palgrave* (London and New York: Macmillan), vol. 3.
Roth, Alvin E. (ed.) (1987): *Laboratory Experimentation in Economics* (Cambridge: Cambridge University Press).
Rubinstein, Ariel (1982): 'Perfect Equilibrium in a Bargaining Model', *Econometrica*, 50 (1), 97–109; reprinted in K. Binmore and P. Dasgupta (eds), *The Economics of Bargaining* (Oxford: Blackwell, 1987).
Schmeidler, David (1969): 'The Nucleolus of a Characteristic Function Game', *Siam Journal of Applied Mathematics*, 17, 1163–70.
Schotter, Andrew, and Schwödiauer, Gerhard (1980): 'Economics and the Theory of Games: a Survey', *Journal of Economic Literature*, 18 (2), 479–527.
Selten, Reinhart (1965): 'Spieltheoretische Behandlung eines Oligopolmodels mit Nachfragetragheit', *Zeitschrift für die gesamte Staatswissenschaft*, 12, 301–24, 667–89.
Selten, Reinhart (1975): 'Re-examination of the Perfectness Concept for Equilibrium Points in Extensive Games', *International Journal of Game Theory*, 4, 25–55.
Shapley, Lloyd S. (1952): 'Notes on the n-person Game. III: Some Variants of the von Neumann–Morgenstern Definition of Solution', *Research Memorandum RM-817*, RAND Corporation, Santa Monica.
Shapley, Lloyd S. (1953): 'A Value for n-person Games', in H.W. Kuhn and A.W. Tucker (eds), *Contributions to the Theory of Games* (Princeton, NJ: Princeton University Press), vol. II.
Stackelberg, Heinrich von (1934): *Marktform und Gleichgewicht* (Vienna and Berlin: Springer).
Stone, Richard (1948): 'The Theory of Games', *Economic Journal*, 58 (230), 185–201.
Stone, Richard (1984): 'Model Design and Simulation', *Economic Modelling*, 1 (1), 3–23.
Thaler, Richard H. (1988): 'The Ultimatum Game', *Journal of Economic Perspectives*, 2 (4), 195–206.
Turnovsky, Stephen J., Basar, Tamer and D'Orey, Vasco (1988): 'Dynamic

Strategic Monetary Policies and Coordination in Interdependent Economies', *American Economic Review*, 39 (3), 341–61.

Williams, J.D. (1954): *The Compleat Strategyst* (New York: McGraw-Hill).

Zeuthen, Frederik (1930): *Problems of Monopoly and Economic Warfare* (London: Routledge and Kegan Paul).

11
Expectations

Frank Hahn

Introduction

A centenary is an occasion for looking where we have got to in relation to our predecessors and this is my assigned task with respect to expectation theory. But what follows is neither a survey nor a complete history. It is a bird's eye map of the past with particular reference to the recent past. Certain aspects are subsequently examined in somewhat greater detail.

One can discern two approaches which have guided work in expectations in recent years. One is favoured by econometricians and especially macroeconometricians. The theory here is rudimentary and highly special. The main concern is to get a model that 'works empirically'. An excellent critical survey is to be found in Pesaran (1987). This line traces its origin to a celebrated paper by Muth (1961). This as well as subsequent developments are based on a number of somewhat implausible *ad hoc* assumptions of which perhaps the most important is that agents know the true structural equilibrium relationships in the economy. I shall refer to these developments largely, I fear, critically because I have not found them interesting or persuasive and also because they appeal to a Friedmanite methodological talisman rather than economic theory with which they seem sometimes to be in conflict.

The other approach has been that of theorists. It has several

Expectations

distinguishing features. For the most part the theories are formulated in a 'states of nature' framework, and due attention is paid to the insurance possibilities provided by an economy and to its information structure. Hardly any of this work deals with 'representative agents', nor is there any role for linearity in economic relations. Thus agents are not generally postulated to be risk neutral. While there is some notable work in partial equilibrium theory, the most solid achievements and insights arise from a general equilibrium framework. It is an approach which I find congenial because it is capable of laying bare the central issues. It is the platform from which I propose to view developments.

In the second part of this chapter, i.e. after 'Retrospect', my discussion is based on a number of principles to which I adhere and which it will be helpful to state at the beginning.

1 Simple models are desirable if they are not inconsistent with the more general theory from which they are derived, if they do not close doors on central issues and if their insights are robust. Their 'predictive' power I regard as secondary (but not of course as unimportant).
2 Axioms should concern fundamentals such as rationality and should not pre-empt further enquiry. For instance market clearing, perfect competition and Pareto efficiency I do not regard as suitable axioms since, if they are so taken, large and central concerns of economics are buried.
3 In particular I am unwilling to leave Adam Smith's celebrated 'invisible hand' in a black box. It is his and his successors' achievement to have shown how the very economical signalling system of prices can indeed be reconciled with an orderly (and sometimes efficient) allocation. But certain conditions must be met. It is a travesty of this branch of theory to proceed 'as if' the economy were centralized in a single agent who knows the economy's feasibility set. This may indeed be a result of proper theorizing in certain circumstances but they are restrictive. When expectations play a role in the model they are downright constricting.
4 When economic theory suggests non-pathological possibilities, e.g. multiple equilibria, great efforts are needed by simple model builders who exclude them not only to 'test for fit' but to explain and to understand why this should be so. Evidence which we cannot understand (e.g. miracles) I am inclined to treat sceptically.

Retrospect

In his *Industrial Fluctuations* (1929) Pigou distinguished between 'real' and 'psychological' components in expectation formation. He wrote:

> In a stationary state, or, more accurately, a state of steady self-repeating movement, real causes of varying expectations could not, by definition exist. Nor, as a matter of fact, though not of logic, could psychological causes exist, because with everything repeating itself regularly, rational beings would be bound to realize that this was happening, and so could not fall into error. In a non-stationary world peopled exclusively by perfectly intelligent persons psychological causes, as defined above, could not exist since they imply error, but there would be nothing to prevent real causes from existing. In the actual world both sorts of causes are present. Moreover they react on one another. (pp. 35–6)

This direct and simple statement has not been bettered in the more recent literature. The last two sentences suggest that, as far as sophistication goes, we have regressed. Keynes of course played a virtuoso tune on their theme:

> Investment based on genuine long term expectations is so difficult today as to be scarcely practicable. He who attempts it must surely lead much more laborious days and run greater risks than he who tries to guess better than the crowd how the crowd will behave; and, given equal intelligence, he may make more disastrous mistakes. (1936, p. 157)

Indeed the whole of chapter 12 of the *General Theory* gives arguments and insights which we have not refuted but ignored.

By 1939 Harrod gave probably the first definition of a (particular) perfect foresight equilibrium: 'The warranted rate of growth is taken to be that rate of growth which, if it occurs, will leave all parties satisfied that they have produced neither more nor less than the right amount' (1939, p. 16). Recall that for Harrod investment was proportional to the expected increase in demand (output). One could therefore paraphrase him as follows: the warranted rate of growth is that rate of growth in expected demand which will lead to actions which will just ensure that demand is equal to supply at each date. Harrod concluded that the warranted growth path was unstable not in the sense that it did not lead to the steady state but in the sense that any departure from it (say due to error) would be magnified and lead to a cumulatively greater error. In this Harrod of course made certain expectational assumptions. From these it emerges that he regarded the warranted path as purely a theoretical reference path.

Hicks (1937) had also paid particular attention to expectations in his study of an economy going from 'week' to 'week'. Although he had important Swedish predecessors this work became the foundation of much subsequent dynamic analysis. Hicks invented the notion of an elasticity of expectations and to its magnitude he attached great significance in the study of stability. It seems clear that he was not here concerned with what Pigou had called the 'real' basis of expectations.

In 1952, reflecting on Harrod's work and on Samuelson's dynamics in his *Foundations*, I attempted a more formal approach to expectations. For the notion of long-run equilibrium I said we must suppose that 'there exists an expectation function such that supply forthcoming at any announced price in any period is exactly taken off the market at that price' (p. 803). I continued:

> As long as the variations in demand are systematic ... it is possible (it should be noted that we do *not* maintain that this actually happens) to learn by experience and thus to evolve a 'rule of thumb' or a mode of routine behaviour which will ensure that the output forthcoming at the planned price was exactly sold.

I thought of long-run equilibrium as a situation in which events did not provide anything new to learn. I then proceeded to study some special cases: Harrod's warranted path, Goodwin's matrix multiplier, tâtonnement stability. I was concerned to show that perfect foresight paths gave rise to 'forward dynamics' and would generally be ill-behaved if the 'backward dynamics' induced by expectations based on past events led to stability. This theme has recently been taken up again (Grandmont, 1986; Marcet and Sargent, 1988; Woodford, 1988; Evans, 1989).

Being mathematically inclined I was greatly impressed by the new rigour making its appearance in America. I regarded it and do regard it as liberating us from generalities and twaddle. But it never occurred to me to take perfect foresight paths as descriptive.

Indeed they seemed so much in contradiction with my historical sense that further formal work on them seemed a waste of time.

Then Muth's famous article (1961) appeared. It was widely read but made little impact. The agent as econometrician was perhaps too novel an idea. The article also seemed rather more addressed to econometricians than to theorists. Indeed subsequent history has shown that econometricians are much more liable to rational expectations fever than are others. Muth's basic idea is well known and its ingenuity exceeds its plausibility. However, Muth did not pretend to know how agents came to know the structural equations describing an economy by means of which knowledge they could all be their own econometricians. In so far as such knowledge is thought of as a consequence of a rationality axiom it seems mistaken. After all, to make an old point, econometricians get paid and the cost of achieving what the Muthian agent is supposed to have achieved is rather high. That leaves 'as if', to which I return again. But it must be admitted that this is not the only economic theory open to such Simonesque objections.

In any case by that time the age of Arrow–Debreu was upon us. The famous model collapsed the (uncertain) future into the present and expectations of market variables ceased to play a role. It seems to me that few people at the time (or perhaps now) understood the true nature of this great intellectual achievement. It was not a description of a market economy but an answer to the old question of what would have to be the case for a decentralized economy responding only to price signals to be capable of the coherence which Adam Smith had hinted at and so many had claimed. It provided a wonderful base camp for expeditions into the world but not a map of the world.

In fact of course macroeconomists whose acquaintance of this model is not always exact or extensive continued to model the economy sequentially. They could see with the naked eye that there was trading and decision making at every date and they were interested in money which could have no being in the Arrow–Debreu world. These economists never lost interest in expectations (see for instance Cagan's important paper (1956)). It would only be a matter of time before they arrived where Pigou had left off and stumbled on Muth.

In 1972 the Lucasian age was ushered in with a brilliant article (Lucas, 1972). It is known that in certain circumstances the equilibrium values of real variables are independent of the money stock. This can also be shown to hold for sequence economies with rational expectation. One assumption, however, as Lucas showed, is that agents can distinguish 'real' from nominal signals. In general, rational expectations prices will depend on both and if agents cannot disentangle them then relative prices and hence real allocations may differ even though the 'real' state is no different. In his model Lucas supposed that agents could not (perfectly) observe the total money stock. It they could, he took it for granted that they would also perfectly predict the price level. If, with some licence, one thinks of the informational deficiency concerning nominal magnitudes as similar to Pigou's 'psychological' component, then Lucas's paper is an important step in formally modelling the interaction of this component with the 'real'.

However, Lucas believed real rational expectations equilibria to be unique, which is not generally the case. Moreover his agents had a belief, held with certainty, that the quantity equation theory of the price level is correct in the sense that a proportional change in the money stock would result in a proportional change in the price level. But there may be other self-fulfilling theories. Nowadays we all know about sunspot rational expectations equilibria which represent the Pigovian 'psychological' component in a pure form. Lucas set the stage for allowing for the interaction of Pigou's two components but he and his followers have been reluctant to perform on it. For the most part there has been a determination to model economies where only the 'real' calls the tune.

There are great difficulties with this. Certainly it is well known that Arrow–Debreu economies can have very many (although, in general, denumerable) real equilibria. The same will *a fortiori* be true of rational expectations sequence economies. It is not easy to see how a theorist can make predictions unless he provides a theory of expectation formation, i.e. a theory of how agents' theories come to be formed. Certainly knowledge on the part of the agent of the 'real' structural equations may be quite insufficient for calculating the 'right' expectations. He would have to know something concerning the expectations of other agents. When insurance markets are not complete even worse problems may arise in an economy with financial assets and only inside money. In that case there is a multi-dimensional continuum of real equilibria (Geanakoplos and Mas-Collell, 1988).

Many of the rational expectations macroeconomists have sought to sidestep these problems by supposing that the (single-good) economy behaves 'as if' a single infinitely lived agent made optimal choices in full knowledge of the real production and consumption possibilities in the economy. It is known that in this case there will, in general, be a unique optimum path to pursue. Since there is only one individual he need not consider expectations of others. The prices that emerge from this exercise are shadow prices which these economists then identify with market prices. I shall return to the matter below. It seems to me, however, that this is not so much sidestepping the problems as turning one's back on them.

However, the line followed in the 'psychological' chapter XII of the *General Theory* also requires great care. Not all such beliefs, although held by all agents, may be capable of being self-fulfilling. For instance, as Tirole (1985) has argued, if it is held that the value of an asset will grow at the rate of interest which itself exceeds the economy's rate of growth, then evidently this cannot be self-fulfilling. In time the value of the asset would exceed the economy's resources. Again sunspots equilibria in overlapping generations models require the 'sunspot-free', i.e. the 'real', economy to have certain characteristics (just as, in Tirole's case, 'bubbles' require the rate of interest to be less than the rate of growth). In contrast, we now know that beliefs concerning others are central in the equilibria of many games and this suggests (no more than that) that a game theoretic formulation of chapter XII may well be possible.

But outside macroeconomics further important advances were being made. Hayek (1937) in a profound paper had argued that the allocation of resources in the textbook manner was not the only role of prices: they also transmitted information. This paper lay relatively unnoticed until Grossman wrote his Ph.D. thesis which led to the paper published in 1976. He considered the question of whether prices constituted a sufficient statistic from which everyone could infer the real situation in so far as it was known to any agent. Radner (1982, summary) then considered more generally the possibility of prices serving to aggregate the information available to different agents. An equilibrium which was identical with that which would obtain if all information were pooled he called a 'full communication equilibrium'. For a finite state space he was able to prove the generic existence of such an equilibrium. It then followed easily that every full communication equilibrium was also a rational expectations equilibrium.

These results were bought at a cost, however. In particular it was supposed that prices imparted their information instantaneously so that they both cleared markets and provided the information which would affect demand and supply simultaneously. This unnatural assumption could also lead to (non-generic) paradoxes. It could happen that, when all agents have the same information, there may be the same equilibrium price vector for two different 'real' situations (states of nature). If then common information of agents depended on being able to deduce real states from prices, the commonality of information would be lost. If, when this is the case, price vectors are uniquely determined by real states, then once again all agents could be equally informed by observing these prices and we are back with common information. So no equilibrium exists. One can escape this and related puzzles by dropping the simultaneity I have mentioned, or by making information of prices 'noisy'. Grossman and Stiglitz (1980), after showing that full communication equilibrium on the stock market implies zero trade, opted for the second.

If equilibrium prices are always one to one with the state of nature (Radner says that then prices are 'non-confounding') it still does not at all follow that any agent in the economy has 'full information' (i.e. the common partition of the set of states of nature may be very coarse). Now suppose that it costs resources to refine the partition. To spend resources in this way requires an agent to benefit by doing so. If the new information, however, is used in changing market behaviour prices will change and reveal the information to everyone else, so possibly making it worthless. In that case no agent will attempt to acquire the finer information. This rather simple and obvious idea is of practical significance. It really is only another aspect of what economists have always known – that information is a public good.

However, in all of this one must take care not to become the captive of the canonical economic model and so miss large chunks of what is likely to be of importance in the world. In the canonical model the production sets are what game theorists call common knowledge. If that were not so, one would not expect prices to reveal technological knowhow (more direct methods like industrial espionage are more appropriate here). The price of Coca-Cola does not reveal its recipe. A price may reveal a technological improvement but not what it is. Patent laws prevent the use of information directly acquired by observation and not indirectly via prices. In other words there is a great deal of information which is not captured by partitions of the set of states of nature and there are a great many signals which are not price signals. In spite of the advances which have occurred in treating information as both endogenous and more embracing, notably by game theorists, these have largely been confined to examples and certainly have not embraced an economy as a whole. But once again beliefs concerning other agents are likely to become very important and the perfect competition world of so much theorizing will almost certainly have to be relegated to the realm of Gedanken Experiment.

In particular it must be hoped that we shall be able to dig more deeply than does, say, the 'efficient market' hypothesis of the stock market. It will be recalled that this maintains that prices there reflect all the information available to traders. The implication is thus that variations in these prices reflect 'innovations', i.e. new information, an implication which must be somewhat in doubt after 1987. But the hypothesis (a) treats information as exogenous and (b) is not very clear what this information is. Moreover it is not easy to reconcile it with Tirole's results which I have already discussed. I return to this matter briefly below.

It is one thing to describe, and even prove, the existence of a rational expectations equilibrium and quite another to give a plausible account of how it came to be. Indeed this is true of much simpler equilibria. The credit belongs to Margaret Bray singly (1983) and in collaboration with Kreps (1984) and Savin (1986) to have looked the question in the face and not to have passed it by. From the start it was clear that learning would affect the information available and in the case of multiple equilibria what the 'truth' was which had to be learned. Bray, and Bray and Savin, considered rather simple cobwebs in which learning was by ordinary least squares. Convergence depended on structural parameters. In the work with Kreps a bounded martingale resulting from Bayesian updating led to convergence given knowledge of the structure of the 'true' model. But the latter was thought of as specified relative to the learning process itself. More recently work by Woodford (1988) and Marcet and Sargent (1988) have made use of a rather powerful theorem to study these matters. Woodford has shown how a statistical learning process on the part of agents in an overlapping generations model can converge on a sunspot equilibrium. Marcet and Sargent study convergence in a more conventional macromodel.

This work has helped to clarify the main issue but no-one would claim that these are settled. The main features (at this stage, I think, unavoidably) are that the economy is perfectly competitive, that all agents learn in the same way from the same signals and that the underlying 'true' model of the economy or market is very simple and known. Implicitly there is also a common knowledge postulate in that every agent knows that other agents are learning in a certain way and behaves rationally in the light of whatever knowledge they have. Without that postulate agents for instance would have to learn the kind of 'mistakes' made by others. But the main obstacle to the whole project is the multiplicity of rational expectations equilibria and, in more complicated settings, the extremely complicated paths that rational expectations equilibria may pursue, including chaotic paths (see the remarks of Kehoe and Levine (1985)). As I have noted already, some of these difficulties can be avoided in a model with infinitely lived agents.

There are of course those who argue that it is unnecessary to have a theory of how rational expectations equilibria come about, just as these same economists would argue that in ordinary models we can treat market clearing as an axiom. This is justified by an appeal to Friedmanite methodology. The implication seems to be that treating rational expectations and rational expectations market clearing as an axiom leads, or can lead, to good predictions. This implication is perhaps not uncontroversial. But even if that were the case, indeed particularly if that were the case, we could not stop where we are being asked to stop. If we did we would be like a biologist who is satisfied with the prediction that, with high probability, members of a species produce members of that same species without being interested in the question of how this comes about. No molecular biology for such philistine predictors! But in any case, as I shall argue below, this methodology is particularly inappropriate here. For we do have a serious theory of equilibrium and this leads us to recognize that it is not capable of predicting. Even when parameters are estimated within the usual margin of error there may be many equilibria and they may be far apart. Samuelson (1947) saw through all this many years ago. He considered that comparative statics (or dynamics) was the only thing in the prediction line that equilibrium analysis was good for. He then added that this always involved further postulates concerning the stability of equilibrium under some adjustment process. Research over the last 40 years has shown that matters are even more complicated.

But it is probably true that in all fields a new insight causes people 'to go over the top', especially if the insight suggests that eminent predecessors were all wrong. If it were not for politicians and bankers taking these enthusiasts at face value, no great harm would result; indeed the resulting disputes would add to the sum total of human happiness. However, one must also beware of the sin of mindless 'common sense'. The idea of a rational expectations equilibrium is a very fruitful one: it allows us to examine, as it were, the laboratory case of an economy in which mistaken expectations play no part. Sunspot equilibria are a good example of a pathology whose origin does not lie in mistaken expectations. Pigou certainly understood the advantage of proceeding in a way which allowed one to distinguish between 'real' and 'psychological' disturbances. Economists can be proud of the progress they have made in this kind of analysis and can perhaps forgive their brethren who have escaped from the laboratory into the 'real' world. But they must continue to maintain rather publicly that while, say, Einstein's theory may turn out to be false (like all theories), the prior probability of this is negligible compared with that which attaches to rational expectations equilibrium macro-theories being false.

Multiple Equilibria and Pareto Efficiency

It is insufficiently appreciated that the very best we can hope for from general equilibrium theory is that generally the number of possible equilibria is countable (Debreu, 1970). That, it will be agreed, leaves a lot of equilibria. As I have already noted several times, when this difficulty is understood by some economists they seek to escape it by the postulate of an infinitely lived agent. Although I have quite recently discussed this matter elsewhere (1989), some points are relevant to the issues under discussion here.

Expectations

It will be useful to make a small detour to the Arrow–Debreu model. It is known that its equilibrium is Pareto efficient. This led Negishi (1960) to propose an ingenious method of proving the existence of an equilibrium (which Arrow and I (1971) imitated). Suppose that there are n agents with utility functions $u^i(x_i)$ where $x_i \in R^l_+$ is the consumption vector of agent i. Let $\alpha_i \geq 0$ ($i = 1, ..., n$) be scalars such that $\Sigma \alpha_i = 1$. Consider the problem

$$\max \Sigma \alpha_i u^i(x_i)$$

subject to '$(x_1 \ldots x_n)$ is feasible given endowments and production sets'. Assume the set of feasible allocations convex and for simplicity assume the maximand strictly concave. It is easy to see that this problem has a unique solution $x_i(\alpha)$, $i = 1, ..., n$, where $\alpha = (\alpha_1 \ldots \alpha_n)$. Moreover it is easy to see that there will have to be a common marginal rate of substitution between goods (common to all agents) which equals the marginal rate of transformation. That is, there will be shadow prices $p_j(\alpha)$, $j = 1, ..., l$ which we can normalize to $\Sigma_{j=1}^l p_j(\alpha) = 1$.

Suppose that $e_i \in R^l_+$ is the endowment of agent i and π_i is his entitlement to the profits of production when $p = p(\alpha) = \{p_1(\alpha) \ldots p_l(\alpha)\}$. Then it may now happen that

$$p(\alpha)x_i(\alpha) \gtreqless p(\alpha)e_i + \pi_i$$

That is, at the shadow prices we would have to redistribute wealth between agents in order that, if shadow prices were market prices, they would just be able to afford the allocation which we want them to have, i.e. $x_i(\alpha)$. Negishi suggested a continuous way of reducing α_i if an agent could afford more than $x_i(\alpha)$ at $p(\alpha)$ and of increasing α_i if he could not afford $x_i(\alpha)$. This led to a straightforward proof that there exists an α^* such that every agent could just afford $x_i(\alpha^*)$ at the prices $p(\alpha^*)$.

This method of proof of existence exemplifies the 'as if' proposition that a competitive economy's equilibrium can be considered as the solution to a social optimization problem. Economic theorists will know that this requires the usual assumptions concerning returns and externalities. We now know that it also requires a 'complete market hypothesis'. But from the viewpoint of this section the important fact is that there is no claim in the Negishi proof that α^* is unique; there may be many equilibrium vectors $p(\alpha^*)$, $x_i(\alpha^*)$.

With this out of the way let us now turn to an economy of infinitely lived agents. Let $x_i(t) \in R_+^l$ be the consumption vector of agent i at t. Let δ be a discount rate and suppose that the economy behaves 'as if' it maximized the Ramsey integral

$$\sum_{i=1}^{n} \alpha_i \int_0^\infty \exp(-\delta t)\, u^i[x_i(t)]\, \mathrm{d}t$$

subject to feasibility and initial endowments. I do not spell out this constraint but take it to be well behaved. Assuming that δ is not too large it can be shown that for every α there will be a unique path of allocations $x_i(t, \alpha)$, $i = 1, \ldots, n$ for $t \geq 0$. Associated with this path there will be a path of shadow prices $p(\alpha, t)$, $t \geq 0$. We can now (with some technical niceties) go through the Negishi argument. In general there will be α^* such that each agent expecting the price path $p(\alpha^*, t)$ can just afford to, and want to, consume $x_i(t, \alpha^*)$ each t. Once again, however, while the solution to the maximum problem is unique for each α, there are in general a number of values of α which mimic the competitive rational expectations equilibrium path.

So infinitely lived agents as such do not result in a unique rational expectations equilibrium. For that we must take the further drastic step, now much favoured by some macroeconomists (see Kydland and Prescott, 1982), of collapsing the economy to a single agent. The only defence for this is that 'it works' and I have already noted why I consider this a pretty poor one.

However, infinitely lived agents in an economy which behaves 'as if' it maximized a weighted Ramsey integral subject to 'real' constraints will be Pareto efficient. Sunspots are out. But something very peculiar has happened. Recall Hayek's claim for the market economy, namely that is prices are carriers of information and indeed that they constitute an informationally efficient mode (i.e. the number of signals to which agents must respond is minimal (Hurwicz, 1973; Mount and Reiter, 1982). But in the Ramsey-like model proposed here agents know the real feasibility set directly (or behave as if they did) – just as an all-seeing central planner would know, and which Hayek claimed not to be possible. In going directly from shadow to market prices the whole Hayekian argument has been short-circuited and put beyond discussion. Indeed the economy is Pareto efficient and sunspot-free for no other reason than that it has been assumed to be so from the start.

These are some of the reasons why I do not believe the infinite agent approach to be one that recommends itself to a serious economist. There are others which I can only mention.

It will be recalled that I stipulated that 'δ should not be too large'. Suppose δ were very large. Then agents would only be interested in the more or less immediate future. The Ramsey model would come to share some of the features of the overlapping generations model. Indeed Boldrin and Montruchio (1986) have shown that by choosing δ of various magnitudes the solution path to the Ramsey problem can take on weird and wonderful forms including amongst these cycles and, for some utility functions, chaos. The estimate of δ and u^i from empirical data has indeed been attempted. But I think it must be agreed that the outcome hardly carries (nor indeed could carry) the conviction which would be required by a Friedmanite methodology.

But matters, as Matsuyama (1989) has shown, are even worse. If, as seems proper, one studies a monetary economy and if money demand is modelled by inserting real balances in the utility function which is not separable in the good and real balances, then there may be multiple steady states and chaotic optimum paths for low discount rates. So, going to the extreme, Ramsey modelling certainly has not yielded the desired theoretical payoff and one would be surprised to find that data rule out the manifold possibilities.

It should now also be noticed that, if by a judicious choice of parameters and structural form the Ramsey approach does yield a unique steady state equilibrium, it will not suffice to have anything less than rational expectations over the infinite future. Indeed the solution, i.e. the path of the economy, must satisfy a 'transversality condition' which is a restriction on the path $p(t, \alpha)$ and $x_i(t, \alpha)$ as $t \to \infty$. While of some interest as a laboratory experiment such a requirement can hardly be taken as empirically interesting.

Even now we have not exhausted the serious problems because we have not included any stochastic elements in the story. It must by now be very widely understood that unless there are sufficient insurance (contingent) markets the resulting rational expectations equilibrium will not generally be Pareto efficient. Indeed as Geanakoplos and Polemarchakis (1986) amongst others have shown, it will not even be constrained Pareto efficient. I have also already noted earlier that in some circumstances the equilibrium set may form a high-dimensional manifold. All of this means that we should not proceed 'as if' the economy were guided by a Ramsey social-welfare function being maximized subject to usual constraints if there are missing markets. It is one of the characteristics of the macroeconomics enthusiasts that the question of the number of markets is never discussed – perhaps because all agents are supposed to be risk neutral. It is of course an open, and important, empirical question and an important theoretical question how to account for 'closed' markets and how complete actual market systems are. But it would be surprising if markets were found not to be seriously incomplete, e.g. in the contingent market for labour services for which labour contracts which respect bankruptcy constraints are not a perfect substitute.

From all this I conclude as follows. Typically traditional equilibrium theory, especially in a stochastic world, allows there to be many equilibria with rational expectations. It is only when markets are 'complete' (e.g. in an overlapping generations model if all generations which will ever be born can trade with each other – see Burnell (1989)) that all these equilibria are necessarily Pareto efficient and so exclude Pigou's 'psychological' equilibria. Completeness of markets in actual economies seems highly doubtful. Hence sunspot equilibria or equilibria related to Keynes's chapter XII are perfectly possible. This in turn means that equilibrium rational expectations theories are likely to require more attention to processes before they can be predictive. It is also likely that these theories leave vast scope for government intervention in the market.

I do not regard these conclusions as 'negative'. Indeed they seem to me to illustrate the power of economic analysis to produce deep insights. In the first instance, the multiplicity of equilibria resulting from 'real' expectations which are correct shows why, even in models giving full scope to economic rationality, we need not be committed to historial determinism: the world could have been other than it is. The explanation of why it is what it is will have to take account of the path which it has taken and will have to combine that with a theory of learning and adaptation. Furthermore, the possibility of 'psychological' or mixed psychological and real equilibria teaches us that man, and in this case his beliefs, is the proper measure of things. We make theories about the world and see it only distantly and partially. The possibility of self-verifying theories is much larger than that which can be deduced from an economy's 'real' feasibility set.

On Transversality and Discounting

I have already several times referred to transversality conditions and to their importance for both much current theorizing and macroeconometrics. I now want very briefly to elaborate on these remarks.

In the fictional Ramsey world of a single agent and single good let $q_t = \exp(-\delta t) p_t$, where p_t is the shadow price of the good at t and δ is the discount rate. A transversality condition is $\lim_{t \to \infty} q_t x(t) = 0$. That is, the present shadow value of future quantities of the good goes to zero as $t \to \infty$. A condition of this sort is often appealed to, as indeed it must be if one claims to have a solution to the Ramsey problem. It then serves to rule out 'explosive' or 'implosive' rational expectations paths. It also serves in calculating rational expectations paths recursively since it guarantees that expected values far enough into the future must become negligible in determining current values.

Now there are certain obvious difficulties. If the discount rate is low enough one sees intuitively that a Ramsey maximizer would arbitrage away any candidate path which fluctuated. Conversely low discount rates put transversality at risk. High discount rates as already noted may have a great variety of optimum paths. It is known that there are well-formulated Ramsey problems without solution, e.g. when there is no discounting. This is so even on 'the overtaking criterion'. It follows from all this that if one wanted to follow the Ramsey 'as if' path to forecasting one would need to be able to give a rather good empirical account of the 'as if' discount rate. This is rarely attempted.

For a long time rational expectations macro-theorists assumed either explicitly or implicitly that the fictional Ramsey problem yields a saddlepoint solution in phase space and so of course a unique path from any initial conditions. Not even Marx embraced so thorough-going historical determinism as do these economists when they suppose that the Ramsey path is also the actual one. Recently, Ramsey cycles have been studied by adding stochastic elements and lags (Kydland and Prescott, 1982). Certainly this is an improvement on the clockwork world modelled hitherto. But the appropriate infinite foresight together with transversality is still needed.

Some Further Implications

It will be obvious that, if the solution to the Ramsey problem represents the way that the world is, then government policy can only affect the path of the economy by changing the 'real' opportunities. Monetary policy, if it is known, cannot it seems affect the real path since adding it to the description of the problem can do no more than change the level of shadow prices but not their relation to each other. However, this conclusion depends on what we mean by monetary policy and how we graft money onto the Ramsey model.

Two routes have been explored: one puts real cash balances in the utility function while another employs the 'Clower constraint'. In either case we obtain a new unknown, namely the optimum path of real cash balances. Now, if indeed the world is mimicked by this more elaborate Ramsey problem, then one must assume that somehow the invisible hand ensures the optimum real cash balances. There is no occasion for policy, monetary or indeed any other. But as Wallace (1988) has noted there are legal restrictions on the issue of money and these, when taken into account as a constraint, may lead to suboptimality. It is well known that the monetary policy advocated here is the payment of interest on money – in steady state, the interest rate is equal to the discount rate. If that policy is included under the heading of 'monetary policy' then it will have 'real effects' since it affects 'real' intertemporal opportunities.

The famous 'Lucas critique' also emerges painlessly from this formulation of an economy. The relations amongst shadow prices at different dates reflect real transformation opportunities since that is what he means by saying that the economy is in rational expectations equilibrium. These transformation opportunities may depend on government policy, and therefore action, at various dates. Hence it follows rather easily that the path of an economy must in such cases depend on policy and therefore cannot be modelled as depending, in a given way, on variables which do not include that policy. This point apparently came as something of a revelation to econometricians. Others were less surprised. It was for instance a commonplace of discussions in the 1950s that if the government committed itself to a given unemployment rate such a commitment would shift the Phillips curve.

The 'Lucas critique' when full blown hangs on 'Ramseyfication' and so is at risk if no solution exists or if, say, the solution is chaotic. But the critique is surely much more generally valid. Indeed it is hard to think of examples of such an economy in which actions of agents depend on the future in which these actions could be taken to be independent of government policy and still be rational. However, this line of thought should not be confused with the earlier 'ineffectiveness proposition'. For instance the 'Lucas critique' applies fully to overlapping generations models but in these models monetary policy, fully foreseen, can be effective by redistribution between the young and the old and a consequent change in the equilibrium path of the economy.

As I have remarked earlier it is quite unclear how a world which behaves 'as if' guided by a Ramsey maximizer has any need for government policy in the usual sense. Indeed something of the same sort can be asked about the actions of agents. Ramsey agents take a decision only once, at the 'beginning'. That decision yields an optimum policy which makes actions at any date a predetermined function of the state of nature. (Recall that prices are assumed to be uniquely determined by the state of nature.) This policy could be put on a computer and in any case specifies routinized behaviour. Firms would have no further need of highly paid executives and no-one need decide anything ever again. Programmed trading on the stock exchange is an example. But it is not easy to think of other cases. It would be very interesting to have some evidence about whether, for instance, boards of directors etc. when claiming to be decision makers are in fact implementing a policy (implicitly) decided upon in the distant past.

The Efficient Market Hypothesis

Rational expectation modelling seems particularly appropriate to stock markets. These markets have many expert traders and information is almost continuously available. The efficient market hypothesis simply says that traders use all the information they have in forming expectations and that therefore prices reflect that information. By itself that seems pretty innocuous. But it has been quickly translated into the proposition that the current price of a share is equal to the information-conditioned present value of expected dividends over the infinite future – a proposition that, as we have already seen, Keynes regarded as false.

Evidently more is involved than prices reflecting all available information. One must suppose that a rational expectations equilibrium over the infinite future is supposed to characterize asset markets. For the argument must go something like this. Given zero transaction costs, an investor need only consider the dividend and price of the asset next period. But if he is right about this price then it again must reflect the dividend and asset price in the period after next. And so on. If time does not have a stop then in the far enough future the present value of the asset price becomes small enough to be ignored. Hence successive substitution yields the desired result. It is not surprising that Keynes, if he ever considered this argument, should have rather decisively rejected it. He knew that the world was not like this and the sophistry of 'as if' had not yet become fashionable.

The crash of 1987 as well as various econometric investigations make the 'as if' approach here particularly open to doubt. But there seems no agreement amongst the empirical investigators and in any case I would find the theory unacceptable even if there were solid empirical support for the prediction.

One may now ask: what is the prediction? It is that asset prices should perform a random walk since the only information which cannot be learned is white noise. It is also believed that the variance of asset prices should be small unless there is new systematic information.

The first thing to do is to get the theory right on its own terms. Asset holders are not sensibly modelled as risk neutral (see, for example, Lucas, 1978). The proper arbitrage condition at each instance of time equalizes (for those holding an asset if no short sales are possible) the utility price of the asset with the expected marginal utility of its return. Small changes in the state of the world (subsumed under noise) may have large utility effects and they may also have large effects on the composition of active investors. In addition states of nature may be serially correlated as they are in sunspots (Azariadis and Guesnerie, 1986). Both these considerations suggest that low variance is not a safe prediction. To this must now be added the results of Tirole's work that I have already cited which do not rule out bubbles.

One now adds to all this the rather obvious observation that information between investors will differ and that it will not, as we have seen, on a sensible view be aggregated by prices. Hence the expected dividend streams will differ over agents. I cannot refrain here from noting that the exclusive concern with time series data has apparently prevented an attempt at a direct enquiry on this point. There is a massive opportunity for such an enquiry by proper survey methods.

It should now be noticed that if the efficient market hypothesis, as it is often stated, were correct, then Keynes's description of expectation formation is as good as – indeed better – than any other. This is because the forecast of the price expected by other agents will turn out to be a forecast of the stream of dividends. But one expert suffices. The rest need only go with the herd and turn out to be right. But of course Keynes was at pains to deny the basic premiss.

Once again one inclines to the view that Pigou was close to a sensible theory. Keynes was surely exaggerating when he gave the impression that 'real' factors played no role whatsoever, i.e. that the market was a pure sunspot. However, the hubris induced by bits of formal modelling has led our contemporaries to the opposite extreme in which they deny any psychological component. I suspect that is due more to the difficulty of modelling the latter with the precision which we have come to expect than to an obtuse refusal to consider the world. After all we all know, to take just one example, that chartists make a good living.

But I do not believe that one need despair of capturing what is needed in a formal manner. Quite evidently expectations are not formed for the infinite future. Computation is hard and costly. In such circumstances one looks for summary information – as indeed do economists in their usual course of business. Knowing something about the price expectations of others would always be useful. There are very many ways in asset markets in which such knowledge is transmitted and it is not just through prices. In most asset markets traders are in close personal contact and they are served by specialized journals and information. The propagation of expectations may well be found to be suitably modelled by a model of the propagation of infectious diseases. It would be not too hard to produce an 'as if' theory on these lines which might have considerable empirical success.

But it would be a mistake since 'real' factors also surely matter. Some of these, however, do not simply refer to facts but to theories of facts. We know that rational expectation macroeconomists believe that agents know the true structural model of the economy. Of course they do not, for the simple reason that no-one does. They may know the model of these macroeconometricians and they may hold the theory that these models are true. I would be inclined to argue that expectations (whether they turn out to be rational or not) on this basis should be firmly classified as 'psychological'. These models may indeed by the ultimate bootstrap.

In general, agents have theories concerning the real world and these theories change only slowly, if for no other reason than that counterfactual evidence is hard to recognize as such in something as complex as an economy. However, they do change (Mrs Thatcher has successfully changed them), and that will be reflected in the behaviour of the asset markets.

All of this leads to a modest suggestion. Let us agree that agents do not peer into the distant future and that, in their asset-holding decisions, they pay a good deal of attention to the expected price. Their information space is complex but certainly includes what they know of the beliefs of others. These, if nothing else, will affect the uncertainty which they attach to the investment. Let us further agree that, for a proportion of the market participants, the error in expectations is larger than could be explained by white noise. But we shall note that this error is in some sense expected by the participants – they know that they are not generally in rational expectations equilibrium. We now think of a much looser equilibrium than is usual, i.e. one in which the fraction of erroneous investment does not vary much. Such an equilibrium may be disrupted not only by new information but by a change in theories held by agents, e.g. when they become persuaded that Keynesian policies can only do harm. We then have to formulate much harder theories of learning and contagion.

The modest suggestion is hardly a theory and certainly not a precise proposal. But I believe that something of this sort should be thought about not by practical financiers (we only want to observe them) but by 'high' theorists.

Expectations and 'Ad Hockery'

Earlier economists used themselves and the experience of talking to others as some guide to sensible expectational postulates. This is not time series evidence nor does the procedure lead to axiomatics. It is frequently said to be *ad hoc* and therefore bad. Econometricians in particular feel that this way of building models places insufficient restrictions on estimation. Added to this is a further argument: the common postulate that agents are rational should not suddenly be abandoned when it comes to expectations. A rational agent will not persist in beliefs which are being systematically disappointed. Equilibrium economics in a stochastically stable environment thus entails not only that agents have been learning but that they have learned.

One must ask whether the rational expectations hypothesis and rational expectations equilibrium are somehow logically entailed by an axiom of rationality.

The hypothesis that rationality implies that the agent in forming his expectations uses all the relevant information which he has seems persuasive. It certainly is convenient. But it is not likely to be a true implication if there are costs (real and psychic) of keeping track of and organizing all the information one has available. This is really connected with the fact that information is likely to be endogenous. I may have ready access to information (in my papers, libraries, newspapers etc.) but not use it. The hypothesis then becomes rather weak: a rational agent will form his expectations on the basis of that part of his information which he chooses to use and that I suppose *is* deducible from rationality. If the hypothesis is strengthened then it is no longer a logical implication of rationality.

Evidently similar problems arise in other branches of economic theory and I am pretty clear that certainly in the first instance we should ignore them. My point is that when we do so we have in mind pragmatic reasons such as ease of analysis and sharpness of results. These considerations lead to *ad hoc* procedures.

When it comes to equilibrium, as I have already argued, matters are more difficult. The clearing of markets is not an axiom nor indeed derivable from rationality except possibly in a continuum exchange economy. We have no satisfactory theory of price formation and if we had it might be rational not to set market-clearing prices. (Think of a search model over a number of periods.) But more serious is the incompleteness of equilibrium analysis when there is a mutliplicity of equilibria. To pick one rather than another requires us to study processes which at the moment are bound to be *ad hoc*. I have difficulties in believing that, for instance, Bayesian learning is an implication of rationality. After all at the foundations are axioms like a *complete* pre-ordering by a belief relation which is not obviously an element in a concept of rationality.

Thus quite properly it seems that all our theories contain '*ad hockery*' for reasons of manageability, ignorance and observations that we use in their construction. There seems to be only one implication of rationality which every theory of expectations should satisfy and that is the requirement that agents should not persist in beliefs which are being systematically falsified by events. If that is agreed than indeed it is true (as I argued in 1952) that only states of the economy in which this does not happen can qualify as *long-run* equilibria. In that sense rational expectations equilibria are really the only candidates for the long run. Whether actual economies are ever in long-run equilibrium is of course another question.

It may now be objected that I have taken various theorists and econometricians to task for *ad hockery* when I am now concluding that in some sense it is necessary if one is to get anywhere. My answer is that there are simplifications and *ad hockery* which close doors and others which do not. The single Ramsey agent takes us away from our main concern: the coordination of a decentralized economy. It commits us to a quite unacceptable historical determinism. It requires the infinite future to play a part in the present and is not in the least robust to modification on this score. The attention given to linear models is perhaps less objectionable and it is certainly understandable. The danger here is forgetfulness: risk neutrality is a strong piece of *ad hockery* and one should not forget that one has made it when reaching for the computer. Samuelson's pure consumption loan model (1958) was simple and *ad hoc*. It has proved possible to use it to derive a truly remarkable number of insights especially concerning expectational equilibria.

It opened (and did not close) doors. It takes a great economist to hit on fruitful simplifications.

A Remark Concerning Stability

Consider a typical perfect foresight model whose laws of motion are

$$x_t = f(x_{t+1})$$

Here x_{t+1} appears on the right-hand side instead of x^e_{t+1} (the expected value) because one assumes that $x^e_{t+1} = x_{t+1}$ for all t. Suppose that $\bar{x}$ satisfies

$$\bar{x} = f(\bar{x})$$

so that we can call $\bar{x}$ the steady state value of x. Then if x is actually in a small neighbourhood of $\bar{x}$ we obtain the perfect foresight path

$$f'(\bar{x})^{-1} \Delta x_t = \Delta x_{t+1}$$

where $\Delta x_t = x_t - \bar{x}$. If $|f'(\bar{x})| < 1$ this path diverges from the steady state.

Now consider a model in which expectations depend on the past and are not necessarily correct. For instance we may adopt the *ad hoc* expectation function

$$x^e_{t+1} = e(x_{t-1}) \text{ with } e(\bar{x}) = \bar{x}$$

Our model now gives rise to the path

$$x_t = f\{e(x_{t-1})\}$$

Proceeding as before we find that, if $|e_x| \leq 1$, this path converges to $\bar{x}$ whenever the perfect foresight path diverges and *vice versa*.

Of course this is schoolroom stuff. But it provides two lessons. One is that mistakes may be stabilizing and the other is that, when they are, they eventually disappear. Now it so happens that in a number of leading models the perfect foresight path starting in the vicinity of the steady state diverges. For instance this is true in overlapping generations models with a single asset. Recently, as I have already noted, a number of very interesting studies of stability of steady states when there is learning have been undertaken

(Grandmont, 1988; Marcet and Sargent, 1988; Woodford, 1988; Evans, 1989). In Woodford's case the 'learning path' converges to a sunspot equilibrium. The pioneer here was Bray (1983). With the exception of Grandmont and Bray the learning agents are assumed to know a good deal concerning the structural characteristics of the economy. But there can be little doubt that these economists are pursuing the right lines.

The trouble with perfect foresight or rational expectations paths which are not steady states is that they are often badly behaved. Kehoe and Levine (1985) show in a many-good overlapping generations model that there is a set of divergent such paths and sensibly note that it is hard to reconcile them with the hypothesis that expectations are correct. This of course applies particularly to chaotic paths. In other words we need to exclude such paths by some means and rational expectations theory gives us no guidance on how to do that. Learning paths, especially routine learning paths, allow greater theoretical freedom but it must be admitted that this is partly due to our not having a generally accepted learning theory.

One of the difficulties here is that different agents may learn differently. At the moment this creates considerable difficulties especially if one keeps in mind the feedback from learning to what there is to be learned. We really need a statistical theory of the economy in which we start with a distribution of characteristics including learning characteristics. This may or may not turn out to be possible but it is worth a try, especially if the opportunity cost of research offer is some representative agent model.

It is of course not at all obvious that actual economies are ever in any sort of steady state equilibrium. For instance Kaldor's arguments (1972), which had less impact than they would have had if they had been more precisely formulated, are nonetheless persuasive. To twist our intellectual concerns to establish convergence to steady state may turn out to be a mistake both theoretically and empirically. The alternative is to study paths in which some sort of learning continues for ever. This will be much harder but not self-evidently impossible.

There are of course now Ramseyesque 'real business cycle' theories. The rational expectation paths here cycle but are by construction 'optimal'. I have not been able to make any sense of this approach and I am rather in the same position as Voltaire, for instance, with regard to miracles when it comes to empirical evidence in its favour.

There remains an important point. Learning generates information. Equilibria must be thought of in relation to the information structure and will depend on it. Hence equilibrium whether steady state or not will in general not be independent of the learning process. Early work by Rothschild (1974) has now been followed by others, e.g. Arthur (1989) and Hahn (1989). It is early days but I for one will consider it a very large forward step indeed if we begin to understand much more thoroughly that where we are is in large measure to be explained by how we got here. The project of a history-free economics does not seem a serious one. It is interesting to note that our role model, physics, seems to have come to a similar conclusion concerning the physical universe.

A Conclusion

There is no doubt that much has been learned since Pigou wrote in 1929. We have a much tighter and comprehensible way of formulating the problems. Its chief virtue to me is that is shows us where to look next and not that it has 'delivered'. Its vice is that is provides a kind of machine whose handles are easy to turn and therefore stops more serious thinking and work. It is also true that older economists were much more conscious of the fact that price signals are only a subset, and often not the most important one, in the set of signals that agents act on in forming beliefs. For instance most took it as obvious that quantity signals also played a part. The postulate of perfect competition has made it very difficult to get to grips with the mechanism of price changes (Arrow, 1959) and has led to a black box market-clearing theory. My main conclusion is this. Much good and sometimes beautiful work has been done, some of which is likely to have been misdirected. What we need now is an end to the timidity which prevents us grappling with the important complexities which we know to be 'out there'. Perhaps it would help if the Swedish Academy confirmed that the taking of intellectual risks is a dominant characteristic of Nobel prize winners.

REFERENCES

Arrow, K.J. (1959): 'Towards a Theory of Price Adjustment', in M. Abramovitz et al. (eds), *The Allocation of Economic Resources* (Stanford, CA: Stanford University Press), pp. 41–51.

Arrow, K.J. and Hahn, F.H. (1971): *General Competitive Analysis* (San Francisco, CA: Holden Day).

Arthur, W.B. (1989): 'Competing Technologies, Increasing Returns and Lock-in by Historical Events', *Economic Journal*, 99 (394), 116–31.

Azariadis, C. and Guesnerie, R. (1986): 'Sunspots and Cycles', *Review of Economic Studies*, 53 (5), 176, 725–38.

Boldrin, M. and Montruchio, L. (1986): 'On the Indeterminacy of Capital Accumulation Paths', *Journal of Economic Theory*, 40, 26–39.

Bray, M.M. (1983): 'Convergence to Rational Expectation Equilibrium', in R. Friedman and E.S. Phelps (eds), *Individual Forecasting and Aggregate Outcomes* (Cambridge: Cambridge University Press).

Bray, M.M. and Kreps, D.M. (1984): 'Rational Learning and Rational Expectations', *Research Paper 616*, Graduate School of Business, Stanford, CA.

Bray, M.M. and Savin, N.E. (1986): 'Rational Expectations Equilibria, Learning and Model Specification', *Econometrica*, 54, 1129–60.

Burnell, S. (1989): 'Sunspots and Rationality', Ph.D. Thesis, Cambridge University.

Cagan, P. (1956): 'The Monetary Dynamics of Hyperinflation', in M. Friedman (ed.), *Studies in the Quantity Theory of Money* (Chicago, IL: University of Chicago Press).

Debreu, G. (1970): 'Economies with a Finite Set of Equilibria', *Econometrica*, 38, 387–92.

Evans, G.W. (1989): 'The Fragility of Sunspots and Bubbles', *Journal of Monetary Economics*, 23, 297–317.

Geanakoplos, J.D. and Mas-Collell, A. (1988): 'Real Indeterminacy with Financial Assets', *Journal of Economic Theory*, 47, 22–38.

Geanakoplos, J.D. and Polemarchakis, H.M. (1986): 'Walrasian Indeterminacy and Keynesian Macroeconomics', *Review of Economic Studies*, 53, 755–79.

Grandmont, J.M. (1986): 'Local Bifurcations and Stationary Sunspots', *Technical Report 513*, IMSSS, Stanford, CA.

Grossman, S.J. (1976): 'On the Efficiency of Competitive Stock Markets where Traders have Diverse Information', *Journal of Finance*, 31, 573–85.

Grossman, S.J. and Stiglitz, J.E. (1980): 'On the Impossibility of Informationally Efficient Markets', *American Economic Reveiw*, 70, 393–408.

Hahn, F.H. (1952): 'Expectations and Equilibrium', *Economic Journal*, 62 (248), 802–19.

Hahn, F.H. (1989): 'Equilibrium and Dynamics', in F.H. Hahn, *The Economics of Missing Markets, Information and Games* (Oxford: Oxford University Press).

Harrod, R.F. (1939): 'An Essay in Dynamic Theory', *Economic Journal*, 49, 14–33.
Hayek, F.A. (1937): 'Economics and Knowledge', *Economica, New Series*, 4, 33–54.
Hicks, J.R. (1937): *Value and Capital* (Oxford: Clarendon Press).
Hurwicz, L. (1973): 'The Design of Mechanisms for Resource Allocations', *American Economic Review*, 63, 1–30.
Kaldor, N. (1972): 'The Irrelevance of Equilibrium Economics', *Economic Journal*, 82 (328), 1237–55.
Kehoe, T.J. and Levine, D.K. (1985): 'Comparative Statics and Perfect Foresight in Infinite Horizon Economies', *Econometrica*, 53 (2), 433–54.
Keynes, J.M. (1936): *The General Theory of Employment, Interest and Money* (London: Macmillan).
Kydland, F. and Prescott, E.C. (1982): 'Time to Build and Aggregate Fluctuations', *Econometrica*, 50 (6), 1345–70.
Lucas, R.E. (1972): 'Expectations and the Neutrality of Money', *Journal of Economic Theory*, 4, 103–24.
Lucas, R.E. (1978): 'Asset Prices in an Exchange Economy', *Econometrica*, 46, 1426–45.
Marcet, A. and Sargent, T.J. (1988): 'Convergence of Least Square Learning Mechanisms in Self-referential Linear Stochastic Models', Mimeo, Hoover Institute, Stanford, CA.
Matsuyama, K. (1989): 'Endogenous Price Fluctuations in an Optimizing Model of a Monetary Economy', *Northwestern University Discussion Paper 825*.
Mount, K. and Reiter, S. (1982): 'The Informational Size of Message Spaces', *Journal of Economic Theory*, 8, 161–91.
Muth, J.F. (1961): 'Rational Expectations and the Theory of Price Movements', *Econometrica*, 29, 315–35.
Negishi, T. (1960): 'Welfare Economics and Existence of an Equilibrium for a Competitive Economy', *Metroeconomica*, 12, 92–7.
Pesaran, M.H. (1987): *The Limits to Rational Expectations* (Oxford: Blackwell).
Pigou, A.C. (1929): *Industrial Fluctuations* (London: Macmillan).
Radner, R. (1982): 'Equilibrium under Uncertainty', in K.J. Arrow and M.D. Intriligator (eds), *Handbook of Mathematical Economics* (Amsterdam: North-Holland), vol. 2.
Rothschild, M. (1974): 'A Two-armed Bandit Theory of Market Pricing', *Journal of Economic Theory*, 9, 185–202.
Samuelson, P.A. (1947): *Foundations of Economic Analysis* (Cambridge, MA: Harvard University Press).
Samuelson, P.A. (1958): 'An Exact Consumption Loan Model of Interest With or Without the Social Contrivance of Money', *Journal of Political Economy*, 66 (5), 467–82.
Tirole, J. (1985): 'Asset Bubbles and Overlapping Generations', *Econometrica*, 53 (5), 1071–100.

Wallace, N. (1988): 'A Suggestion for Oversimplifying the Theory of Money', *Economic Journal*, 98 (Supplement), 25–36.

Woodford, M. (1988): 'Learning to Believe in Sunspots', Mimeo, Columbia University, New York.

12
Trimming Consumers' Surplus Down to Size

Paul A. Samuelson

I wrote in my salad days that consumer's surplus should appear only in beginner's books, being replaced in intermediate treatises by the analysis of revealed preference under general equilibrium. Like the itch to scratch in wet cement, the sight of a dd' demand curve invites measuring the area inside it. And there appears in the literature, at time intervals governed by the Poisson distribution, articles with titles like 'Consumers Surplus Without Apologies', 'C-S Rehabilitated' or 'The 25 Different Definitions of C-S'. That is why I was not so rash as to call this piece 'The Last Word on C-S'.

Authors deploy such titles because to this day consumers' surplus discussions involve ambiguities, confusions, approximations, redundancies and Napoleonic pretensions hard to match in other parts of economic theory. At the same time there is great intrinsic interest in going beyond instantaneous *marginal* conditions at an equilibrium point to analyse and compare positions at a *finite distance from each other* – which is the true task of revealed-preference and consumer surplus efforts. Therefore an informal ramble through the literature of the subject can be useful. And some mathematical notes in an appendix can carry on the tradition of Marshall in the era when the *Economic Journal* and the Royal Economic Society were founded a century ago.

Orientation

Figure 12.1 poses the problem we address. In Figure 12.1(a) Marshall's demand curve is shown as dd': the CS area at E is supposed to be given by the triangle dϵe (usually a curvilinear triangle); the total utility of consuming ϵ's amount of q_1 (tea) is given by the trapezoidal area dEϵ0; because the consumer pays only the rectangle of eEϵ0 for the good, the excess over this of the total utility area is the triangular area CS.

Figure 12.1(b) pictures in a general equilibrium diagram the typical uses hoped to be accomplished by means of CS. On the horizontal axis is q_1 or tea; on the vertical axis is the other good(s), shown here as q_2. A production possibility frontier is shown as DZ, depicting society's trade-off between the goods as dictated by production technology. The dd' locus in figure 12.1(a) translates into the ED' locus of figure 12.1(b).

If DZ were a frontier concave (from below) as under constant returns to scale and perfect competition, there would be no CS problem. The convex indifference contours of Robinson Crusoe – or of each symmetric consumer – could be superimposed on figure 12.1(b). Smith's invisible hand of *laissez faire* would find its best-welfare equilibrium at a unique point where DZ is tangent to the highest attainable indifference counter. (Postpone any problems of interpersonal equity between persons of divergent tastes and resource endowments.)

Because DZ is shown to be convex at lowest levels of q_1 production, we must decide whether there is any point on it involving positive q_1 consumption that yields greater welfare (greater ordinal utility) than does the intercept point D with the q_1 industry absent. Is a point like E on a higher or lower indifference contour than D? CS is an ambitious attempt to throw light on this question; and on which of the local maxima, each representing tangencies of a wavy DZ locus to a convex indifference contour, is the true *maximum maximorum*.

A second main use that devotees of CS hope for it is the following. Suppose government needs some of the producible goods: for battleships, police or army service, public parks and so forth. After such public goods are provided out of society's limited resources, the menu of possibilities for private (q_1, q_2) is more

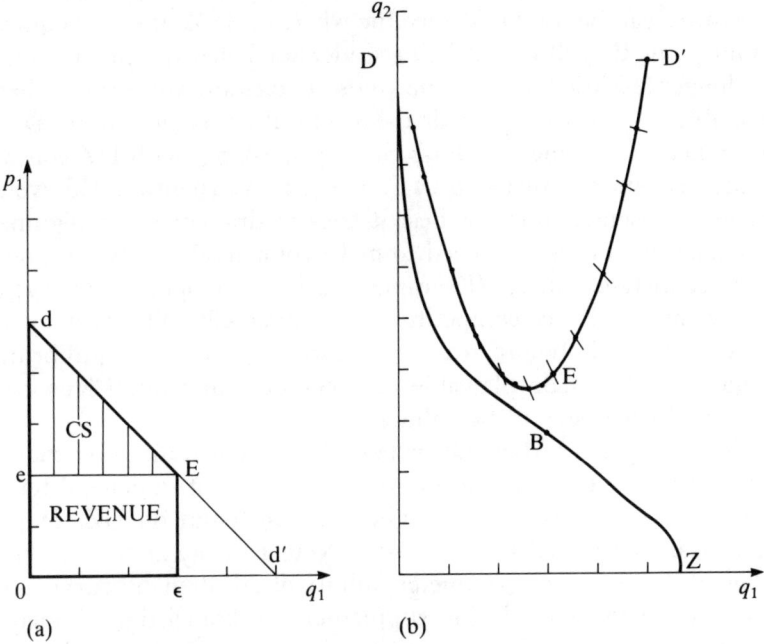

Figure 12.1 (a) Marshall's dd' demand curve defines at E three areas: the triangular area dEe of consumers' surplus; the rectangular *revenue* area of eEϵ0; and the dEϵ0 sum of these areas purporting to give the *total utility* of good q_1. (b) The trade-off frontier of technology and cost between q_1 and q_2 is shown as DBZ. When increasing returns (to scale) makes it lose its concavity, we need knowledge of the indifference contours to decide whether subsidizing q_1 to mitigate its losses at some point on DBZ is better than shutting down its production to be at D. Part (a)'s dd' is shown on (b) as the general equilibrium demand locus ED', each point on which shows the p_1/p_2 slope pointing vaguely toward D. These Marshallian data are seen to be unable to show whether the uninferable indifference contour through D ever passes below the DBZ locus. So, in general, Marshall–Dupuit CS cannot answer whether q_1 should be produced at all. QED. (If we had an ED' locus for *every* income level (for every D-like intercept point), we would know *all* indifference slopes everywhere and be able to infer all indifference contours.)

limited. DZ is shifted inward, say to D'Z'. Various alternative tax measures can be used to determine where on D'Z' the new equilibrium point E' will fall, it being understood that the previous E is no longer feasible for us. Some kinds of taxes are worse than others, possibly leaving society inside the technically feasible frontier D'Z'. Why need CS come into this? Strictly speaking, with DZ concave under constant returns to scale and no externalities, CS would have no essential role. At best it tries to dramatize for beginners the analysis that has *no* need to make comparisons between points a finite distance apart. (Example: tea is a monopoly industry; all others are perfectly competitive, including salt. The *prima facie* case to tax salt before tea is a theorem in general equilibrium, which can be made plausible for beginners in Santa Claus cases where CS happens to be valid.)

A century after Marshall, experts know that translating the dd' data of figure 12.1(a) onto figure 12.1(b) cannot in general tell us whether D is or is not the highest-welfare point on DZ. Dupuit and Marshall hoped for too much. Note I in my appendix shows that, if we had a one-parameter infinity of dd' demand curves, one for each income level, the supplementary knowledge of income elasticities additional to own-price elasticities would enable us to pencil into figure 12.1(b) each point's indifference slope – thereby providing us with the general equilibrium data concerning indifference contours and all market behaviour. Abram Bergson (1966, 1975) and J.A. Hausman (1981) discuss some of the ways that this may be done; R. Willig (1976) gives the approximation bounds entailed. To the observation by Ian Little (1950) that it is often impractical to suppose that we have knowledge of people's indifference contours, we must reply that pretending to use knowledge that is irrelevant, merely because we think we have it and we do not have relevant knowledge, is to perpetrate an irrelevancy if not a fraud.

In my youth it was customary to treat Alfred Marshall as a god. That was a long time ago and the Statute of Limitations has run out. My intention here is to take him more seriously as a creative scholar, judging him by exactly the same standards that we apply to a Hotelling, Hicks, or promising new thesis writer. How many, for example, have read in the last half-century Marshall's Mathematical Appendix, Note II, where the foundation of his analysis of consumer's rent is laid – and laid faultily? Copies of the *Prin-*

ciples in the Harvard libraries show little dirt on those pages, and no doubt the same pattern prevails in London and Cambridge. Now that serious scholars like John Whitaker (1975) and Richard Howey (1960) have provided the data to judge Marshall's claims to originality in the years before Jevons, we see that those pretensions would be unsustainable in other than a Marshall – and hence they must be judged to be that in Marshall. Alas, he was only a very great economist – and, for reasons of health and temperament, one who fell short of his potential creativity and scientific achievement.

Early History of Consumers' Surplus

Production and exchange is not a zero-sum game. Peters and Pauls are made better off by it, even though at the equilibrium position itself no further incremental benefit can be achievable by any one person without hurting some other person. This is trite in the age after Pareto. It is natural to try to quantify some of the economic gains achieved, and consumers' surplus is one of the attempts to do so.

Alfred Marshall's *Principles* (in nine editions: 1890, ..., 1920; variorum 1961, ed. C.W. Guillebaud) gave consumers' surplus a central role – an exaggeratedly central role. Jules Dupuit (1844), as Marshall acknowledged, had already elaborated the same concept; A.A. Cournot (1838), more unevenly, had touched upon it; the brilliant engineer Fleeming Jenkin (1871) had anticipated the intersecting demand and supply curves of partial equilibrium, and their enclosed CS area integrals. In less detail Marshall (1879) had earlier exposited CS.[1]

Critics everywhere immediately jumped on the non-optimalities in Marshall's notions. Indeed, John Neville Keynes, when reading proofs for Marshall, had warned him before publication of obvious vulnerabilities, points that came as no surprise to him (see Guillebaud, 1961, 260, 832). Simon Patten (1893) in America, J. Shield Nicholson (1893, 1894) in Britain, Leon Walras, Vilfredo Pareto and Enrico Barone on the continent raised similar critiques. Reserved until just after Marshall's death were the similar objections of Edwin Cannan (1924) and Allyn Young (1924).

Marshall, grudgingly, took notice of criticisms in early revisions.

But never did he give the subject a careful recasting: the evidence is unclear that he knew how to do so. Francis Edgeworth, as editor of the *Economic Journal*, refused to publish the important contribution by Enrico Barone (1894), and himself gave a defence of Marshall's CS (Edgeworth, 1894). Mathematical pupils of Marshall – C. Sanger (1895) and A. Berry (1891) – were encouraged to defend his formulations. Although the enemy was held at bay for the four decades in which the *Principles* dominated world economic teaching, mortal flaws remained: producers' rent or surplus was particularly faulty in Marshall's text, in part because of his confused treatments of external economies, external diseconomies and the incompatibility of perfect-competition equilibrium and firm's increasing returns. A zealous reader who accepted Marshall's logic would have to believe in the nonsense that an increasing-cost industry should be taxed so that a constant-cost industry can be subsidized – a *non sequitur* resulting solely from Marshall's forgetting to reckon *producers'* surplus areas properly. A.C. Pigou (1912, 1932) perpetuated this erroneous conclusion after shifting its logic to encompass (pecuniary) externalities induced for each firm by expanded industry output. Young (1913) immediately corrected Pigou, pointing out that rises in rents are beneficent instruments of Smith's invisible hand; but Pigou threw in the towel only after Dennis Robertson (1924) and Frank Knight (1924) reiterated Young's admonition.

Deeper than the flaws in Marshall's treatment of CS was the related basic flaw in the concept of partial equilibrium itself. Except for elementary beginners, economic teachers today, as in figures 12.1(b) and 12.1(a), replace partial equilibrium models by simplified models of general equilibrium. And they are right to do so. What CS depicts imperfectly or complexly on a (q_i, p_i) diagram is seen transparently and validly on the diagram of indifference contours and production possibility frontiers. Piero Sraffa's (1926) paper remains a classic in its insistence that increasing returns requires the replacement of perfect competition by some version of imperfect competition. But, as shown in Samuelson (1987, 1989), his attempt to deduce the emptiness of the category of increasing-cost industries is a failure in logic and relevance. The young Sraffa had a valid misgiving, but he should have traced his disquiet with Marshall to the empirical and theoretical superiority of *general* equilibrium over *partial* equilibrium.

The second era for consumers' surplus began with such works as those of Harold Hotelling (1932, 1938), John Hicks (1939, 1941, 1943, 1946), Maurice Allais (1943, 1981), Samuelson (1942, 1947, 1971, 1983), A.M. Henderson (1941), R.L. Bishop (1943), M. Sono (1943, in Japanese), J.N. Morgan (1948) and Arnold Harberger (1971). For an excellent guide to the literature of this century's last half, see the *New Palgrave Dictionary*'s item on CS by A. Takayama (1987); see also the item on Dupuit by R. Ekelund (1987). How far economics has come since 1923 is seen by contrasting these last two with the respective items by Neville Keynes and Edgeworth in the previous *Palgrave*. I recommend enthusiastically, but not unreservedly, the useful survey of Marshall's critics by Peter Dooley (1983).

REMARKS
Connected with some of the issues of CS, but not really reliant on that concept, is the problem of the 'second best' solved by the best-feasible theory of taxation of Frank Ramsey (1927). Elsewhere, Samuelson (1982) has reviewed subsequent related works by Hotelling, both Hicks's, Marcel Boiteux, Samuelson, Gerard Debreu, James Mirrlees and Peter Diamond, Will Baumol and others. The vast literature on the economic theory of economic index numbers, including the theory of Divisia (1925–6) line-integral indexes, is also relevant but can only be mentioned here.

Categories of Criticism

From Nicholson on, the following objections to Marshall's CS are reiterated in the literature.

1 Utility is not measurable.
2 No money measure of utility is valid.
3 Much of the Marshallian thinking rests on the doubtful legitimacy and relevance of his relying on additively independent cardinal utility $- \Sigma_1^n u_j[q_j]$ of the present mathematical note II – in the fashion of Gossen, Jevons, Walras, Fisher and Frisch. Early on, Patten (1893) insisted that what he would pay for one and two units of bread would be much affected by how scarce meat might be.
4 Almost all writers recognized that the Marshall–Dupuit integral inside the demand curve does not measure the extra amount that the consumer would pay *in toto* to consume q_1 of this good rather than do

without any of it (or do with a specified lesser amount of it). My mathematical note IV addresses all-or-none offer functions.

5 The marginal utility of income, which Marshall's procedure took to be constant or to be 'almost constant' (up to a 'second-order' divergence when the fraction of income spent on q_1 is 'small', $p_1q_1/\Sigma_i^n p_j q_j \ll 1$), cannot be relied on to validate Marshall's procedures.

6 For 'indispensable' goods, CS is infinite; and what is the use of saying that my £1,000 income is really worth £10,000?; and even if one good's CS is measurable, the CS of all goods cannot be computed – or, in the Young (1924) version, the CS of all goods nets out exactly to zero. So go the critics.

7 Marshallians display grave errors of commission and omission in the treatment of *producers' surplus*.

8 Whatever the legitimacy of consumer's surplus for each person, it is ethically illegitimate to sum money consumer's surpluses for each to arrive at a money sum for all purporting to measure consumers' surplus – the problem of where to put the apostrophe in consumer's or consumers' surplus.

9 Whereas Marshall (1890) writes loosely of three distinguishable concepts of CS, in the writings of Hicks, Henderson, Samuelson and Bishop there are at least half a dozen distinguishable concepts; in J.N. Morgan there are more than a score, and in Sono literally an infinity of different CS measures depending upon which arbitrary path of integration is chosen for the relevant line integral.

10 No model can exist for which Marshall's CS measurements are exact for *all n* goods; and one can always specify counterexamples in which, although each good is positive and uses up a negligible fraction of total income, the discrepancy between the $\int q_i \, dp_i$ integral and the all-or-none demand offer will be indefinitely great.

Every one of these criticisms has points. Several can be replied to with varying degrees of cogency and relevance. Briefly, I shall try to sample some of the more interesting queries raised.

Readers who skip my mathematical note IV need only note that the all-or-nothing offer measure is given by the vertical distance between our known DD' curve in figure 12.1(b) and the indifference curve through D there (which is unknowable unless we have more than one Marshallian DD' or dd' curve).

All-or-None Demand Responses

Marshall somewhat confusedly deals with three CS concepts.

1 There is the geometric area or integral of the dd' curve, $\int q_i \, dp_i$.
2 There is the excess of what money could be extracted from the consumer (to consume q_i rather than zero of good i) by an all-or-none offer over the $p_i q_i$ he actually does pay for q_i.
3 There is the q_i good's actual independent-additive utility, $u_i[q_i]$, alleged to be unaffected by changes in other q_j.

Marshall understands shakily the relationship between (1) and (2), in approximation or exactitude; he nodded in relating (3) and (2), somehow falling into the belief that constancy of the marginal utility of money spent on the other goods would suffice to make (1) and (2) identical. Since the all-or-none offer function is the basic one of the triad in Marshall's thinking, we can begin with it. My note IV provides rigorous definition.

Suppose I can buy 0, or 1, or 2 units of tea when you have specified for me the prices of other goods, $(p_2, ..., p_n)$ and my total spendable income M. At p_1 above £3, I buy 0 tea; at p_1 between £1 and £3 I buy 1 tea; at p_1 below £1, I buy 2 tea.

Marshall and Dupuit pretend that from these data they can infer how I will respond to all-or-none offers. They at first claim that

1 rather than do without 2 of tea I can be forced to pay £4 (equal to £3 for the first unit and £1 for the second);
2 rather than do without 1 of tea, I can be forced to pay £3.

The second statement is correct. The first statement, as they occasionally recognize, in general is not true. (When I am spending $M - £1$ on other goods, I would rather take one of those pounds and buy a second unit of tea; but when I have only $M - £3$ to spend on other goods, it will not be worth my while to spend one of those scarcer pounds to buy that second unit of tea.)

Marshall will reply: 'You are formally correct. But this is a quibble. You forget that my fine print says "I am supposing the marginal utility of money is constant". As long as the dd' curve shows that only a small fraction of income is ever spent on tea, my statement 1 is a close approximation to the truth.'

Is it *necessarily* a close approximation to the truth? Nicholson said early on that indispensable goods ought to have the most CS. For them Marshall's $\int q_1 \, dp_1$ would be infinite. How can one with a finite income of M offer an infinity of pounds rather than do without 2 of q_1?

Marshall has this reply: Always, I specify that we handle indispensable goods by measuring CS not back to $q_1 = 0$ but rather back to q_1 = subsistence (or = subsistence + epsilon).

Nicholson grumbled in rebuttal: where we need it most, you disqualify your concept. Actually, Nicholson received no cogent answer at all.

Consider salt rather than tea. We never spend much on it. But tribes have died in history to attain that first pinch of it. Their correctly computed all-or-none offers for it involve expenditures that become large relative to total M *even though the dd' shows everywhere a minuscule fraction of M spent on q_1.*

Doubts about logic are confirmed by the standard Mill–Marshall–Cobb–Douglas case of invariant fractional expenditures on every good. Marshall's proposed integral, even when calculated back to specified positive (q_1, p_1) levels of pseudo-subsistence, can be made to exceed a billion times available M of income.

Impossible Constancy of the Marginal Utility of Money

To defend orthodox CS analysis as a good approximation, Marshallians usually base their case on some constancy of the marginal utility of money λ. When Henry Schultz died in a 1938 auto accident, I investigated this possibility for a posthumous *Festschrift*. Since the marginal utility of money income is halved when all prices and income double, Samuelson (1942) elucidated the impossibility that λ could be constant, or approximately constant, with respect to all $n + 1$ of the variables $(M, p_1, p_2, ..., p_n)$.

What, so to speak, is the most constancy that λ can have with respect to variations in (M, P)? Of the $n + 1$ partial derivatives $(\partial \lambda / \partial M, \partial \lambda / \partial p_j)$, we can at most specify that n out of $n + 1$ of them are literally zero; λ must then be maximally sensitive to the remaining variable, being its inverse. I worked out how special are the two possible extreme cases: when there exists a utility indicator whose λ is unaffected by all prices and is additively independent of the form $\Sigma_1^n u_j[q_j]$, we have to be in the Mill–Marshall–Bernoulli case of logarithmic or Cobb–Douglas utility with unitary income and own-price elasticities. All empirical experience is against this case; and for it the $\int p_i \, dq_i$ integral infinitely overstates what an all-or-none offer can elicit from the consumer's finite M.

The second extreme case is when there exists a utility indicator whose λ is unaffected by M and by variations in $p_2, \ldots, p_n$, being of the form (constant)$/p_1$. This is the extreme Auspitz–Lieben–Berry–Hotelling case where all goods but the first one have zero income elasticity – again a bizarre empirical curiosum. The Santa Claus examples that we put in the beginners' textbooks to elucidate CS, tacitly or brazenly, involve this form. The mutliple-variable line integrals of my note III and of the Hicks–Hotelling–Allais expositions go most smoothly in this case. The $\int p_i \, dq_i$ integral does equal all-or-none offers for all independent Marshall goods other than q_1.

Fifty years later, I realize that we ought to investigate a third case, possibly important for approximation purposes. Suppose that λ is symmetric in the goods, symmetric in $(p_1/M, \ldots, p_n/M)$. Combine such symmetry with homotheticity, all income elasticities being exactly unity. Then when n is large, each single $\partial \lambda / \partial p_i$ might be regarded as almost zero. Let us now grant Marshall his special assumption of additive independence. Then we are in the constant elasticity of substitution (CES) case of Bergson (1936), by virtue of the combination of homotheticity and additivity. Now grant Marshall as rope the further assumption that no good is indispensable. Our utility function then becomes the Bergson fractional power series $\Sigma_1^n q_j^a$, $0 < a < 1$. Only if we add the final symmetry assumption that the ps all begin equal or nearly so can we ensure that each q_i stays near to zero as $n \to \infty$. As shown in my section on approximations, the percentage discrepancy between all-or-none offers and $\int p_i \, dq_i$ integrals goes to zero as $n \to \infty$, a relationship definitely glimpsed by Marshall. Without relying on such extreme assumptions, we can at best hope to use knowledge about all income elasticities (e.g. that they are all unity in the CES case) to alter Marshall's integral – as suggested by Hicks's many writings, Willig (1976), and Hausman (1981).

Second-Order Errors When $p_i q_i/M$ is Small?

Marshall was a Second Wrangler. When he used a mathematical expression like 'changes in the marginal utility of income are of a "second order of smallness" when $p_1 q_1/M$ is "small"', that should have a definite mathematical content. Alas, it does not in general.

Is there nothing at all to Marshall's heuristics? Have economists been all taken in over a century?

I think I can make a small case for him, perhaps itself only of a second order of smallness. Here is how a strict logician might argue.

1. Suppose in figure 12.1(b) that the intercept point D has an indifference curve that pierces into it at a finite angle. Then the observable DD' locus begins with that same angle, being tangential to the indifference curve when q_1 starts out at zero.
2. Therefore, as we start our $\int q_1 \, dp_1$ integral nearer and nearer to q_1 of zero, its error in approximating the relevant all-or-none offer curve becomes of less and less percentage importance.
3. This formal victory is nearly an empty one. What we are trying to measure in this incipient-q_1 case itself goes to zero. So to speak, we can say that the wart must be small when the face itself is very small. However, that is to miss the point of the incipient tangency. It permits us to say validly: as the face gets very small, the wart necessarily occupies an ever smaller *fraction* of its surface.

If the reader begins to weary at what seems reminiscent of medieval conundrums concerning the number of angels supportable on the point of a pin, I say join the club. My note IV shows how from the beginning we can infer analytically the exact functions for all-or-none offers when we have the full data of figure 12.1(b); and it suggests how, lacking data on other than a single ED' locus, we can try to deploy the axioms of revealed preference to infer what ordinal comparisons can be made.

One point needs to be clarified. Most of Marshall's expositions can be understood on the supposition that he has in mind as his *approximating* model

$$\text{utility} = u_1[q_1] + Cq_{II} \qquad u_1'' < 0 \qquad (12.1)$$

where C is a strict constant and q_{II} is a pre-Hicks composite commodity. My note III deals with this model, which is associated with Auspitz and Lieben (1889), Berry (1891), Hotelling (1932) and others.

For *this* model the Dupuit integral $\int p_1 \, dq_1$ does give an *exact* measure of the consumer's all-or-none offer. But this exactitude has naught to do with the smallness of p_1q_1/M, which can be indefinitely near to unity without destroying the exactitude.

Again, Marshall's inadequacies are not without merit. He undoubtedly had in mind loose heuristics of the following vague type: as the number of goods becomes large, $n \to \infty$, the expected $p_i q_i/M = e_i$ becomes small, $e_i \to 0$; and then the quasi-constant C in Cq_{11} becomes insensitive to a stipulated p_i change. Therefore, the marginal utility of income, which relates the nominal p_1 ordinate in dd' to the marginal utility function $u'_1[q_1]$, becomes virtually constant.

Marshall seems to have reasoned as follows:

> When the marginal utility of income is constant – as with unitary elasticity of demand for q_1 – the integral $\int p_1 \, dq_1$ does correctly measure the $u[q_1] - u[\bar{q}_1]$ difference *and therefore we have correctly measured the consumer's all-or-none offer function*.

Up to the italicized clause, one cannot object. But the last and crucial clause is a logical *non sequitur*. Marshall hopelessly confuses his additive-psychological utility with his all-or-none offer *money* measure of utility. Only under the strict model of (12.1) are they the same. The Mill–Bernoulli case of unitary price and income elasticity was seen to entail a different story. (Marshall's Note VI, prompted by Keynes's warnings, proposes to multiply the ordinate of dd' by some appropriate function of p_1q_1 when elasticity is not unity. What data give us that function? And when we have it, Marshall ends with the correct $u_1[q_1]$ and not with its *money* measure.)

Still once again, Marshall's mistakes are not without reason. Suppose he considers a consumer with CES utility following Abram Bergson (1936, 1975): $u = \Sigma_1^n q_j^{1/2}$. Let $n \to \infty$ with fixed prices and income. Then every $(q_i^*) \to 0$. Now as our q_1 is ever nearer to the level of $q_1 = 0$, my earlier tangency-at-intercept argument becomes ever more relevant.[2]

We must ask this: in saving the face of the formal argument by concentrating on ever smaller industries, are we emasculating the welfare purposes that CS is supposed to address?

This is a fair question. Dr Johnson defined a patron as someone who throws you a lifeline when you are already near to shore. But we need to remember that near to shore is not quite on the shore. Particularly in the domain of increasing returns, Edward Chamberlain can pose the problem: would it be better to have twice as many differentiated products at some multiple of the present unit costs? CS approximations might possibly apply in some of these investigations.

As Young (1924) pointed out, even at the end of his life Marshall proposed approximations at best defensible for ultra-small industries to the *totals* of a country's trade.

To sum up, moderns are right to jettison use of dd′ in favour of new curves whose shapes we cannot infer without income elasticity data estimatable only from *shifts* in dd′ curves.

Consumers' Surplus For Everything?

There is something about consumers' surplus that, like the devil, brings out the worst in each of us. Allyn Young, at the peak of his great powers, in that same 1924 article adds to his valid points the nonsensical assertion that CS as applied to all goods must cancel out to zero.

Hicks, a true hero of the CS saga, in unguarded moments writes sentences which seem to assert that two situations near the same indifference curve must have nearly the same marginal utility of income. Milton Friedman (1949), puzzled by the ambiguities of Marshall's expositions, convinced himself that Marshall must have meant his dd′ curve to involve no change in well-being of the consumer. As I reread Friedman and Marshall, I judge it absurd to suppose that Marshall would want the point E in figure 12.1(a) to be no better than the point d, a supposition that ignores his whole purpose of measuring the CS between them. If Marshall is a Slutskian, so are Mill, Mrs Fawcett and a myriad others who, Bishop showed, before 1879 used the same *ceteris paribus* language that he does. The totality of textual evidence puts Marshall nearer to Dupuit and Gregory King than to Eugen Slutsky.

Marshall conceded too much in sometimes admitting that his CS could not apply to *all* industries. When a Nicholson or Cannan asks, 'What sense is there to say that my £1,000 of income is worth £10,000?', Marshall is entitled to reply:

It makes sense for an average Englishman with £1,000 to reflect that, with £100, he could live as well at English prices as he could live in India on average pay there. It makes sense for me to estimate that Schumpeterian innovations will give my grandchildren an income that is quadruple my present dollar income. These are CS for totals.

Technically, I can infer for all n the *total* function $\Sigma_1^n u_j[q_j]$ if I have the observable indifference-contour data that they generate. But this is not to deny that adding together the total of all-or-none offers, to form what my note IV defines as $\Sigma_1^n N_j(q_j)$ in the pretence of arriving at the all-or-none offer for the vector of goods $(q_1, q_2, ...)$, would be to fall victim to the fallacy of composition – as Marshall may have feared.

The Mill–Marshall case, where $u = \Sigma_1^n k_j \log q_j$, does admit of a beautifully simple money measure of total utility – namely, $q_1^{k_1} \ldots q^{k_n}$, where $\Sigma_1^n k_j = 1$. And any case of homothetic preferences admits of a similar *unique* money-metric utility that is a homogeneous-first-degree function of its qs. Far from Marshall's being right in admitting that CS cannot apply to all goods at once, a principal merit of the general CS concept is to deflate our hubris in failing to recognize that we each owe our high modern standard of living to the productivity environment that we are lucky enough to live in.

'Money-metric' Utility

When the eminent mathematical biologist Joel E. Cohen was still a young member of Harvard's Society of Fellows, he amused me by saying: 'I envy you economists, because you have a metric.' He had in mind money, which is not coined in Darwin's jungle. Only a trained economist, I reflected at the time, can appreciate the treacheries involved in money as a metric.

A basic objection to the assertion that 'total utility' can be measured (exactly or approximately) by some kind of integral area of observable money-denominated demand functions is the modern one that *you as a consumer possess no unique cardinal measure of utility*.

Modern this objection may be, in the sense that it became standard after Hicks and Allen (1934), or after W.E. Johnson (1913) who concentrated solely on indifference curves, or after a stream of writings by Pareto covering the 1893–1918 period, or after certain recognitions in the Ph.D. thesis of Fisher (1892), inspired presumably by Willard Gibbs. Actually, long before the present age, in the original criticism of Marshall's CS, Nicholson (1893) seems in some of his passages to be asserting that only *ordinal* utility comparisons are ever involved in a consumer's demand behaviour, saying for example (p. 59): 'The utility of the last piece of money given may no doubt ... equal the utility of the last portion of the commodity acquired [each and every commodity, PAS]; but ... tells nothing as to how much he [the consumer] likes either.' This could well be Nicholson's way of saying that $\text{price}_{\text{tea}}/\text{price}_{\text{coal}}$ equals the marginal-rate-of-substitution-or-indifference [or *relative* marginal utilities] 'twixt tea and coal. Giving Nicholson full credit for this may be overly generous, since in his reply to Edgeworth Nicholson (1894, 344) says that his objection is not so much to [cardinal] utility as to the misguided attempt to measure any version of it by *money* calculation of Marshall's $\int q_i \, dp_i$ type.

The impeccable modern position is not to deny that *any* cardinal utility function exists for me, but to recognize that there are an *infinity* of such utility indicators; and that, in general and in the absence of stochastic risk, there is no one of them of privileged interest that could be the special object of an approximation by money.

When you glance at a diagram showing my family of indifference contours, you realize that those indifference contours could be given cardinal utility numbers that agree with the (minimum) *money* required to buy some point on them. To discuss tacit notions of 'complementarity', Samuelson (1974) defined such cardinal concepts as coming under the title of 'money-metric utility'. But again, we face an embarrassment of riches. There are an infinity of different Engels paths of consumption and income – essentially an $(n-1)$-fold infinity corresponding to that many different relative price configurations $(1, p_2/p_1, ..., p_n/p_1)$.

One particular species of the genus of money-metric utility has been prominent in the historic discussions of CS. Distances along the vertical q_2 axis in figure 12.1(b) can give cardinal numbers to the indifference contours that pierce that axis. (The q_2 axis is the Engels path when p_1/p_2 is prohibitively large.) When there are more than two goods, all the goods but q_1 purchasable at frozen prices can define (in terms of the total expenditure on them) a Hicksian composite q_{11} infelicitously called 'money' (see my note I). Then any combination such as (3 tea, 20 'money') is indifferent to some intercept point involving 0 of tea, i.e. indifferent to (0 tea, X 'money'), where X marks the intercept at which the relevant indifference contour pierces the vertical axis. X is thus an objective observable indicator of ordinal utility. This X is used in all four of the Hicks–Henderson CSs, but the logic of revealed preference accords it no qualitative pre-eminence.

We shall see that, often in the simplest textbook applications of CS, it is labour or some other measure of resources that provides the convenient metric – if by some miracle there singularly happens to exist such a metric. My appendix concludes with the observation and warning that, in general, arithmetic differences between costs and benefits are not valid.

Quantum Economics

Just as Max Planck was about to discover the irreducible graininess of physical reality, Marshall put on his shield, *Natura non facit saltum*. Treating economic variables as continuum real variables is at bottom an idealization. You consume a pinch of salt but not $\sqrt{2}$ of salt. Suppose, with Dupuit, we take seriously the integer nature of consumption, contemplating 0, 1, 2, ... train rides. Having in Samuelson (1967, 1973) touched on quantum economics, I here provide a bare sketch in which Marshall's limit approximations for CS fail logically.

Strictly speaking, if q_1 is integral so should be q_2 in figure 12.1(b). We shall gain brevity and sacrifice little realism, however, if we let q_2 be a real variable. Figure 12.2 redoes figure 12.1 in the quantum mode. Only the three meridians, $q_1 = 0, 1, 2$, count: instead of continuous indifference contours, the broken straight lines (such as Dac) provide the loci of indifference, with only the endpoints of the line segments counting. The straight lines joining two meridians do indicate the critical p_1/p_2 indifference 'slopes' at which q_1 consumption jumps from j to $j + 1$. Now in figure 12.2(b)

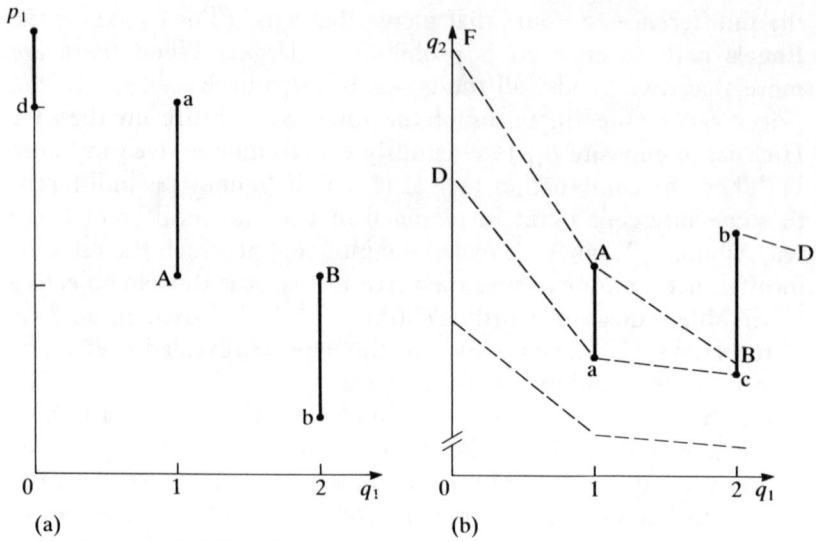

Figure 12.2 In this quantum-economic version of figure 12.1, the smooth dd' curve of 12.1(a) becomes the vertical line-segments: above d on the intercept; aA; Bb; and so forth. The smooth indifference contours of 12.1(b) here become the broken line segments that meet at points like a or A; now 12.1(b)'s D'ED locus of demand becomes the verticals above D, through A and a, b and B, and so forth. Because AB more realistically has a steeper slope than ac, Marshall's correct Bc distance of money CS is much less than his integral area, which is Aa. The break in b's vertical scale just above 0 in part (b) shows that Marshall's error can stay great even when we find $p_1 q_1 / M$ to be very small!

the DD' locus of demand consists of vertical straight line segments like DaABb..., where the broken line segment BA points directly to the intercept point D.

If the broken indifference slopes in each slab were all parallel, we would be in the Auspitz–Hotelling case where the Dupuit–Marshall areas (now summations rather than integrals) do exactly calculate correct all-or-nothing offers. However, the ac slope along the indifference locus going through D is here much less than the AB slope of the indifference locus going through B, A and F. Therefore, Marshall's area measure of $\Sigma q_j \Delta p_j$ involves a percentage error that could be 99 per cent or more.

Query: Must the percentage error shrink when $p_1 q_1 / M$ stays very small? The answer is, 'No; once we notice the break in the scale along the vertical axis, we realize that p_1q_1/M can be made to be as tiny as we wish without diminishing our finite percentage error.'

In the end, second-order-of-smallness logic has not salvaged Marshall's approximation. The lifeline of intercept tangency that I threw him fails when q_1 is integral. Why? Since q_1 can only drop discretely from 1 to 0, being incapable of going through a limit sequence like (1/2, 1/4, 1/8, ...), intercept tangency has no meaning. That is simply, as philosophers say, the way the cookie crumbles.

Consumers' Surplus Put to Work

Space constraint mandates concentrating on most important applications. Figure 12.3 can illuminate the problem of whether to produce a good subject to persisting increasing returns that render marginal cost pricing unable to cover total costs. This has assuredly been the single most important use claimed for consumers' surplus.

First, concentrate only on the heavy lines in the diagram. In figure 12.3(c), leisure is shown with a marginal utility that is strictly constant, the singular case most favourable to the autonomy of Marshall's partial equilibrium analysis. The other two goods show declining $d_i d_i'$ lines: using the constant utility of leisure as our numeraire of numerical utility, and using a unit of leisure as our market numeraire (so that p_1 and p_2 really also represent p_1/p_3 and p_2/p_3), there is nothing at all approximate about our triangular CS, as discussed in Samuelson (1971).

In our first best-case for CS, we suppose the $s_i s_i'$ supply curves all to be horizontal. Since there is then no producers' surplus in this constant-cost scenario, we cannot yet misuse the concept. Labour is the obverse of leisure, and its total is what is allocated transferably between the goods. The equilibrium shown at E_1, E_2 and E_3 cannot be improved on in a one-person Crusoe world. We can say, 'Crusoe maximizes his total ordinal utility', or, 'Crusoe maximizes his total CS', or, 'Crusoe minimizes his socially desirable labour, and maximizes his leisure'. He can do all this by playing the game of market competition. Biologist Cohen can indeed envy us economists our rock-solid metric, which is not really 'money'

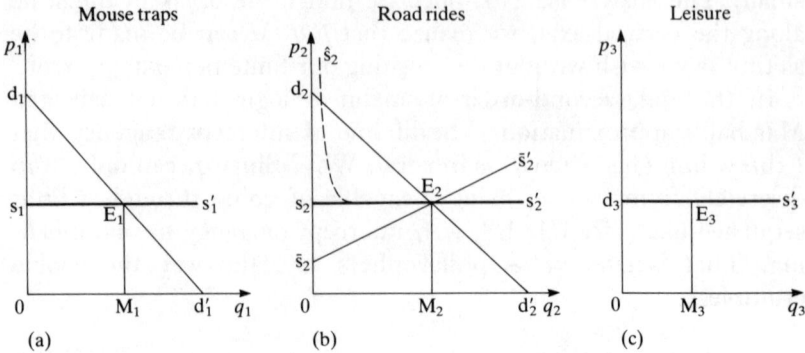

Figure 12.3 In the first scenario all supply curves are horizontal, consisting of constant unit costs of transferable labour. Competitive equilibrium at (E_1, E_2, E_3) will maximize Crusoe's ordinal utility, and also maximize the sum of Marshallian CSs. In the second scenario, q_2 is produced by transferable labour, working on limited specialized land and resulting in the rising $\bar{s}_2 \bar{s}_2'$. If Marshall taxes q_2 to subsidize q_1, he can increase summed CS only by destroying some Crusoe welfare (and destroying some summed CS plus producers' surplus). In a further scenario of increasing returns along $\hat{s}_2 E_2 s_2'$, society will decide to produce positive q_2, selling it at the E_2 level that will fail to cover costs, only if the CS area exceeds the $\hat{s}_2 E_2$ area of full costs, thereby justifying the use of lump-sum taxes to finance the initial labour needed. A final scenario, in which the leisure graph of (c) is irrelevant and the total of labour is fixed (at $0M_1E_1s_1 + 0M_2E_2s_2$), or in which *both* industries need the same limited land, destroys the validity of Marshall's partial equilibrium analysis and of his crude $\int q_i \, dp_i$ cost–benefit approximations.

but rather labour–leisure–utils stuff in this contrived Santa Claus case.

In the second scenario, replace the solid line $s_2 s_2'$ in figure 12.3(b) by the lighter rising line $\bar{s}_2 \bar{s}_2'$. We are still to be in a world of constant returns *to scale*, but I now specify in the Jones–Samuelson fashion that good 2 has to be produced by using the transferable labour on a land specialized to be capable of producing only good 2. As before, good 1 needs only transferable labour as input. As before, the market equilibrium of E_1, E_2, and E_3 maximizes Crusoe's total utility. Marshall momentarily forgot to mention that the area that should be maximized is $\Sigma CS_j + \Sigma PS_j = [d_1E_1s_1+0] +$ $[d_2E_2s_2+\bar{s}_2E_2s_2] + [0+0]$. Bemused by externalities and having a block against recognizing that increasing returns to scale (and *its* decreasing cost curves) is incompatible with ss' supply curves of perfect competition, Marshall chose at a crucial point to forget about producers' surplus (PS) in his optimality calculus. His logic, which his pen forbore from writing down except in a decreasing-cost context, was to maximize just the CS areas. If Marshall gave a per-unit subsidy in figure 12.3(a), financing it by a compensating per-unit tax in figure 12.3(b), the loss in CS in figure 12.3(b) would be much smaller than the gain in CS in 12.3(a); however, taking account of the loss in producers' surplus in 12.3(b), Crusoe and society would lose by the interference!

Now consider a third scenario. In it, figure 12.3(b) contains neither the $s_2s'_2$ nor the $\bar{s}_2\bar{s}'_2$ marginal cost curves. Instead (much as in figure 12.1(b) near the intercept D of DED'), let there be an indivisible labour cost C_2 if anything at all of q_2 is to be produced – followed by a marginal cost like that shown in E_2s_2. The broken line $\hat{s}_2E_2s_2$ suggests the story. Should Crusoe shut down the second industry? We can measure the CS triangle of $D_2E_2s_2$ in labour units because of our strong assumptions about labour–leisure's constancy of marginal utility. If this exceeds C_2, Crusoe should incur the indivisible cost and consume q_2 at the level shown at E_2. (If he wants to play the game of a market economy, he imposes on himself a lump-sum tax of C_2 labour units, giving up that much leisure, and uses the labour thus provided to the State to provide the public utility producing q_2 with the indivisible labour needed to start off the industry.)[3]

Has CS been vindicated? A general equilibrium diagram like figure 12.1(b) can beautifully handle this case and others as well. But, under my trumped-up story's assumptions, yes, CS will work here.

Isn't this kind of a vindication? Not in general. Suppose both industries can use the same quality of land along with the transferable labour. Now *no* partial equilibrium diagrams have the autonomy to provide us with measurable producer's surplus areas to take into account. And this is in the perfect case of strictly constant Marshall–Dupuit marginal utility of money.

Enough is enough. Still a final scenario imparts a vital message. Drop figure 12.3(c) from figure 12.3. Replace its variable supply of labour–leisure by a strict constancy of total labour supplied to be used in figures 12.3(a) and 12.3(b). Now, as Walras kept telling the Marshallians, the dd' curves in 12.3(a) and 12.3(b) are *not* market demand curves. Marginal utility curves may be straight lines, but the demand curves they entail in (p_i, q_i) space are no longer straight lines. Nor are they autonomous and independent of (endogenous!) p_j changes, even when additively independent utility functions miraculously exist.

All roads reach to Rome. General equilibrium, not partial equilibrium, must be our tool.

Concluding Reflections

Have I been too hard on consumers' surplus? Has it not had a historic role in the development of welfare economics?

Here is a list of important landmarks in the history of modern welfare economics.

Adam Smith's notion of the invisible hand as somehow leading under *laissez faire* to some kind of optimum is an important early contribution – despite its manifest imperfections. Smith had no need for CS.

Neoclassical economists – notably Pareto, Barone and Wicksell – glimpsed the truth that competitive equilibrium achieved efficiency in production and consumption allocations; thus, if and only if the initial endowments of individuals were contrived to be ethically optimal, the competitive market system could be used under capitalism or socialism to achieve an optimum of a proposed ethical system.

These fundamentals were sorted out for the first time in Bergson (1938), following upon quasi-independent enunciations by Lerner, Kaldor, Hicks, Hotelling, Samuelson, Little and Scitovsky – and, for that matter, by Mill, Marshall, Pareto and Viner – that elimination of deadweight loss by competition's achieving what has for four decades been dubbed Pareto optimality implies that gainers can in some sense bribe losers. Gerard Debreu and Kenneth Arrow provided the rigorous closure for standard welfare economics.

The track described above represented a gradual reformulation of the naive welfare hedonism of Bentham, Sidgwick and Edgeworth, which supposed that there really did exist a scientifically definable cardinal function of utility for each individual, which could somehow be objectively given its appropriate weight factor so that science could hope to define a privileged total-utility sum for the universe. Pigou's welfare economics worked tacitly within this framework, and traces of it lived on in the works of Lerner and Meade even after Robbins's 1932 *Essay on the Nature and Significance of Economic Science* had persuasively questioned the possibility of a scientific basis for value judgements.

I terminate my chronicle prior to the current developments in Rawlsian welfare economics, and its foreshadowing in the writings of Harsanyi, Vickrey, Arrow, Samuelson, Sen, Mirrlees and many others. And I exclude from this discussion the breakthroughs in mathematical politics by Kenneth Arrow and other scholars in the social choice field.

Where in the above chronicle did consumers' surplus play an important historical role? What is not the same question, where might it have done so?

The answer to both questions is essentially this: consumers' surplus was not intrinsically involved in the major breakthroughs, nor need it have been.

Accuracy requires mention of one constructive part played by the consumers' surplus concept. It came in at the very beginning of CS. An appreciation of marginal cost pricing and the useful role to be played in increasing returns situations by two-tier and other schemes of price discrimination appeared already in the mid-nineteenth-century writings of Dupuit. Dupuit's readers were alerted to the qualitative truth that, as one first departs from an optimum – by taxation, monopoly or whatever – the deadweight loss is quadratically negligible, being the square of a variable that is already small. These truths could have been perceived without consumers' surplus, but it is factually the case that CS did play a key role in the making of this innovation and in its spread.[4]

The various editions of my *Economics* will also bear witness to my belief that, for beginners, consumers' surplus is a concept with pedagogical value. If this damns the concept with faint praise, so be it.

Appendix: Mathematical Notes

I

Here it is shown how complete knowledge of the maximizing person's observable demand functions does suffice to determine complete knowledge of his/her ordinal utility (or preference) function. Goods $(q_1, \ldots, q_n) = Q$ are each determinate smooth functions of prices and income, $(p_1/M, \ldots, p_n/M) = P/M = Y = (y_j)$, where $\Sigma_1^n y_j x_j = 1$:

$$Q = f(Y) = [q_i] = \left[f^i\left(\frac{p_1}{M}, \ldots, \frac{p_n}{M}\right) \right] \tag{I.1}$$

Under specific regularity conditions, these implicit equations will be uniquely invertible,

$$Y = f^{-1}(Q) = F[Q] : 0 \leqslant Q \leftrightarrow Y \geqslant 0$$

$$= (y_i) = (F^i[q_1, \ldots, q_n]) \tag{I.2}$$

I have shown (Samuelson, 1947; 1983, 459–62) that $F[\ ]$ and $f(\ )$ are dual functions and possess the same qualitative properties. Under our regularity conditions, almost everywhere the testable Slutsky–Hicks conditons are to hold:

$$S(Y) = [s_{ij}(Y)] = M\left[\left(\frac{\partial q_i}{\partial p_j}\right) + q_j\left(\frac{\partial q_i}{\partial M}\right) \right]$$

$$= [s_{ji}(Y)] = S(Y)' \tag{I.3}$$

$$= \left[f^i_j(Y) - f^j(Y) \sum_{k=1}^n y_k f^i_k(Y) \right] \tag{I.4}$$

$[a_1, \ldots, a_n] S(Y) [a_1, \ldots, a_n]' < 0$ for $[a_1, \ldots, a_n] \neq bY$

where the following subscript notation denotes partial differentiation:

$$\left[\frac{\partial f^i}{\partial y_j} \right] = [f^i_j(y_1, \ldots, y_n)] = f_Y(Y) \tag{I.5}$$

When $n = 2$, (I.3) reduces to $s_{11}(y_1, y_2) < 0$ almost everywhere (a.e.).

Similar symmetry and definiteness conditions hold for $F[Q]$. In particular, the more familiar Allen–Antonelli integrability conditions can be expressed by

$$\frac{y_i}{y_1} = \frac{F^i[q_1, \ldots, q_n]}{F^1[q_1, \ldots, q_n]} \tag{I.6}$$

$$= R^i[Q] \quad i = 2, \ldots, n$$

$$A[Q] = (R^i_j[Q] - R^j[Q]R^i_1[Q]) = A[Q]' \tag{I.7}$$

Almost everywhere in Q

Trimming Consumers' Surplus Down to Size

$$[z_2 \ldots z_n] A[Q][z_2 \ldots z_n]' < 0 \quad \text{for } z \neq 0 \qquad (I.8)$$

Given (I.7)'s integrability conditions, we know from the Pfaff theory of partial differential equations that we can construct an 'exact' ordinal-utility differential from the condition

$$du[Q] = \left(dq_1 + \sum_{j=2}^{n} R^j[Q]\, dq_j\right) I[Q] \qquad (I.9)$$

where $I[Q]$ is any one of an infinity of existent 'integrating factors'.

Therefore, from the observable demand functions alone, the general theory of revealed preference demonstrates that we can infer *all* the 'better-or-worse' relationships between alternative Q situations:

$$Q^A \text{ better than } Q^B \text{ iff } u[Q^A] > u[Q^B]$$

$$\text{or iff } v(u[Q^A]) > v(u[Q^B]),\ v'(u) > 0 \qquad (I.10)$$

$$Q^A \text{ indifferent to } Q^B \text{ iff } u[Q^A] = u[Q^B] \text{ etc.}$$

The usual consumers' surplus exposition of the textbooks tries to push its luck too far: from sole knowledge of a (q_i, p_i) demand locus, premised on certain constancies of *other* (p_j) or (q_j) in the $Q = f(Y)$ domain, it is hoped to be able to make (Q^A, Q^B) comparisons that will guide public utility decision making. Only in Santa Claus cases are the purported calculations valid, as figure 12.1(b) showed. Thus, Hausman (1981) has not made Marshall's CS exact: rather he has stipulated the general equilibrium knowledge of $[\partial q_j/\partial M,\ \partial q_j/\partial p_j]$ that is involved in Note I to infer the indirect utility function $V(M, p_1, \ldots, p_n)$ whose $[\partial V/\partial p_j]$ gradient is proportional to (I.1)'s demand vector.

Hicks's beautiful trick of a composite commodity makes a two-dimensional picture possible. Here is a long-needed proof that the trick works in the most general of contexts.

Define a mixed-dual function, in the fashion of Samuelson (1960), by the following:

$$u^*(q_1, \ldots, q_{r-1}, M_r; p_r, \ldots, p_n) \qquad 1 < r < n$$

$$= \max_{q_r, \ldots, q_n} u[q_1, \ldots, q_r, \ldots, q_n] \text{ subject to } \sum_r p_j q_j = M_r$$

$$= u[q_1, \ldots, q_{r-1}, q_r^*, \ldots, q_n^*] \qquad (I.11)$$

where

$$0 < [q_r^*, \ldots, q_n^*] = [F^{r+j}(q_1, \ldots, q_{r-1}, M_r; p_2, \ldots, p_n)] \qquad (I.12)$$

$$= F(q_1, \ldots, q_{r-1}, M_r) \text{ for short} \qquad (I.13)$$

is the unique vector root of the $n - r$ implicit relations for $[q_r, \ldots, q_n]$

$$\frac{u_j[q_1, \ldots, q_r, \ldots, q_n]}{\sum_r^n q_k u_k[q_1, \ldots, q_r, \ldots, q_n]} = \frac{p_j}{M_r} \qquad j = r, \ldots, n \qquad (I.14)$$

Essentially, what we must show is that, if $u[\ ]$ is strictly quasi-concave in all its variables, then

$$u[\tfrac{1}{2}A + \tfrac{1}{2}B, \tfrac{1}{2}a + \tfrac{1}{2}b] > u[A, a] = u[B, b] \qquad (I.15)$$

where $u[A_1, \ldots, A_{r-1}, a_r, \ldots, a_n] = u[A, a]$, ... From (I.11)'s strong maximum property,

$$u[\tfrac{1}{2}A + \tfrac{1}{2}B, F(\tfrac{1}{2}A + \tfrac{1}{2}B, \tfrac{1}{2}M_r^\alpha + \tfrac{1}{2}M_r^\beta)]$$

$$= u^*(\tfrac{1}{2}A + \tfrac{1}{2}B, \tfrac{1}{2}M_r^\alpha + \tfrac{1}{2}M_r^\beta; p_r, \ldots, p_n)$$

$$\geq u[\tfrac{1}{2}A + \tfrac{1}{2}B, \tfrac{1}{2}a + \tfrac{1}{2}b] \qquad (I.16)$$

Combining (I.15) and (I.16), we arrive at our desired quasi-concavity of u^*:

$$u^*(\tfrac{1}{2}A + \tfrac{1}{2}B, \tfrac{1}{2}M^\alpha + \tfrac{1}{2}M^\beta; p_r, \ldots) > u^*(A, M^\alpha; p_r, \ldots)$$

$$= u^*(B, M^\beta; p_r, \ldots) \qquad (I.17)$$

REMARK

It is the linearity of the budget constraint imposed by M_r that is crucial to the validity of the Hicks theorem. It can be verified that the observable marginal rates of substitution $[\partial u^*/\partial q_j]/[\partial u^*/\partial M_r]$ will be proportional to the observed vector $(p_1/p_n, \ldots, p_{r-1}/p_n)$.

II

Demand when a strongly separable additive utility function can be specified. Gossen, Jevons, Walras and Marshall were beguiled by this very special case. Marshall mistakenly asserted that it had realistic properties: he never wrote down its exact theory but no doubt did comprehend its simplicities. Here is a terse modern treatment: one cardinal utility indicator $u[Q]$ is to be of the (strongly separable) additive-independent form

$$u[Q] = u_1[q_1] + \ldots + u_n[q_n] \qquad (II.1)$$

$u_i'[q_i] > 0$ a.e. for $q_i > 0$; $u_i'[q_i] \to \infty$ as $q_i \to 0$

$u''_i[q_i] < 0$ a.e. for $q_i > 0$; $u_i'[q_i] \to 0$ as $q_i \to \infty$

I shall assume that $u_i[0]$ is finite to avoid infinities in the CS integrals, and obviate having to get around infinities by Marshall's device of presupposing q_i is above a specified indispensable level of subsistence.

A calculable example is a Bergson CES case such as

$$u = \sum_{1}^{n} q_j^{1/2} \tag{II.2}$$

It can be shown, as in Pollak (1971), that this entails the (non-independent!) demand functions

$$q_i = \frac{y_i^{-2}}{\sum_{1}^{n} y_k^{-1}} \qquad i = 1, \ldots, n \tag{II.3}$$

$$\frac{\partial q_i}{\partial p_j} \neq 0 \qquad \text{for } j \neq i$$

Note that, when p_1 alone changes, the *summed* effects on the demand curve shifts for goods 2, ..., n do *not* constitute welfare effects that Marshall can ignore – even when n goes towards infinity! As n gets large, any single cross-derivative like normalized $\partial q_2/\partial p_1$ may go to zero while the *summed* cross-welfare effects may stay large.

Marshall realized that coffee and cream, tea and lemon, and coal could not be $[q_1, q_2, q_3, q_4, q_5]$ in (II.1). He supposed that complements and substitutes could somehow be components of certain composite commodities, and then these composites could be expected to fit the additive utility straitjacket that Patten (1893) and other critics deplored. Thus consider needs for 'drink' and 'warmth', defining their composites as, say,

$$q_{\mathrm{I}} = [\min(\text{coffee, cream})^{1/2} + \min(\text{tea, lemon})^{1/2}]^2 \tag{II.4}$$

$$q_{\mathrm{II}} = \text{coal}$$

Then Marshall would want to try

$$u_{\mathrm{I}}[q_{\mathrm{I}}] + u_{\mathrm{II}}[q_{\mathrm{II}}] \tag{II.5}$$

From 1868 to 1924 he never showed any sophisticated understanding of the special and exotic implications of the $\Sigma u_j[q_j]$ specification, implications spelled out for example in Samuelson (1974) and elsewhere; in this regard apparently Marshall seems to have been as confused as any gullible reader.

Never mind. From (II.1) what follows for $f(Y)$? Alas, in general the *autonomy* of partial equilibrium two-dimensional demand relations,

$$q_i = f_i(y_i) \qquad \frac{\partial q_i}{\partial y_j} = 0, \ j \neq i, \ i,j = 1, \ldots, n \tag{II.6}$$

is valid only in the Mill–Cobb–Douglas case where

$$u_i = k_i \log q_i \qquad \sum_{1}^{n} k_j = 1 \tag{II.7}$$

and Marshall's CS integral areas are infinite!

Here is how the $f(Y)$ functions are derivable for a maximizing individual with $u = \Sigma_1^n u_j(q_j)$:

$$\max_{q_i} \sum_{1}^{n} u_j(q_j) \text{ subject to } \sum_{1}^{n} y_j q_j = 1 = \sum_{1}^{n} \frac{p_j}{m} q_j$$

$$= \sum_{1}^{n} u_j(q_j^*) = \sum_{1}^{n} u_j[f_j(Y)] = \hat{u}(M;P)$$

$$= \hat{u}(M) \text{ for short} \tag{II.8}$$

where the vectors $[Q^*; \lambda^* M]$ and $[f(Y); \Gamma(Y)]$ are each the unique root of the following $n + 1$ independent implicit equations

$$u_i(q_i) = \lambda p_i \qquad i = 1, \ldots, n \tag{II.9a}$$

$$= y_i \sum_{1}^{n} q_j u_j(q_j) \tag{II.9b}$$

$$\lambda = \sum_{1}^{n} \frac{q_j u_j(q_j)}{M}$$

For the general case of (II.1), or (II.8), we may suppose that the Second Wrangler of 1865 glimpsed the truth almost everywhere of

$$\frac{\partial q_i}{\partial M} > 0 > \frac{\partial q_i}{\partial p_i} \qquad i = 1, \ldots, n \tag{II.10}$$

$$\frac{\partial \lambda}{\partial M} < 0 \qquad \text{sgn}\left(-\frac{\partial q_j}{\partial p_i}, \frac{\partial \lambda}{\partial p_i}\right) = \text{sgn}\left[\frac{\partial(p_i q_i)}{\partial p_i}\right]$$

In words, for additive independence:

> All income elasticities are positive. All own-price elasticities are negative. A rise in income and each good's consumption pushes down the (equalized) marginal utility of income. When a rise in p_i raises what is spent on q_i, that lowers the amount left to spend on every other good and raises income's marginal utility; when it lowers expenditure on q_i, the opposite happens to each q_j and λ falls. When p_i's elasticity is unity, all q_j's are unaffected and the marginal utility of income is constant; however, such a constancy in λ does *not* imply that Marshall's CS integral correctly measures what a consumer would just pay for the privilege of consuming q_i of the ith good. Even though $\partial \lambda / \partial p_i$ be zero and the income effect definitely positive, the $\int q_i \, dp_i$ integral does overstate the consumer's all-or-none offer – as will be shown.

III

An extreme case where a good exists with strict constancy of marginal utility. To defend the face of his partial equilibrium and CS procedures, let him assume à la Auspitz and Lieben (1889), Berry (1891) and Hotelling (1932):

$$u = q_1 + \sum_2^n u_j[q_j] \qquad u_1'' \equiv 0 > u_j'' \qquad (\text{III.1})$$

Then for M not so small as to wipe out all demand for q_1, (II.9) can be expressed as

$$\frac{y_i}{y_1} = u_i'[q_i] \qquad i = 2, \ldots, n \qquad (\text{III.2})$$

$$= g_i[q_i] = \frac{p_i}{p_1}$$

For i and j greater than 1 and unequal,

$$q_i = g_i^{-1}\left(\frac{p_i}{p_1}\right) \qquad \frac{\partial q_i}{\partial p_i} < 0 = \frac{\partial q_j}{\partial p_i} \qquad (\text{III.3})$$

$$\frac{\partial q_i}{\partial M} = 0 < \frac{\partial q_i}{\partial p_1} \qquad (\text{III.4})$$

The demand for q_1 lacks (III.3)'s independence from other ps, being the residual

$$q_1 = \frac{M}{p_1} - \sum_2^n \left(\frac{p_j}{p_1}\right) g_j^{-1}\left(\frac{p_j}{p_1}\right) \qquad (\text{III.5})$$

$$\frac{Eq_1}{EM} = \frac{1}{(p_1 q_1)/M} > 0 > \frac{\partial q_1}{\partial p_1} \qquad (\text{III.6})$$

$$\operatorname{sgn}\left(-\frac{\partial q_1}{\partial p_i}\right) = \operatorname{sgn}\left(\frac{\partial [p_i q_i]}{\partial p_i}\right) \qquad (\text{III.7})$$

If M shrinks enough to make q_1 vanish in (III.5), then for all lower M Marshall is back in the general case of (II.1) where all his partial equilibrium dd curves lack autonomy.

REMARKS

This case of (III.1) violates my specification in (I.1) that $f(Y)$ is to be uniquely invertible. Where q_1 just vanishes, an infinity of (y_i/y_1) vectors will generally be admissible in (III.2). I leave to the interested reader to work out the still more bizarre case where $u_1''[q_1]$ is allowed to be positive: the indifference contours will still be nicely convex in regions where the negativity of the vector $(u_2''[q_2], \ldots, u_n''[q_n])$ is sufficiently strong to outweigh the positivity of u_1''. In such regions all goods but q_1 are inferior goods! And a rise in income raises rather than lowers the marginal utility of income λ! Being a superior good, q_1's $\partial q_1/\partial p_1$ cannot display Giffenosity. The sign of its $\partial(p_1 q_1)/\partial p_1$ term will govern the sign of all elements in the $[\partial q_2/\partial p_1, \ldots, \partial q_n/\partial p_1]$ vector. The sign of $\partial q_1/\partial p_i$ will be governed by the sign of $-\partial(p_i q_i)/\partial p_i$. The sign of $\partial q_{2+i}/\partial p_2$ will be seen to be opposite to that of $\partial q_1/\partial p_2$. Since any q_{1+i} is an inferior good, any and all may display

Giffenosity. As with the case where u''_1 vanishes, the global unique invertibility of $f(Y)$ is lost here.

After this last digression, let us return to the case of a good with strictly constant u'_1. Marshall's heart cannot have really been in this lifeline thrown to him by Berry (1891) since it denies his cherished view that more income means a rise in most goods' consumptions and means a diminution in the marginal utility of income λ. Hicks's 1939 *Value and Capital* (1939, 38–40) throws Marshall this same lifeline of strict constancy of $\partial u/\partial q_1$, but primarily only for geometrical exposition purpose preparatory to Hicks's espousal of a *compensational* measure of CS. Hotelling (1932) can be construed, as can Auspitz and Lieben (1889), to be using a strictly constant $\partial u/\partial q_1$ in the background. Eschewing additive independence for goods $(2, \ldots, n)$, Hotelling is then effectively working with

$$u = q_1 + v[q_2, \ldots, q_n] \qquad v \text{ strictly concave} \qquad (III.8)$$

$$\frac{\partial^2 v}{\partial q_i \partial q_j} \gtreqless 0$$

$$\frac{y_i}{y_1} = \frac{\partial v[q_2, \ldots, q_n]}{\partial q_i} \qquad i = 2, \ldots, n \qquad (III.9)$$

By (Hotelling) duality, the inverse of these last functions can be written as

$$q_i = \frac{\partial v^*(y_2/y_1, \ldots, y_n/y_1)}{\partial (y_i/y_1)} \qquad (III.10)$$

where $v^*()$ is an existent function dual to $v[\ ]$. The following residual defines q_1:

$$q_1 = \frac{1}{y_1} - \sum_2^n \frac{y_j}{y_1} q_j \qquad (III.11)$$

When m is so small as to make q_1 negative in (III.11), (III.10) has to be replaced by

$$v_i[q_2, \ldots, q_n] \Big/ \sum_2^n q_j v_j[q_2, \ldots, q_n] = y_i \qquad i = 2, \ldots, n \qquad (III.12)$$

and all bets are off on path independence of CS line integrals.

For sufficiently large M, Hotelling generalizes Marshall's one-variable integral

$$\int_{\bar{p}_i}^{p_i} f^i(\ldots, t_i, \ldots) \, dt_i = C(p_i) - C(\bar{p}_i) \qquad (III.13)$$

to the following line integral that is independent of path between endpoints $(y_1^a, \ldots, y_n^a)$ and $(y_2^b, \ldots, y_n^b)$:

$$v^*(Y^b) - v^*(Y^a) = \int \sum_2^n v_j^*(y_2, ..., y_n) dy_j \qquad (III.14)$$

Later Allais and Hicks similarly generalized to multiple price changes under constrained budgets. Most, but not all, of the failures of Marshall's one-variable case carry over to the *general n*-variable case – where the requisite line integrals of observable demand generally are *not* independent of path.

IV

Deriving 'all-or-nothing' offer curves. Marshall's critics fell into his erroneous belief that constancy of the marginal utility of income would validate his disparate definitions of consumer surplus. This is a treacherous argument. Under Millian or logarithmic utility, along the (p_i, q_i) demand curve the marginal utility of income is strictly constant. However, as we have seen, what the consumer will offer in pounds or dollars rather than consume less of good q_i is not remotely approximated by the $\int p_i \, dq_i$ integral. (By contrast, consider the Hotelling–Marshall case of note III where u is $q_i + \Sigma_2^n u_j[q_j]$. Again, marginal utility of income, λ, is unaltered by a rise in p_i. But this time the demand curve's integral does measure what the consumer would pay in money to enjoy $u_i[q_i]$ rather than $u_i[0]$!)

Here is a formal derivation of my all-or-none offer function $N_1(q_1)$ for good q_1 that an omnisciently discriminating monopolist could just extract from me for the privilege of receiving q_1 rather than zero good 1, it being understood that my given income of M is freely spendable on all the other goods at specified prices for them of $(p_2, ..., p_n)$ and that additive-independence properties of (II.1) hold.

N_1 is the root of the following relation:

$$u_i[0] + \hat{u}_1(M; p_2, ..., p_n) = u_1[q_1] + \hat{u}_1[M - N_1; p_2, ..., p_n] \qquad (IV.1)$$

where

$$\hat{u}_1(M; p_2, ..., p_n) = \max_{q_2, ..., q_n} \sum_2^n u_j[q_j] \text{ subject to } \sum_2^n p_j q_j = M \qquad (IV.2)$$

For short, write $\hat{u}_1(M)$ for $\hat{u}_1(M; p_2, ..., p_n)$. The inverse function of $\hat{u}_1(M)$ is well defined and can be denoted by $\bar{u}_1\{\ \}$. This enables us to write

$N_1[q_1]$ (short for $N_1[q_1; M, p_2, ..., p_n]$)

$$= M - \bar{u}_1\{u_1[0] - u_1[q_1] + \hat{u}_1(M; p_2, ..., p_n)\} \qquad (IV.3)$$

Similarly, for any good, its all-or-none offer is

$$N_i[q_i] = M - \bar{u}_i\{u_i[0] - u_i[q_i] + \hat{u}_i(M; p_1, ..., p_{i-1}, p_{i+1}, ..., p_n)\} \qquad (IV.4)$$

Since $\bar{u}_i'\{\ \}$ has the same sign as $u_i'[\ ]$, it is easy to verify that

$$N'_i[q_i] = \frac{\partial N_i[q_i; M, p_2, \ldots, p_n]}{\partial q_i} > 0 \qquad N''_i[\ ] < 0 \qquad (IV.5)$$

$$\frac{\partial N_i}{\partial M} > 0$$

For all positive $\bar{q}_i$, it can be verified that

$$N_i[\bar{q}_i] < \int_0^{q_i} p_i \, dq_i \qquad (IV.6)$$

However, if one of the other goods had strictly constant marginal utility as in note III, the last inequalities would become an equality for $i > 1$.

One of my interpretations of the bizarre mathematical Note II of Marshall is that he was trying to derive what I here write as $N'_i[q_i]$. If so, he did not succeed in the attempt.

For the general case of not-necessarily-additive utility, here is how the $N_1(q_1; M, p_2, \ldots, p_n)$ all-or-none offer function is derived. For this general case, we might as well partition $[q_1, \ldots, q_n]$ into two sets, $[q_1, \ldots, q_{r-1}]$ and $[q_r, \ldots, q_n]$ for $1 < r < n$; what we seek is $N(q_1, \ldots, q_{r-1}, M; p_r, \ldots, p_n)$, the amount I will pay to consume positive $(q_1, \ldots, q_{r-1})$ when I can spend the rest of my M on the remaining goods at their frozen $(p_r, \ldots, p_n)$ prices, rather than consume zero of each $(q_1, \ldots, q_{r-1})$ and spend all my M on the other goods at their frozen $(p_r, \ldots, p_n)$ prices.

The u^* function defined back in (I.11) dealing with Hicks's composite good is precisely the tool I now need. The desired all-or-none offer function, N, can be written as $N^r(q_1, \ldots, q_{r-1}, M; p_2, \ldots, p_n)$. It is defined as the unique N root of the following implicit equation:

$$u^*(0, \ldots, 0, M; p_2, \ldots, p_n) = u^*(q_1, \ldots, q_{r-1}, M - N; p_2, \ldots, p_n) \qquad (IV.7)$$

The excess of $N^r(\ )$ over $p_1 q_1 + \ldots + p_{r-1} q_{r-1}$ actually being spent on $(q_1, \ldots, q_{r-1})$ is the CS Marshallians often seek and give names to. Not only does this represent an unnecessary enthusiasm for a particular cardinal $u[\ ]$ or $u^*(\ )$, but even when we provide the CS analyst with the general equilibrium knowledge of $(\partial q_i/\partial M, \partial q_i/\partial p_j)$, in a truly general 'general equilibrium' there is generally *not* a definable money-stuff (or scalar transferable labour) in terms of which net costs and benefits can be measured. Figure 12.3 is too indulgent toward the CS neophytes.

NOTES

I owe thanks to the MIT School of Management for partial aid, and to Eva Hakala for editorial assistance.

1 An astonishingly subtle understanding of the deadweight losses entailed by a tariff is to be found in the pre-Cournot writing of Albert Gallatin (1831), the Swiss-American financier who had been President Thomas Jefferson's Secretary of the Treasury and who was born in 1761 – earlier even than David Ricardo! Doubtless someone will discover CS in Homer and the Talmud.
2 Milton Friedman (1935), in his first venture into print, questioned the deduction of A.C. Pigou (1910) that, under additively independent utilities, the ratio of two (unimportant) good's own-price elasticities would be closely approximated by the ratio of their income elasticities. He was right to question Pigou's result and constructive in stating what is exactly rather than approximately true. But Pigou, we can now perceive, was not wrong in his Marshallian heuristics. To see this, first consider the trivial case where the marginal utility of income is strictly independent of each and every price change: as shown in Samuelson (1942), this logarithmic case implies that all own-price elasticities are precisely unity; since income elasticities are also unity, Pigou's theorem is singularly true. Second, consider the case where there are n general goods with identical marginal utility functions $\phi'[q_j]$ and n with marginal utility functions $\Phi'[q_{n+j}]$: $\phi'' < 0$, $\Phi'' < 0$. To assure Pigou's Marshallian proviso that little is spent on any one good, suppose that $q\phi'[q]$ and $q\Phi'[q]$ have finite upper bounds. Then Pigou would be right to assert that, as $n \to \infty$, every $p_j q_j/M \to 0$ and $[\partial \log q_i/\partial \log p_i]/[\partial \log q_{n+j}/\partial \log p_{n+j}] \to [\partial \log q_i/\partial \log M]/[\partial \log q_{n+j}/\partial \log M]$. Using Pigou's authorized understanding of what Marshall was assuming, we would be little tempted to suppose with Friedman (1949) that Marshall ever meant to be Slutzkian.
3 Can this analysis be applied to a more-than-one-person case? Yes, delicately. Let the demand curves be the horizontal summation of individual's demands. Each person can calculate his/her all-or-nothing CS amounts. Since each such area represents labour units, and since the C_2 total cost is in labour units, we can add consumer's surplus to get a total of consumers' surplus. If this CS total exceeds C_2, the public good q_2 can be produced and sold at its marginal cost, the loss being subsidized by lump-sum taxes on each citizen somehow allocated so as to be each less than their CS. The resulting Lindahl-public-good decision is Pareto optimal, but of course no claim can be made that it is a Bergson-optimal equilibrium. We have a sufficient condition, but not a necessary condition for a decision to produce positive q_2. Marshall and Harberger, tacitly or explicitly, presume that if all Pareto-optimal decisions are made, by the law of large numbers most citizens stand to gain. Maybe so. ('You should live so long,' is one cynical observation.) Every time society opts to use a non-ideal system of taxes and to transfer from rich to poor, naive

readers of Harberger can calculate a net second-order destruction of consumers' surplus – even though an ethical calculus may reckon there to be a positive surplus of welfare of the first order of magnitude. (*Warning*: After an ethically mandated transfer is made from one person to another, the new summed CS might fail the C_2 test. Then, whether some positive q_1 should be produced will depend on ethical decisions made.)

4 Peggy (M.F.W.) Joseph (1939) provided the pivotal insight that deadweight loss in taxation is crucially related to *substitution* elasticities (curvature of indifference contours) and not to the *ceteris paribus* elasticities of dd' addressed by pre-1930 CS analysis.

REFERENCES

Allais, M. (1943): *A le recherche d'un discipline economique* (Paris: Ateliers Industria).
Allais, M. (1981): 'La théorie générale des surplus, tome I et II', *Economies et Sociétés*, Cahiers de l'Institut de sciences mathematiques et economiques appliquees, Laboratoire associe au CNRS, vol. XV, nos 1–5, pp. 17–718.
Auspitz, Rudolf, and Lieben, R. (1889): *Untersuchungen über die Theorie des Preises* (Leipzig: Duncker and Humblot).
Barone, E. (1894): 'Sulla "Consumers' Rent"', *Giornale degli Economisti, 2nd series*, 9, 211–24.
Bergson, A. (1936): 'Real Income, Expenditure Proportionality, and Frisch's "New Methods of Measuring Marginal Utility"', *Review of Economic Studies*, 4, 33–52.
Bergson, A. (1938): 'A Reformulation of Certain Aspects of Welfare Economics', *Quarterly Journal of Economics*, 52, 310–34.
Bergson, A. (1966): *Essays in Normative Economics* (Cambridge, MA: Harvard University Press).
Bergson, A. (1975): 'A Note on Consumer's Surplus', *Journal of Economic Literature*, 13 (1), 38–44.
Berry, A. (1891): 'Alcune Brevi Parole sulla Teoria del Baratto di A. Marshall', *Giornale degli Economisti, 2nd series*, 2, 549–53.
Bishop, R.L. (1943): 'Consumer's Surplus and Cardinal Utility', *Quarterly Journal of Economics*, 57, 421–49.
Cannan, E. (1924): '"Total Utility" and "Consumer's Surplus"', *Economica*, 4, 21–6.
Cournot, A.A. (1838): *Researches into the Mathematical Principles of the Theory of Wealth* (New York: Macmillan) (1929 English translation of 1838 French text).
Divisia, F.J. (1925–6): 'L'indice monétaire et la théorie de la monnaie', *Revue d'Economie Politique*, 39, 842–64, 980–1008 and 1121–52; 40, 49–81.

Dooley, P.C. (1983): 'Consumer's Surplus: Marshall and his Critics', *Canadian Journal of Economics*, 16 (1), 26–38.

Dupuit, A.-J.-E.J. (1844): 'On the Measurement of the Utility of Public Works', translated by R.H. Barback from the *Annales des Ponts et Chaussées*, in *International Economic Papers No. 2* (London: Macmillan, 1952).

Dupuit, A.-J.-E.J. (1849): 'On Tolls and Transport Charges', translated by Elizabeth Henderson from the *Annales des Ponts et Chaussées*, in *International Economic Papers No. 11* (London: Macmillan, 1962).

Dupuit, A.-J.-E.J. (1853): 'On Utility and its Measure – on Public Utility', *Journal des economistes*, 36, 1–27.

Edgeworth, F.Y. (1894): 'Professor J.S. Nicholson on "Consumers' Rent"', *Economic Journal*, 4, 151–8.

Ekelund, R.B., Jr (1987): 'Arsene-Jules-Emile Juvenal Dupuit', in *The New Palgrave Dictionary of Political Economy* (London: Macmillan), vol. I, pp. 143–4.

Fisher, I. (1892): *Mathematical Investigations in the Theory of Value and Prices* (New York: Augustus M. Kelley, 1965).

Friedman, M. (1935): 'Professor Pigou's Method for Measuring Elasticities of Demand from Budgetary Data', *Quarterly Journal of Economics*, 50, 151–63.

Friedman, M. (1949): 'The Marshallian Demand Curve', *Journal of Political Economy*, 57, 463–95. Also in *Essays in Positive Economics* (Chicago, IL: University of Chicago Press, 1953).

Gallatin, A. (1831): 'Free Trade Memorial to Congress', reproduced as ch. XVIII in F.W. Taussig (ed.), *Selected Readings in International Trade* (Boston, MA: Ginn, 1921).

Guillebaud, C.W. (1961): *Notes* [on Marshall's *Principles*, vol. 2 of 1961 variorum edition] (London: Macmillan).

Harberger, A.C. (1971): 'Three Basic Postulates for Applied Welfare Economics: an Interpretative Essay', *Journal of Economic Literature*, 9, 785–97.

Hausman, J.A. (1981): 'Exact Consumer's Surplus and Deadweight Loss', *American Economic Review*, 71, 662–76.

Henderson, A. (1941): 'Consumer's Surplus and the Compensating Variation', *Review of Economic Studies*, 8, 117–21.

Hicks, J.R. (1939): *Value and Capital* (Oxford: Oxford University Press).

Hicks, J.R. (1941): 'The Rehabilitation of Consumers' Surplus', *Review of Economic Studies*, 8, 108–16.

Hicks, J.R. (1943): 'The Four Consumer's Surpluses', *Review of Economic Studies*, 11, 31–41.

Hicks, J.R. (1946): 'The Generalized Theory of Consumer's Surplus', *Review of Economic Studies*, 13, 68–74.

Hicks, J.R. and Allen, R.G.D. (1934): 'A Reconsideration of the Theory of Value: I and II', *Economica*, New Series, 1, 52–76.

Hotelling, H. (1932): 'Edgeworth's Taxation Paradox and the Nature of Demand and Supply Functions', *Journal of Political Economy*, 40, 577–616.

Hotelling, H. (1938): 'The General Welfare in Relation to Problems of Taxation and of Railway and Utility Rates', *Econometrica*, 6, 242–69.

Howey, R. (1960): *The Rise of the Marginal Utility School, 1870–1889* (Lawrence, KS: University Press of Kansas). (Reprint forthcoming New York: Columbia University Press, 1989).

Jenkin, F. (1871): 'On the Principles which Regulate the Incidence of Taxes', in *The Graphic Representation of the Laws of Supply and Demand and Other Essays on Political Economy* (London: London School of Economics, 1931).

Johnson, W.E. (1913): 'The Pure Theory of Utility Curves', *Economic Journal*, 23, 483–513.

Joseph, M.F.W. (1939): 'The Excess Burden of Indirect Taxation', *Review of Economic Studies*, 6, 226–31.

Knight, F.H. (1924): 'Some Fallacies in the Interpretation of Social Cost', *Quarterly Journal of Economics*, 38, 582–606.

Little, I.M.D. (1950): *A Critique of Welfare Economics* (London: Oxford University Press).

Marshall, A. (1879): *Pure Theory of Foreign Trade and Domestic Values*, privately printed.

Marshall, A. (1890, ..., 1920): *Principles of Economics*, ed. by C.W. Guillebaud (London: Macmillan, ninth variorum edition, 1961).

Morgan, J.N. (1948): 'The Measurement of Gains and Losses', *Quarterly Journal of Economics*, 62, 287–308.

Nicholson, J.S. (1893): *Principles of Political Economy* (London: Macmillan), vol. I.

Nicholson, J.S. (1894): 'The Measurement of Utility by Money', *Economic Journal*, 4, 342–7.

Patten, S. (1893): 'Cost and Utility', *Annals of the American Academy of Political and Social Science*, 3, 409–28.

Pigou, A.C. (1910): 'A Method of Determining the Numerical Value of Elasticities of Demand', *Economic Journal*, 20, 636–40.

Pigou, A.C. (1912): *Wealth and Welfare* (London: Macmillan).

Pigou, A.C. (1932): *Economics of Welfare* (London: Macmillan).

Pollak, R.A. (1971): 'Conditional Demand Functions and the Implications of Separate Utility', *Southern Economic Journal*, 37, 423–33.

Ramsey, F.P. (1927): 'A Contribution to the Theory of Taxation', *Economic Journal*, 37, 47–61.

Robertson, D.H. (1924): 'Those Empty Boxes', *Economic Journal*, 34, 16–30.

Samuelson, P.A. (1942): 'Constancy of the Marginal Utility of Income', in O. Lange et al. (eds), *Studies in Mathematical Economics and Econometrics in Memory of Henry Schultz* (Chicago, IL: University of Chicago Press). Reprinted as chapter 5 in *Collected Scientific Papers of Paul A. Samuelson* (CSP) (Cambridge, MA: MIT Press), vol. I, ed. J. Stiglitz, 1966.

Samuelson, P.A. (1947, 1983): *Foundations of Economic Analysis* (Cambridge, MA: Harvard University Press).

Samuelson, P.A. (1960): 'Structure of a Minimum Equilibrium System', in R.W. Pfouts (ed.), *Essays in Economics and Econometrics: A Volume in Honor of Harold Hotelling* (Durham, NC: University of North Carolina Press).

Reprinted as chapter 44 in *CSP*, vol. I.

Samuelson, P.A. (1965): 'Using Full Duality to Show that Simultaneously Additive Direct and Indirect Utilities Implies Unitary Price Elasticity of Demand', *Econometrica*, 33, 781–96. Reprinted as chapter 134 in *CSP*, vol. III, ed. R.C. Merton, 1972.

Samuelson, P.A. (1967): 'The Monopolistic Competition Revolution', in R.E. Kuenne (ed.), *Monopolistic Competition Theory: Studies in Impact. Essays in Honor of Edward H. Chamberlin* (New York: Wiley). Reprinted as chapter 131 in *CSP*, vol. III.

Samuelson, P.A. (1971): 'An Exact Hume–Ricardo–Marshall Model of International Trade', *Journal of International Economics*, 1, 1–18. Reprinted as chapter 162 in *CSP*, vol. III.

Samuelson, P.A. (1973): 'A Quantum-theory Model of Economics: Is the Coordinating Entrepreneur Just Worth his Profit?', in J. Bhagwati and R. Eckhaus (eds), *Development and Planning, Essays in Honour of Paul Rosenstein-Rodan* (London: Allen and Unwin). Reprinted as chapter 214 in *CSP*, vol. IV, eds. H. Nagatani and K. Crowley, 1977.

Samuelson, P.A. (1974): 'Complementarity: an Essay on the 40th Anniversary of the Hicks–Allen Revolution in Demand Theory', *Journal of Economic Literature*, 12, 1255–89. Reprinted as chapter 208 in *CSP*, vol. IV.

Samuelson, P.A. (1982): 'A Chapter in the History of Ramsey's Optimal Feasible Taxation and Optimal Public Utility Prices', in S. Anderson et al. (eds), *Economic Essays in Honour of Jørgen H. Gelting* (Copenhagen: Danish Economic Association). Reprinted in *CSP*, vol. V, ed. K. Crowley, 1986.

Samuelson, P.A. (1987): 'Sraffian Economics', in *The New Palgrave Dictionary of Political Economics* (London: Macmillan), vol. 3, pp. 452–61.

Samuelson, P.A. (1989): 'Revisionist Findings on Sraffa', in K. Bharadwaj and B. Schefold (eds), *Proceedings of the Conference on Sraffa's 'Production of Commodities by Means of Commodities' After Twenty-Five Years, Florence, Italy, 1985* (London: Unwin Hyman).

Sanger, C.P. (1895): 'Recent Contributions to Mathematical Economics', *Economic Journal*, 5, 113–28.

Sono, M. (1943): 'On Dupuit's Relative Utility from the Point of View of Choice Theory', *Economic Essays (Keizai Ronso)*, 57, 88–97.

Sraffa, P. (1926): 'The Laws of Returns under Competitive Conditions', *Economic Journal*, 36, 535–50.

Takayama, A. (1987): 'Consumer Surplus', in *The New Palgrave Dictionary of Political Economics* (London: Macmillan), vol. 1, pp. 607–13.

Whitaker, J. (1975): *The Early Economic Writings of Alfred Marshall, 1867–1890* (two volumes, London: Macmillan).

Willig, R.D. (1976): 'Consumer's Surplus without Apology', *American Economic Review*, 66 (4), 589–97.

Young, A.A. (1913): 'Pigou's Wealth and Welfare', *Quarterly Journal of Economics*, 27, 672–86.

Young, A.A. (1924): 'Marshall on Consumers' Surplus in International Trade', *Quarterly Journal of Economics*, 39, 144–50.

13
The Econometrics of DHSY

David F. Hendry,
John N.J. Muellbauer and
Anthony Murphy

It is a pleasure to participate in the *Economic Journal's* Centenary celebrations even if the suggested topic of our paper is a mere stripling of a decade old. We have chosen to focus on *recent methodological* developments in econometrics in the context of aggregate consumers' expenditure in the United Kingdom (primarily in terms of expenditure on non-durables and services) for three reasons. Firstly, the early history of the consumption function is now well documented (see Spanos, 1989; Thomas, 1989). Further, the two papers by Davidson et al. (1978) (since known by its acronym DHSY) and Hall (1978) delineated the framework for most subsequent empirical research, albeit along different lines. Finally, DHSY based their work on intuitive rather than formal notions, many of which have since been formalized, extended and interrelated, and a synthesis could prove useful.

At the time that DHSY commenced their study, in practical terms consumption functions in the United Kingdom were forecasting badly with persistent over-prediction of expenditure relative to its historical relationship with income. In methodological terms, the proliferation of incompatible models was puzzling: at most one of them could be correct, and it was unclear why conventional methods applied to a common data set delivered different outcomes. Using a 'detective story' approach to account for existing evidence, DHSY developed a conditional model with a servomechanistic interpretation which exhibited empirically constant parameters and explained the properties of extant equations. The main justification of the model was its empirical success, and although the many concepts they used were discussed and empirical evaluation was attempted, it was clear that considerable theoretical work would be needed to make the concepts formal and testable. And like Pooh Bear's attempts at descending stairs on his backside, 'there had to be a better way' to do empirical research.

The DHSY model was (Δ_k denotes a k-period difference; i.e. $\Delta_k c_t = c_t - c_{t-k}$)

$$\Delta_4 c_t = \alpha_1 \Delta_1 i_t + \alpha_2 \Delta_1 \Delta_4 i_t - \alpha_3 \Delta_4 p_t$$
$$- \alpha_4 \Delta_1 \Delta_4 p_t + \alpha_5 (i - c)_{t-4} + \epsilon_t \qquad (13.1)$$

where it was claimed that the α_i were constant over time and $\{\epsilon_t\}$ was a homoscedastic white-noise error process. In (13.1) c, i and p respectively denote real consumers' expenditure on non-durables and services, the implicit deflator thereof, and real personal disposable income; lower case letters are logs of the corresponding capitals. Equation (13.1) involves seven conceptual developments meriting comment:

1 error correction mechanisms like $(i - c)_{t-4}$ and the related notion of cointegration;
2 exogeneity formalized as valid contemporaneous conditioning on variables such as $\Delta_4 i_t$;
3 constancy and invariance of the $\{\alpha_i\}$ parameters, leading on to recursive estimation;
4 encompassing, or accounting for the properties of rival models to (13.1);
5 expectations formation, and the legitimacy of its absence;
6 methodology of dynamic modelling including the theory of reduction;
7 model discovery and evaluation procedures, in a progressive research strategy.

The structure of the paper is as follows: the first section documents the main theory models of consumers' behaviour under consideration. Then, in the following section, we discuss the econometric methodological developments related to the DHSY study, the close interplay in this area between theory and evidence, and the seven concepts noted above. Next we apply recent approaches to the original DHSY equation and data set to replicate their findings and check the congruency of their model using more powerful tests. Finally we re-evaluate the DHSY equation on annual UK data.

The Economics of Consumers' Expenditure

Under the usual assumptions of life-cycle theory (see Ando and Modigliani, 1963), the target level of real non-durable consumption C^* is proportional to real life-cycle wealth W:

$$C^* = K\left(\frac{P_n}{P_d}, \rho\right) W \qquad (13.2)$$

where the factor of proportionality $K(\ ) > 0$ depends on the relative price of non-durables P_n to durables P_d and on the long-run real rate of return ρ. W consists of financial and physical wealth A, and human capital defined as the discounted present value of current and expected future real non-property income I_n. If I_n were a random walk with constant drift, then for an infinitely lived consumer $W = A + I_n/(\rho - g)$ where g is the long-run growth rate of I_n. To obtain a log-linear functional form for consumption, we use the approximation

$$\ln W = \ln\left(A + \frac{I_n}{\rho - g}\right) \approx \ln\left(\frac{I_n}{\rho - g}\right) + (\rho - g)\frac{A}{I_n}$$

$$\approx i_n + (\rho - g)\frac{A}{I_n} - \ln(\rho - g) \qquad (13.3)$$

so that the linear combination of i_n and A/I_n proxies $w = \ln W$. If i_n does not follow a random walk with constant drift, A/I_n will help to forecast future values of income. From (13.2) and (13.3)

$$c^* = \beta_0 - \beta_1 \rho - \beta_2\left(\frac{p_n}{p_d}\right) + \beta_3 i_n + \beta_4 \frac{A}{I_n} \qquad (13.4)$$

where β_0 depends on g. In (13.4), β_1 is greater than zero because of the higher discounting of future incomes as ρ rises; β_2 is greater than zero because of substitution between non-durables and durables; $1 > \beta_3 > 0$ since previous empirical work on non-durables suggests an income elasticity of less than unity (e.g. Bollerslev and Hylleberg, 1986) and research on durables reveals an income elasticity greater than unity; and $\beta_4 > 0$ as $K( ) > 0$.

Five potentially important influences on consumers' behaviour are omitted from (13.3): (a) income uncertainty; (b) credit constraints; (c) demographic changes; (d) liquidity; and (e) dynamic adjustment. We consider these in turn.

Theorists have written extensively on income uncertainty (see, for example, Samuelson, 1969; Merton, 1969; Sandmo, 1974; Flemming, 1973, 1974). Although income uncertainty could increase consumption (see Deaton and Muellbauer, 1980, 405–9), precautionary saving in response to income uncertainty seems more likely, and may confound negative real interest rate effects.

The total consumption of credit-constrained households can be approximated by their income, but could also vary with credit availability. To aggregate across the consumption of rationed and unrationed households, we use weights of π and $1 - \pi$ where π is the consumption share of rationed households, and although variations in π over time need to be modelled (e.g. due to strikes of long duration) it also has a constant component.

Changes in population demography also may alter aggregate consumption (see Currie, Holly and Scott (1989) and Muellbauer and Murphy (1989) for UK evidence). Although older households often have accumulated more wealth than other households, their expenditure-to-income ratios are surprisingly low and US evidence matches this finding for those aged 65 or more. Relevant elements in explaining this apparent contradiction of life-cycle theory include bequest motives, uncertainty about age of death, anticipated health expenditures, physical frailty reducing expenditure and the inability of house owners to unlock their housing wealth. Thus, higher proportions of the population in some of the younger age categories, say under 45, are likely to be associated with a higher level of expenditure relative to income and wealth.

Equation (13.4) imposes equal weights on different assets even though, for example, wealth in a pension fund may be less relevant than liquid assets for spending decisions, suggesting the use of different weights on liquid assets (LA), on illiquid assets (IA) and on debt (DB).

It is convenient to postpone the discussion of dynamics until after the next section.

The Formalization of an Econometric Methodology

Error Correction Mechanisms

A key factor in the predictive success of DHSY and their ability to explain other findings was an error correction mechanism (ECM). Such models originated in the control theory literature (see Phillips, 1954, 1957) and were used by, for example, Stone (1964) although not explicitly as an ECM. Sargan (1964) introduced a real wage feedback term in a wage inflation equation to ensure long-run homogeneity, and interpreted the model as an extension of partial adjustment. Hendry and Anderson (1977) derived a similar formulation from a satisficing model of UK building societies, and Hendry (1977) and DHSY characterized these models as members of a class of error correction processes which ensured coherence between long-run targets in what were otherwise growth rate models.

An ECM is an adjustment process linking realized and target values of an economic variable y_t with y_t^* where $y_t^* = \Sigma_j \beta_j z_{jt}$ is a linear combination of the determinants of long-run plans. The simplest ECM takes the form

$$\Delta y_t = \theta_1 \Delta y_t^* + \theta_2 (y_{t-1}^* - y_{t-1}) \qquad (13.5)$$

where $\theta_1 > 0$, $\theta_2 > 0$, or more generally

$$\Delta y_t = \sum_{j=1}^{n} \theta_j \beta_j \Delta z_{jt} + \theta_{n+1} (y_{t-1}^* - y_{t-1}) \qquad (13.6)$$

where (13.6) has the same steady state implications as (13.5) but allows different adjustment speeds for different zs (e.g. more volatile or more certain zs have smaller θs). ECMs are a generalization of the partial adjustment mechanism[1]

$$\Delta_1 y_t = \theta_0 (y_t^* - y_{t-1}) = \theta_0 \Delta_1 y_t^* + \theta_0 (y_{t-1}^* - y_{t-1}) \qquad (13.7)$$

Expectations and forward-looking behaviour need to be embedded in the ECM target y^* to which adjustment takes place. The ECM can be interpreted as a servomechanism representing the behaviour of agents who face costs of cognition and decision making and may not be rational in the short run but ultimately respond to economic constraints and incentives. Equations (13.5) and (13.6) capture both the short-run discrepancy and the long-run process of reconciliation. In this interpretation, y^* is not just the forward looking but long-run target towards which agents adjust as in the partial adjustment hypothesis; instead, y^* is what the outcome would be if agents were economically rational and took into account the various constraints, including costs of adjustment, which they face. The distinction between this interpretation of the target and more traditional interpretations is subtle, but can be important.

Recent research on *cointegration* of economic time series concerns the existence of long-run solutions of the form $y = \Sigma \beta_j z_j$ (see Granger, 1981, 1986; Hendry, 1986; Engle and Granger, 1987; Phillips, 1987, 1988; Aoki, 1988; Johansen, 1988; *inter alia*). For the long run to make sense, y_t and $\Sigma \beta_j z_{jt}$ must have the same order of *integration*. A series is said to be integrated of order 1, denoted I(1), if the autoregressive representation has a single unit root. Thus, $y_t = y_{t-1} + u_t$, where u_t is stationary,[2] has a single unit root since $\Delta_1 y_t = u_t$ which is I(0) and has a finite and non-zero spectrum at all frequencies. If y_t and $\Sigma \beta_j z_{jt}$ are I(1), then $\Delta_1 y_t$, $\Sigma \beta_j \Delta_1 z_{jt}$ are I(0). In general, $\omega_t = y_t - \Sigma \beta_j z_{jt}$ will be I(1), but y_t is said to be *cointegrated* with $\Sigma \beta_j z_{jt}$ if ω_t is I(0), a hypothesis which can be tested.

A range of tests for unit roots, and hence for cointegration by applying analogous tests to ω_t-type variables, has been proposed. Consider a one-variable case denoted by $\omega_t = y_t - \phi z_t$, where in fact

$$\Delta_1 y_t = \beta_0 + \beta_1 \Delta_1 z_t + \beta_2 (y - \phi z)_{t-1} + \epsilon_t \quad (13.8)$$

The basis of the tests is to form the least squares combination linking y_t and z_t (which calibrates ϕ) and apply the relevant tests to the residuals from the static regression:

$$y_t = \gamma_0 + \gamma_1 z_t + \omega_t \quad (13.9)$$

Letting a circumflex denote least squares estimates, then $\hat{\omega}_t = y_t - \hat{\gamma}_0 - \hat{\gamma}_1 z_t$ is tested for a unit root; if that is rejected, $\hat{\omega}_t$ is the ECM and $\hat{\gamma}_1$ is the estimate of ϕ. One widely used test is the augmented Dickey–Fuller (ADF) statistic (Dickey and Fuller, 1979, 1981), which is the t test on $\lambda_0 = 0$ in[3]

$$\Delta_1 \hat{\omega}_t = \lambda_0 \hat{\omega}_{t-1} + \sum_{i=1}^{n} \lambda_i \Delta_1 \hat{\omega}_{t-i} + v_t \qquad (13.10)$$

The ADF test coincides with the test of $\beta_2 = 0$ in (13.8) (when ϕ is known) if $\beta_1 = 1$ as then there is a *common factor* (COMFAC) in the dynamics (Hendry and Mizon, 1978; Mizon and Hendry, 1980; Sargan, 1980). Thus, one might anticipate (13.10) to be better/poorer as the mean lag is close to/far from zero.[4] Consequently, it may be preferable to analyse (13.8) or, when the homogeneity of y with respect to z is unknown,

$$y_t = \alpha_0 + \alpha_1 z_t + \alpha_2 z_{t-1} + \alpha_3 y_{t-1} + \epsilon_t \qquad (13.11)$$

and test $1 - \alpha_3 = 0$ (is there a unit root?) and $\alpha_1 + \alpha_2 = 0$ (does the level of z matter?).

If y_t and $\Sigma \beta_j z_{jt}$ are cointegrated, then $y_t - \Sigma \beta_j z_{jt}$ will be an ECM, and conversely when the ECM is indeed I(0). Engle and Granger (1987) propose the approach to testing for and estimating cointegrated relationships in (13.9) and (13.10) above and establish an isomorphism between cointegration of I(1) variables and the existence of an I(0) ECM as an aspect of the Granger representation theorem. Consider an n-vector process $\mathbf{x}_t$ which is I(1) such that $\Delta_1 \mathbf{x}_t$ has the Wold decomposition $\Delta_1 \mathbf{x}_t = \mathbf{C}(L)\mathbf{v}_t$, where $\mathbf{C}(L) = \Sigma \mathbf{C}_i L^i$, L is the lag operator and $\mathbf{v}_t \sim \text{ID}(0, \Sigma)$: if there are r cointegrating relationships, then $\mathbf{C}(1) = \Sigma \mathbf{C}_i$ has rank r, and there exists an ECM representation (and conversely) given by

$$\mathbf{A}(L)\Delta_1 \mathbf{x}_t = \mathbf{\Pi} \mathbf{x}_{t-1} + \epsilon_t \qquad (13.12)$$

where $\mathbf{\Pi} = \alpha \beta'$ and α, β are $n \times r$ of rank r.

Johansen (1988) derives an estimator of r by estimating the rank of α and β in the vector autoregressive representation (VAR) (13.12). His method formulates β as the eigenvectors of a positive-definite matrix, where the corresponding ordered eigenvalues μ_i lead to asymptotic test statistics based on $T \ln(1-\mu_i)$; if r such terms are not rejected (using tables reported in, for example, Johansen and Juselius (1989)) then there are r cointegrating linear combinations of $\mathbf{x}_t$, of which $\beta' \mathbf{x}_t$ is one transformation (an application is reported in the next section). Phillips (1988) derives a full information maximum likelihood estimator in a structural ECM system.

In economics, it is unreasonable to treat cointegration as a purely *statistical* phenomenon which happens by chance: ECMs allow an *economic behavioural* explanation for cointegrated time series, which can focus on the *structural* parameters of agents' decision processes (see 'Constancy and invariance', below). Interpreted as embodying cointegrating relationships corresponding to long-run solutions based on economic theory, ECMs have been widely used in empirical research: the current version of HM Treasury's macroeconomic model is specified using a methodology which focuses on the existence of coherent long-run solutions.

Kennan (1979) and Nickell (1985) interpret ECMs as partial adjustment models derived under adjustment costs, rational expectations and intertemporal optimization. Yet another interpretation is as a Euler equation (i.e. an intertemporal first-order optimization condition) modified for liquidity constraints as in Muellbauer and Bover (1986). Suppose that an *un*constrained consumer maximizes expected utility in the form

$$E_t\left(\sum_{i=0}^{T-t} \alpha^i U(C_{t+i}^u)\right)$$

subject to the budget constraint

$$A_t^u = (1 + \rho)A_{t-1}^u + I_{nt}^u - C_t^u$$

Then the Euler equation is

$$E_t[(1 + \rho)\alpha U'_{t+1}] = E_t(U'_t) \qquad (13.13)$$

where $U' = \partial U/\partial C^u$. Hansen and Singleton (1982) show that with homothetic preferences and a log-normal distribution of U'

$$E_{t-1}c_t^u - c_{t-1}^u = \frac{\ln \alpha(1 + \rho) + \sigma_t^2/2}{\gamma} \qquad (13.14)$$

where σ_t^2 is the variance of $\ln U'$ expected at $t - 1$ and $1/\gamma$ is the intertemporal elasticity of substitution. If σ_t^2 is constant

$$\Delta_1 c_t^u = \alpha_0 + \epsilon_t^u \qquad (13.15)$$

where ϵ_t^u is an innovation error. This is a logarithmic form of the Hall (1978) consumption function.

When there are both credit-constrained and unconstrained households, average consumption is approximately given by

$$\Delta_1 c_t = (1 - \pi)\Delta_1 c_t^u + \pi \Delta_1 c_t^c \qquad (13.16)$$

If credit-constrained households consume their non-property income, $c_t^c = i_{nt}^c + \epsilon_t^c$, and so

$$\Delta_1 c_t = (1-\pi)(\alpha_0 + \epsilon_t^u) + \pi\Delta_1 i_{nt}^c + \pi\Delta_1 \epsilon_t^c$$

$$= (1-\pi)(\alpha_0 + \epsilon_t^u) + \pi E_{t-1}\Delta_1 i_{nt}^c + \pi\Delta_1 \epsilon_t^c + \pi\eta_t$$

$$= (1-\pi)(\alpha_0 + \epsilon_t^u) + \pi\{E_{t-1}i_{nt}^c - c_{t-1}^c\} + \pi(\epsilon_t^c + \eta_t) \quad (13.17)$$

where η_t is the prediction error on income (see, for example, Hall and Mishkin (1982), who interpret their evidence as suggesting $\pi \approx 0.2$). Although the { } term is not observable, it can be approximated by $E_{t-1}i_{nt} - c_{t-1}$ or a weighted average of that plus $E_{t-1}\Delta_1 i_{nt}$. This form induces an ECM of the type estimated by Muellbauer and Bover (1986), who also note that the incidence of credit rationing may depend on expected income relative to current so that π may vary with the regressors in (13.17).

Exogeneity

The treatment of $\Delta_4 i_t$ and $\Delta_4 p_t$ and their first differences as valid conditioning variables in (13.1) is open to question both because of potential contemporaneous feedback from $\Delta_4 c_t$ and because agents' decision variables might be the expected values rather than the outcomes.[5] We proceed as follows: denote the vector of contemporaneous variables by $\mathbf{x}_t' = (\Delta_4 c_t: \Delta_4 i_t, \Delta_4 p_t) = (y_t: \mathbf{z}_t')$, the available information by $\mathbf{X}_{t-1}^1 = (\mathbf{x}_1, ..., \mathbf{x}_{t-1})$ and the joint density function by $D_X(\mathbf{X}_T^1|\boldsymbol{\Theta})$ where $\boldsymbol{\Theta}$ denotes the parameterization[6] of $D_X(\ )$. Sequentially factorize $D_X(\mathbf{X}_T^1|\boldsymbol{\Theta})$ as

$$D_X(\mathbf{X}_T^1|\boldsymbol{\Theta}) = \prod_{t=1}^{T} D_X(\mathbf{x}_t|\mathbf{X}_{t-1}^1, \boldsymbol{\Theta})$$

where $\mathbf{x}_t - E(\mathbf{x}_t|\mathbf{X}_{t-1}^1) = \mathbf{v}_t$ is a mean innovation process by construction (Hendry and Richard, 1982). Next, contemporaneously factorize $D_X(\mathbf{x}_t|\mathbf{X}_{t-1}^1, \boldsymbol{\Theta})$ as

$$D_X(\mathbf{x}_t|\mathbf{X}_{t-1}^1, \boldsymbol{\Theta}) = D_Y(y_t|\mathbf{z}_t, \mathbf{X}_{t-1}^1, \boldsymbol{\lambda}_1) D_Z(\mathbf{z}_t|\mathbf{X}_{t-1}^1, \boldsymbol{\lambda}_2) \quad (13.18)$$

Then Engle, Hendry and Richard (1983) defined $\mathbf{z}_t$ as *weakly exogenous* for $\boldsymbol{\alpha}$ (the parameter of interest in (13.1)) if (a) $\boldsymbol{\alpha}$ is a function of $\boldsymbol{\lambda}_1$ *alone*, and (b) $\boldsymbol{\lambda}_1$ and $\boldsymbol{\lambda}_2$ are *variation free*. Condition (a) involves obtaining $\boldsymbol{\alpha}$ from *only* analysing the conditional model, whereas (b) requires that there are no cross-links between the conditional and marginal models so that nothing about α could be learned from the latter. Thus, when z_t is weakly exogenous for α, there is no loss of information about α from only analysing the conditional process $D_Y(y_t|z_t, X_{t-1}^1, \lambda_1)$ and neglecting to model the marginal process $D_Z(z_t|X_{t-1}^1, \lambda_2)$. Note that lagged feedback from y to z is permissible.[7] Cases where it is invalid to condition include the following: if the ECM from the conditional model also enters the marginal model (this violates (b) and necessitates joint estimation for full efficiency); if there is cross-equation contemporaneous or serial correlation (denying (b) again, since the parameters of the conditional and marginal distributions are functions of the parameters of the other); or where current-dated variables represent solved out expectations.

Since (a) represents what is of interest to the investigator, it is not testable (although it may fail in any given formulation). To test (b) requires the complete specification of the marginal density, and the advantage of conditioning was precisely to avoid doing so! Thus, only aspects of (b) can be tested and care is necessary to avoid rejecting due to mis-specification of the marginal process. Engle (1982a) proposed a Lagrange multiplier (LM) test equivalent to incorporating in the y equation the elements of ν corresponding to the z process and testing their significance: an extension of this test is discussed below and applied in the next section. Alternatively, a Hausman (1978) test of least squares versus instrumental variables estimates would deliver a similar conclusion, and DHSY adopted this approach to the extent of reporting both sets of estimates and noting their close similarity. However, since parameters are of little interest unless they are constant, and from (13.18) a more penetrating analysis is feasible when λ_1 is constant but λ_2 is not, we turn to that.

Constancy and Invariance

DHSY stressed the *constancy* of their parameters as an essential property of (13.1), particularly since other models of the consumption function were mis-predicting. They relied on one post-sample[8] predictive failure test asymptotically equivalent to a Chow (1960) test for non-constant coefficients over the period where inflation increased. One test might not reject because of 'good luck' in selecting the post-sample period, but Bean (1978) and Davis (1982) showed that the equation held over longer post-sample periods.

Three developments help clarify the basis of their approach. Firstly, Hendry (1979) showed that model mis-specification was necessary but not sufficient for predictive failure to arise, and also required the post-sample data process to behave differently from that in-sample. Secondly, the personal computer and its ready provision of graphical output facilitated a rapid proliferation of recursive estimation and testing techniques (Terasvirta, 1970; Brown, Durbin and Evans, 1975; Hendry and Neale, 1987), so that detailed analyses of constancy issues became a routine rather than a nightmare. Thirdly, the distinction between *constancy* and *invariance* was reiterated by the analysis of exogeneity: parameters could vary over time but be invariant to (say) policy changes, or be constant over time but alter for a class of interventions. The concept of invariance or *autonomy* has a long history (Frisch, 1938; Haavelmo, 1944; Aldrich, 1989), and building on that basis Engle et al. (1983) defined z_t as *super exogenous* for α if z_t is weakly exogenous for α, and λ_1 is invariant to changes in λ_2. Thus, super exogeneity could be violated by a failure of weak exogeneity or by a lack of invariance (either of which would necessitate joint modelling) and tests of super exogeneity could be tests of either or both aspects.

Lucas (1976) criticized conventional macroeconomic models on the grounds that agents' expectational mechanisms would alter as policies changed, so that policy simulations would yield misleading inferences in models where the behavioural parameters were not separately distinguished from the parameters of the expectations processes. Thus, super exogeneity characterizes when a conditional model should be immune to the Lucas critique. Consider the scalar example

$$y_t = z_t \beta + u_t \qquad (13.19)$$

where the invariance of β to a policy change is questioned. Denote a policy variable by ζ_t where $E(\zeta_t|I_t) = \mu_t$ is the mean of ζ_t, σ_t^2 its variance and I_t denotes available information, and consider the expansion (Engle and Hendry, 1989)

$$\beta = \psi + \psi_1 \mu_t + \psi_3 \mu_t \sigma_t^2 \qquad (13.20)$$

The null of invariance entails the joint hypothesis that $\psi_1 = \psi_2 =$

$\psi_3 = 0$, so that $\psi_0 = \beta$; otherwise, β varies with the moments of the policy rule. Under rational expectations, $E(z_t|I_t)$ rather than z_t should enter the model (13.19), and (13.20) would detect that if z depended on ζ. To construct a test, when I_t is observable, μ_t can be estimated by regression or $\zeta_t = \mu_t + \xi_t$ can be used to eliminate μ_t in (13.20); var(ζ_t) (about a constant) or Engle's (1982b) ARCH model could be used for modelling σ_t^2, the latter allowing a split of σ_t^2 into predictable and unpredictable components.[9] However, expectations models also entail intermodel comparisons and hence encompassing, and so we first consider the issue.

Encompassing

The theory of encompassing concerns whether one model can explain the empirical findings of rival models of the same phenomena (Hendry and Richard, 1982; Mizon, 1984; Mizon and Richard, 1986; Hendry and Richard, 1989). If so, the latter are encompassed; if not, they contain specific information excluded by the former. The analysis treats each model as the data generation process (DGP) in turn to see whether it can account for the rival models' empirical results.

DHSY's first encompassing attempts involved standardizing the data set used and embedding the rival models in a common framework. Hendry and Richard (1982) formalized that approach by treating all models as reductions of the DGP (see 'Dynamic modelling methodology', below). Consequently, both nested and non-nested models come under the remit of encompassing analyses. Cox (1961, 1962) analysed tests for separate families of hypotheses, proposing a modified likelihood ratio statistic,[10] and many related one-degree-of-freedom non-nested tests now exist (see MacKinnon (1983) for a survey). Mizon (1984) and Mizon and Richard (1986) analysed the encompassing principle and developed a test-generating formula which itself encompassed virtually all extant tests; Hendry and Richard (1989) offer a survey.

Consider two rival models, denoted M_1 and M_2 with parameter vectors $\boldsymbol{\alpha}$ and $\boldsymbol{\beta}$, of a variable y_t generated by $D_Y(\boldsymbol{Y}_T^1|\boldsymbol{\Theta})$. Since both models are created by reduction from $D_Y(\ )$, $\boldsymbol{\alpha}$ and $\boldsymbol{\beta}$ are functions of $\boldsymbol{\Theta}$ denoted by $\boldsymbol{\alpha}(\boldsymbol{\theta})$ and $\boldsymbol{\beta}(\boldsymbol{\theta})$,[11] and by an equivalent argument applied to M_1, $\boldsymbol{\beta}(\boldsymbol{\alpha})$ represents what M_1 anticipates M_2

should find when M_1 is treated as the DGP. Let $\psi_\alpha = \boldsymbol{\beta}(\boldsymbol{\theta}) - \boldsymbol{\beta}[\boldsymbol{\alpha}(\boldsymbol{\theta})]$ denote the population encompassing difference, and let $\mathscr{E}$ denote *encompasses*; then $M_1 \mathscr{E} M_2$ if and only if $\psi_\alpha = 0$. If $M_1 \sim\mathscr{E} M_2$ (i.e. does not encompass) then M_2 reflects specific features of $D_Y(\ )$ not accounted for by M_1, and if $M_1 \mathscr{E} M_2$ then either $M_2 \sim\mathscr{E} M_1$ or M_1 and M_2 are reparameterizations. If neither model encompasses the other, a more general (or very different) model is needed.

Let M_m denote the minimal nesting model[12] of M_1 and M_2. If $M_1 \mathscr{E} M_2$, M_2 provides no information about y beyond M_1, and since M_m reflects information from $D_Y(\ )$ in addition to that in M_1 only to the extent that M_2 does, then M_1 will also encompass M_m. This concept, called parsimonious encompassing and denoted $\mathscr{E}_p$, requires that a *small* model M_1 can account for the results of the *larger* model M_m within which it is nested, and in linear models $M_1 \mathscr{E} M_2$ if and only if $M_1 \mathscr{E}_p M_m$.

The relationship defined by $\mathscr{E}$ is not transitive, but this reflects the problem of proceeding from the simple to the general. The converse route of general $\rightarrow$ simple argues for using parsimonious encompassing and involves testing the validity of any reduction from M_m to M_1 to check whether $M_1 \mathscr{E}_p M_m$ since $M_m \mathscr{E} M_1$ must hold because of nesting. Let M_3 denote an intermediate model between M_1 and M_m; then if $M_3 \mathscr{E}_p M_m$ and $M_1 \mathscr{E}_p M_3$, it follows that $M_1 \mathscr{E}_p M_m$. Consequently, parsimonious encompassing *is* transitive, antisymmetric and reflexive (Florens et al., 1987), and defines a partial ordering over models which sustains a progressive research strategy.

It is possible to apply encompassing to a broader model than that actually developed under a rival theory. This is what Davidson and Hendry (1981) did in their test of the Hall model against an ECM to show that it is encompassed by the latter but cannot account for the latter's coefficients being the relevant derived function of the income generation process. Another example is that M_2 may treat $\boldsymbol{\beta}$ as constant but if (say) M_1 implies that $\boldsymbol{\beta}$ cannot be constant, then M_1 must predict that M_2 should fail a test of parameter constancy. This use of encompassing recurs in the next section as part of a strategy for testing the importance of changes in expectations formation in conditional models.

Expectations

If expectations are at least cointegrated with outcomes, aspects of the Lucas critique become testable in a framework of cointegration where some of the expectations variables are subject to regime shifts: if agents form expectations about future policy but econometric models condition on policy-related variables, predictive failure will ensue when such rules change. To apply the above approach to the Lucas critique, consider the conditional model (Hendry, 1988)

$$E(y_t|\mathbf{z}_t) = \boldsymbol{\beta}'\mathbf{z}_t \qquad (13.21)$$

where $\zeta_t \in I_t$ is an admissable element in the agents' information set, so that

$$E(y_t|\zeta_t) = \boldsymbol{\beta}'E(\mathbf{z}_t|\zeta_t) \qquad (13.22)$$

Note, therefore, that the conditional model sustains an expectations interpretation, though the converse does not necessarily hold (e.g. if $\mathbf{z}_t$ is not available information). To see that regime shifts sustain powerful encompassing tests for discrimination between feedback and feedforward models let

$$\mathbf{z}_t = \boldsymbol{\Pi}_t\zeta_t + \mathbf{u}_t \qquad (13.23)$$

be the marginal process for $\mathbf{z}_t$. If (13.21) and (13.23) hold, then the regression of y_t on ζ_t cannot be constant since the coefficient would be $\boldsymbol{\beta}'\boldsymbol{\Pi}_t$ and would vary with t. Conversely, if (13.22) and (13.23) hold and $\mathbf{z}_t \notin I_t$, then the regression of y_t on $\mathbf{z}_t$ cannot be constant, which is precisely the logic of the Lucas critique. Thus, an encompassing test can discriminate between expectations and feedback provided there *are* regime shifts, a conclusion reinforced by the presence in the behavioural model of expectations about future events (Favero, 1989). The joint application of exogeneity and encompassing also clarifies the role of expectations versus feedbacks in stationary processes (Hendry and Neale, 1988).

Dynamic Modelling Methodology

The approach in DHSY was far from structured, although it adopted ideas from Leamer (1976), Mizon (1977) and Sargan (1980). The model search process was an iterative one, and they made at least one serious mistake: when new information was introduced, it was analysed in the context of the adopted model; and DHSY *did not return to the general model* implicit in the extension. This led to erroneous inferences about the role of liquid assets, and related mistakes about the treatment of seasonality (Hendry and von Ungern-Sternberg, 1981). Many of the methodological developments since DHSY have served to emphasize the essential role of the general model and the need for simplification approaches to model discovery (Hendry, 1979; Mizon and Hendry, 1980; Sargan, 1980; Hendry and Richard, 1983; Hendry, 1987; Pagan, 1987; *inter alia*). Not to do so allows 'holes' to appear in the σ-field of information which can generate apparent paradoxes; two items of information might individually corroborate a model yet jointly refute it (Ericsson and Hendry, 1989), which is related to the intransitivity of $\mathscr{E}$ above.

Once the imperative of general to simple is adopted, many previously puzzling problems are clarified. For example, the theory of reduction not only accounts for the properties of empirical models as reduced reparameterizations of the DGP, it also explains the 'symptomatology' which pervades the elementary econometrics textbooks. Further, parsimonious encompassing re-emerges as the limit to valid model reduction; most major econometrics concepts (innovations, exogeneity, Granger-causality, constancy etc.) are revealed as corresponding to measures of no loss of information from the associated reduction; and a taxonomy of information sets for model evaluation arises due to the sequence of reductions so that the complete range of null hypotheses for diagnostic testing can be delineated (Hendry, 1987; Hendry, 1989; Hendry and Ericsson, 1989). The results above on invariance, super exogeneity and encompassing (and earlier results on COMFAC and predictive failure) thus fit neatly into a structured framework as evaluating the potential losses from the associated reductions. Empirical models which adequately characterize the evidence on all the criteria are said to be *congruent*.

Discovery and Evaluation

The discovery of useful empirical models is not a mechanistic procedure but involves important elements of creativity and a researcher's own value added. Since the validity of an empirical model is a property of that model and not of how the model was found, the primary role of methodology in the context of discovery is to advise on research strategies that might be more efficient or less prone to difficulties. In the general to simple approach, two main steps are involved: the formulation of the initial congruent general model, which depends on previous empirical knowledge and theoretical reasoning, and determines the usefulness of the framework within which modelling occurs; and the simplification route adopted to formulate the interpretable parsimonious econometric model, which should satisfy the design criteria and be publicly tested in due course.

Once a model is in the public domain, it is open to evaluation by deriving functions of as yet unused information that its proprietor would accept as legitimate tests of the model. Thus, tests for constancy on out-of-sample data, invariance against novel regime changes, encompassing of new rival specifications, or even new test statistics all allow genuine evaluation of a claimed congruent model. In this context of justification, the standard principles of Neyman–Pearson testing as quality control apply and are an essential step in ascertaining whether models are sustainable or require revision.

DHSY Revisited

To illustrate the methodological developments in above, we re-evaluated the model in DHSY using the new approaches and tests. Firstly, the re-estimates of equation (13.1) over their final sample period, 1959, quarter 2, to 1975, quarter 4, were as follows (compare DHSY equation (45*)):

$$\Delta_4 c_t = 0.48\Delta_4 i_t - 0.23\Delta_1\Delta_4 i_t - 0.12\Delta_4 p_t - 0.31\Delta_1\Delta_4 p_t$$
$$(0.028) \quad\quad (0.038) \quad\quad\quad (0.022) \quad\quad (0.098)$$

$$- 0.094(c - i)_{t-4} + 0.006\Delta_4 DV_t$$
$$(0.012) \quad\quad\quad\quad (0.002) \quad\quad\quad\quad\quad\quad (13.24)$$

$$R^2 = 0.956 \quad \sigma = 0.00601$$
$$F(6,65) = 235.0 \quad DW = 2.00$$

In (13.24), DV is a dummy variable for indirect tax changes,

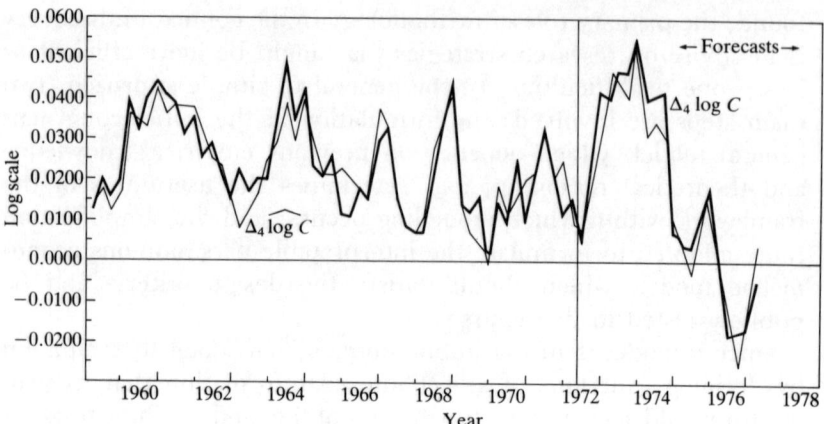

Figure 13.1 Actual and fitted values from DHSY over the period 1958, quarter 2, to 1976, quarter 2.

coefficient standard errors are in parentheses, σ is the standard deviation of the residuals, R^2 is the squared multiple correlation coefficient but for an equation without an intercept, the F test checks the significance of (13.24) and DW denotes the Durbin–Watson statistic. Figure 13.1 shows the fitted and actual outcomes from estimating (13.24) over 1958, quarter 2, to 1971, quarter 2, and forecasting over the remaining sample to 1976, quarter 2. All the empirical calculations and graphs are from PC-GIVE 6.01 (Hendry, 1989).

The re-analysis proceeds in five stages as follows: firstly, we examine the cointegration of c_t with i_t and $\Delta_4 p_t$ and evaluate the legitimacy of the unit coefficient for the ECM; secondly, we consider a reduction sequence from an unrestricted representation with five lags; then we use recursive procedures to investigate the constancy of (13.24) more rigorously; next we examine the weak and super exogeneity of income and inflation for the parameters of (13.24); finally, we consider the constancy of the marginal processes for income and annual inflation to test the encompassing implications against expectations alternatives.

Cointegration

Following the Johansen (1988) approach of 'Error correction mechanisms', above, to retest DHSY's choice a fifth-order VAR was estimated for $(c_t, i_t, \Delta_4 p_t)$ including a constant and three seasonals in every equation. The eigenvalues of the long-run matrix π and its factorization into the (standardized) matrices α and β' as in (13.12) yielded (for T = 1959, quarter 2, to 1976, quarter 2) for the eigenvalues of π

j	μ_j	$-T\log(1-\mu_j)$	$T\sum_{r=1}^{j}\log(1-\mu_r)$
1	0.039	2.77	2.77
2	0.101	7.32	10.09
3	0.204	15.77	25.86

The null of zero cointegrating vectors can be rejected in favour of one, whereas the null of one is only marginally rejected against two. The matrix of cointegrating weights β is

Variable	c_t	i_t	$\Delta_4 p_t$
c_t	1.00	−0.93	0.66
i_t	−1.30	0.00	0.11
$\Delta_4 p_t$	−0.63	2.75	1.00

and these corresponded to the following feedback coefficients (α matrix)

Variable	c_t	i_t	$\Delta_4 p_t$
c_t	−0.047	−0.069	−0.005
i_t	0.330	−0.339	−0.007
$\Delta_4 p_t$	−0.190	−0.084	0.003

The first row of β suggests a cointegrating equation of the form $c_t = 0.93 i_t - 0.66 \Delta_4 p_t$, consistent with the derived long-run solution form (13.24) and supporting a near unit coefficient on income in the ECM: the cointegrating linear combination is plotted in figure 13.2. The first element in α yields a feedback coefficient of -0.047 which is somewhat smaller than in equation (13.24) but supports cointegration.

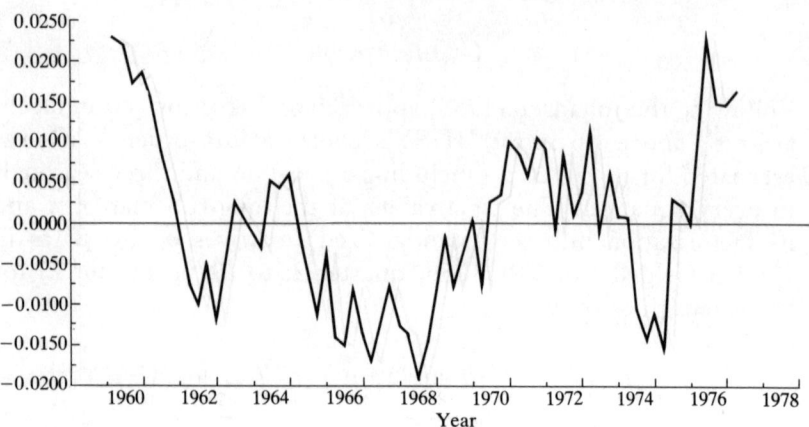

Figure 13.2 First cointegrating vector in UK consumers' expenditure.

A Reduction Sequence

Given this evidence in favour of c, i and $\Delta_4 p$ being cointegrated despite only 17 years' data, we commence single equation modelling with five lags on every variable, obtain the long-run solution and then sequentially simplify to a parsimonious interpretable econometric representation. While anachronistic, the results highlight several modelling issues. Firstly, the estimates of the unrestricted autoregressive-distributed lag model, denoted AD(5, 5, 5), are shown in table 13.1 (the constant and seasonals are not reported).

The tests conducted are as follows: AR 1–5 is an F test for fifth-order residual autocorrelation; ARCH 1–4 is an F test for fourth-order ARCH residuals, White is the F test for heteroscedasticity in White (1980), Reset is an F test for functional form misspecification (Ramsey, 1969), and $\chi^2(2)$ is a test for normality (see Hendry (1989) for details and references). A set of F tests confirms the joint significance of each variable in the table, although the t tests on the sums of coefficients are not significant at even conventional levels for c and i, which would not allow the null hypothesis of no cointegration to be rejected at this stage. The tests on the constant and the seasonals were not significant. F tests also revealed

Table 13.1 Unrestricted AD(5, 5, 5) estimates

Lag	0	1	2	3	4	5	Σ
c	−1.000	0.132	−0.032	0.058	0.731	−0.026	−0.136
	−	(0.127)	(0.090)	(0.091)	(0.097)	(0.122)	(0.097)
i	0.272	0.151	0.038	0.044	−0.106	−0.196	0.125
	(0.040)	(0.056)	(0.050)	(0.047)	(0.052)	(0.056)	(0.081)
$\Delta_4 p$	−0.316	0.166	0.023	−	−	−	−0.127
	(0.087)	(0.151)	(0.096)	−	−	−	(0.040)
$\Delta_4\text{DV}$	0.0070	−	−	−	−	−	0.0070
	(0.0023)	−	−	−	−	−	(0.0023)

$R^2 = 0.9984$; $\sigma = 0.0058$; $F(18, 53) = 1836.1$; DW = 2.15; AR1–5 $F(5, 48) = 1.67$; ARCH 1–4 $F(4, 45) = 2.28$; White $F(33, 19) = 0.82$; Reset $F(1, 52) = 11.85$; Normality $\chi^2(2) = 0.495$.

Standard errors in parentheses.

that each lag except the third was significant at least at the 0.5 per cent level. The mis-specification checks are acceptable, except for the Reset test which indicates an inappropriate functional form choice (this converged on insignificance as the reduction proceeded, and a separate test for long-run price level homogeneity did not reject).

The solved static long-run equation was (Q denotes the net seasonal coefficient):

$$c = 0.920i - 0.933p + 0.051\text{DV} + 0.765 - 0.418Q \quad (13.25)$$
$$(0.089) \quad (0.536) \quad (0.042) \quad (0.697) \quad (0.379)$$

The coefficients are close to those of the Johansen procedure,[13] and the standard errors are consistent with the existence of a long-run relationship.

Since the seasonals were insignificant in the unrestricted equation, these were eliminated (mimicking the DHSY decision); the 'obvious' transformations were then made to fourth differences, ECM and levels, without any eliminations, and these were followed by a sequence of further deletions and any suggested transformations. Altogether, nine steps were taken to return to DHSY, and figure 13.3 records the graph of the Schwarz (1978) criterion (which balances goodness of fit and parsimony) during the reduction. The upturn at the last step (which is significant at a high level) is due to deleting Δi_{t-4} which is absent from (13.1);

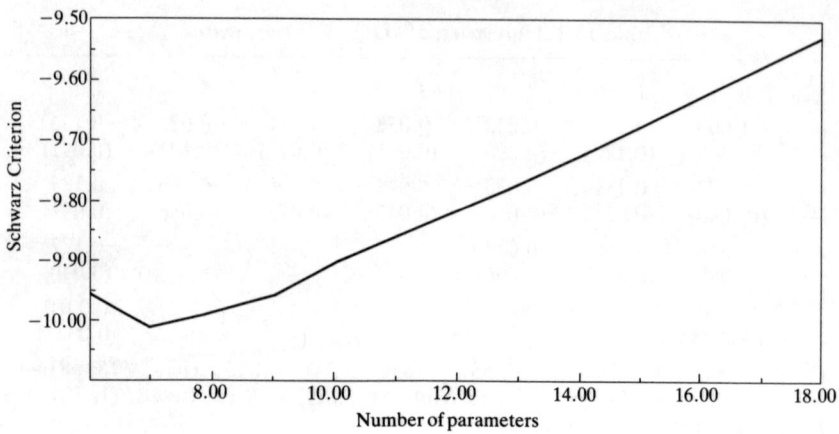

Figure 13.3 Reduction from AD(5, 5, 5) to DHSY.

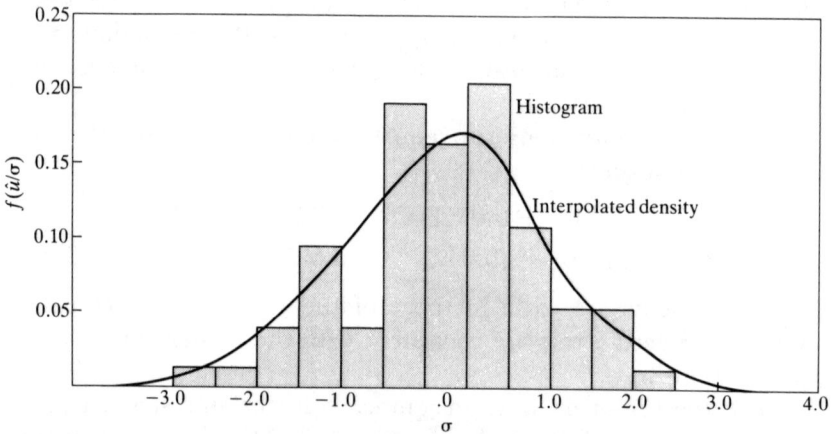

Figure 13.4 DHSY residual frequency plot, 1958, quarter 2, to 1976, quarter 2.

otherwise, the reduction sequence monotonically and almost linearly improved the criterion value (and hence σ). Figure 13.4 records the histogram and interpolated density for the final set of residuals as further evidence about their normality.

Nevertheless, if the constant and seasonals had been retained

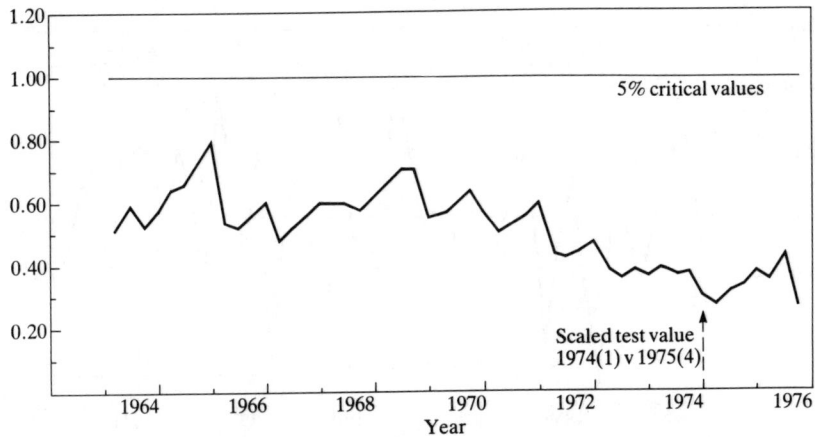

Figure 13.5 Scaled sequence of 'break-point' Chow tests over the period 1963, quarter 1, to 1975, quarter 4.

throughout, the final σ would have been 0.567 per cent (which is significantly smaller than (13.24)), with an ECM coefficient of -0.15 (0.03) consistent with later findings (cf. for example Hendry and von Ungern-Sternberg, 1981). Moreover, although the predictive failure test was large ($\chi^2(20) = 121$), the Chow test was only 1.14 for the last 20 observations, suggesting that this expanded model is constant, but the numerical values of the subsample coefficients differed markedly (but not significantly) from the whole-period results (the Chow test for (13.24) was 1.06).

Tests for COMFAC reductions were also tried: a static baseline with fifth-order error autoregression was strongly rejected, but if one lag of both i and inflation were included and a simple fourth-order process was estimated, $\sigma = 0.7$ per cent could be achieved, although the model was somewhat less constant than (13.24).

Recursive Estimation and Constancy

Next, we estimated (13.24) recursively over the sample 1959, quarter 2, to 1975, quarter 4, matching DHSY and figure 13.5 shows the sequence of 'break-point' Chow (1960) tests, scaled by their critical values at the 5 per cent level: no value is significant, confirming the constancy of (13.24) claimed by DHSY on this more stringent analysis. This outcome is supported by figure 13.6

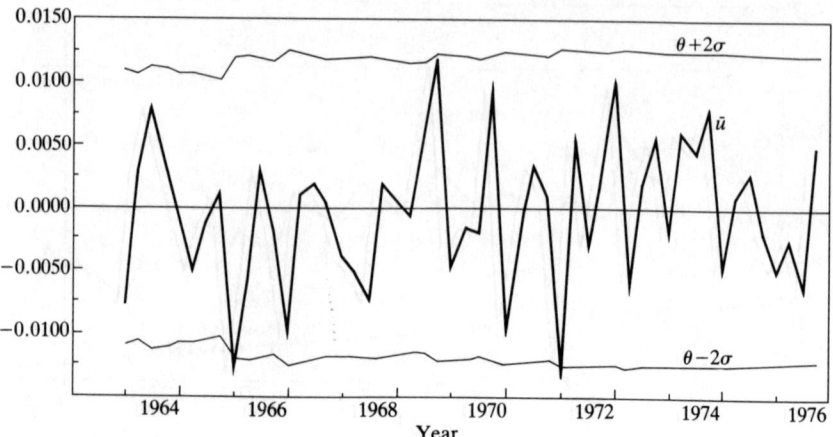

Figure 13.6 One-step-ahead forecast errors from DHSY with $\pm 2\sigma$.

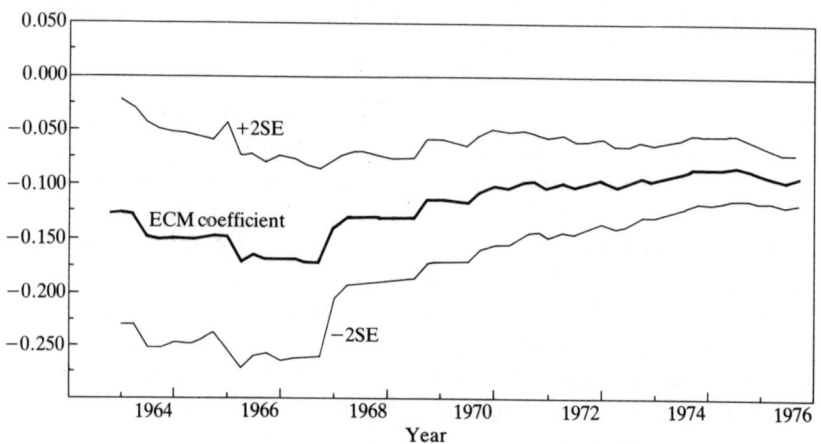

Figure 13.7 DHSY error correction coefficient +2SE by recursive least squares.

which records the sequence of one-step-ahead forecast error with $0 \pm 2\sigma_t$ for each feasible t, and by the graph of the ECM coefficient $\pm$ 2SE in figure 13.7; its recursively computed t value is reported in figure 13.8 and confirms that it was significant for the entire sample on conventional critical values, and from 1966 on for

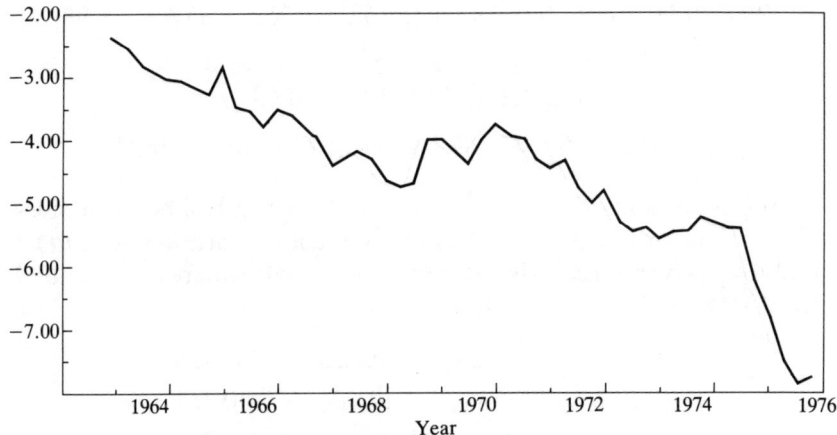

Figure 13.8 Recursively computed t statistic on the DHSY error correction mechanism, 1963, quarter 1, to 1975, quarter 4.

Dickey–Fuller critical values. Overall, therefore, (13.1) is acceptable on this criterion.

Super Exogeneity and Invariance

Fourthly, to test weak and super exogeneity against parameter alternatives, we developed single equation models of i_t and $\Delta_4 p_t$:

$$\Delta_1\Delta_4 p_t = \underset{(0.06)}{0.18\Delta_4 p_{t-1}} - \underset{(0.16)}{0.48\Delta_4 p_{t-4}} + \underset{(0.14)}{0.35\Delta_4 p_{t-5}} - \underset{(0.002)}{0.0004}$$
(13.26)

$R^2 = 0.21 \quad \sigma = 0.0086 \quad F(3, 63) = 5.52 \quad DW = 1.60$

$\chi^2(2) = 3.69 \quad \text{AR 1–5}, F[5, 58] = 1.64$

$\text{ARCH 4}, F[4, 55] = 1.75$

$X_i^2, F[6, 56] = 2.12 \quad X_i^* X_j, F[9, 53] = 1.69$

and

$$\Delta_4 i_t = \underset{(0.14)}{0.68\Delta_4 i_{t-1}} - \underset{(0.13)}{0.64\Delta_4 i_{t-4}} + \underset{(0.003)}{0.01\Delta R_{t-3}} - \underset{(0.006)}{0.001}$$
$$- \underset{(0.22)}{1.1\Delta\Delta_4 p_t} + \underset{(0.27)}{0.46\Delta_4 c_{t-1}} + \underset{(0.29)}{0.92\Delta_4 c_{t-4}}$$
(13.27)

$R^2 = 0.70 \quad \sigma = 0.0178 \quad F(6, 62) = 24.5 \quad DW = 1.98$

$\chi^2(2) = 0.72 \quad AR\ 1\text{-}5,\ F[5, 5] = 1.23$
$ARCH\ 4,\ F[4, 54] = 0.63$

$X_i^2,\ F[12, 49] = 1.02 \quad Reset,\ F[1, 61] = 0.23$

In (13.26) and (13.27), X_i^2 is an F test for residual heteroscedasticity. The residuals from these two equations are denoted $\hat{u}[p]$ and $\hat{u}[i]$ and these and distributed lags of their squares were added to (13.24) and tested for significance:

$\Delta_4 c_t = 0.47 \Delta_4 i_t - 0.22 \Delta\Delta_4 i_t - 0.12 \Delta_4 p_t - 0.32 \Delta\Delta_4 p_t$
$\qquad [0.04] \qquad [0.06] \qquad\quad [0.03] \qquad\quad [0.15]$
$\quad - 0.09(c - i)_{t-4} + 1.0\hat{u}[p]_t + 0.019\hat{u}[i]_t - 0.27\hat{u}[p]_t^2$
$\qquad [0.02] \qquad\qquad [2.0] \qquad\quad [0.103] \qquad\quad [0.33]$
$\quad + 0.11\hat{u}[p]_{t-1}^2 - 2.2u[i]_t^2 + 1.6u[i]_{t-1}^2$
$\qquad [0.14] \qquad\quad [2.3] \qquad\quad [1.5] \qquad\qquad\qquad (13.28)$

$R^2 = 0.947 \quad \sigma = 0.00686 \quad F(11, 52) = 83.8 \quad DW = 2.21$

Longer or shorter lags on the squared residuals yielded similar outcomes – in no case were any of the added terms testing for weak or super exogeneity significant (terms in [ ] denote heteroscedastic-consistent standard errors; see White, 1980).

Testing the Lucas Critique

Finally, we tested the constancy of the marginal models for i_t and $\Delta_4 p_t$ following the procedures described earlier. Scalar autoregressions, VAR models and dynamic single equation models were investigated and with one exception (the VAR equation for i_t) all revealed considerable non-constancy of these marginal processes, inconsistent with any attempted interpretation of the contemporaneous terms in (13.24) as proxies for expectations. Figures 13.9 and 13.10 show two typical plots of sequences of 'break-point' Chow tests: none of the breaks coincides with a period where (13.24) has any constancy problems. Thus, the Lucas critique can be rejected for (13.24) for the claim that it will alter if expectations formation changes.

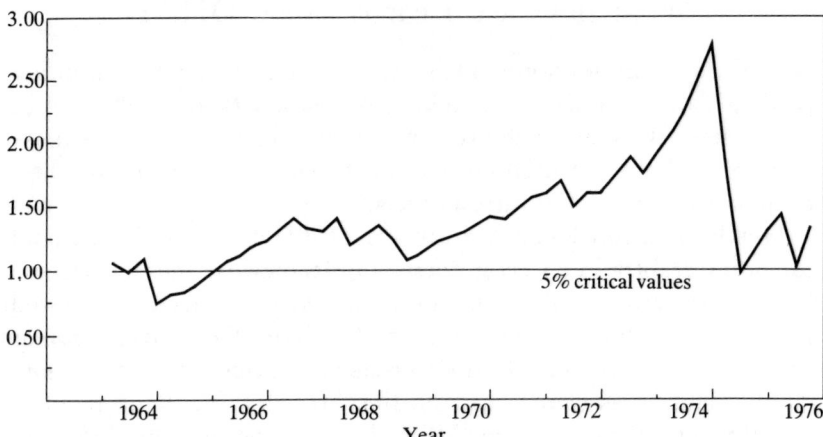

Figure 13.9 Sequence of 'break-point' Chow tests for AD(5) model of $\Delta_4 \log P$.

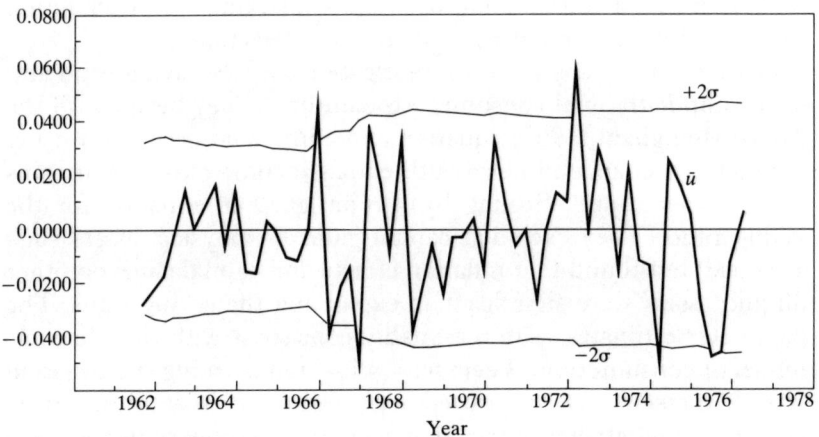

Figure 13.10 One-step forecast errors $\pm 2\sigma$ from AD(1) model of $\Delta_4 \log I$.

What have we Learnt Since DHSY

One of the main developments since DHSY has been the attention paid to data on and the modelling of the assets and liabilities of consumers. We now briefly review studies which make use of these data in the United Kingdom, within the context of solved out life-cycle consumer expenditure models.[14]

Hendry and von Ungern-Sternberg (1981) modelled the demand for non-durables in an error correction framework incorporating a liquid asset effect and an inflation correction to income weighted by the level of liquid asset holdings. The latter has proved popular in recent research, even if liquid assets have been replaced by more comprehensive asset measures in the Treasury and Bank models. Muellbauer (1981) examined the demand for non-durables and durables in a two-equation system in which relative prices, liquid and illiquid assets played important roles. However, the main objective of that paper was theoretical, namely to demonstrate that the cross-equation restrictions implied by simple neoclassical intertemporal consumption theory was rejected by the data. It was suggested that a combination of credit constraints and transaction costs for durables might account for this rejection.

Pesaran and Evans (1984) investigated the UK saving ratio and hence implicitly total consumer expenditure. They began with the Ando–Modigliani (1963) equation and eliminated net wealth using the identity 'change in net wealth equals income plus capital gains minus expenditure'. Scaling by income gave an equation for the saving ratio. They excluded capital gains on physical assets such as houses but found that inflation effects and capital gains on other illiquid assets were significant in explaining the saving ratio. The parameter estimates were reasonably consistent with the life-cycle model of consumption. Their reason for transforming the equation was that assets were measured with error and that these errors built up cumulatively so that they were non-stationary in a statistical sense. Quasi-differencing, they argued, reduced them to stationarity. Whether these errors were important enough to throw away the long-run information content in the data is an open question, though we have our doubts. Also, if in the basic consumption function in levels, different asset types have different coefficients, their data transformation would not be valid. Furthermore, their approach was not as general as our ECM framework.

Patterson (1984) investigated the separate roles of net liquid assets (gross liquid assets minus non-mortgage debt) and net illiquid assets (gross liquid assets minus mortgage debt) in the non-durable consumption function on annual data for 1959–80. He found that, with income adjusted for both inflation-induced losses on liquid assets and the depreciation of durable goods, both types of wealth had a significant effect on consumption with a larger coefficient on liquid wealth. His best equation had a standard error of 0.47 per cent and like most UK research did not include relative price effects, income volatility, demography or interest rates.

Observed in 1988, non-durable consumer expenditure models at HM Treasury and the Bank of England were roughly on the lines of Patterson (1984) though for quarterly data. Unlike Patterson, though, housing and other physical wealth were excluded from net wealth (perhaps due to data limitations) and liquid assets were not distinguished. However, following Hendry and von Ungern-Sternberg (1981), inflation losses on liquid assets were subtracted from personal disposable income. No relative price effects were incorporated.

In the section on economics of consumers' expenditure, we suggested a somewhat more general framework for modelling non-durable consumption allowing for relative prices, income volatility, the incidence of credit constraints on households whose earnings are affected by long-duration strikes, some disaggregation of assets and liabilities, and demography. Admittedly with the hindsight of access to a much longer run of data analysed by Muellbauer and Murphy (1989), we can ask what might conceivably have been discovered in 1977 from examining annual data from 1957 to 1976, roughly the DHSY estimation period.

In table 13.2 we provide estimates for such a general model in column (a). Income I_n here is real per capita disposable non-property income and the feedback takes the form $(0.95 i_{nt-1} - c_{t-1})$. The long-run effect (though not the impact effect) of relative prices (rp) is insignificant. From the perspective of later data, we can now understand that this was the result of insufficient variation over the 1957–76 sample rather than because relative prices are unimportant, and one can see why DHSY omitted them. The ratios of liquid assets minus debt to income $(LA - DB)/I_n$ and of

Table 13.2 Re-estimation of DHSY for 1957–1976

	(a)	(b)	(c)	(d)[a]	(e)[a]
Constant	−0.187 (1.6)	−0.025 (0.2)	−0.054 (3.0)	−0.040 (2.2)	−0.046 (2.2)
Δi_{nt}	0.533 (17.6)	0.526 (14.0)	0.495 (7.1)	0.415 (8.1)	0.427 (8.2)
$(c - 0.95 i_n)_{t-1}$	0.342 (6.6)	0.257 (4.1)	0.259 (2.6)	0.052 (1.3)	0.107 (1.4)
$\Delta \mathrm{rp}_t$	−0.110 (3.1)	–	–	–	0.025 (0.3)
rp_t	−0.014 (0.6)	–	–	–	−0.012 (0.8)
$\Delta \left(\dfrac{LA-DB}{I_n} \right)_t$	0.064 (1.4)	0.029 (0.5)	0.110 (1.3)	–	–
$\left(\dfrac{LA-DB}{I_n} \right)_{t-1}$	0.091 (2.4)	0.039 (0.9)	0.054 (2.6)	–	–
$\Delta \left(\dfrac{IA}{I_n} \right)_t$	0.022 (10.9)	0.021 (7.6)	0.023 (4.8)	0.027 (6.0)	0.027 (5.9)
$\left(\dfrac{IA}{I_n} \right)_{t-1}$	0.009 (4.3)	0.008 (3.2)	0.009 (2.2)	0.011 (2.5)	0.011 (2.4)
σ_t	−0.205 (2.1)	−0.261 (2.9)	–	–	–
WR_t	0.004 (0.2)	0.030 (1.1)	0.023 (0.5)	0.023 (0.5)	0.032 (0.6)
Dem_t	0.0056 (1.2)	−0.0007 (0.1)	–	–	–
Strik_t	−0.00245 (5.6)	−0.00207 (4.6)	–	–	–
$\hat{\sigma}$ (%)	0.131	0.182	0.342	0.374	0.375
DW	2.93	2.38	2.39	2.41	2.56
R^2	0.9966	0.9916	0.9604	0.9447	0.9524

t values are in parentheses.
[a] Columns (d) and (e) use $\Delta(A/I_n)_t$ and $(A/I_n)_{t-1}$ in place of $\Delta(IA/I_n)_t$ and $(IA/I_n)_{t-1}$.

illiquid assets (including physical wealth) to income IA/I_n are significant, however, with substantially smaller coefficients on the latter than the former. Income volatility (σ) measured over the previous four years lowers consumption, as expected, and is significant. Demography (Dem) in the form of the population proportion aged 15–29 has the expected sign but is not significant. The measure of long-duration strikes deflated by employment is quite significant. It enters in the form $x_t - (x_{t-1} + x_{t-2})/2$ so that the effect is only temporary, because aggregate income correctly incorporates the income losses of strikes and so we would not expect the long-run relation of consumption to income to shift. The weighted change in the nominal interest rate (WR) is insignificant.

Column (b) examines the effect of omitting relative prices: it makes liquid assets–debt insignificant and reduces the size of the error correction to income. Column (c) further omits income, volatility, demography and the strike variable. This makes liquid assets–debt show up more strongly again though the fit deteriorates sharply.

Column (d) incorporates net assets in a single wealth measure including physical wealth as in models of 1989 vintage at HM Treasury and the Bank of England. In this formulation, the error correction to income is sharply weaker while column (e) shows that not even an impact effect of relative prices now survives.

On annual data for 1957–76 (and using non-property income I_n in place of disposable income i) DHSY is as follows:

$$\Delta c_t = \underset{(3.2)}{0.0072} + \underset{(10.5)}{0.444\Delta i_{nt}} + \underset{(3.7)}{0.188(i_n - c)_{t-1}} - \underset{(5.3)}{0.163\Delta p_t}$$

$$\hat{\sigma} = 0.409\% \quad R^2 = 0.9244 \quad DW = 1.78 \qquad (13.29)$$

Note that more general dynamic effects are insignificant. Relative prices are insignificant as the following confirms:

$$\Delta c_t = \underset{(0.4)}{0.004} + \underset{(10.2)}{0.458\Delta i_{nt}} + \underset{(2.9)}{0.279(i_n - c)_{t-1}} - \underset{(5.0)}{0.174\Delta p_t}$$

$$- \underset{(0.6)}{0.048\Delta rp_t} - \underset{(1.2)}{0.021 rp_{t-1}} \qquad (13.30)$$

$$\hat{\sigma} = 0.418\% \quad R^2 = 0.9311 \quad DW = 1.84$$

However, income volatility and the strike variable are significant:

$$\Delta c_t = 0.009 + 0.565\Delta i_{nt} + 0.310(i_n - c)_{t-1} - 0.128\Delta \bar{p}_t$$
$$\quad\quad (0.8) \quad (10.9) \quad\quad (3.4) \quad\quad\quad\quad (3.4)$$
$$\quad - 0.075\Delta\mathrm{rp}_t - 0.032\mathrm{rp}_{t-1} - 0.328\sigma_t - 0.00217\mathrm{Strik}_t$$
$$\quad\quad (1.1) \quad\quad (1.7) \quad\quad (1.8) \quad\quad (2.6)$$
$$\hat{\sigma} = 0.353\% \quad R^2 = 0.9578 \quad DW = 1.67 \quad\quad (13.31)$$

Here inflation is measured as a two-year average.[15] The most remarkable feature of this last equation is the similarity of the coefficients with those of table 13.1, column (a), which replaces inflation by $(LA-DB)/I_n$ and IA/I_n. This suggests a valuable insight into the role of inflation effects in consumption functions: as foreshadowed by Hendry and von Ungern-Sternberg (1981), inflation effects appear to be primarily an imperfect proxy for real assets and debt. In the last 30 years inflation has had a strong negative correlation with ratios of both liquid and illiquid assets to income.

NOTES

Support for this research from the UK Economic and Social Research Council through grant B00220012 is gratefully acknowledged. We are indebted to Neil R. Ericsson, Carlo Favero, Adrian J. Neale and Jean-François Richard for helpful comments on an earlier draft.

1 Useful references include Kennan (1979), Salmon (1982), Currie (1981), Hendry, Pagan and Sargan (1984), Nickell (1985), Pagan (1985), Wickens and Breusch (1988) and Hylleberg and Mizon (1989).
2 Stationarity is not necessary, since the unconditional variance of a process may alter over time and yet the process have no unit roots in its autoregressive representation; the notation $I(k)$ refers to the presence of k unit roots without entailing constancy of unconditional moments of k-period difference.
3 However, the critical values are not conventional ones in general and can be

found in the Dickey–Fuller references cited above.

4 We are indebted to Neil Ericsson for this point. Banerjee and Dolado (1988) show that the test of $\beta_2 = 0$ is close to a conventional t distribution.
5 DHSY investigated the hypothesis of pure measurement errors, and had earlier unsuccessfully tried relative prices and asset measures.
6 θ should allow for any possible transients or parameter changes.
7 z_t is strongly exogenous for α if z_t is weakly exogenous for α and Y_{t-1}^1 does not Granger-cause z_t.
8 In fact, since Chow tests have LM interpretations, it was inefficient to retain the last 20 observations for forecasts only as comparison of DHSY equations (45) and (45**) reveals.
9 The test will have power to detect non-linearities and non-constancies as well as invariance failures, especially as I_t could be a set of dummy variables for policy regimes or a Chow test.
10 Pesaran (1974) compared the Cox test with an F test in the embedding model and found that the former had high power to discriminate between two rival specifications.
11 We assume their estimators converge almost surely on the corresponding parameters.
12 Recreating M_m from M_1 and M_2 may be difficult since several models with equal dimensional parameter spaces may exist, but this reflects the usual problems of a specific $\rightarrow$ general route and not a difficulty peculiar to encompassing. Since models are reductions of processes, M_m arises prior to the further reductions of M_1 and M_2 and is implicit in their creation.
13 The static regression estimates were $c_t = 0.85 i_t - 0.2 \Delta_4 p_t$ and had a DW statistic of 2.3 (!), although conventional Engle–Granger tests are not applicable owing to the quarterly frequency of the data.
14 Considerable CSO resources have been devoted to measuring the flow of funds and annual balance sheets and semi-official annual data now go back to 1957 (Bryant, 1987). Quarterly series back to 1966 are available and, with some work, can be extended back to 1963.
15 Similar results were obtained for Δp_t instead of $\Delta \bar{p}_t$.

REFERENCES

Aldrich, J. (1989): 'Autonomy', *Oxford Economic Papers*, 41, 15–34.
Ando, A. and Modigliani, F. (1963): 'The "Life-cycle" Hypothesis of Saving: Aggregate Implications and Tests', *American Economic Review*, 53, 55–88.
Aoki, M. (1988): 'Cointegration, Error Correction and Aggregation in Dynamic

Models', *Oxford Bulletin of Economics and Statistics*, 50, 89–95.

Banerjee, A. and Dolado, J. (1988): 'Tests of the Life Cycle–Permanent Income Hypothesis in the Presence of Random Walks: Asymptotic Theory and Small Sample Interpretations', *Economic Record*, 64, 81–101.

Bean, C.R. (1978): 'The Determination of Consumers' Expenditure in The United Kingdom', *Government Economic Service, Working Paper 4*, London, HM Treasury.

Bollerslev, T. and Hylleberg, S. (1985): 'A Note on The Relation Between Consumer's Expenditure and Income in the UK', *Oxford Bulletin of Economics and Statistics*, 47, 153–70.

Brown, R.L., Durbin, J. and Evans, J.M. (1975): 'Techniques for Testing the Constancy of Regression Relationships Over Time (with Discussion)', *Journal of the Royal Statistical Society B*, 37, 149–92.

Bryant, C.G.E. (1987): 'National and Sector Balance Sheets 1957–1985', *Economic Trends*, 403, 92–119.

Chow, G.C. (1960): 'Tests of Equality Between Sets of Coefficients in Two Linear Regressions', *Econometrica*, 28, 591–605.

Cox, D.R. (1961): 'Tests of Separate Families of Hypotheses', in *Proceedings of the Fourth Berkeley Symposium on Mathematical Statistics and Probability* (Berkeley, CA: University of California Press), vol. 1, pp. 105–23.

Cox, D.R. (1962): 'Further Results on Tests of Separate Families of Hypotheses', *Journal of the Royal Statistical Society B*, 24, 406–24.

Currie, D. (1981): 'Some Long Run Features of Dynamic Time Series Models', *Economic Journal*, 91, 704–15.

Currie, D., Holly, S. and Scott, A. (1989): 'Savings, Demography and Interest Rates', *Working Paper*, London Business School, Centre for Economic Forecasting.

Davidson, J.E.H. and Hendry, D.F. (1981): 'Interpreting Econometric Evidence: Consumers' Expenditure in the UK', *European Economic Review*, 16, 177–92.

Davidson, J.E.H., Hendry, D.F., Srba, F. and Yeo, S. (1978): 'Econometric Modelling of the Aggregate Time-Series Relationship between Consumers' Expenditure and Income in the United Kingdom', *Economic Journal*, 88, 661–92.

Davis, E.P. (1982): 'The Consumption Function in Macroeconomic Models: A Comparative Study', *Bank of England Technical Series Discussion Paper 1*.

Deaton, A.S. and Muellbauer, J.N.J. (1980): *Economics and Consumer Behaviour* (Cambridge: Cambridge University Press).

Dickey, D.A. and Fuller, W.A. (1979): 'Distribution of the Estimators for Autoregressive Time Series with a Unit Root', *Journal of the American Statistical Association*, 74, 427–31.

Dickey, D.A. and Fuller, W.A. (1981): 'Likelihood Ratio Statistics for Autoregressive Time Series with a Unit Root', *Econometrica*, 49, 1057–72.

Engle, R.F. (1982a): 'A General Approach to Lagrange Multiplier Model Diagnostics', *Econometrica*, 50, 83–104.

Engle, R.F. (1982b): 'Autoregressive Conditional Heteroscedasticity, with Estimates of the Variance of United Kingdom Inflations', *Econometrica*, 50, 987–1007.
Engle, R.F. and Granger, C.W.J. (1987): 'Cointegration, and Error-correction: Representation, Estimation and Testing', *Econometrica*, 55, 251–76.
Engle, R.F. and Hendry, D.F. (1989): 'Testing Superexogeneity and Invariance', Unpublished Paper, Nuffield College, Oxford.
Engle, R.F., Hendry, D.F. and Richard, J.-F. (1983): 'Exogeneity', *Econometrica*, 51, 277–304.
Ericsson, N.R. and Hendry, D.F. (1989): 'Encompassing and Rational Expectations: How Sequential Corroboration can Imply Refutation', *Discussion Paper 354*, Board of Governors of the Federal Reserve System.
Favero, C. (1989): 'Testing for Superexogeneity: The Case of the Term Structure of Interest Rates', *Discussion Paper 67*, Oxford Institute of Economics and Statistics.
Flemming, J.S. (1973): 'The Consumption Function when Capital Markets are Imperfect', *Oxford Economic Papers*, 25, 160–72.
Flemming, J.S. (1974): 'Portfolio Choice and Liquidity Preferences: a Continuous Time Treatment', in H.G. Johnson and A.R. Nobay (eds), *Essays in Monetary Economics* (Oxford: Oxford University Press).
Florens, J.P., Hendry, D.F. and Richard, J.-F. (1987): 'An Information Matrix Approach to Parsimonious Encompassing', *ISDS Discussion Paper 8709*, Duke University.
Frisch, R. (1938): 'Statistical versus Theoretical Relations in Economic Macrodynamics', in *Autonomy of Economic Relations*, Memorandum published in 1948, University of Oslo.
Granger, C.W.J. (1981): 'Some Properties of Time Series Data and their Use in Econometric Model Specification', *Journal of Econometrics*, 16, 121–30.
Granger, C.W.J. (1986): 'Developments in the Study of Cointegrated Economic Variables', *Oxford Bulletin of Economics and Statistics*, 48, 213–28.
Haavelmo, T. (1944): 'The Probability Approach in Econometrics', *Econometrica*, 12 (Supplement), 1–118.
Hall, R.E. (1978): 'Stochastic Implications of the Life Cycle–Permanent Income Hypothesis: Theory and Evidence', *Journal of Political Economy*, 86, 971–87.
Hall, R.E. and Mishkin, F. (1982): 'The Sensitivity of Consumption to Transitory Income: Estimates from Panel Data on Households', *Econometrica*, 50, 461–81.
Hansen, L. and Singleton, K. (1982): 'Generalized Instrumental Variables Estimation of Non-linear Rational Expectations Models', *Econometrica*, 50, 1269–86.
Hausman, J. (1978): 'Specification Tests in Econometrics', *Econometrica*, 46, 1251–71.
Hendry, D.F. (1977): 'On the Time Series Approach to Econometric Model Building', in C.A. Sims (ed.), *New Methods in Business Cycle Research* (Federal Reserve Bank of Minneapolis).

Hendry, D.F. (1979): 'Predictive Failure and Econometric Modelling in Macroeconomics: The Transactions Demand for Money', in P. Ormerod (ed.), *Modelling the Economy* (London: Heinemann Educational), ch. 9.

Hendry, D.F. (1986): 'Econometric Modelling with Cointegrated Variables: An Overview', *Oxford Bulletin of Economics and Statistics*, 48, 201–12.

Hendry, D.F. (1987): 'Econometric Methodology: A Personal Perspective', in T.F. Bewley (ed.), *Advances in Econometrics* (Cambridge: Cambridge University Press), ch. 10.

Hendry, D.F. (1988): 'The Encompassing Implications of Feedback versus Feedforward Mechanisms in Econometrics', *Oxford Economic Papers*, 40, 132–49.

Hendry, D.F. (1989): *PC-GIVE. An Interactive Econometric Modelling System*, University of Oxford, Institute of Economics and Statistics.

Hendry, D.F. and Anderson, G.J. (1977): 'Testing Dynamic Specification in Small Simultaneous Systems: An Application to a Model of Building Society Behavior in the United Kingdom', in M.D. Intriligator (ed.), *Frontiers in Quantitative Economics* (Amsterdam: North-Holland), vol. 3A, pp. 361–83.

Hendry, D.F. and Ericsson, N.R. (1989): 'An Econometric Analysis of UK Money Demand in *Monetary Trends in the United States and the United Kingdom* by Milton Friedman and Anna Schwartz', *American Economic Review*, forthcoming.

Hendry, D.F. and Mizon, G.E. (1978): 'Serial Correlation as a Convenient Simplification, Not a Nuisance: a Comment on a Study of the Demand for Money by the Bank of England', *Economic Journal*, 88, 549–63.

Hendry, D.F. and Neale, A.J. (1987): 'Monte Carlo Experimentation using PC-NAIVE', *Advances in Econometrics*, 6, 91–125.

Hendry, D.F. and Neale, A.J. (1988): 'Interpreting Long-run Equilibrium Solutions in Conventional Macro Models: A Comment', *Economic Journal*, 98, 808–17.

Hendry, D.F., Pagan, A.R. and Sargan, J.D. (1984): 'Dynamic Specification', in Z. Griliches and M.D. Intriligator (eds), *The Handbook of Econometrics* (Amsterdam: North-Holland), vol. II, ch. 18.

Hendry, D.F. and Richard, J.-F. (1982): 'On the Formulation of Empirical Models in Dynamic Econometrics', *Journal of Econometrics*, 20, 3–33.

Hendry, D.F. and Richard, J.-F. (1983): 'The Econometric Analysis of Economic Time Series', *International Statistical Review*, 51, 111–63.

Hendry, D.F. and Richard, J.-F. (1989): 'Recent Developments in the Theory of Encompassing', in B. Cornet and H. Tulkens (eds), *Contributions to Operations Research and Econometrics. The XXth Anniversary of CORE* (Cambridge, MA: MIT Press).

Hendry, D.F. and von Ungern-Sternberg, T. (1981): 'Liquidity and Inflation Effects on Consumers' Expenditure', in A.S. Deaton (ed.), *Essays in the Theory and Measurement of Consumer Behaviour* (Cambridge: Cambridge University Press), ch. 9.

Hylleberg, S. and Mizon, G.E. (1989): 'Cointegration and Error Correction

Mechanisms', *Economic Journal*, 99 (Supplement), 113–25.

Johansen, S. (1988): 'Statistical Analysis of Cointegration Vectors', *Journal of Economic Dynamics and Control*, 12, 231–54.

Johansen, S. and Juselius, K. (1989): 'Maximum Likelihood Estimation and Inference on Cointegration – With Applications to the Demand for Money', *Oxford Bulletin of Economics and Statistics*, forthcoming.

Kennan, J. (1979): 'The Estimation of Partial Adjustment Models with Rational Expectations', *Econometrica*, 47, 1441–55.

Leamer, E.E. (1976): *Specification Searches: Ad Hoc Inference with Non-Experimental Data* (New York: Wiley).

Lucas, R.E. (1976): 'Econometric Policy Evaluation: A Critique', in K. Brunner and A.H. Meltzer (eds), *The Phillips Curve and Labor Markets*, Carnegie–Rochester Conference Series on Public Policy, vol. 1 (Amsterdam: North-Holland), pp. 19–46.

MacKinnon, J.G. (1983): 'Model Specification Tests against Non-nested Alternatives', *Econometric Reviews*, 2, 85–110.

Merton, R.C. (1969): 'Lifetime Portfolio Selection Under Uncertainty: The Continuous Time Case', *Review of Economics and Statistics*, 57, 247–57.

Mizon, G.E. (1977): 'Model Selection Procedures', in M.J. Artis and A.R. Nobay (eds), *Studies in Modern Economic Analysis* (Oxford: Basil Blackwell), ch. 4.

Mizon, G.E. (1984): 'The Encompassing Approach in Econometrics', in D.F. Hendry and K.F. Wallis (eds), *Econometrics and Quantitative Economics* (Oxford: Basil Blackwell), pp. 135–72.

Mizon, G.E. and Hendry, D.F. (1980): 'An Empirical Application and Monte Carlo Analysis of Tests of Dynamic Specification', *Review of Economic Studies*, 49, 21–45.

Mizon, G.E. and Richard, J.-F. (1986): 'The Encompassing Principle and its Application to Non-nested Hypothesis Tests', *Econometrica*, 54, 657–78.

Muellbauer, J.N.J. (1981): 'Testing Neoclassical Models of The Demand For Consumer Durables', in A. Deaton (ed.), *Essays In The Theory And Measurement Of Consumer Behaviour* (Cambridge: Cambridge University Press), pp. 213–36.

Muellbauer, J.N.J. and Bover, O. (1986): 'Liquidity Constraints and Aggregation in the Consumption Function Under Uncertainty', *Discussion Paper 12*, Oxford Institute of Economics and Statistics.

Muellbauer, J.N.J. and Murphy, A. (1989): *Why Has UK Personal Saving Collapsed?* (London: Credit Suisse First Boston).

Nickell, S.J. (1985): 'Error Correction, Partial Adjustment and All That: An Expository Note', *Oxford Bulletin of Economics and Statistics*, 47, 119–30.

Pagan, A.R. (1985): 'Time Series Behaviour and Dynamic Specification', *Oxford Bulletin of Economics and Statistics*, 47, 199–211.

Pagan, A.R. (1987): 'Three Econometric Methodologies', *Journal of Economic Surveys*, 1.

Patterson, K.D. (1984): 'Some Properties of Consumption Functions with Integral Correction Mechanisms', *Manchester School of Economic and Social Studies*, 52, 347–62.

Pesaran, M.H. (1974): 'On the General Problem of Model Selection', *Review of Economic Studies*, 41, 153–71.

Pesaran, M.H. and Evans, R.A. (1984): 'Inflation, Capital Gains, and U.K. Personal Savings: 1953–1981', *Economic Journal*, 94, 237–57.

Phillips, A.W. (1954): 'Stabilization Policy in a Closed Economy', *Economic Journal*, 64, 290–323.

Phillips, A.W. (1957): 'Stabilization Policy and the Time Form of Lagged Responses', *Economic Journal*, 67, 265–77.

Phillips, P.C.B. (1987): 'Time Series Regression with a Unit Root', *Econometrica*, 55, 277–301.

Phillips, P.C.B. (1988): 'Optimal Inference in Cointegrated Systems', *Working Paper 88-42*, University of Auckland.

Ramsey, J.B. (1969): 'Tests for Specification Errors in Classical Linear Least Squares Regression Analysis', *Journal of the Royal Statistical Society B*, 31, 350–71.

Salmon, M. (1982): 'Error Correction Mechanisms', *Economic Journal*, 92, 615–29.

Samuelson, P.A. (1969): 'Lifetime Portfolio Selection by Dynamic Stochastic Programming', *Review of Economics and Statistics*, 51, 239–46.

Sandmo, A. (1974): 'Two-period Models of Consumption Decisions under Uncertainty: A Survey', in J.H. Drèze (ed.), *Allocation Under Uncertainty: Equilibrium and Optimality* (New York: Macmillan), pp. 24–35.

Sargan, J.D. (1964): 'Wages and Prices in the United Kingdom: A Study in Econometric Methodology', in P.E. Hart, G. Mills and J.K. Whitaker (eds), *Econometric Analysis for National Economic Planning* (London: Butterworths).

Sargan, J.D. (1980): 'Some Tests of Dynamic Specification for a Single Equation', *Econometrica*, 48, 879–97.

Schwarz, G. (1978): 'Estimating the Dimension of a Model', *Annals of Statistics*, 6, 461–4.

Spanos, A. (1989): 'Early Empirical Findings On The Consumption Function, Stylized Facts or Fiction: A Retrospective View', *Oxford Economic Papers*, 41, 150–69.

Stone, J.R.N. (1964): 'Private Saving in Britain: Past, Present and Future', *Manchester School of Economic and Social Studies*, 32, 79–112.

Terasvirta, T. (1970): *Step-wise Regression and Economic Forecasting*, Economic Studies Monograph 31 (Helsinki: Finnish Economic Association).

Thomas, J.J. (1989): 'The Early History Of The Consumption Function', *Oxford Economic Papers*, 41, 131–49.

White, H. (1980): 'A Heteroskedastic-consistent Covariance Matrix Estimator and a Direct Test for Heteroskedasticity', *Econometrica*, 48, 817–38.

Wickens, M. and Breusch, T. (1988): 'Dynamic Specification, the Long-Run and the Estimation of Transformed Regression Models', *Economic Journal*, 98 (Conference Papers), 189–205.

14
Reflections on Macroeconomics and Share Systems

Martin L. Weitzman

It was with a strange mixture of delight and dismay that I set about trying to reflect on my 'contributions' to the *Economic Journal* (*EJ*) (the articles 'Increasing Returns and the Foundations of Macroeconomic Theory' in December 1982 and 'Some Macroeconomic Implications of Alternative Compensation Systems' in December 1983) – delight because being asked is obviously an honour; dismay because, well, what was I going to say that I hadn't already said before, in the recent past, and typically more than once (Weitzman, 1984, 1985).

For better or worse I decided to build my reflections around a narrative of how these ideas developed in my own mind and how with benefit of hindsight I might recast their essence today. That is at least superficially different from repeating the models themselves. And such introspective personal history leads naturally to introspective personal ramblings about what it all means. Since the latter is what I think I am supposed to be doing here, this way seems as good as any other.

Involuntary unemployment has been, is now, and perhaps always will be an extraordinarily difficult concept for economists (and almost anyone else) to handle. It seems that just about every sort of explanation has been tried but no single approach comes up with an entirely consistent, convincing, consensus-building account. In prosperous times, it is perhaps not so entirely preposterous to think of unemployment as an economically normal, largely voluntary, free choice activity. The rational expectations school has made this sort of market-clearing equilibrium vision the centrepiece of a now well-known paradigm of unemployment and business cycles. For a wide variety of reasons, most of which have been articulated by others in the literature, I have not found this approach very palatable as a description of economic reality even during relatively good times. And during bad times the idea that very high unemployment rates are essentially voluntary seems way off the mark. Then the phrase 'coordination failure' seems to me to have a much more authentic ring. But what, exactly, is the idea supposed to mean?

If there is such a thing as a coordination failure, then the Great Depression was surely the biggest coordination failure of all time. This extreme event has long been in the back of my mind, asking to be explained. The puzzle of it all served as an image of what I thought I was trying to model.

I was too young to live through the Great Depression, but I feel as if I practically did because of the vivid profound effects it had on my parents and their contemporaries. As the orphaned son of a very poor tubercular mother, I later perceived some vague connection between our overall condition and the hard times everyone seemed to have passed through. My adoptive parents were among those who experienced first hand the mass unemployment of the 1930s, and it left them with a bitter cynicism about the ability of the capitalist system to provide a stable environment and to meet basic needs. To them the market system seemed irrationally and dangerously out of control. While their radical views moderated over time, as a young boy growing up in the 1940s and 1950s I was regaled with plenty of first-hand stories about 'failures of coordination'.

What, to my father, was the cause of the Great Depression? His basic story of what was actually happening comes down to me through the years as something like the following. The shoe factory was shut down because customers could not afford to buy shoes. The unemployed worker who needed shoes could not afford to buy them because he did not have a job. Since the system was unplanned and anarchistic, there was no good way to get workers, factories and buyers together. If the worker would agree to take all of his pay in some of the shoes he produced, then just maybe something could be arranged. But that, of course, was ridiculous because what would the worker do with all those shoes?

The paper 'Increasing Returns and the Foundations of Unemployment Theory' was conceived in the spring of 1981 and a first draft was written that summer. The basic idea was then in the air. Around that time, Peter Diamond's (1982) seminal paper 'Aggregate Demand Management in Search Equilibrium' had a catalysing influence on my thinking.

Diamond's work showed that multiple equilibria could be endemic in a non-Walrasian environment. His milieu was a search-theoretic coconut economy. Individuals could either work for themselves and abstain from the market or shake down coconuts from trees. Unfortunately, anyone's shaken-down coconuts could not be consumed right away but had to be traded for somebody else's shaken-down coconuts, which could then be consumed. This was meant to reflect some sort of division of labour specialization.

The model displays a kind of externality that gives rise to multiple equilibria. If a lot of people are shaking down coconuts, it will be more worthwhile for me to shake down coconuts and try to trade with them because it will be relatively easy for me to find a trading partner. But if others are not shaking down coconuts, then neither should I, because it will be difficult to locate a trading partner and I may be stuck with my own coconuts, which I cannot consume.

Diamond's model struck me as an extremely interesting and perhaps important allegory. But it was at too high a level of abstraction for my tastes. What, exactly, was the source of the division of labour trading constraint? Where did preferences fit in? Where were prices and wages? What was the role of increasing returns (which the system as a whole displayed)? Where were ordinary looking firms and workers?

This intellectual inspiration led me to think seriously about how to integrate monopolistic competition into a general equilibrium type framework that would permit closer examination of Keynesian style coordination failures. It had always seemed to me, as it did to many others, that the natural habitat of a Keynesian macroeconomy is an imperfectly competitive microeconomy, just as classical macroeconomics and perfect competition are natural counterparts.

But the details were not really worked out. In principle it seemed as if it should be interesting to look carefully at the macroeconomic side of a Hotelling–Chamberlin monopolistically competitive circle economy. A model with endogenously determined product diversity and division of labour would appear to be a natural vehicle for studying failures of coordination. The heart of the matter seemed to me to be the idea that, while firms are specialists in production, workers are generalists in consumption; therefore an unemployed worker is unable to communicate to his potential employer his effective demand. Such failures of coordination are difficult to describe, much less to explain, in an artificially aggregated economy that produces essentially one good. From the beginning I thought that modelling the failure of coordination implicit in an inability to communicate effective demand required increasing returns and product diversity. It is true that, with enough ingenuity, unemployment can be generated in models by various forms of asymmetric information combined with adverse selection or moral hazard, but division of labour struck me as a rather more relevant foundation.

Naturally, with benefit of hindsight I would have presented the model somewhat differently. The transportation cost function on the circumference was assumed for simplicity to be linear; it makes more sense and is even neater for the appropriate loss function to be of exponential decay. Because I wanted to emphasize features of the real economy, I left out monetary considerations altogether; in retrospect it would have been better to bite this bullet by building in some crude representation of a monetary economy. A more serious drawback is that the model was vague about what exactly is supposed to be the definition of an unemployment equilibrium and just what had been proved. At that time I took it as sufficient to show how the model was hinting strongly at some problems in automatically adjusting to full employment, and left it at that. Since then there have been a number of serious attempts to deal carefully with expectations and to give a rigorous game-theoretic account of unemployment equilibrium.[1]

Despite these and other misgivings, I believe there remains a basic germ of truth from this paper concerning the relative difficulty of full employment adjustments in an environment of increasing returns and imperfect competition. What comes out of the model, I hope, is a framework explaining how increasing returns, product diversity, monopolistic competition, failures of coordination and hysteresis-like unemployment all fit together in a fairly consistent story. With benefit of hindsight, let me restate the essential argument about the macroeconomic role of increasing returns.

Suppose, just for the sake of argument, that we lived in a world where there was strict constant returns to scale–down to the level of a person or even a grain of sand, or even, if that were necessary, an atom. The standard reasons for macroeconomic failure would continue to hold. Money might be non-neutral, there could be a genuine role for government as a Pareto-improver of social welfare, and so forth. But it is truly difficult to imagine involuntary unemployment with strict constant returns to scale in all aspects of technology, including borrowing and lending of capital. Note that the claim is that some form of increasing returns is a necessary, but by no means sufficient, condition for genuine involuntary unemployment.

Under strict constant returns, the macroeconomic inefficiencies would show themselves in the form of 'wrong' labour–leisure choices (or, more generally, wrong substitution choices among various factors and commodities). An economy of blueberry pickers, mushroom gatherers, clam diggers and the like cannot exhibit involuntary unemployment no matter what else is present or absent. It can show fluctuations, inefficiencies, poverty, even starvation, but it cannot show involuntary unemployment. Any 'involuntarily unemployed' resource would merely form itself into a mini-firm, hire (with non-increasing returns to scale in borrowing) a few grains of cooperating input and sell its mini-output on competitive markets. Balanced expansion would take care of the rest. Involuntary unemployment is logically impossible in a strict constant returns to scale world of one-person firms.

Now it seems to me that the really damaging macroeconomic inefficiencies of advanced capitalist countries are caused by involuntary unemployment, and not by the wrong labour–leisure choice. I doubt that Keynes would ever have written his book if he had lived in a strict constant-returns-to-scale world because there probably never would have been a Great Depression. It seems to me that if we could magically turn our economy into a constant-returns system – if the automobile worker laid off from a 1,000-man plant could produce in his home workshop one-thousandth of what that plant produces (by using in his home workshop one-thousandth of its capital) – we would have eliminated the lion's share of macroeconomic losses due to coordination failures. Other coordination inefficiencies admittedly might remain, but my casual empiricism tells me they would be orders of magnitude smaller in terms of welfare losses.

So I see increasing returns and imperfect competition as not just another minor detail, but as crucial aspects of the Keynesian story. That story simply cannot be told credibly or completely without something like increasing returns blocking unemployed labourers from working on their own or in small groups. It was to focus as sharply as possible on the underlying 'real' role of increasing returns and imperfect competition that I attempted (perhaps unsuccessfully) to trim away as much as possible of all else from the model. (Certainly there is a crucial place, in any complete story, for expectations, money, sticky wage contours and so forth – my basic point is that increasing returns constitutes a necessary, but by no means sufficient, condition for the existence of involuntary unemployment.) Furthermore, as I tried to show in the paper, the quantity-adjustment mechanisms which play such an important role in the operational part of Keynesian theory can be grounded more solidly in imperfect competition than in perfect competition, where they really do represent an artificial intrusion.

In most reasonable models of an economy with non-trivial increasing returns to scale, there is going to be a theorem showing that higher levels of equilibrium employment are associated with higher real wages. This aspect comes out quite clearly in the model under discussion and I believe it obtains under fairly general circumstances. The existence of economies of scale will generally mean that higher levels of long-run economic activity go together with higher real pay. This has at least two important implications, one for the long run and the other for the short run.

On the long-run side, consider the implications of an upward-sloping supply of labour schedule for the monopolistically competitive sector. The upward-sloping supply might come from the idea that labour not employed in the advanced increasing-returns sector can employ itself with diminishing returns in various small-scale self-contained activities. The combination of an upward-sloping long-run supply of labour schedule with a condition relating higher levels of equilibrium employment to higher real wages means that it is easy to generate multiple equilibria. The situation is analogous to combining upward-sloping supply and demand curves. There can easily be multiple intersections. Between each pair of stable equilibria will be an unstable equilibrium. The stable equilibria can be ranked, so that some of them are inferior to others. All this is roughly consistent with a Keynesian world view and provides some support for the idea of government policy to move an economy from a bad to a good equilibrium.

On the short-run side, pro-cyclical real wages is a very unclassical feature which not only corresponds empirically to what we frequently observe in the real world but makes it theoretically difficult to accept the idea that the economic system can automatically, and relatively easily, adjust itself toward full employment. After all, the classical argument is that unemployment will be eliminated by downward pressure on wages. Arguing where burdens of proof lie is always tricky, but it seems to me that the burden of proof here might rest on whomever would assert that downward-pressed (money) wages spontaneously cause the increased real wages that accompany higher employment. For that to happen, prices must decline even faster than wages. It is of course possible, but some good stories have to be told. Here is yet another indication that economies of scale form a natural backdrop for Keynesian macroeconomics.

As I perhaps did not sufficiently stress in in my original paper, but have been at pains to emphasize here, it is not increasing returns alone that causes involuntary unemployment. Other ingredients like money, expectations of other firm's responses, reasonable specifications of tastes, a sticky wage contour of equal pay for equal work, and so forth are also needed to give a credible account of involuntary unemployment. Yet, I would maintain it is important not to lose sight of the forest for the trees. Large-scale division of labour makes for an economic environment in which, contrasting with constant returns, it really is quite fundamentally difficult to tell reasonable stories about how a market economy naturally adjusts to create full employment.

While writing this paper on the foundations of unemployment theory in the summer of 1981, I was once again struck by how the seemingly innocuous assumption of a wage system actually carries a lot of implications. The institutional detail of a wage system seemed to matter. The basic argument about how an economy can get stuck in a low level equilibrium trap reflecting a failure of coordination was quite dependent upon the wage system of paying labour. I vaguely made a connection with the depression story about the unemployed shoe factory worker being hirable but for the fact that he would not take payment in shoes. This story always seemed to trail off into oblivion at some point and the basic strand of argument was never fully developed. At the time I did not attach any great significance to the observation. Some time way back, perhaps in student days, it had seemed peculiar how, when you got right down to it, so much of standard marginal productivity theory seemed to depend on the institution of a wage contract. Labour was supposed to be hired to the point where the marginal revenue product of an extra worker was equal to the wage rate. But what happened if labour was paid entirely in shares of revenues or profits instead of wages? Then the maximand changed. There were no wages as such. Was more labour then hired, to the point where the marginal revenue product of labour was zero? This question was filed away as one more economic puzzle that had no practical implications and presumably could be resolved if one took the time to think about the problem the right way.

The basic ideas behind the share economy came in a sudden flash of Eureka-style inspiration. It happened at the end of January 1982. I can place the date fairly accurately because I remember it was right around the time of the one-hundreth anniversary of Franklin D. Roosevelt's birth. I recall thinking through the ideas while watching a documentary television film on the New Deal.

The beginning of 1982 was a very inauspicious time for the economy. Unemployment was soaring to heights that were unmatched since the Great Depression. A severe tightening had been instituted by monetary authorities who could see no other way to break the back of inflation. I well recall that several colleagues who later came grudgingly to praise Paul Volcker at that time criticized him bitterly for raising interest rates so high and causing so much unemployment. People were scared because no end to the recession was in sight. Economists were widely condemned for not coming up with better solutions to the then seemingly intractable problem of stagflation.

The automobile industry was hit very hard by this most serious recession since the Great Depression. It was quite clear that there were going to be even more layoffs and plant shutdowns. The

United Automobile Workers (UAW) union proposed to General Motors (GM) that they, the UAW, would moderate their wage demands provided GM kept down the prices of its autos; but if the prices of new models went up the UAW would be their usual aggressive selves in asking for higher wages. This proposal was floated as a trial balloon in late January of 1982. Probably the union was motivated by a combination of trying to appear generally helpful in the fight against stagflation and attempting to reach out specifically in a novel face-saving way to preserve jobs. Nothing much came of the idea, and the story itself was meagerly reported as a little-noted article buried in the business pages.

As soon as I saw this rather obscure news story, a flash went off in my mind. If workers agreed to contracts that in effect tied their pay to the prices of what they were producing, that could help with stagflation because it was just like product wages. While from the beginning I never thought this kind of idea represented a magic bullet, I did immediately become quite excited by the prospects. But first it was off to the drawing board to work out the details.

A bunch of questions immediately suggested themselves. It seemed intuitively clear that product wages, revenue sharing, profit sharing, cost sharing etc. were generically related to each other – but just what was the connection? And then I recollected that Japanese workers were paid by some kind of unusual system that somehow resembled profit sharing – could that have anything to do with why Japan seemed always to be able to maintain such high rates of employment? Most importantly, what were the theoretical properties of these kinds of unorthodox payment systems and how did they differ from wage systems?

When I tried to plug in product wages or profit sharing into the general equilibrium monopolistic competition model previously developed, some paradoxical results came out. Suppose a wage economy was in 'unemployment equilibrium'. Workers are unemployed because there is not adequate demand for what they produce and there is not adequate demand for what they produce because other unemployed workers lack purchasing power. Now substitute an identical-pay level of profit or revenue sharing for wages. The effect is equivalent to simultaneously lowering the base wage paid by a firm and transfer-taxing its pure profits so that each employed worker in the previous equilibrium configuration is paid the same as before. But now the firm will want to expand production and employment, because the marginal revenue product of labour exceeds its marginal cost. If every firm in the economy converts over to the new system, a balanced expansion occurs out of the unemployment equilibrium trap with final pay actually at higher levels than before.

But now comes the paradox. Where does the expansion end? Obviously when the economy runs out of labour. But then how can there be an equilibrium? The firms want to hire more labour, but no more is available. Would there not then be a bidding up of profit-sharing coefficients? To what level? Intuitively there ought to be some kind of isomorphism with a full employment wage system, but a sharing system looks as if it would then be displaying an excess demand for labour. To what kind of macroeconomics does this correspond? What is going on here anyway? Things had reached that supremely exciting point where the theory I had created was taking on a life of its own, becoming strong enough to talk back to me while I, its creator, was not quite sure what the artificial creature was trying to say. Of course, later everything became obvious. And, after all, this is economics, so that no amount of theorizing is a match for the complications of the real world. But at the time I felt the unmistakable thrill of discovery. I really felt I was on to something.

It seemed fairly obvious that in a classical, deterministic, frictionless equilibrium, profit-sharing and wage economies should be isomorphic. Workers and capitalists should end up with the same remuneration under both arrangements. But how was this compatible with there being a seemingly eternal desire for expansion under profit-sharing? The essence, I reckoned, had to do with the difference between a Hicksian short run where pay parameters were essentially quasi-fixed, for whatever reason, and a Marshallian long run where they were subject to basic market forces. In the short run it could make sense to talk about an excess demand for labour even if the concept was essentially meaningless for the long run. Equilibrium, I reminded myself, does not mean demand equals supply. After all, the monopolist in equilibrium always wants to sell more at the price he has chosen than his customers want to buy, but that does not mean he wishes to lower his price.

In my view the concept of 'excess demand for labour' under a share economy is essentially a heuristic device that may be useful as a way of thinking about what is happening in a share economy in a short run when pay parameters are quasi-fixed relative to everything else. But nothing substantive depends on using this phrase or even understanding what it means. The properly fastidious way to think about the matter is, I think, as follows. A short-run equilibrium is defined for a situation where pay parameters are quasi-fixed and every other variable in the system, including labour, can be freely changed. (This is obviously an extreme situation but it serves to make a basic point that hopefully holds for less extreme situations.) Then a long-run equilibrium, where pay parameters are also free to vary, is defined. The basic result is that small changes in the neighbourhood of a long-run equilibrium may produce short-run unemployment in a quasi-fixed wage system but not in a quasi-fixed share system.

Because the concept of 'excess demand for labour' is controversial, let me rephrase the essential argument without ever making use of that phrase. Suppose there are two kingdoms, Old Lakeland and New Lakeland, which are physically identical in every way. The economies of both identical-twin kingdoms consist exclusively of fishing from the numerous privately owned lakes and exporting all the fish at given world prices. For each lake, fishing production functions are stable and known.

In Old Lakeland, the monarch has decreed that the money wages to be paid throughout the year at each lake are to be posted on 1 January of that year and cannot be altered until 1 January of the next year. In New Lakeland, the monarch has decreed that payment of each lake shall consist of a share of the value of the fish caught per worker; the share fraction applying throughout the year is to be posted on 1 January of that year and cannot be altered until 1 January of the next year. In both economies, once the pay parameters (wages or share fractions) are posted, workers are free to migrate to that highest-paying lake which will employ them.

Suppose that the world price of fish has been steady for as long as anyone cares to remember. Then Old Lakeland and New Lakeland will settle into a (long-run) competitive equilibrium that is exactly identical in every respect except that pay is called 'wages' in Old Lakeland and 'shares' in New Lakeland.

Suppose next that, suddenly and without warning, in the middle of one year the world price of fish drops. By royal decree, pay parameters cannot be changed to reflect the new situation until next 1 January. What happens in this (short-run) disequilibrium? Lake owners in Old Lakeland will choose to lay off workers, so that Old Lakeland exhibits unemployment. But at the same time New Lakeland remains at full employment.

This basic parable can be amended in a number of ways without destroying its essential message. A share economy will have a tendency to remain at full employment after contractionary shocks, because share employers want to retain workers, while a wage economy will probably exhibit unemployment during a recession because it is then profitable for wage firms to shed labour.

Let me turn to the issue of how a share economy might affect the NAIRU. In the highly idealized frictionless world of a perfectly competitive labour market with perfect information, long-run equilibrium is the same under wage and share systems. In a idealized long run, Old Lakeland and New Lakeland are isomorphic and both have zero rates of unemployment. But what about somewhat more realistic situations. Is the 'share natural rate' of unemployment lower than the 'wage natural rate'? The formal analysis of unemployment comparisons between Old Lakeland and New Lakeland that I have described has been based on short-run disequilibrium considerations, when pay parameters are quasi-fixed. But might widespread sharing also lower the natural rate under a more realistic concept of long-run equilibrium than was treated in the Lakeland example?

The answer is: Yes, it presumably would. Furthermore, the short-run and long-run unemployment problems are probably related.

In order to talk meaningfully about the effects of profit-sharing on the natural rate of unemployment, one has first to have some idea about what is causing a positive natural rate in the first place. There are several theories. Some are more persuasive than others, and they are not mutually exclusive.

A leading theory contends that long-term unemployment is largely inertial or hysteresis-like. Whatever initial disequilibrium caused the increased unemployment in the first place, once unemployment continues long enough it almost gets built into the system, perhaps because the long-term unemployed outsiders cannot or do not act effectively as a disciplining force in wage setting, perhaps because working skills or desires atrophy without work, perhaps because the plight of the unemployed eventually gets forgotten by the electorate, perhaps for other reasons. In this view the rate of change of unemployment typically has a more powerful effect on wage settlements than the absolute level of unemployment.

If this kind of inertial effect lies behind the too-high natural rate, then presumably widespread profit-sharing would lower or eliminate it. The long-term unemployment would have difficulty developing in the first place out of an initial contractionary shock because profit-sharing firms are more reluctant to let go of workers. Taking as given this kind of natural rate unemployment, leaving aside how it got started in the past, the ingrained expansionary bias of a profit-sharing system should act as a built-in counterforce to help absorb the unemployed. The absorption process could of course be speeded by traditional expansionary macroeconomic policies which, under profit-sharing, presumably pose less danger of causing prices to accelerate because the employment–inflation trade-off has been improved. So any way you look at it, profit-sharing looks as if it ought to help diminish long-term inertial unemployment.

Another theory of why the natural rate is so high is that labour has too much bargaining power. Whether a switch from a wage system to profit-sharing would lower this kind of NAIRU depends on what it is that labour and management bargain over. If they bargain over pay parameters but management controls the employment decision, a switch to profit-sharing would lower the NAIRU. If labour and management bargain over both pay parameters and employment levels, the NAIRU would be the same under either system. In-between bargaining would yield in-between results, with the NAIRU then being somewhat lower under profit-sharing than under a wage system.

A third class of theories, based on the so-called 'efficiency wage hypothesis', holds that long-term unemployment is caused by companies themselves choosing to pay above market-clearing wages to discourage bad worker behaviour like shirking or quitting. Within this kind of model the equilibrium natural rate would in principle be the same under a wage or a profit-sharing system, although short-term disequilibrium dynamics could differ.

To the extent that too-high unemployment in some economies is aided by 'overly generous' unemployment and welfare benefits, which creates some voluntary unemployment, presumably the labour payment mechanism *per se* makes little or no difference. So 'the revenge of the welfare state' kind of unemployment should not be affected by a switch to profit-sharing.

Finally, there is the long-standing identification of the 'natural rate' with semi-permanent frictional or structural unemployment, due to continously occurring microeconomic changes. This kind of unemployment, it is usually said, cannot be reduced by pure macroeconomic policies except temporarily and at the cost of increasing inflation. As with inertial unemployment, however, the wage system is heavily implicated in frictional or structural concepts of the NAIRU. After all, both wage and profit-sharing systems respond to shifts in relative demands by sending a signal that eventually transfers workers out of a losing firm or sector and over to a winner. With a wage system the signal to workers that their firm is a loser in the game of capitalist roulette and that it is time to look for a new job with a winning firm is the boot – the worker is laid off and must suffer through an unemployment spell of some duration while searching for the new job. Under a profit-sharing system, the firm does not voluntarily let go of a worker because of weak demand. Instead it is the worker who chooses to leave because pay is too low relative to what is available elsewhere at relatively more successful firms.

Summing up, in none of the standard scenarios does a profit-sharing system cause a higher NAIRU than a wage system, and in most of the more reasonable descriptions a profit-sharing system generates a lower NAIRU than a wage system. In addition, the profit-sharing system has better disequilibrium properties when pay parameters are sticky in the neighbourhood of the NAIRU unemployment rate.

From all of these theoretical exercises considered together it seems difficult not to draw the conclusion that a profit-sharing economy is more likely to have lower unemployment than a wage economy. Yet these are theoretical exercises. What, realistically, is the possible role that profit-sharing might play in improving economic performance?

When it comes down to it, when all is said and done, I guess I think the moral of the story is that profit-sharing is likely to be a 'good thing'. The formal theory gives a veneer of respectability, a flavour of overall coherence, to a general idea that is easy enough to understand on a common-sense level. Profit-sharing can help the unemployment–inflation trade-off because the built-in profit-sharing cushion makes it less cost-saving for the employer to lay off workers during bad times.

What causes unemployment or slack labour markets? There is one basic answer but, like a coin, the answer has two sides. Side one is that unemployment is caused when firms face insufficient demand for their products relative to their marginal costs of production. Side two is that unemployment is caused when firms have too-high marginal costs of production relative to the demand for their products. Sometimes it is useful to stress one side of the coin, sometimes the other. But it is essentially the same coin.

In either case, the key to non-inflationary full employment is an economic expansion that holds down the marginal cost to the firm of acquiring more labour. Macroeconomic policy alone – the purposeful manipulation of financial aggregates – can be very powerful in achieving full employment or price stability, but cannot be reliably depended upon to reconcile both simultaneously. Why? Because of the two-headed monster – stagflation. Illusions of being able to fine tune aside, we know how to get unemployment down and output up by the usual expansionary monetary and fiscal measures. We also know how to break inflation by policy-induced recessions. What we do not know – and this is perhaps the central economic dilemma of our time – is how simultaneously and reliably to reconcile reasonably full employment with reasonable price stability. Expansionary policies often dissipate themselves, to an excessive degree, in too-large wage and price increases rather than expanded employment and output.

When one thinks seriously about it, the wage system of paying labour does not seem like a very good idea. We try to award every employed worker a predetermined piece of the income pie before it is out of the oven, before the size of the pie is even known. Our 'social contract' promises workers a fixed wage independent of the health of their company, while the company chooses the employment level. This stablizes the money income of whomever is hired, but only at the considerable cost of loading unemployment on low-seniority workers and inflation on everybody – a socially inferior risk-sharing arrangement that both diminishes and makes more variable the real income of workers as a whole. An inflexible money wage system throws the entire burden of economic adjustment on employment and the price level. Then macroeconomic policy is called upon to do what is often very difficult – reconcile full employment with low inflation.

Any economy is full of uncertainty. There are no absolute guarantees, and if the uncertainty does not come out in one place it will show up in another. I am saying that it is much better, much healthier, if everyone shares just a little bit of that uncertainty right at the beginning rather than letting it all fall on an unfortunate minority of unemployed workers who are drafted to serve as unpaid soldiers in the war against inflation. It is much fairer if people will agree that only 80 per cent of their pay is going to be tied directly to the funny looking green pieces of paper – which are themselves an illusion, although a very useful illusion – and 20 per cent will be tied to company profits per employee. Then the economy can be more easily controlled to have full employment and stable prices. Society will be producing, and hence consuming, closer to its full potential. If people will face up to the uncertainty, and if everyone accepts some small part of it, then society as a whole can end up with higher income and less uncertainty overall.

A profit-sharing system, where some part of a worker's pay is tied to the firm's profitability per employee, puts in place the right incentives to resist unemployment and inflation. If workers allow some part of their pay to be more flexible by sharing profits with their company, that could improve macroeconomic performance by directly attacking the economy's central structural rigidity. The superiority of a profit-sharing system is that it has enough built-in flexibility to maintain full employment even when the economy is out of balance from some shock to the system. When part of a worker's pay is a share of profits, the company has an automatic inducement to take on more employees in good times and, what is probably more significant, to lay off fewer workers during bad times. A profit-sharing system is not anti-labour and does not rely for its beneficial effects on lowering workers' pay. The key thing is not to get total worker pay down – it could even go up within reason – but to lower the base wage component relative to the profit-sharing component. The marginal cost of labour is approximately the base wage, more or less independent of the profit-sharing component.

While it is possible to dream up unlikely counterexamples and to interpret the existing evidence perversely, the bulk of economic theory, empirical evidence and common sense argue that widespread profit sharing will help to improve macroeconomic performance. The bottom line is that if is easy to envision situations where profit-sharing helps macroeconomic performance while it is difficult to imagine scenarios where profit-sharing damages an economy, which is as much as can be claimed for any economic idea.

The British Chancellor of the Exchequer stated the case for profit-sharing as follows in his 1986 annual budget speech before the House of Commons:

> The problem we face in this country is not just the level of pay in relation to productivity, but also the rigidity of the pay system. If the only element of flexibility is in the numbers of people employed, then redundancies are inevitably more likely to occur. One way out of this might be to move to a system in which a significant proportion of an employee's remuneration depends directly on the company's profitability per person employed. This would not only give the workforce a more direct personal interest in their company's success, as existing employee share schemes do. It would also mean that, when business is slack, companies would be under less pressure to lay men off; and by the same token they would in general be keener to take them on.

It is no mystery why profit-sharing makes the employer view things fundamentally differently. In a profit-sharing system the young school graduate looking for work comes with an implicit message to the employer saying: 'Hire me. I am reasonable. Your only absolute commitment is to pay me the base wage. That is my marginal cost to you. The profit-sharing bonus is like a variable cost, depending to some extent on how well the company is doing. So you have a built-in cushion or shock absorber if something should go wrong. You won't be under such pressure to lay off me or other workers during downswings.' By contrast, the young school graduate looking for work in a wage system now comes to a potential employer with the implicit message: 'Think very carefully before you hire me. I am expensive and inflexible. You will have to pay me a fixed wage independent of whether your company is doing well or poorly.' Is it difficult to deduce in which situation companies might be expected more eagerly to recruit new hires and to retain them, and in which situation new hiring commitments are likely to be avoided when possible? The essence of the case for profit-sharing is the basic idea that on the margin the profit-sharing firm is more willing than the wage firm to hire new workers during good times and, more importantly, to lay off fewer workers during bad times. From a social point of view, a wage system is poorly designed because it is inherently so rigid. There has to be a precise relation between the wage level and the level of aggregate demand to hit the full employment target exactly without causing inflation. By contrast, a profit-sharing system is inherently much more forgiving. Full employment can be maintained even if base wages and profit-sharing parameters are somewhat 'too high' relative to aggregate demand or, equivalently, aggregate demand is 'too low' relative to pay parameters.

Without getting into the more controversial issue of whether profit-sharing causes increased hiring and excess demand for labour, even a one-sided worst-case scenario where profit-sharing 'merely' dampens economic downturns by encouraging employers to lay off fewer workers during recessions still represents a potentially large economic benefit. In periods of recession and other kinds of squeeze, the 'insiders' risk becoming 'outsiders' and they may well be glad of a system which, without painful renegotiations, will enable an automatic adjustment in pay to be made – which would be self-reversing in recovery – to preserve jobs. Also, even in periods of normal growth there will always be firms under pressure to reduce employment, and anything which lessens that pressure will help overall employment. To ratchet an economy toward a tight labour market and improve the employment–inflation trade-off so that macroeconomic policies can be used more effectively requires only that, on the margin, during downswings a few less old workers are laid off and during upswings no fewer new workers are hired.

The basic story being told is subject to a host of potential criticisms and objections. The model is incomplete and *ad hoc* at certain crucial points. Nevertheless, I think the basic message rings true. Sharing arrangements generally make it easier to consummate and less desirable to dissolve an economic union of those who are hired with those who do the hiring.

When someone asks of an ordinary wage system 'why is company X hiring so many workers rather than fewer or more?', the first instinctive response of the economist is to say that labour is being hired to the point where its marginal revenue product to the company is equal to its marginal cost. We economists know there are many caveats to be made and that a large number of models can be constructed that weaken or even negate this simple classical answer. Still, in the end, most of us come back to the marginal revenue product equals marginal cost explanation as the basic 'big picture' employment story we keep in the back of our minds.

The profit-sharing story that I am trying to tell attempts to push through to its logical conclusion the simple standard classical marginalist paradigm under conditions when there is an alternative 'sharing' payment mechanism. It then turns out that the resulting share system adheres closer to full employment than a corresponding wage system as various underlying parameters (including pay parameters) are perturbed around their long-run equilibrium values. If we try to tell the simple Econ-10 employment story with a money wage replaced by an equivalent amount of profit-sharing, the resulting macroeconomy has better employment-stabilizing properties because the marginal cost of labour is lower. The standard IS–LM story can be told 'as if' the underlying short-run cost of labour is the base wage.

The idea that profit-sharing is generally a 'good idea' has obviously caught on to some degree. I think there must be several reasons for this. People seem to be much more aware that the well-being of a company's workers depends, ultimately, on the well-being of the company itself, and that it is probably healthier to recognize this mutual dependence explicitly by some form of profit-sharing than to go on pretending that it does not exist. There is much speculation, and some evidence, that profit-sharing leads to improved productivity because workers feel that they have more of a stake in the outcome.[2] (At the very minimum, workers in a profit-sharing company seem to take an interest in company profits, whose existence and determinants they are often only dimly aware of otherwise.) Finally, there is the sense that macroeconomic performance may be improved under profit-sharing. Not, of course, exactly in the mechanical highly formal description of the models. Reality is more than a match for any model, at least in economics. My hope is that the overly crisp models of profit-sharing are at least pointing in the right direction of an internally consistent economy with better macroeconomic properties than the more conventional wage system.

NOTES

1 See, for example, Cooper and John (1988), Kiyotaki (1988), Roberts (1987), and the further references cited therein.
2 See Weitzman and Kruse (1989) for a broad survey of the evidence.

REFERENCES

Cooper, R. and John, A. (1988): 'Coordinating Coordination Failures in Keynesian Models', *Quarterly Journal of Economics*, 103, 441–63.
Diamond, P. (1982): 'Aggregate Demand Management in Search Equilibrium', *Journal of Political Economy*, 90, 881–94.
Kiyotaki, N. (1988): 'Multiple Expectational Equilibria Under Monopolistic Competition', *Quarterly Journal of Economics*, 103, 881–94.
Roberts, J. (1987): 'An Equilibrium Model with Involuntary Unemployment at Flexible, Competitive Prices and Wages', *American Economic Review*, 77, 856–74.
Weitzman, M.L. (1982): 'Increasing Returns and the Foundations of Unemployment Theory', *Economic Journal*, 92, 787–804.
Weitzman, M.L. (1983): 'Some Macroeconomic Implications of Alternative Compensation Systems', *Economic Journal*, 93, 763–83.
Weitzman, M.L. (1984): *The Share Economy* (Cambridge, MA: Harvard University Press).
Weitzman, M.L. (1985): 'The Simple Macroeconomics of Profit Sharing', *American Economic Review*, 75, 937–53.
Weitzman, M.L. and Kruse, D. (1989): 'Profit Sharing and Productivity', in A. Blinder (ed.), *Worker Compensation and Productivity* (Washington, DC: Brookings Institution).

Index

Acworth, William 40, 53
Adams, Henry Carter 93, 94, 95, 102
Addis, Sir Charles 150, 161
ad hockery, expectations and 253–5
agents: in expectation theory 233; infinitely lived 242, 244–5; Ramsey 249, 254
Allen–Antonelli integrability conditions 284
Allen, Roy 208
all-or-none offer functions 269–70, 271, 272, 275; derivation of 291–2
American Economic Association (AEA) 7, 9, 27, 34, 93, 172, 175
American economics profession 9, 92–105
American Federal Reserve Board's multicountry model 222–3
Anderson, G.J. 302
Ando-Modigliani equation 324
Argyll, Duke of 32, 51–2, 63 n10
Armstrong, W.E. 149
Arrow, K.J. 243, 257, 282–3
Arrow–Debreu model 236, 242–3
Ashley, William 14, 54–5, 63 n29, 143; on trusts 96–7
Association of University Teachers of Economics (AUTE) 19, 186
automobile industry 342–3
autonomy *see* invariance
Axelrod, Robert 218, 225

Baird, Joyce 173, 175
Balducci, R. 221

Balfour, Arthur J. 32, 163
Ball, Sidney 83–4
Bank of England model 324, 325, 327
Banzhaf–Coleman index 207
bargaining 213–16; in cooperative games, Nash solution 204, 222, 227
bargaining power of labour 347
bargaining set 207
Barone, Enrico 266
Basar, Tamer 223
Bastable, C.F. 41, 112
Bayesian learning 254
Bean, C.R. 308
Bergson, Abram 264, 271, 273, 282, 286
Bernstein, Eduard 77
Bertrand, J.L.F. 210
Beveridge, William 16, 166, 170
Bickerdike, C.F. 56–7, 117, 149–50, 151
bimetallism 39
Binmore, K. 224
Birmingham Airport 219
Böhm-Bawerk, Eugen von 76, 112
Boldrin, M. 245
Bonar, James 6, 32, 41, 78–9, 112, 161, 166, 168–9, 188
Bortkiewicz, Ladislaus von 123–4, 126, 128–9
Bover, O. 305, 306
Bowley, Arthur 113, 118, 210
Bowley's conjectural variation 211
Brand, Lord 173
Bray, Margaret M. 240, 256
British Association for Advancement of Science, Section F 7–8, 12–13, 29, 31

British Economic Association, precursor of Royal Economic Society, foundation and early years 3, 22–43, 65, 93, 151
Brown, A.J. 185
bubbles, Tirole's 238, 251
Butlin, F. 75–6
Buttress, S.J. 173

Cagan, P. 236
Caine, Sydney 177, 178
Cairnes, John Elliot 95, 126
Cambridge University 12, 13, 18, 22, 34; Economics Tripos 11, 14–15, 32; school of economics 10–11, 60–1, 168
Cambridge University Press 172
Canada 207, 224
Candela, G. 221
Cannan, Edwin 32, 37, 41, 51, 55, 63 n8, 143, 148, 151–2, 163, 166–7, 170
Cantillon, Richard 168
Carr-Saunders, A.M. 174
Carter, Charles 175, 180, 182, 184
Cassel, Ernest 75, 116, 125, 150
Chamberlain, Joseph 9
Chamberlain, Edward 273
Champernowne, David 180, 185
Chancellor of the Exchequer 351
Childers, H.C.E. 32, 163
Chow tests, 307, 322–3
Clapham, J.H. 146, 152, 167
Clark, J.B. 38, 92, 95, 102–5
Clark, J.M. 116, 118
Clower constraint, 248
Coats, A.W. and S. 153
Cohen, Joel E. 275
cointegration 299, 303–5, 314, 315
Cole, G.D.H. 84–6, 89
Collet, Clara E. 42, 168
Collison Black, R.D. 178
common factor 304, 312
commonsense, sin of 242
conjectural variation 210, 211, 212
Conrad, Johannes 93
constancy of parameters 299, 314, 319–21; and invariance 299, 307–9
constant-sum games 199, 201
consumers' expenditure, economics of 298, 300–1, 324
consumers' surplus 196, 261–97; criticism of 267–8; early history of 265–7
consumption functions 298
cooperation 78–81; versus self-interest 216–18

coordination failure 336, 338, 340, 342
core, the 204–5, 207
costs: keeping down 218–19; overhead, allocation of 219–20
Cournot, Antoine A. 5, 210, 265
Cournot equilibrium 211, 212
Cournot–Nash equilibrium 211, 212
Cournot reaction curve 210, 212, 213
Courtauld, Samuel 148
Courtney, Leonard H. 31, 66–8, 163
Cox, D.R. 309
credit constraints, 301, 305–6
Cunningham, William 30, 143
Cunynghame, Henry 49, 116
cycles 220–1

Dam, Kenneth W. 220
Davidson, J.E.H. 310
Davis, E.P. 308
Deane, Phyllis 179, 185
demography, population 301
DHSY 197; econometrics of 298–334; re-estimation of 326
Diamond, Peter 337
Dickey–Fuller statistic 303–4
discounting 247–8
Dore, Mohammed 221
D'Orey, Vasco 223
Dorfman, R. 200, 210
Douglas, Paul 150
Dresher, Melvin 216
duopoly 202; and oligopoly 210–13
Dupuit, Arsene-Jules-Emile Juvenal 264, 265, 267, 277, 283
dynamic modelling methodology 299, 311–12

econometric methodology, formalization of 302–7
Economic Advisory Council 16, 185
economic history 10, 40–1, 144
Economic History supplement 10, 144
Economic Journal, as professional arena in 1920s and 1930s 4; early years of 8–12, 23, 26–8, 30, 32–3, 35–7, 39–43, 49–62; last 50 years of 195: treatment of socialism in 65–87; *see also under* Edgeworth as editor *and under* Keynes as editor
Economic Review 8–9, 30
economics, as profession 3–4, 10, 12–15, 19 n5, 20 n11, 22, 57–8, 153; institutionalization of 14–15; official use of 16–17, 187; mathematics in 5, 18; methodological debate 8–9

Edgeworth, Francis Ysidro, as editor of *Economic Journal* 5, 9, 11, 18, 20 n15, 29, 32–4, 37–8, 41–2, 53–5, 60, 65, 163–4, 214, 266; on Marxism 77–8, 80–1; as reviewer 109–32
efficiency wage hypothesis 347
efficient market hypothesis 240, 249–53
Einaudi, Luigi 148
Elliot, Sir Thomas 165
Ely, Richard T. 93, 94, 95, 99–100
encompassing 299, 309–10, 312
Engel, Ernst 52, 93
Engels, Friederich 52, 75, 76–7
Engels path 276
Engle, R.F. 304, 306–7, 308–9
English Historical Review 23
equilibria 256–7, 266, 282, 292
error correction mechanisms 299, 302–6
Euler equation 305
excess demand for labour 344–5
exogeneity 299, 306–7, 308
expectations 232–60, 299, 311; and *ad hockery* 253–5; in equilibrium 196
experimental economics, use of to test game theory 223–6

Fawcett, Millicent 151
Fay, C.R. 169
Feinstein, Charles 185
Fisher, Irving 38, 60–1, 148
Fleming, J.M. 148, 150
Flemming, John 180, 185
Flood, Merill 216
Flux, A.W. 32, 50–1, 116
Foxwell, Herbert Somerton 6, 15, 23, 32–3, 59, 163, 166, 170
Frankel, Jeffrey A. 223
Freeman, Richard 6, 9
Friedman, Milton 150, 274, 293 n2
Friedmanite methodology 232, 241, 245
full communication equilibrium 238
Fuller, Arthur 173, 182

Gallatin, Albert 293 n1
Galton–Pearson theorem 122
games: and linear programming 208–10; types of 202–3
game theory 196, 198–231; solution concepts in 203–8; use of experimental economics to test 223–6
General Theory 234, 238
German historical school 9, 93, 98, 104
Gide, Charles 38, 81, 124, 128
Giffen, Robert 32–3, 39, 112; his paradox 119–21

Gillies, D.B. 204
Goldsmith Library 25
Gonner, E.C.K. 25–6, 28
Goodwin, Richard M. 220, 221
Goschen, George Joachim, as first President of British Economic Association 6, 31–3, 161, 163
Grandmont, J.M. 235, 256
Granger, C.W.J. 304
Granger representation theorem 304
Graziani, A. 119, 122–3
Great Depression 336, 342
Green, A.R. 146
Gregory, T.E. 168
Grossman, S.J. 238, 239
growth model, Neumann's 221–2
Guillebaud, Claude 172

Hadley, Arthur T. 93
Hahn, F.H. 185, 186, 235, 243, 257
Haldane, R.B. 163
Haldane Committee on machinery of government 16
Hall consumption function 305
Hall model 310
Hall, Robert 174, 176, 178
Hamilton, C.J. 165–6
Hansen, L. 305
Hardie, Jeremy 186
Harrod, Roy 143, 146–7, 166, 170, 172, 175, 178, 188, 234
Hausman, J.A. 264, 285, 307
Hawtrey, Ralph 16, 166, 170, 171
Hayek, Friederich von 15, 238, 244
Henderson, Hubert 16, 171
Hendry, D.F. 302, 306, 308, 309, 310, 324, 325, 328
Hewins, W.A.S. 32
Hey, J.D. 185
Hicks, J.R. 111, 115, 125, 166, 178, 235, 274, 290
Hicks's theorem 285–6
Higgs, Henry 6, 32, 38, 43, 161, 163, 164, 166, 168, 170, 188
Hicks's theorem 285–6
HM Treasury's macroeconomic model 305, 324, 325, 327
Hoare, Alfred 161, 165, 166, 170, 188
Hobson, John Arthur 53, 61, 97, 105
Hotelling, H. 290
Howson, Susan 185

imperfect competition 337–8, 340
income uncertainty, 301
increasing returns, macroeconomic role of 339, 340

indifference contours 262–3, 276
individualism 65–70
international policy coordination 222–3
Intriligator, Michael D. 207, 210, 213
invariance of parameters 299, 312, 314, 321–2; and constancy 299, 307–9

Jaffe, William 172
James, Patricia 178, 186
Japan, payment system in 343
Japanese Economic Planning Agency model 222–3
Jenkin, Fleeming 265
Jenks, E. 40
Jenks, J. 101, 102
Jevons, Stanley 5, 6, 7, 111, 112, 116, 144, 178, 181
Jewkes, John 170
Johansen, S. 304
Johnson, Elizabeth 16, 172, 181
Johnson, Harry 131–2, 181
Joseph, Peggy (M.F.W.) 294 n4
Journal des Economistes 7

Kadish, Alon 6, 9
Kahn, Richard 172, 181
Kaldor, Nicholas 146, 185, 256
Kalecki, M. 145–6, 149
Kehoe, T.J. 256
Kennan, J. 305
kernel 207
Keynes, John Maynard 3, 4, 5, 15, 16–17, 130, 227, 234, 246, 250, 251; as editor of *Economic Journal* 60–1, 143–53, 161, 166, 167; edition of his economic writings 16, 181, 182
Keynes, John Neville 9, 26, 115, 164, 265
Koopmans, Tjalling 125, 210
Kreps, David M. 240
Kress Library 25

labour economics 38–9
labour–leisure choice 339
Lagrange multiplier test 307
Lavington, Frederick 60–1, 62
Levine, D.K. 256
linear programming and games 208–10
liquidity 301
Little, Ian 264
Littlechild, S.C. 219
Llewellyn Smith, Hubert 16
London School of Economics 14–15, 34, 173
long-run equilibrium 235, 254

Loria, Achille 77
Lotka–Volterra predator–prey model 220–1
Lucas, R.E. 236–7, 250, 308
Lucas critique 248–9, 308, 311; testing of 322–3

MacDonald, Ramsey 16
MacDougall, Donald 182
Macgregor, D.H. 143, 152, 161, 164; on trusts 98–9, 103–4
Macmillan, publishers 33, 182
macroeconomics 197; and share systems 335–54
Madge, Charles 148
Maitland, F.W. 40
Malinowski, Bronislaw 151
Maloney, John 9, 10
Malthus, T.R. 169, 178, 186
Marcet, A. 240–1
marginal revenue product 342, 353
marginal utility of money 268, 270–2, 281
market clearing 233
Marris, Denny 174, 177
Marshall, Alfred 6, 8–9, 10–11, 16, 25–31, 32, 50–2, 58, 59, 60, 66, 111, 115, 119–21, 143, 163, 165, 261; on consumers' surplus 262–6, 286–7, 290; Economics Tripos 14–15, 16; *Principles of Economics* 4–5, 41–2, 172; as a Second Wrangler 271–3, 288; on socialism 73–5; on trusts 92, 97–8, 103, 105
Marshall–Dupuit integral 267–8, 271, 272
Marshall, Mary 52
Marshall's demand curve 262, 263
Martin, John Biddulph 30, 32–3
Marx, Karl 68, 70, 71; *Capital* 75–8, 95
Matsuyama, K. 245
Matthews, Robin 174–5, 185, 186
McKenzie, L.W. 112, 125
McMillan, John 219
Meade, James 148, 178
Mill, John Stuart 6, 72, 80; on natural monopoly 94–5
Mind 23
mixed strategies 200
Mizon, G.E. 309
Moggridge, Donald 5; editor of Keynes edition 16, 181, 182
models, discovery and evaluation procedures for 299, 312–13
'money-metric' utility 275–7

Montruchio, L. 245
Moore, Henry Ludwell 121–2
Morgenstern, Oscar 195
Morley, John 32, 163
Muellbauer, J.N.J. 305, 306, 324, 325
multiple equilibria 337, 340–1; and Pareto efficiency 242–7
Murphy, A. 325
Muth, J.F. 232, 236
Mynors, Humphrey 170, 174

Nash, John 203, 204, 214
Nash equilibrium 203, 204, 220, 223
Nash solution 203–4, 216, 221
natural rate of unemployment 346–7
Negishi, T. 243, 244
Neumann, John von 125, 195
Neumann–Morgenstern cardinal utilities 214
Neumann–Morgenstern theory 196
Neumann's growth model 221–2
Newman, Peter 5, 9, 18
New Palgrave, The 227, 267
Neyman–Pearson testing 313
Nicholson, John Shield 42, 50, 59, 62 n4, 269–70, 276; on Marxism 77–8, 112
Nickell, S.J. 305
non-cooperative games 203–4, 211, 216, 220, 222
nucleolus 207, 219

O'Brien, Dennis 172
Oman, Helen 170
Oudiz, Gilles 222, 223
overlapping generations models 238, 255
Owen, Guillermo 206, 207, 219
Oxford University 12, 13, 18, 22

Palgrave, Robert Inglis, 23–4, 164
Pantaleoni, Maffeo 38, 81
Pareto efficiency 233; and multiple equilibria 242–7
Patterson, K.D. 325
perfect competition 233
perfect foresight equilibrium 234
perfect foresight paths 235, 255, 256
Pesaran, M.H. 232, 324
Petty, William 33
Pfaff theory of partial differential equations 285
Phelps, L.R. 30
Phelps Brown, E.H. 182
Phillips, P.C.B. 304
Pigou, Arthur Cecil 10, 56, 58–9, 62,
105, 109, 116, 118–19, 146, 151, 168, 214, 234, 236, 242, 251, 257, 266, 293 n2; 'psychological' component 237, 246
Plant, Arnold 166, 178
Political Economy Club 6, 7, 29
predator–prey model 220–1
Prest, Alan 182, 184
Price, L.L. 32, 40–2, 51–2, 55, 58–9, 62 n7, 78–9, 84–5, 116
prisoner's dilemma 213, 216, 225–6, 227
producers' surplus 268, 281
profit-sharing *see* share economy
Pullen, J.M. 186

Quarterly Journal of Economics 7, 15, 27, 144
Quesnay, François 178

Radner, R. 238
Rae, John 49–50, 76
railways 39, 60
Ramsey, Frank 146
Ramsey model 244, 245, 247–9
Rapoport, Anatol 226
rational expectations equilibrium 239, 240, 241, 253, 256
rational expectations hypothesis 249–50, 253
Rea, Russell 57, 119–20
recursive estimation 299, 314, 319–21
Reddaway, Brian 180, 185
reduction sequence 314, 316–19
Revue d'Economie Politique, 7
Ricardo, David 6, 41, 52, 95, 113; edition of his works 172
Ricci, G. 221
Richard, J.-F. 306, 308, 309
Robbins, Lionel 15, 66, 146, 166, 168, 170, 171, 173, 174, 179
Robertson, Dennis H. 82–3, 85–6, 111, 146, 147–8, 168, 171, 266
Robinson, Austin 5, 11–12, 16, 19, 143; as editor of *Economic Journal* and Secretary to Royal Economic Society 161–88
Robinson, Joan 145–6
Rockett, Katharine 223
Roscher, Wilhelm 33
Royal Economic Society, early role of 17; Royal Charter 43, 66, 177–8; changes in internal organization 161–88; modern role 19, 186–8; officers 1891–1990 189–92; scholarly publications of 24, 33–4, 178, 179, 181–2, 185–6

Royal Statistical Society 7–8, 24, 38, 49, 167
Rybczynski, T. 184, 186

Sachs, Jeffrey 222, 223
saddlepoint 200
Salter, Sir Arthur 16
Samuelson, Paul A. 72, 200, 210, 235, 241, 254, 270, 276
Sargan, J.D. 302
Sargent, T.J. 240–1
Savin, N.E. 240
Schwarz criterion 317–18
Scott, W.R. 167
self-interest, versus cooperation 216–18
Senior, Nassau 72
Shaked, Avner 224
Shapley, Lloyd S. 204, 205
Shapley value 205–7, 208, 219
share economy 342, 345–7
sharing the cake 224–5
Shaw, G.B. 31
Sidgwick, Henry 8, 31, 42, 66; on socialism 71–3, 101–2, 112, 126
Silberston, Aubrey 185, 186
Singer, Hans 147
Singleton, K. 305
Slutsky–Hicks conditions 284
Smart, William 32
Smith, Adam 6, 41, 59, 167, 233, 282
Socialism 18, 65–87
Solow, Robert M. 200, 210
Sorel, Georges 82–4
Sraffa, Piero 172, 266
stability 255–7
Stackelberg, H. von 210
Stackelberg reaction curve 213
stagflation 342–3, 349
Stamp, Josiah 167
Stark, William 172
stationarity 328 n2
Steedman, Ian 9, 10
Stigler, George 111, 112, 129
Stigler, Stephen 117, 119
Stiglitz, J.E. 239
Stone, J.R.N. 145, 185, 202, 221, 302
Sturges, Paul 185
sunspot equilibrium 238, 241, 242, 251
super exogeneity 308, 312, 314, 321–2
Sutton, John 224
syndicalism 82–6

tariffs 39, 55–6

tariff wars, game of 220
Taussig, F.W. 38, 99
Thaler, Richard H. 223
Theory of Games, The 195
Tirole, J. 238, 240, 251
Tit for Tat 226
transversality and discounting 247–8
trends 220–1
Tress, Ronnie 184–5
trust movement in Britain and America 92–105
Tucker, A.W. 216
Turnovsky, Stephen J. 223
two-person zero-sum games 199, 203, 207, 208–9

ultimatum game 224–5
unemployment: causes of 349; involuntary 335–6, 339, 341
unemployment equilibrium 338, 343
von Ungern-Sternberg, T. 324, 325, 328
United Kingdom 298, 301, 302, 316, 324–5; game theory applied to 224
United Nations Security Council 207
United States 222, 224, 235, 301

Verein fur Sozialpolitik 7

wage contract 342
wage system of paying labour 349, 351–2
Wagner, Adolf 93
Walker, General Amassa 52
Wallace, N. 248
Walras, Leon 5, 112, 123–5, 128–9; edition of his correspondence 172
Webb, Beatrice 15, 42, 79, 112–13
Webb, Sidney 15, 32, 42, 66–71, 82, 105, 112–13
Wedgwood, J.C. 147
Whitaker, John R. 97, 178, 186
Wicksell, Knut 60, 117, 118, 172
Wicksteed, Philip 112, 116
Williams, J.D. 218
Williams, Philip 9
Willig, R. 264
Winch, Donald 179, 180, 185
Woodford, M. 240–1, 256
Worswick, David 185

Young, Allyn A. 118–19, 266, 274

Zeuthen, Frederik 214–16